The Advanced Art of Baking & Pastry

The Advanced Art of Baking & Pastry

R. ANDREW CHLEBANA

PHOTOGRAPHY BY ANTHONY TAHLIER

WILEY

Library of Congress Cataloging-in-Publication Data

Names: Chlebana, R. Andrew, author.
Title: The advanced art of baking and pastry / R. Andrew Chlebana.
Description: Hoboken, New Jersey : Wiley, [2018] | Includes bibliographical references and index. |
Identifiers: LCCN 2017015523 (print) | LCCN 2017021342 (ebook) | ISBN 9781119400738 (epub) | ISBN 9781119400714 (pdf) | ISBN 9781118485750 (cloth : alk. paper)
Subjects: LCSH: Baking. | Pastry.
Classification: LCC TX763 (ebook) | LCC TX763 .C4935 2018 (print) | DDC 641.86/5—dc23
LC record available at https://lccn.loc.gov/2017015523

ISBN: 978-1-118-48575-0
Printed in the United States of America

10 9 8 7 6 5 4 3 2 1

To Heather: My rock.

Contents

Foreword

Pastry Chef/Professor Andy Chlebana has written a dynamic new textbook called *The Advanced Art of Baking & Pastry*.

This is the most up-to-date information written by a chef and author who has worked at the top of the hospitality industry and competed at the highest level. Pastry chefs of every level will benefit from the depth and variety of pastry experience inside.

Andy Chlebana served as Team USA Coupe du Monde de Patisserie Captain and has won numerous awards, working both in chocolate and in sugar. Due to this singular experience, he delivers two excellent chapters, "Chocolate Work" and "Sugar Work." Every aspect on the subject is detailed in Chapters 13 and 14, from design and structure to advanced techniques like airbrushing chocolate and creating pastillage.

A subject close to my heart, modern pastry techniques, is given due diligence in Chapter 4 with detailed explanation of the most innovative techniques developed in the past decade.

Chapter 10 on plated desserts is a refreshingly up-to-date discussion on presentation, balance, and flavors of hot and cold desserts.

There's an ample amount of solid, classic techniques and recipes as well. "Bread for the Pastry Chef" (Chapter 2) is an artisan bakery primer that explains the function and science of the bread, fermentation, mixing methods, and numerous recipes. Additional chapters cover "Assembling Cakes," "Frozen Desserts," and "Vienoisserie."

The Advanced Art of Baking & Pastry is visually stunning, with artistic photographs by one of the top photographers in the county. There's no one in the world more qualified to write this than Chef Chlebana, and there's no pastry textbook to date that encompasses so much of the sweet world!

JIMMY MACMILLAN
Top Ten Pastry Chef by *Dessert Professional Magazine*
Emmy® Award-winning creator of The Chicago Restaurant Pastry Competition

Acknowledgments

I would like to express my gratitude to the many people who assisted me throughout the process of writing this book. There are many people to thank, and I don't want anyone to feel that they have been left out, so thank you to everyone who helped in some way, no matter how big or small. Your assistance was greatly appreciated and has given me the ability to complete this project.

I would like to thank my wife, Heather, and my children, Abigail, Annabel, Andrew, and Adler, who supported and encouraged me in spite of all the time it took me away from them. It was a long, difficult journey for them.

Thank you to my editors at Wiley. My first contact with the company, Mary Cassells, kept on me until I submitted the proposal and was with me until the rough draft of the manuscript. Andrea Brescia helped me put all the pieces together and get everything in order to look the way it does now. I could not have done this without either of you encouraging me along the way. There is a team of people behind the scenes at John Wiley and Sons who have contributed countless hours to the completion of this book; I thank you all for your efforts.

The photo shoot was a big undertaking for this project. Many people were involved, and everyone contributed to the beautiful images that I hope will inspire the reader. First I need to thank the most talented photographer I have had the pleasure of working with, Anthony Tahlier. He and his first assistant, Sean Henderson, truly worked magic behind the lens. They made the food that a team of my lab assistants and students helped me prepare look fantastic.

Thanks to Joliet Junior College and the Culinary Arts Department for giving me the time to work on this book. Several friends, coworkers, and other departments contributed to my efforts. Brooke Hoekstra and Heather Schreiner helped from the early steps of testing and developing recipes, creating the schedule for the photo shoot, and preparing the food we shot; additional assistance was provided by Brooke Ball and Eileen Braski. Tim Bucci, my partner in crime at the college, always made me think about what I was doing and pushed me to become a better pastry chef. Additional help was provided during the development stages by Anthony Kozlowski and Stacey Lyons.

Math is an important part of baking and pastry. Donna Katula from the Joliet Junior College Math Department helped to clean up some of the formulas and make them more user friendly.

We are all students and continue to learn all throughout our careers. Nancy Carey helped a great deal with the breads in this book. Stephanie Pintoy provided technical assistance for Chapter 4, "Modern Pastry Techniques."

Products and services were also provided by the following companies; their commitment to industry and education is greatly appreciated. Thank you for all the products and time you donated during the production of this book:

Chicago Culinary FX—Michael Joy & Beatrice Schneider

John E. Koerner & Co. Inc.—Tim Koerner

SiliKoMart

Tomric Systems, Inc.—Tom Elsinghorst

CHAPTER 1

Introduction

How do you go from making a simple éclair to a plated dessert in a fine-dining restaurant? How do you go from learning to temper chocolate to creating an elegant showpiece? The answer is simple—continued mastery of one skill after another. Mastering the skills required to be a pastry chef requires a strong foundation built on professionalism, techniques, understanding ingredients, and constant improvement. In this chapter the groundwork will be laid, and you will begin your journey to mastering the advanced art of pastry.

LEARNING OBJECTIVES

After reading this chapter, you should be able to:

1. **Identify** the fundamental skills necessary to be successful in the pastry shop.
2. **Identify** specialty equipment and tools.
3. **Describe** how to prevent foodborne illness.

Professionalism

Pastry chefs and chefs have a great deal of pride in the work they do. The job of a pastry chef is not to simply provide good food. Formulas and techniques are used to transform ingredients that can be found in most home kitchen pantries into something extraordinary. Having the ability to create these edible works of art is only a small portion of pastry chef's responsibilities. They must also be able to manage their staff, entertain the guest, and create revenue for the business—all while working long hours and holidays. This is a considerable amount of responsibility for one person to orchestrate.

Every kitchen has its own stories that span across the industry—the long days, impossible workloads, malfunctioning equipment, being a pastry cook short for a shift, or orders not getting delivered, all while being able to serve the food to the guest without them knowing the chaos in the back of the house. To the uninitiated, it sounds like a nightmare; however, those that work in a kitchen tell these stories and wear them like a badge of honor.

I am constantly asked: "Why would you choose a job like this?" What draws people to work in the hospitality industry? A closer examination in the name of the industry reveals the answer. The *hospitality* industry is based on the principles of service. It is the job of the pastry chef, executive chef, baker, and cook to provide *service* to the guest. It is our job not only to serve food but also to cater to the needs and tastes of the guests and entertain them as well.

"We are Ladies and Gentlemen serving Ladies and Gentlemen." This is the motto of the Ritz-Carlton Hotel Company; it clearly defines the function of all employees. Not only are employees responsible for serving the guest but they must also treat their fellow staff members with the same courtesy and respect. Professionalism starts with the attitude of the employee.

Dedicated employees who demonstrate pride in their craft will advance quickly through the ranks of the pastry shop.

Skills for Success in the Pastry Shop

A good attitude and understanding of the expectations of the hospitality industry provide a solid foundation to succeed in the pastry shop. Ensuring cleanliness and safety as well as understanding ingredients and striving to improve are foundational skills. When starting out in your career, take the time to develop skills in these areas and build on them as you continue learning. You will find that these areas are all intertwined—one relies on and impacts the others. The ability to demonstrate an understanding of these skills is the first step in the start of your career.

Mastering Cleanliness

One word that could easily describe the kitchen environment would be *hectic*. Multitasking is essential, but when working on more than one task at a time, it is easy to become disorganized. It is important to focus not only on technique and properly executing the process of a recipe but also on maintaining a clean and organized work area. A clean work area is the sign of an efficient work area—and a safe one. Cleanliness encompasses more than an individual's personal uniform and workspace; it also means that all members are contributing to the cleanliness of the pastry shop.

Uniform The uniform of the kitchen has evolved over many years. While there is a wide range of what is worn in the kitchen, there are five elements that make up proper kitchen attire. The professional image of the pastry chef is based on sturdy shoes, pants, chef jacket, apron, and hat. While different uniforms can be found in culinary schools and restaurants throughout the country, some form of each of these elements is typically used.

Just as the uniform of the pastry chef has changed over the years, so has the role of the pastry chef. The pastry chef is no longer kept "trapped" in the kitchen. Kitchen spaces are more open and accessible, making the back of the house more visible to the guest. Television shows have increased the popularity of the food service industry, and, as a result, the diner may request to meet the chef and even tour the kitchen. Guests often want to meet the people who have made their food, adding to their experience of the meal. A clean uniform benefits the individual as well as the industry as a whole. When we wear our kitchen uniforms we represent the professionalism of the industry. A clean uniform not only makes the individual look good, it increases the positive perception of the industry.

Your uniform is the first thing that guests will see when they meet you. All clothing, including shoes, must be clean. Professionalism is demonstrated partly through appearance. It is understood that flour will get on pants and shoes, and chocolate will get on a white chef's coat. This happens to everyone on occasion, but the goal is to develop work habits that will maintain the cleanliness of the uniform.

Work Area Organization In addition to maintaining a clean uniform, it is important to maintain a clean work area. Not only are clean work areas sanitary and free from debris, but they also include the organization of equipment and ingredients. Keeping the work area clean will help to keep your uniform clean. A clean work area demonstrates good organizational skills, respect for ingredients, and collaboration with coworkers.

The expectation of work in a professional pastry shop is to execute a recipe correctly and as quickly as possible. When assembling a recipe, organize ingredients and equipment to minimize the possibility of having to do the recipe again. Ingredients not arranged in an organized way can easily be left out of a recipe, resulting in wasted food. A recipe that needs to be remade adds to the labor cost as well as food cost. The fundamentals of understanding ingredients and mixing methods will ensure the mise en place of equipment and ingredients is correct.

The pastry shop is not a one-person operation; all team members come together, working like a machine to provide the necessary products to the guest. A clean work area shows a great deal of respect and professionalism among coworkers.

Pastry Shop Organization In addition to maintaining individual workstations, the members of the team must work together to keep the pastry shop clean and organized. Restaurants, country clubs, and bakeries may have limited staffing. Consequently, this requires all team members to partake in daily removal of trash, cleaning of floors, and storage of inventory. In larger operations, cleaning the shop is a cooperative effort between the stewarding department and kitchen staff.

A clean pastry shop will provide a safe working environment for team members. Food products and debris on floors increase the chances of accidents caused by slipping or falling, and they attract rodents and pests. Cleaning any food or debris from worktables and floors will create a safer work environment and will be less likely to attract vermin.

In an effort to maintain the common areas of the pastry shop, designing a schedule of daily and weekly maintenance will ensure that these areas are cleaned. Additional areas of responsibility that may need to be included on this list would be rotating of storeroom items, inspecting cooler production for freshness, and organizing freezer space. Properly training staff to clearly label and date products will reduce the amount of time required to clean and organize these areas. If all team members do their part, when it comes time to clean the shop, it can be done quickly and effortlessly.

Focusing on Safety

A safe work environment will contribute to reduced workplace injuries. The pastry kitchen is a dangerous place to work—sharp knives, mechanical equipment, and even dirty floors can all cause injury. Safety starts with the individual. Good personal habits and maintenance of personal tools are both necessities.

Earlier, we discussed the importance of the uniform and how a clean uniform reflects directly on the professionalism of the pastry chef. Your tools are an important part of your uniform. Without them, you would not be able to complete your daily tasks. All personal tools should be cleaned and stored and in proper working order before leaving for the day. Cleaning and drying tools will help them to last longer and reduce the possibility of cross contamination.

In addition to being clean, knives should be properly sharpened. A dull knife will make it more difficult to accurately cut items and is more dangerous than a sharp knife.

Understanding Ingredients

When starting out in your career, it is important to understand *why* something is being done just as much as *what* is being done. Take pie dough, for example, which is a simple combination of flour, fat, and liquid. To mix pie dough, the fat is cut into the dry flour. Once this mixture has reached pea-sized particles, liquid is then added. That sounds simple enough, and it is, really. The *what* is simple to explain and can be learned through demonstration.

But as you continue in the profession, it is important to analyze the *why*. Why are these ingredients used? Why do I mix them this way?

To make changes to the recipe, you must first understand the function of the ingredients. Each chapter in this text examines the ingredients used in the formulas and explains their function and benefits. This places the information right alongside the theory and formulas for easy reference.

The simplicity of pie dough makes it a good example for this exercise. First, let's look at what makes a good pie dough. Descriptors of pie dough would be *flaky* and *tender*. Developing these textures in the dough is achieved through the ingredients used and method of assembly. Mixing the dough using the same method and different ingredients will yield a different result.

Pie dough is made from a ratio of 3 parts flour, 2 parts fat, and 1 part liquid. First we will examine the flour. A flaky dough is made by using low-protein flour, such as cake or pastry. However, even with low-protein flour, a tough dough can be created. If liquid is added earlier in the mixing or the dough is mixed too long after the liquid is added, the result will be a tough crust. While pie dough can be made with stronger flours, mixing must be observed very closely to prevent overmixing, which can happen very easily.

The second ingredient is fat. Fat comes in many forms—solid vegetable fat, oil, butter, and lard. What does the fat do in pie dough? It creates layers inside the dough to make the baked dough flaky. Oil will be instantly absorbed into the flour and will not contribute to a flaky dough. We are thus left with solid fats, each of which must be analyzed to determine the best selection.

Analyzing Fats in Pie Dough

Type of Fat	Characteristics	Cost	Source
Butter	Hard when cold, soft when room temperature, good flavor	High	Animal
Solid vegetable fat	Hard when cold, firm when room temperature, neutral flavor	Low	Vegetable
Lard	Hard when cold, firm when room temperature, neutral flavor	Low	Animal

Solid vegetable fat is the most commonly used fat in the production of pie dough. It works well under a wide range of temperatures and is low in cost. While butter will give additional flavor, it quickly transitions from a firm consistency when refrigerated to very soft at room temperature and can be easily overmixed. Lard has many of the same characteristics as the vegetable fat and will produce a very flaky dough. The source of the lard and vegetable fat may help in the decision making process. For example, if producing pies to be marketed as vegetarian, vegetable fat would be a better choice.

The last ingredient is liquid. Liquid is used to pull the flour and fat together to form a dough. Water is typically used for this function. It is easily accessible in the pastry shop and carries a very minimal cost. In some instances, pie dough may contain milk—the fat in milk will contribute to a softer crust. The lactose present in the milk will cause the crust to brown more than if water was used.

It is amazing the difference that changing one ingredient in a recipe has on the final results. In addition to possible changes in flavor or texture, ingredients interact with each other in a recipe and create a system. Changing one can impact how the others work and ultimately change the final result. Understanding ingredients will help you to make an informed decision as to what can be added or taken away, and provide insight into the results of the final product.

Striving to Improve

To achieve success in the pastry shop, it is important to continuously strive for improvement. Some of the tasks found in the pastry shop may come naturally to an individual while others may not. Generations of pastry chefs have worked hard to master the challenges of the bakeshop and innovate new techniques. Many others will continue behind them and build on what they have done. Working on your skills and continuing to improve and develop new skills is what will make you successful in this industry.

The skills you learn in culinary school are the foundation of your new career. Students learn the fundamentals of working cleanly, proper scaling, use of equipment, mixing techniques, piping—the list goes on and on. To truly master these skills takes years of practice. Apply the same techniques an athlete uses: Practice will make you surer and more precise.

When preparing formulas in class or at work, mistakes will happen. These mistakes should be used as a learning experience to prevent the mistake from happening again. Carefully analyzing the result should result in an understanding of what went wrong. Learning from mistakes will make you a stronger pastry chef.

Food Safety

The food service profession relies on more than food that looks and tastes good. As professionals, we also guarantee that the food being served is safe for consumption. Serving food that is unsafe can result in sickness, fines, and lawsuits. Observing safe food-handling practices will protect our customers, the reputation of the business, and your bottom line.

State and local governments are responsible for determining the sanitation standards that must be observed by food service operations under their jurisdiction. Sanitation inspections are conducted to ensure that the laws are being followed to provide the public with safe food. While inspectors are not always welcome, remember that these visits are in place to protect the customer and the operation. It is through recognizing and understanding the causes of foodborne illness that it can be prevented.

Food can become contaminated through three hazards: physical, chemical, and biological.

Physical Contamination

Physical contamination occurs when foreign matter enters a food item, which may cause illness or injury to a person consuming the product. Physical contaminants may include glass, metal flakes, bone chips, shells, wood, and stone. Illness may not be directly connected to these items, but they can cause illness through cross contamination.

Chemical Contamination

Chemical contamination is caused by cleaning chemicals or by cooking food using pans and utensils not approved for cooking. Chemicals should always be stored away from food and food preparation areas. When they must be used, be sure to thoroughly rinse the area with water before use. Since different foods react with metals, it is recommended to use stainless-steel pots, pans, and utensils to reduce the likelihood of chemical contamination.

Biological Contamination

Biological contamination is caused by ingesting food or water that contains bacteria, parasites, viruses, or toxins produced by microorganisms or plants (such as poisonous mushrooms). While no one is immune from contracting a foodborne illness, pregnant woman, the elderly, small children, and those with chronic illness are more susceptible. The symptoms often present the same as the flu—cramping, upset stomach, vomiting, and diarrhea—which can lead to dehydration. In some instances, neurological symptoms such as dizziness or difficulty breathing may occur and require immediate medical attention.

The pastry shop is a hands-on operation, and food that is constantly handled can become easily contaminated if the proper guidelines are not followed. Personal hygiene, time–temperature abuse, and cross contamination are the main causes of foodborne illness.

Personal Hygiene

Good personal hygiene is the first step in preventing the spread of foodborne illness. Bacteria are present on our skin, hair, eyes, nose, mouth, and hands. These bacteria can be transferred to food and food contact surfaces and, given the right conditions, can multiply in food and make people sick. Regular hand washing is the most effective defense against the spread of foodborne illnesses.

Here are 10 ways to reduce foodborne illness:

1. Do not work if you are sick.
2. Wear a clean uniform.

3. Properly restrain hair with a hat or hairnet.

4. Keep facial hair neatly trimmed.

5. Do not touch your face or head at work.

6. Remove jewelry at work.

7. Cover your mouth when coughing or sneezing.

8. Wash hands as needed when working:
   - After eating, drinking, break
   - After using restroom
   - After working with anything that may be contaminated

9. Wear rubber gloves when working with finished food items.

10. Wear rubber gloves when wearing a bandage.

Rubber gloves are not a complete solution to stopping the spread of foodborne illness. In fact, if used improperly, they can be just as bad as not washing your hands. Gloves are not a substitute for hand washing. Gloves should be worn when working with foods that are not going to be heated again for service. This will reduce the risk of contaminating the food with bacteria on your hands. The gloves should only be worn when handling food—opening doors and gathering equipment should be done prior to putting the gloves on.

Time–Temperature Abuse

There are ideal conditions under which bacteria will grow; however, through the use of time and temperature, we can control the bacteria's ability to reproduce. In addition to time and temperature, bacteria require a moist, neutral environment, and oxygen. Bacteria can grow in the presence (aerobic) or absence (anaerobic) of oxygen, and this is true for the bacteria that cause foodborne illness as well.

The best tool in the kitchen to fight against microorganisms is a thermometer. When storing food, keep it under 41°F (5°C) in the refrigerator or above 140°F (60°C) for serving. When

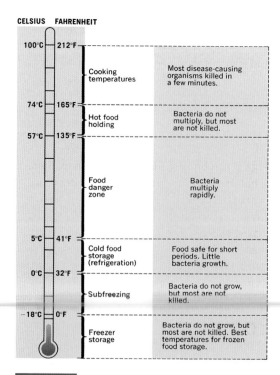

FIGURE 1.1 Thermometer showing temperature ranges for bacteria growth

held at these temperatures, the bacteria will not be killed but the growth will be slowed down. Food stored between this range—41°F (5°C) to 140°F (60°C)—is in the **food danger zone**. The maximum time for food to be stored in the danger zone is 4 hours. This range is ideal for the reproduction of bacteria and it grows at a very fast rate. Food stored in this range for more than 4 hours should be discarded.

Cross Contamination

Cross contamination is the process of unknowingly transferring bacteria or microorganisms from one surface to another surface or food. It usually occurs between raw and cooked foods and can occur during storage. Raw items in the bakeshop—for example, egg products—should be stored on the bottom shelf of coolers to prevent raw egg product from getting on finished items. Preventing cross contamination can be done by washing hands, changing cutting boards, and washing and sanitizing workstations throughout the day. The proper use of rubber gloves can also reduce the possibility of cross contamination.

Food Allergies

A food allergen is an exaggerated immune response triggered by certain proteins in food. The most common symptoms of food allergies include tingling in the mouth; hives; itching; swelling of the lips, tongue, or face; wheezing or trouble breathing; abdominal pain, nausea, or diarrhea; and dizziness, lightheadedness, or fainting. In severe cases, some people will go into anaphylactic shock, with difficulty breathing, a drop in blood pressure, rapid pulse, and loss of consciousness. In cases of severe reaction, emergency medical treatment is necessary, as severe allergic reactions can lead to death.

Some people have an intolerance to certain foods. There is a difference between intolerance and an allergy. An allergic reaction comes on every time the food is eaten. Intolerance only manifests itself gradually, or only after consuming large quantities of the food. Both may exhibit similar symptoms. Although food intolerance can lead to chronic health issues, it is not imminently life threatening, as food allergies sometimes are.

As a commitment to keeping the customer safe, it is important that food service workers are aware of allergens in the food they serve. There are over 160 foods that can cause allergic reactions—the Food Allergen Labeling and Consumer Protection Act of 2004 (FALCPA) identifies the eight most common allergenic foods. The U.S Food and Drug Administration (FDA) states that 90 percent of all food allergies originate from this group of eight foods:

- Milk
- Eggs
- Fish
- Crustacean shellfish
- Tree nuts
- Peanuts
- Wheat
- Soybeans

Many of these allergens can be found in the pastry shop. Some may not be used as an ingredient on their own but they may be part of a prepared item used in a recipe. Understanding ingredients goes further than just understanding how the ingredients work together. It also includes knowing what is in another ingredient. For example, many pistachio pastes are made with almonds or almond oil, and a person might not be allergic to pistachios but might be to almonds. The same holds true for items produced in the pastry shop. While peanuts may only be contained in a few items, they are present in the shop. Cross contamination can be enough to cause some people to go into anaphylactic shock.

Tools and Equipment

Looking back in time, baking bread without any equipment was a laborious task. Dough was mixed by hand and ovens were heated with wood. Fast forward to the modern pastry shop, where mixers knead the dough, dividers portion the dough, proof boxes reduce fermentation time, and oven temperatures are precisely controlled. The tools and equipment of the pastry shop facilitate the job of the pastry chef, reducing production times and helping to regulate consistency.

Tools

Air Tools

Airbrush An airbrush is used for adding detail to pastillage, bonbons, chocolate showpieces, and plated desserts. There are two types of airbrushes, single action and double action. A single-action airbrush only controls the amount of air pressure and will always spray a certain amount of color. A dual-action airbrush controls the amount of colorant as well as the air pressure. Pressing down allows the air to flow and pulling back sprays the color. The more the button is pressed down, the more airflow will increase. The further the button is pulled back, the more paint will be released.

Air compressor The air compressor provides the air pressure for the airbrush.

Heat Tools

Alcohol Wick Burner A small burner filled with denatured alcohol is used to melt and attach a small piece of sugar to a showpiece.

Blowtorch The blowtorch is used to caramelize sugar on a crème brûlée, unmold frozen cakes from metal rings, and fasten sugar pieces on a showpiece. A large **propane blowtorch** and smaller butane blowtorch are used throughout the book. The smaller butane torch is useful for connecting delicate sugar pieces.

Hair Dryer The hair dryer with a cool setting is used to cool sugar work. It can be used to rapidly cool pieces that have been attached, blown sugar, and larger cast pieces.

Heat Gun The heat gun is used for warming melted chocolate and to keep it tempered. It can also be used to warm tools when working with chocolate or to unmold frozen cakes from metal rings.

Scales and Thermometers

Digital Scale A digital scale is a battery-powered device used to measure ingredients by weight. Use a digital scale that is made of kitchen-safe materials with a maximum weight of at least 5 lb (2.267 kg). A smaller scale that can measure 0.003 oz (0.1 g) will be needed for the recipes in Chapter 4, "Modern Pastry Techniques."

Digital Thermometer with Probe A digital thermometer with probe can be used for cooking sugar, checking oil temperature when frying, and checking the temperature of ganache. Many of these thermometers can be switched between Fahrenheit and centigrade.

Infrared Thermometer Infrared thermometers can be used to quickly check the temperature of chocolate when tempering. They only read surface temperature, so it is important to stir thoroughly before checking the temperature to get an accurate reading. Infrared thermometers are not good for checking the temperature of boiling liquids.

Specialty Hand Tools

Chocolate-Dipping Forks Chocolate-dipping forks are used for hand-dipped chocolates. They can be purchased in sets or as individual pieces. The shape of the fork is designed specifically for the candy they are used to dip. A hoop is used for round truffles and forks are used for square or elongated pieces.

Metal Bars Food safe metal bars of varying thickness can be used for spreading cake layers, chocolate, and casting sugar.

Microplane A **microplane** is a very fine grater used for removing the zest of citrus fruits or grating chocolate.

Sauce Gun A **sauce gun** is a funnel-shaped device that can dispense a liquid. The sauce gun is useful for casting sugar, depositing liquor bonbons, glazing pastries, and saucing dessert plates for large functions.

Sugar Pump A sugar pump is a rubber air bladder connected to a copper tip by a rubber hose. It is used to inflate blown sugar.

Equipment

Mixers

Mixers are found in every pastry shop. Their sizes range from small, 5 qt (4.73 L) table-top models up to 60 qt (56.78 L) floor models. The mixer can perform the work of a person in a fraction of the time. Pastry chefs are able to mix large quantities of doughs in short periods of time, which reduces the amount of time a product is in the danger zone.

Vertical Mixer **Vertical mixers** come in countertop, table, and floor models. In these models, the bowl remains in place while the attachment moves in a planetary motion, thoroughly mixing all ingredients in the bowl. There are three attachments used in vertical mixers: paddle, whip, and dough hook.

FIGURE 1.2 Countertop mixer (Image courtesy of Hobart)

FIGURE 1.3a–c Dough hook, paddle, and whip (Images courtesy of Hobart)

1. **Paddle**—a flat attachment that can be used to combine ingredients. Using the paddle at a higher speed will incorporate air into a batter. It is not able to incorporate as much as air as the whip.

2. **Whip**—also known as a wire whip. The whip is used to incorporate air into cream, eggs, and batters. When using the whip attachment, be sure to not overfill the bowl. There needs to be enough space in the bowl for the whip to work properly and aerate the product. This is dependent on the ingredient you are whipping; it is recommended that the bowl not be filled over halfway for most applications.

3. **Dough hook**—a hook-shaped attachment used for developing gluten.

Spiral Mixer **Spiral mixers** are used for developing gluten in bread doughs. The bowl of the mixer turns while the mixing attachment stays in a stationary position. Spiral mixers can quickly develop gluten while not overmixing the dough. They create less friction, resulting in a lower final dough temperature and ensuring a more consistent fermentation. The shortened mixing time also prevents oxidation of the flour, leaving the interior of the bread with a darker color.

FIGURE 1.4 Spiral mixer (Image courtesy of Hobart)

Dough Handlers

The production of bread can be facilitated through the use of dough-handling equipment. This line of products covers a wide range of items to assist in fermentation and shaping.

Divider The divider does exactly what the name implies: It divides the dough. Scaling dough by hand for rolls can be a tedious task, but by using a divider, this process can be handled quickly and produce uniform pieces of dough. After fermenting the dough, it is scaled into a large press: Making the press larger will result in larger rolls. The dough is then briefly rested. The dough is placed into the divider and cut into equal pieces. The number of pieces can vary, depending on the size of the machine and the cutter head that is being used.

Divider Rounder The divider rounder takes the dividing process one step further. After cutting the dough into equal portions, it then mechanically rounds the dough.

Dough Sheeter A dough **sheeter** is a mechanized rolling system. It consists of two conveyer belts with a pair of adjustable rollers in the middle. The front of the sheeter has a dial control that adjusts the opening between the rollers; the numbers refer to the thickness in millimeters. The lower the number, the thinner the dough will become. The dough sheeter can reduce rolling times and produce a uniform thickness throughout the entire piece of dough.

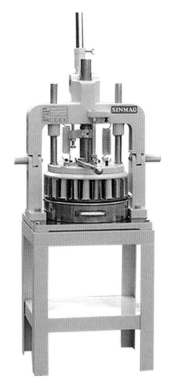

FIGURE 1.5 Divider (Image courtesy of American Baking Systems, Inc.)

FIGURE 1.6 Divider rounder (Image courtesy of American Baking Systems, Inc.)

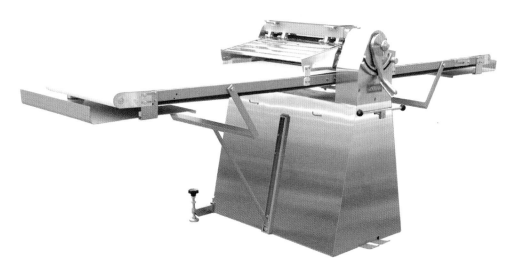

FIGURE 1.7 Dough sheeter (Image courtesy of American Baking Systems, Inc.)

Proof Box A proof box provides the ideal humidity and temperature for fermenting yeast doughs. The temperature and humidity can be adjusted depending on the type of dough. There are portable and fixed-mounted proof boxes.

A proofer retarder is closely related to a proof box, with the added feature of being able to retard the dough. A retarder is a refrigerator that contains moisture to prevent the dough from drying out. Dough can be placed in the proofer retarder at the end of an evening shift, and a timer can be set to switch the retarder off and turn on the proof box. This provides the pastry chefs with dough ready to go into the oven when they arrive in the morning.

FIGURE 1.8 Proof box (Image courtesy of LBC Bakery Equipment, Inc.)

Ovens

The oven is the heart of the pastry shop. There are many styles of ovens available. Often times, the deciding factor on the type of oven is the amount of space in the pastry shop. Many shops contain two types of ovens, one conventional and one convection, to meet the baking needs of different products.

Deck Oven A **deck oven** is also known as a hearth oven. This oven contains a ceramic deck. Sheet pans are placed directly on the deck, and in the case of artisan-style breads, they are baked directly on the deck with no pan. This allows the heat to quickly transfer into the bread dough. Deck ovens are also equipped with steam injection. Steam injection helps in crust formation of breads.

FIGURE 1.9 Deck oven (Image courtesy of LBC Bakery Equipment, Inc.)

Rack Oven A rack oven is a convection oven with steam injection. A rack filled with sheet pans of product is loaded into the oven. The rack is then spun on a carousel inside the oven. This movement, combined with the convection, provides a good circulation of air and promotes even baking. The rack allows for quick loading of larger quantities of pastries, making it ideal for production.

FIGURE 1.10 Rack oven (Image courtesy of Baxter)

Mechanical Oven The interior of a **mechanical oven** is similar to a Ferris wheel. Metal trays inside the oven rotate the product around the oven, which helps to reduce hot spots. There can be four to six shelves inside a mechanical oven. Mechanical ovens have a large footprint; they take up a considerable amount of space in the bakeshop. However, they can also bake a large quantity of baked goods at one time.

Convection Oven A **convection oven** forces air through the oven cavity. Pushing hot air around the food increases the heat transfer. As a rule of thumb, convection ovens are

FIGURE 1.11 Convection oven (Image courtesy of Baxter)

50°F (10°C) warmer than a conventional oven. Products baked in a convection oven will bake slightly faster than a conventional oven, resulting in more moisture retention in the final product.

Combi Oven A **combi oven** is a multipurpose oven that can function as a steamer or convection oven, or it can be used as both a steamer and convection oven at the same time. It is an extremely precise piece of equipment. Combi ovens can also be used to cook sous vide (under vacuum) in combi mode.

FIGURE 1.12 Combi oven (Image courtesy of Vulcan)

Freezers

Blast Freezer A blast freezer is an extremely cold freezer that rapidly decreases the temperature of foods. Blast freezers can be used to quickly set ice cream extruded from a batch chiller without losing air, or to set mousses and creams for quick unmolding. The speed at which the water is frozen in the food produces small crystals, which results in less damage to the food. Once the food is frozen in the **blast chiller**, it is transferred to a conventional freezer for storage.

FIGURE 1.13 Blast chiller (Image courtesy of Irinox North America)

Food Processors

Robot Coupe A Robot Coupe is a professional-grade food processor. It can be used to chop nuts, purée fruits, and emulsify ganache.

Robot Coupe Blixer The Robot Coupe Blixer is a combination food processor and blender. It has adjustable speeds and can quickly purée food. It is especially useful for processing chocolate for rollouts.

FIGURE 1.14 Robot Coupe and Blixer (Photos courtesy of Robot Coupe USA, Inc.)

Vitamix A Vitamix is a high-speed blender that can be used for purées and blending dense ingredients. It has adjustable speeds and is more powerful than a regular blender.

FIGURE 1.15 Vitamix (Photo courtesy of Vitamix)

Immersion Blenders Immersion blenders, also known as stick blenders, are used to blend ingredients. They can be used in the container the products were initially mixed in. They can be used to emulsify frozen dessert bases, ganache, fruit sauces, and to temper chocolate using the seeding method. Immersion blenders do not possess the same power as a Vitamix.

FIGURE 1.16 Immersion blender (Image courtesy of Waring)

Mise en Place

Mise en place is the French term for "putting in place." This term is used in professional pastry shops to refer to the organization of ingredients, equipment, and the individual workstation, as well as the mental preparation required. All of these things help to reduce the time needed to prepare items correctly.

If you recall earlier in the chapter, understanding ingredients is a skill that is important in being successful in the pastry shop. An understanding of ingredients and their function in a recipe can direct the pastry chef as to how they are to be assembled in a recipe. Now we begin to connect the dots. We know the ingredients and the method, so the next step is to gather the tools to complete the recipe. Understanding the method will ensure that the tools are gathered and the workstation is organized to produce the recipe.

An important part of mise en place is mental preparation. In classes, mental preparation includes covering reading material before class, arriving to class on time ready to go, and taking notes to assist with the daily proficiencies. Work is similar—mentally preparing before work for the day ahead. Whether it is banquet production, cake orders, or service on the line, a great deal of thought, planning, and preparation goes into making every day successful. Organizing the production of banquet items to have a smooth flow of work, or organizing prep work and station setup prior to dinner service for working on the line, is critical to the success of the operation.

Key Terms

Physical contamination
Chemical contamination
Biological contamination
Food danger zone
Cross contamination
Propane blowtorch
Microplane

Sauce gun
Vertical mixer
Paddle
Whip
Dough hook
Spiral mixer
Sheeter

Deck oven
Mechanical oven
Convection oven
Combi oven
Blast chiller
Mise en place

Questions for Review

1. List the eight major food allergens.

2. There are five types of ovens used in the pastry shop. Select two and discuss the differences between them.

3. Why is good personal hygiene so critical in stopping the spread of bacteria?

4. How can foodborne illness be prevented?

5. What are the four skills necessary for being successful in the pastry kitchen?

CHAPTER 2

Bread for the Pastry Chef

The importance of bread can be easily observed by looking back in history to the Roman Empire. In order to keep the citizens happy, free bread was given at the Coliseum. The importance of bread cannot be ignored; historically, it has been shown that bread has influenced the success and failures of war and the ability to feed the hungry. Today, the art of bread baking is returning to its roots. Pastry chefs and bakers are producing excellent products combining old-world skills and modern technology.

LEARNING OBJECTIVES

After reading this chapter, you should be able to:

1. **Convert** a recipe using baker's percentage.
2. **Determine** desired dough temperature for straight doughs and doughs with multiple factors.
3. **Identify** the difference between a sourdough and preferment.
4. **Properly** mix dough using the short, intense, and improved mixing methods.
5. **Present** the 14 steps of bread baking.

Introduction to Bread

As part of a sandwich or an accompaniment with a meal, bread is a part of everyday life. Bread's production can be considered more complex than many other items in the pastry kitchen because it is alive. Yeast is used in bread baking to leaven the bread and develop flavor—this can only be done by feeding it and providing the correct environment for it to grow. Understanding what is happening and how each process impacts the following step will help to ensure the proper flavor and texture are developed in the baked loaf. Many variables affect the production of bread. To control the process, it is critical to thoroughly understand ingredients, formula percentages, fermentation, and mixing methods.

Ingredients and Function

Wheat Flours

Flour can come from a wide variety of sources; it is produced by grinding grains, seeds, or roots. The earliest evidence of flour was over 30,000 years ago. Throughout history, the rise and fall of civilizations can be traced back to a simple grain. Napoleon's quickly advancing army could not maintain the grain supply. As a result, starvation set in; his troops were weakened, and this eventually led to their defeat. The Civil War was also won by grain; the North had the grains to feed the troops while the South had cotton. Grains played an important role in history; today, we still rely on grains for nourishment.

Wheat flour is the main ingredient in bread. Today, flour is easily accessible in many forms and is grown throughout the United States. It is broken down into six classes: hard red winter, hard red spring, soft red winter, hard white winter, soft white spring, and durum.

Hard flours are higher in protein content and are best suited for breads. Soft wheat flour is lower in protein and is milled for use in cakes, cookies, and pastries. Winter wheat is grown in the southern United States as far north as Kansas. Seeds are planted in October. The wheat begins to grow, and once winter arrives and temperatures drop, it goes dormant. Once spring arrives, the wheat continues growing until it is harvested in May. Spring flours are grown from the same southern region and continue north into parts of Canada. Seeds are planted in spring and grow during the spring and summer. Harvesting is completed during mid to late summer.

There is no noticeable difference between red and white flours, other than the color. Nutritional values are comparable: The difference lies in the protein contents. Winter wheats have an average protein content of 11% to 12%, while the average protein in spring wheat is 13% to 15%. Wheat protein holds up better under long fermentation times. The extra protein in spring wheat makes it ideal for bread baked in pans and breads that contain grains. The extra strength of the flour helps to support the additional weight of the grains.

When the wheat kernel is harvested, it must be processed into flour. The inner portion of the wheat kernel is protected by the **pericarp**. The pericarp is composed of seven layers. Its main purpose is to protect the wheat kernel. Directly under the pericarp is the bran. **Endosperm** is located under the bran. The starch and protein found in white flour is milled from this layer. The endosperm provides the food for the wheat germ. **Wheat germ** contains fats, vitamins, and minerals—this is the part of the embryo of the wheat kernel that creates the next plant.

When milling white flours (bread, all-purpose, cake, and pastry), many nutrients are lost through the removal of the bran. Many of these flours will state that they are "enriched." Enriched foods have the nutrients that were naturally present in the unprocessed state returned after processing. In the case of wheat flour, thiamin, riboflavin, niacin, folic acid, and iron are replaced after milling. The requirements for labeling a product as enriched are regulated by the FDA.

Specialty Flours

Wheat isn't the only grain milled to make bread. Many other grains and seeds can be milled to produce flour that will change the texture and flavor of the finished product. Utilizing different flours can provide more than just a different flavor—they contribute to the structure, texture, and nutritional value of the bread.

Rye Flour

Rye flour comes in many different forms—pumpernickel, dark, medium, light or white rye, whole rye berries, or cracked rye berries. Rye can be used at lower levels (5% to 10%) and flavor the bread while providing a slightly darker color. When used in higher percentages, the difference between rye and wheat flour will be very clear.

Compared to wheat flour, rye is considerably lower in gluten and requires more liquid to properly hydrate. The gluten formed is also very delicate. Mixing at a high speed will cause the gluten to tear and release water back into the dough, resulting in a sticky dough. This can be prevented by mixing at lower speeds for shorter periods of time. As the percentage of rye flour increases, more care must be taken.

Semolina Flour

Semolina is a finely ground wheat flour produced from durum wheat. When used in bread recipes, it gives the bread a slightly yellow tint and adds crunch to the crust. It can be used in small quantities or to replace the flour 100%. The high protein content requires more hydration and longer mixing times to properly develop the gluten.

Protein Contents in Flours

Protein Content	Flour
7%	Cake
9%	Pastry
11%	Rye flour
11%	All-purpose
13%	Patent
14%	High-gluten
15%	Clear flour
21%	Semolina flour

Grains and Seeds

Grains and seeds are often used in bread to add texture and flavor. Common grains and seeds used in breads are sunflower, sesame, flax, oats, millet, cracked wheat and rye, wheat berries, and corn meal. Before using these in bread making, they must first be placed in water. Placing grains or seeds in an equal amount of water and allowing them to soak for several hours is known as a *soaker*. Using the soaker allows the seeds and grains to absorb water. Not soaking these products will cause moisture to be pulled from the dough during the first fermentation. When mixed this dough had the proper hydration, but now will be dry and stiff. Soaking also softens the grains, prevents cutting the gluten strands during mixing, and provides a better texture to the grains and seeds in the finished product.

Cold and Hot Soakers

There are two ways that grains and seeds can be soaked, cold and hot. A cold soak is the process of soaking the grains or seeds in room-temperature water, 72°F (22°C), for several hours or overnight. The cold soak method does require more time; to speed up the process, a hot soak can be used. To hot soak, bring the water to a boil, pour over grains and seeds to cover, and allow to soak for a few hours. Be sure the soaked grains have cooled completely before mixing into the dough. Adding a soaker that is still warm or hot will increase the dough temperature and speed fermentation.

Which method is the best to use? That depends on how much time you have. If needed quickly, a hot soak is recommended. What are you soaking? The size and type of grain will determine which to use. If your grains are still crunchy in the finished product after a cold soak, test the next time with a hot soak. Ultimately, it comes down to personal preference. The recipes in this book are presented with what was felt to yield the best results after testing.

Liquid

It would be impossible to create bread dough without any liquid. The primary liquid used in the production of breads is water. Flour is hydrated with liquids, allowing for the formation of gluten. It goes much further than this; liquids dissolve the yeast, salt, and sugars and disperse them throughout the other ingredients. Water begins the enzymatic activity. The ratio of flour to water can create a stiff dough with a tight crumb or a slack dough with a loose crumb and crispy crust. Water is also used to control fermentation. It is the medium that makes the sugars available to the yeast. Adjusting water temperature is the simplest way to control fermentation. If the kitchen is too hot, cold or even ice water can be used. If it is too cold in the kitchen, warmer water can be used to achieve the desired dough temperature after mixing (more on desired dough temperature on pages 30–32).

Milk, which is primarily water, is also used in producing bread. Milk is composed of water, lactose (sugar), fat, and milk solids. The small percentage of fat in milk, 3.6%, is enough to soften the crust of the dough. Lactose present in the milk browns during baking and gives the soft crust its deep color and flavor.

Salt

Salt is used to enhance the flavor of the bread that develops during fermentation and baking. If the bread does not have enough salt, it will have a flat flavor. In most recipes, the salt can range from 1.8% to 2% of the weight of the flour. This depends on the dough—formulas that include grains and seeds will have a higher percentage of salt to account for the additional ingredients.

Flavor is only one benefit of salt; this small percentage of salt has profound impacts on the dough. It strengthens the gluten structure of the bread. Without salt in the dough, it will be difficult to work and be sticky. Salt can be added directly to the dry ingredients at the start of the mixing process or at the end. The addition of salt at the end of mixing allows the gluten to begin forming and allows more time for enzymatic process to occur. (See Autolyse on page 35.)

Yeast also benefits from the addition of salt. Many older bakers will say that salt kills yeast, but this is not the case: Salt does not technically kill the yeast. Instead, it slows the fermentation process by water absorption. Too much salt in bread will give a salty flavor, but it will also hinder fermentation and significantly reduce the final size and extend the fermentation time. The color of the final loaf is also affected by salt. As a result of salt slowing the sugar consumption by the yeast, there is more sugar available to create a brown crust.

Yeast

Without yeast, bread would not develop the flavor and texture we have come to know and love. The pastry chef must fully understand yeast to produce great bread. In addition to providing flavor and leavening, yeast also strengthens and develops gluten in the dough. The role of yeast is critical in bread baking. A closer examination into how yeast works will provide the information necessary to understand and control the fermentation process.

Commercial kitchens most commonly purchase yeast in four forms, fresh or cake yeast, active dry, osmotolerant, or instant. Fresh yeast is a highly perishable but consistent product. It should be combined with a small amount of the liquid from the recipe to create a paste before using. Fresh yeast has traditionally been the preferred yeast of bakers and pastry chefs.

However, improvements in the quality of active dry and instant yeast have replaced the use of fresh yeast for many bakers because they provide convenience and an increase in consistency. Active dry yeast requires rehydration prior to being added to the dough, while instant yeast can be directly added to the dough. These yeasts products all have different strengths and cannot be substituted equally in a recipe. The following table provides conversions for yeasts.

Fresh yeast is available through local distributors and is sold in 1 lb (454 g) units, with a shelf life of 1 to 2 weeks under refrigeration. Active dry and instant yeasts are sold in 1 lb (454 g)

FIGURE 2.1 Instant, active, and fresh yeast.

vacuum bags. They are stored at room temperature. Once opened, they can be refrigerated for up to 4 months. If unsure if any of these yeasts have expired, combine a small amount of yeast, sugar, flour, and some water. If the mixture does not begin to ferment after 20 minutes, it is time to replace it.

Yeast Conversions

	Fresh	Active Dry	Instant
Fresh	1 oz	2 oz	3 oz
Active Dry	0.5 oz	1 oz	1.5 oz
Instant	0.33 oz	0.66 oz	1 oz

Recipes that contain more than 10% sugar and/or fat benefit from using osmotolerant yeast. Sugar and yeast compete for the available water in the formula, but the sugar can more easily absorb the water, making it difficult for the yeast to grow. Osmotolerant yeast is able to ferment in these doughs despite the lack of water. If you do not have osmotolerant yeast available, substitute instant yeast and increase the quantity by 30%.

In addition to water, yeast requires food. The primary foods for yeast are sugar and carbohydrates. Fermentation occurs when the yeast consumes the sugar and carbohydrates. During the early stages of fermentation, simple sugars are consumed by the yeast. The more complex carbohydrates are enzymatically broken down into simple sugars and consumed later in the fermentation process.

When the dough is first mixed, there is oxygen in the dough and the yeast is aerobic. During this phase, the yeast produces carbon dioxide and alcohol as byproducts. The oxygen is quickly consumed and the yeast switches over to an anaerobic state. This means the yeast does not need oxygen to grow. It is also during this stage that organic acids begin to form. These organic acids contribute a great deal to the flavor and aroma of the bread as well as strengthen the dough and increase shelf life.

Sugars

Sugar provides sweetness to the bread and a rich brown crust. It can be found in bread in many forms, such as granulated sugar, molasses, honey, or malt syrup. Sugar is the primary food for yeast, but like salt, it absorbs water and can slow down fermentation by pulling water away from the yeast. As the percentage of sugar increases in the recipe, so will the amount of yeast.

Most breads contain 5% or less of sugar. The more sugar in a recipe, the more it will brown. Oven temperature may need to be reduced to prevent the crust, or bottom of the bread, from burning before it fully bakes. Recipes that include a large amount of sugar (20% to 30%) need to have the sugar added in two steps. Up to 12% can be mixed at the beginning of the mixing, with the remainder added at the end. Sugar is hygroscopic and absorbs water, adding too much at the beginning of the mixing will reduce the amount of water available to the flour, creating a weak gluten structure.

Malt

Malt is produced by germinating grains, typically barley. The grains are soaked in water until they begin to sprout. Once sprouted, the grains are dried with hot air to stop the sprouting. At this point, the grain has developed the enzyme amylose, which is necessary to convert the starch in the grain to maltose. Malt can be purchased in two forms, diastatic and nondiastatic. Nondiastatic malt is dried at a higher temperature than diastatic malt; as a result, all the enzymes are destroyed. Nondiastatic malt will provide easily processed sugars to the yeast and sweetness to the bread. Diastatic malt has some additional benefits due to the some of the enzymes remaining active. It still maintains the primary function of providing nutrients for the yeast and aids in converting starch in the dough into sugar, and the additional sugar provides a boost to the yeast.

Eggs

Eggs provide structure, color, and flavor to the bread. The flavor of the egg comes from the yolk and the fats it contains. These fats also tenderize the bread. If used in larger quantities, they can also give a rich yellow color to the dough. The white is mostly water and does not contribute any flavor. Breads with eggs will also develop a brown crust more quickly, and, as a result, reduced oven temperature may be needed for breads containing eggs.

Fats

Fats are used in bread to add flavor and shorten the gluten. There are many fats available for baking bread, yet unsalted butter and olive oil are typically used. Unsalted butter is preferred over salted butter, because it allows greater control over the addition of salt. The function of fat in the dough is to add flavor and tenderize the dough. All fats shorten the gluten. In small amounts, the fat controls how much gluten can form, while in larger quantities it can almost prevent it from forming. In the case of bread dough, too much fat in the recipe added too early can create a dough with a very weak gluten structure. For more information on adding fat to bread dough, see the brioche mixing method. Doughs that include fat tend to have a softer crust and texture.

Math

Baker's Percentage

Introduction to Baker's Percentages

As a student starting out in a new career, a recipe is viewed as a list of ingredients and a method for assembling them. Yet there is much more information contained in this "simple" list of ingredients, such as *baker's percentages*. The recipes included in this text will have ingredients in

U.S. and metric quantities alongside baker's percentage. **Baker's percentage** is the percentage of the weight of an ingredient in relation to the weight of the flour. Through an understanding of baker's percentage, a chef can increase or decrease the yield of a recipe, make adjustments to the ratios, and even know what the recipe produces just by the list of ingredients and the percentages.

When working with baker's percentage, there are three rules to remember:

1. The weight of the flour is always 100%, due to the fact that almost all recipes include flour. If there is more than one flour in the recipe, the total of all flour weights is 100%.

2. To find the percentage of an ingredient, always divide the ingredient by the flour weight. Example = Sugar weight/Flour weight.

3. The total percentage for the recipe will always be over 100%.

Baker's percentage is used in recipes that contain flour. As your career continues and you start to become more familiar with baker's percentage, you will be able to predict the consistency of the final product. For example, when examining the percentage of an ingredient such as water to the flour, the final consistency of the product can be determined. A recipe that is 50% water would produce a final product having the characteristics of a dough. It can be rolled and cut. As the percentage of water increases, the mixture will become more of a batter that can be scooped and baked, or even poured. Recipes in this text that do not contain flour will be based on the total weight of the recipe being 100%.

Calculating Ingredient Percentages

In the following example, we will calculate baker's percentage for a baguette formula.

Baguette

Ingredient	Pounds	Ounces
Bread Flour	2	2
Salt		0.67
Instant Yeast		0.15
Water	1	4

Yields: Five 11 oz loaves

The first step is to convert the amounts to the same unit of measure. When using U.S. measurements, this can be done by converting all ingredients to pounds or ounces. Due to the small quantities of yeast and salt in the recipe, it would be best to convert all of the ingredients to ounces. To begin, multiply the pound weight of the flour by 16 ounces and add this to the 2 ounces.

Bread flour

2 lb 2 oz

2 × 16 = 32 oz

32 oz + 2 oz = 34 oz

The total weight in ounces of bread flour is 34 ounces. Now perform the same process for the water.

Ingredient	Ounces
Bread Flour	34
Salt	0.67
Instant Yeast	0.15
Water	20

The second step is to calculate the percentages of all ingredients. Refer to the rules of calculating baker's percentage on the preceding page. Remember, the flour is always 100%. So to calculate the percentage of salt, yeast, and water, divide the weight of these ingredients by the weight of the flour and multiply this number by 100.

Salt

(0.67 / 34) × 100 = Percentage of salt

0.0197 × 100 = 1.97% salt

Note: It is recommended to keep at least two decimal places when calculating percentages. When converting a recipe from a small test batch to large production batch, rounding the salt to 2% could result in the dough having too much salt. The same is true when rounding down. Therefore, when increasing and decreasing recipes, results will be more consistent when they are not rounded to whole numbers. Using a spreadsheet such as Excel will help you to simplify recipe conversions.

Yeast

(0.15 / 34) × 100 = Percentage of instant yeast

0.0044 × 100 =

0.44% Instant yeast

Water

(20 / 34) × 100 = Percentage of water

0.5882 × 100 =

58.82% Water

After calculating the percentage of all the ingredients, a new table can be created. At this point, the weights of the ingredients can be discarded; the percentages provide all the information needed to calculate the quantities.

Ingredient	Percentage
Bread Flour	100.00%
Salt	1.97%
Instant Yeast	0.44%
Water	58.82%

The percentages are then added together to calculate the formula's total percentage. Remember, when using baker's percentage, the total percentage of a formula will always be more than 100%.

Ingredient	Percentage
Bread Flour	100.00%
Salt	1.97%
Instant Yeast	0.44%
Water	58.82%
Total	161.23%

Calculating a Formula Using Percentages

The total percentage can now be used to scale the recipe up or down, which is an important function in the bakeshop. In this next step, we need to know the total amount of dough needed. The calculations for this example will need to yield a total of 50 baguettes; each baguette will be scaled at 11 ounces.

To calculate the total weight of dough needed, multiply the amount of loaves by the weight per loaf:

Total dough needed = loaves × Weight per loaf

Total dough needed = 50 × 11 oz

Total dough needed = 550 oz

The 550 oz of total dough needed is then divided by the total percentage. This will provide the conversion factor.

Conversion factor = Total dough needed / Total percentage

Conversion factor = 550 oz / 161.23%

Conversion factor = 3.41

The next step is to multiply the percentages of the ingredients.

Ingredient	Percentage	Conversion Factor Multiplied by Percentage	Ounces
Bread Flour	100.00%	3.41 × 100 =	341
Salt	1.97%	3.41 × 1.97 =	6.72
Instant Yeast	0.44%	3.41 × 0.44 =	1.5
Water	58.82%	3.41 × 58.82 =	200.58
Total	161.23%		549.8

The total dough needed to produce 55 baguettes was 550 ounces. The impact of carrying only two decimal points before rounding can be witnessed with how close the conversion was to the original needs. It is always better to have a little extra product than what is needed when producing bread; making a few ounces of extra dough would be acceptable.

Lastly, convert the ounces to pounds by dividing the ingredient totals by 16. Then multiply the remaining decimal (0.31 × 16) to convert the decimal back to ounces.

Ingredient	Percentage	Ounces		Final Weights
Bread Flour	100.00%	341	341/16 = 21.31	21 lb 2 oz
Salt	1.97%	6.72		6.72 oz
Instant Yeast	0.44%	1.5		1.5 oz
Water	58.82%	200.58	200.58/16 = 12.54	12 lb 8.5 oz
Total	161.23%			

Calculating a Formula with Two or More Flours

Some formulas contain more than one type of flour. In these instances the total of the flours are totaled to equal 100%.

Example

Calculating Percentage with More Than One Flour

Ingredient	Weight
Bread Flour	9.0 lb
Whole Wheat Flour	5.5 lb

The flours above are used together in a formula. Since both are flours, they are combined. Add the bread flour and the whole wheat flour together: 14.5 pounds represents 100%. To calculate how much each of the two ingredients contributes, divide the individual flour weight by the total of the flours.

Bread flour/Total flour weight

(9.0 / 14.5) × 100 = Bread flour percentage

62% = Bread flour percentage

Whole wheat flour/Total flour weight

(5.5 / 14.5) × 100 = Whole wheat flour percentage

38% = Whole wheat flour percentage

The percentages of the flours are only used when calculating the weight of bread flour or whole wheat flour is needed when converting a formula. When calculating the percentage of the remaining ingredients in the formula, divide them by the total of the flours, in this case 14.5 pounds.

Desired Dough Temperature

The pastry chef needs to understand and control all processes of bread production—scaling, mixing, dough temperature, shaping, and baking. The series of steps involved in making bread are affected by the preceding step. When mixing bread dough, it is important to account for room temperature, ingredient temperature, and friction from mixing. The goal is to provide the **desired dough temperature (DDT)** in the range of 75 to 78°F (24–26°C).

This temperature range provides the ideal temperature for fermentation. If the dough is too hot, fermentation occurs too quickly. The flavor of the bread will be lacking and the dough will be weak. Dough that is coming off the mixer too cold will ferment slowly and will take considerably longer to process.

The only variable the pastry chef/baker can truly control is the temperature of the water. While a certain level of control can be placed on room temperature, there will be changes throughout the course of a day as well as seasonal changes. The temperature of the flour is often constant with the room temperature.

DDT is nothing more than the average of the temperatures of the three components. When calculating for a straight dough the variables are the room temperature, flour temperature, water temperature, and friction from mixing. For this example we will use a DDT of 75°F (24°C). When calculating for a straight dough, multiply the DDT by 3. This is known as the **total temperature factor**.

75°F × 3 = Total temperature factor

225°F = Total temperature factor

Room temperature and flour temperature are taken with a thermometer and recorded into the formula. Depending on the type of mixer used, speed and time of mixing will change the temperature increase from friction. Unless calculating the friction factor manually, the average increase of dough temperature during mixing is 26°F (14.4°C) for most mixers. To calculate the friction factor manually, scale a batch of dough using the average of 26°F (14.4°C). Calculate the water temperature from the following table. If the dough is 2°F (1°C) warmer than the DDT, increase the friction factor for this mixer by 2 degrees to 28°F (15.4°C).

DDT for Straight Dough

Total Temperature Factor	225°F
Minus Flour Temperature	72°F
Minus Room Temperature	70°F
Minus Friction Factor	26°F
Water Temperature	57°F

Desired Dough Temperature with Multiple Factors

When calculating the DDT for straight dough, the temperature of the flour, room, and friction must be accounted for. Many breads contain a preferment or sour. Due to adding another component into the dough, adjustments need to be made to calculate water temperature. When calculating with multiple factors, multiply the DDT by 4 to determine the total temperature factor. For this example, we will use a DDT of 75°F (24°C).

75°F × 4 = Total temperature factor

300°F = Total temperature factor

DDT with Multiple Factors

Total Temperature Factor	300°F
Minus Flour Temperature	72°F
Minus Room Temperature	70°F
Minus Friction Factor	26°F
Minus Preferment Temperature	78°F
Water Temperature	54°F

In this example, the flour, room, and friction factor remained the same from the straight dough example. The addition of the preferment has decreased the temperature of the water by 3°F (1.6°C). Calculating the DDT is not a proven science. The process helps to create consistency in fermentation times and flavor of the bread. The best results are achieved through testing and recording temperatures in a log. This will facilitate the calculation of the water temperature.

Sour Starters

Sourdough bread can be traced back several thousand years. While there is no clearly defined origin, sourdough starters provided a way to ferment bread when yeast was not commercially available as it is today. Sourdough bread is often shrouded in mystery. Where does it come from? How can I make it? Why are there so many steps?

Sour starter is the mixture used to leaven sourdough bread, comprised of flour and water. Commercial yeast is not used in the production of sourdough bread; instead, it relies on naturally occurring yeast. Yeast is present all around us, on fruits and vegetables, on table surfaces—even in the air. In nature, the concentrations of the yeast are very low. When making a sour the natural yeast present on the rye flour is activated when combined with water. Over a period of 24 hours, the yeast begins to ferment and grow, increasing in strength. The yeast, along with bacteria, begin working together to create the distinctive flavor of sourdough and leaven the bread. This mixture is then fed over a series of days, increasing the amount of yeast and developing the flavor of the starter.

FIGURE 2.2 A sour starter (left); and (at right) after fermenting for 12 hours.

The flavor of the starter comes from the bacteria *lactobacilli,* which is responsible for producing lactic acid. There are two types of lactobacilli, homo-fermentive and hetero-fermentive. Homo-fermentive converts sugars in the dough and produces a mild-flavored lactic acid with yogurt characteristics. Hetero-fermentive converts sugars into lactic acid, acetic acid, and carbon dioxide. As the starter is fed and ages, the flavor will continue to become more complex.

In some cases, starters can be made with additional items such as honey, apples, grapes, or even potatoes. These additional items add flavor to the starter and additional yeast. How does this happen? Think of the wine-making process: Grapes are crushed, and over a period of time, the mixture begins to ferment. This is due to wild yeast present on the outside of the grapes. When making a sour, we capture the yeast that is all around us and provide it with an ideal environment to multiply. When beginning a starter, it is suggested that you use whole grain flours such as whole wheat or rye; unbleached white flour is not recommended. Whole grain flours contain more nutrients and microorganisms than more processed flours and will facilitate the growth of the starter. The following process is a starter that uses rye flour and honey.

Starting the Sour

Schedule	Ingredients	Starter	Time before Next Feeding
Day 1	3 oz (85 g) White Rye Flour 3 oz (85 g) Bread Flour 0.3 oz (8.5 g) Honey 3 oz (85 g) Water		24 hours
Day 2	5 oz (142 g) Bread Flour 3 oz (85 g) Water	5 oz (142 g)	24 hours
Day 3	5 oz (142 g) Bread Flour 3 oz (85 g) Water	5 oz (142 g)	24 hours
Day 4	5 oz (142 g) Bread Flour 3 oz (85 g) Water	5 oz (142 g)	24 hours
Day 5	5 oz (142 g) Bread Flour 3 oz (85 g) Water	4 oz (113g)	Ferment for 12 hours; starter is now ready to produce bread

Note: After the first day, a portion of the starter is discarded. This is a normal practice. Keeping all of the starter would result in a large amount of sour that would need to be discarded.

The process listed above depends on many factors; a sour is a combination of science and art. As a result, the sour starter and feeding procedure may need to be adjusted. The sour will continue to develop flavor with each feeding. The sour is considered ripe when it is domed in the container and the center is just starting to collapse. At this point, the yeast is most active and the flavor is not too acidic. Adjustments to the initial mix quantity in the recipe and temperature of the storage of the sour can help maintain the sour starter, so that it is ready when it is needed. For example, if the sour is not active enough, you can add a small additional amount of the previous batch to the feed, or increase the amount of water slightly. Increasing the water will make the carbohydrates and nutrients in the sour more available to yeast and bacteria, making them easier to process.

Dough temperature and time will also have an effect on when the sour is mature. The warmer the temperature, the quicker it will mature. The goal is to have the sour mature when you are ready to mix the final dough; schedule feedings at the correct time. Temperature is always an issue in the bakeshop—summers are hot and winters are cold. Try to find a consistent temperature for your starter. This may mean setting a low temperature in proof box during winter months or near a cold air vent in the summer. Remember, making adjustments is acceptable and often times needed. Document what you have done so you can be consistent in future feedings. Maintaining the sour starter can be done indefinitely—observe the ripeness and make adjustments as needed.

Preferments

Preferments are an easy way to improve bread flavor, aroma, dough strength, and shelf life. Most are made with flour, water, and yeast. The consistency can range from a dough to a loose batter. The common types of preferments used in bread production are prefermented dough, poolish, biga, and sponge.

Prefermented dough, also known as pâte fermentée or old dough, is used in products that require a shortened first fermentation. It can be made from a simple dough that is water, flour, yeast, and salt. The dough is allowed to mature and is added during mixing. A more straightforward approach would be to save a piece of dough from the day's production. After mixing the dough, a piece large enough for the next day's production is removed and allowed to ferment at room temperature for two hours. It is then placed in the refrigerator overnight. The next day, the prefermented dough is added to the next batch and the process continues. The old dough provides flavor (bacteria and fermentation) and strength to the next batch of dough, and the new dough provides additional food for the yeast. Prefermented dough can be 20% to 30% of the flour weight.

Poolish is of Polish origin, but was quickly adopted by the French and Austrians. A poolish is equal parts flour and water, 100% hydration, which creates a very loose batter. The resulting bread is lighter and less acidic compared to a traditional fermented dough. The Italian counterpart to the poolish is a biga. A biga can range from 50% to 100% hydration. At the lower percentage, it will be somewhat stiffer, and at higher percentages it will be looser. The biga adds structure and flavor to the bread. Breads using poolish and biga are highly extensible and have an increased dough volume. Maturity is noted by these preferments just beginning to collapse in the center. Undermaturing results in less flavor; overmaturing will cause the poolish to have an unpleasant acidic flavor.

Mixing Methods

Straight

The simplest mixing method is the **straight mixing method**. In this method, all the ingredients are added together. There are no additional preferments added to the dough. As a result, the dough lacks flavor, extensibility, and shelf life.

Sponge

The **sponge mixing method** is used primarily for rich doughs. These doughs are high in fat and sugars. The sponge allows the yeast to get a "head start" before being added to the final dough. The use of a sponge allows the yeast to multiply and begin developing flavor before the fat and sugar are added, which will slow down fermentation. A sponge is yeast, flour, and liquid, and as it reaches maturation, the preferment looks like a sponge. There are easily identifiable holes in the sponge as it just begins to collapse. In addition to increased yeast activity, the sponge provides strength to an otherwise compromised dough and flavor to the final bread.

Brioche

Brioche is classified as Viennoiserie, and can have as much as 50% of the flour weight in butter. This is a significant amount of fat. To assist with leavening, the sponge method is used. Adding all the fat at the beginning of the mixing would make it difficult to develop the dough and would take a long time. In the **brioche mixing method**, after the sponge has matured, all ingredients, with the exception of the butter, are added and developed into a dough. At this point, we can test the dough with the window test to see if the gluten has fully developed. Once the dough is developed, the butter is added slowly. Be sure the cold butter is incorporated evenly throughout the dough and that mixing is done quickly. The mixing time for brioche is long—as much as 15 minutes. Any additional mixing will cause excess friction and increase the final dough temperature. This will make the dough ferment too quickly.

Double Hydration

Soft doughs like ciabatta and pugliese can contain over 70% water. Developing gluten in a highly hydrated dough can be difficult. To overcome this, in the **double hydration** method, add 60% water to the weight of the flour. Allow the dough to develop fully, then add the remaining water.

Minimal Mixing with Folds

Minimal mixing breads are also referred to as no-knead breads. These breads are hydrated above 70%. When combining the ingredients, they are simply folded together and should look like a shaggy mass. The dough is then left to rest for 30 minutes. The high hydration of this dough allows the gluten to develop easily. At the end of the 30 minutes, the dough is folded; this procedure is done a total of six times. Use care when working with doughs, using the minimal mixing method to prevent degassing the dough fully and retaining some of the large air cells.

Autolyse

Raymond Calvel developed **autolyse** in 1974. In his procedure, the water and flour are combined and rested for 30 minutes without fully mixing. He observed that the gluten developed while resting. At the end of the rest period, the remaining ingredients are added. The benefit of autolyse is a shortened mix time. This results in a less oxidized dough, giving the dough a creamier color, large open crumb, and improved flavor. It affects enzymes and hydration rates as well.

Degrees of Mixing

Looking back to the early history of bread baking, all of the mixing was done by hand. Bread baking was a labor-intensive job. Hand kneading left the dough with very little gluten development and was a laborious task. The bread would undergo a long first fermentation, sometimes as long as five hours, with several folds to develop the strength of the bread. This time-consuming process produced excellent-tasting breads. As mechanical mixers were introduced, the process was sped up, but this decreased the quality of the bread. As the customer's appreciation for artisanal breads has increased, the pastry chef has employed new techniques to meet this need.

There is no right or wrong way to mix a dough, and each method will have a dough that corresponds to it. The times given in the following sections are estimates and may need some adjustment, depending on the type of mixer used or dough hydration.

Short Mix

In an effort to get back to the quality produced by a hand-mixed bread while still using mechanical mixers, the **short mix** was created. Doughs produced using a short mix are mixed on low speed for 5 minutes. The short mixing time doesn't heat up the dough and prevents

FIGURE 2.3 Short mix (l); improved mix (c); intense mix (r)

oxidizing the dough, creating a cream-colored bread. Short mix doughs require several folds during the longer fermentation to create strength in the bread. The final product is artisan bread with an open crumb and excellent flavor.

Intense Mix

In an effort to dramatically shorten production times, the **intense mix** was created. Intense mix doughs are mixed for 5 minutes on low speed, then 5 to 10 minutes on second speed. While fermentation times are shorter, the bread produced lacks flavor and has a tight, uniform crumb. The color of these breads is white due to overoxidizing the flour. Doughs made using the intense mix method have a first fermentation time of 10 to 30 minutes. This short time does not allow for the production of organic acids. The overdeveloped gluten allows these doughs to trap a large amount of air, producing a larger loaf.

Improved Mix

The **improved mix** is the best of both worlds—the longer fermentation of the short mix with the proper gluten development of the intense mix. In this method, the dough is mixed for 5 minutes on first speed and 2 minutes on second speed. The final bread has an open crumb with slightly more volume than short mix, and the flour is somewhat more oxidized due to the longer mixing time.

Note: All mixing times are dependent on the mixer being used. Adjustments may need to be made to time or speed.

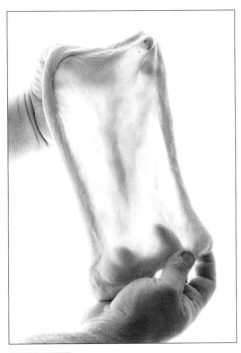
FIGURE 2.4 Proper gluten window

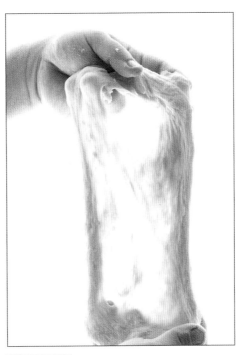
FIGURE 2.5 Underdeveloped dough

Gluten Development

The main goal of mixing bread dough is to develop gluten. Several factors contribute to **gluten** development. When water is combined with flour and mixed, the gluten is activated. Think of gluten as a bowl of spaghetti, only this spaghetti has small hooks on the end. As the dough is worked in the mixer, the gluten is aligned and the ends connect to the gluten next to it. This creates the network inside the bread that gives the bread the ability to retain gas and structure to maintain shape after baking.

When testing gluten development of dough, a simple visual examination of the dough is made. A piece of dough is removed from the mixer and stretched by hand. This is known as a *window pane test*. The dough is stretched to a thin membrane—light will easily pass through the "window." If the dough tears during the test, additional mixing is required.

Bread Production Stages

14 Steps

There are 14 steps involved in producing yeast breads. The final product will determine how many steps are used. In some products, there may be less. Some recipes may include several folds, while others may remove this step entirely. Fermentation times may be long and span several hours; others may be a short 15-minute rest. Be sure to follow the procedures specified in the recipe, as each step will impact the following step, and ultimately the final product.

Selecting the Right Ingredients

Bread is often made from just a few ingredients: flour, liquid, salt, and yeast. Many breads are created with these four ingredients; by changing the ratio or methods, many variations can be created. Things to consider when selecting ingredients are the type of flour, type of salt, water or milk, and type of yeast.

Scaling

Properly scaling ingredients is the most important step to any recipe: when properly scaled, the recipe will yield consistent results and quantity of dough. Recipes are balanced based on how ingredients interact within the recipe and what the final desired results are. Changing one ingredient can result in a completely different product. Pay particular attention to ingredients with the smallest quantities, such as salt and yeast.

Mixing

While this might seem like one of the easier steps, mixing begins the process of transforming the ingredients into a dough. Before combining the ingredients, the DDT must be calculated. During the mixing phase, emphasis is placed on gluten development. Gluten is the protein in flour that gives dough elasticity, extensibility, and the ability to trap gas, and it provides structure when combined with liquid. When mixing, the bread ingredients are equally dispersed throughout the dough, dry ingredients hydrate, and oxygen is introduced to the dough.

Bulk Fermentation

After the dough has been mixed, it is rounded and allowed to ferment. Fermentation is the process of yeast converting carbohydrates into carbon dioxide, alcohol, and organic acids. Carbon dioxide provides the leavening for the bread while the alcohol and organic acids contribute to the flavor. Organic acids add a significant amount of flavor and aroma to the bread. Additionally, they strengthen dough development and increase shelf life of the final product.

Folding

Folding is a relatively new term—this step was originally referred to as punching. The dough was literally punched to release the built-up gas. While this method is effective, folding provides more benefits. Doughs that ferment for longer than 90 minutes, are made with a weak flour, or are highly hydrated (75% or higher) benefit from folding.

Dough Folding Process:

1. Place dough with the smooth rounded side down on a generously floured worktable.
2. Take one-third of the dough from the close side and fold it over into the center. Gently press out some of the gas; do not completely degas the dough. Dust any excess flour from the dough.
3. Complete the same process for one-third of the far side of the dough.
4. Next, work from the left side and fold one-third in toward the center.
5. Finally, from the right side fold in one-third.
6. Carefully turn the folded dough over so the smooth surface is on top.

    Note: If this process is completed multiple times on the dough, follow the same procedure.

Folding the dough correctly will accomplish four things. It will first degas the dough. The high quantity of carbon dioxide present in the dough can retard fermentation. The second benefit is redistributing the yeast throughout the dough, ensuring equal fermentation. The third benefit is temperature equalization. The center of the dough will retain heat while the outside cools; folding makes sure the dough is a consistent temperature. A fourth benefit is development of gluten. The folding process continues aligning the gluten strands and strengthens the dough.

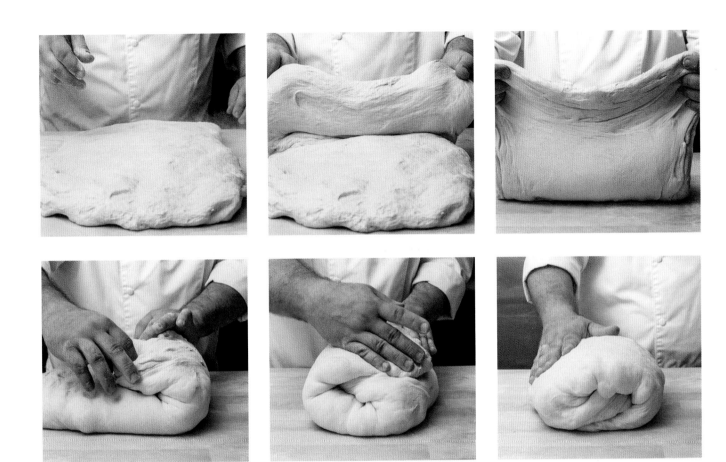

Dividing

To divide the dough, place the dough onto a lightly dusted worktable. At this point, avoid folding or overworking the dough; the dough is rested. Gently flatten the dough, but do not completely degas it. With a metal bench scraper, cut the dough into strips, then place a piece of the dough on a scale. If it is too light, add additional dough; if too heavy, remove some of the dough. After this first piece of dough is scaled to the correct weight, the size can be used to judge the next piece. With some practice, scaling dough can be done quickly and accurately by eye, and then verified on the scale without needing to make adjustments.

Dividing it quickly will prevent the dough from drying out. If there is a large quantity of dough to be divided, cover the dough with plastic. Dividing is an important step because it determines the size of the final loaf. Consistent scaling will produce breads that proof and bake at the same rate.

Preshaping

The dough is now ready for preshaping. Preshaping is the process of taking the randomly shaped pieces of divided dough and forming them into consistent shapes. This step is important in preparing the dough for final shaping. The final shape of the loaf can change the preshaping form—almost any shape can be made from simply rounding the dough. However, longer shapes like a baguette can benefit from an oblong preshaping. Regardless of the shape selected, it is important to keep the dough as even as possible; this will facilitate final shaping.

Intermediate Fermentation

Intermediate fermentation is often referred to as *bench proofing*. This step is a short fermentation that allows the gluten in the dough to relax after preshaping. Stiffer doughs will require a longer rest, while slack doughs could be as short as 15 minutes. After the preshaping is completed, the dough is placed on a dusted bench, sheet pan, or board and covered to prevent drying.

Final Shaping

After the dough has relaxed enough to be shaped, we move onto the next step. In this step, the dough is shaped into the final design, a boule, baguette, loaf pan, roll—there are countless

Bâtard and Baguette Shaping

FIGURE 2.7 Degassing dough

FIGURE 2.8 Beginning to roll the dough for bâtard and baguette

FIGURE 2.9 Shaping a straight bâtard

FIGURE 2.10 Continue rolling the bâtard thinner to form the baguette

Football-shaped Bâtard

FIGURE 2.11 Final step: tightening the dough on a football bâtard

FIGURE 2.12 Starting the "v" shape for a football-shaped bâtard

Boule

FIGURE 2.13 Shaping a boule: tightening the degassed dough into a round

FIGURE 2.14 Shaping a boule: final process using hands to tighten the dough

shapes for breads. After shaping, the dough is transferred into bannetons, baker's couche, metal pan, or parchment-lined sheet pan.

Proofing

Proofing is the final fermentation of the dough. After shaping the dough, it is allowed rise. Most pastry shops use proof boxes to facilitate the fermentation. Proof boxes can be adjusted to provide the ideal temperature and humidity for fermentation while preventing a skin from forming on the dough. If a proof box is not available, place the covered dough in a warm area and allow the dough to ferment. A proof box will shorten the amount of time required for the bread to rise, but the same results can be achieved by allowing the dough to rise at room temperature.

Scoring

Before placing the dough in the oven, score it with a razor blade or lame. While scoring does add a decorative element to bread, it also serves other functions. Scoring allows the bread to expand and reach its maximum fullness. The scoring creates a weakness in the structure of the bread, this allows the pastry chef to control where and how the dough will expand.

Baking

Once the bread has fully proofed, it is ready to load into the oven. This can be done with a peel, a mechanical loader, or by placing the sheet pans in the oven. Use care when transferring dough from bannetons and couches to prevent deflating the dough. Evenly space the dough on the peel. The dough will not be moved again prior to placing in the oven. Properly spaced dough will bake evenly and form an evenly browned and crispy crust.

When baking bread, a steam-injected oven can help develop a rich color and crisp crust. Most breads benefit from steam, with the exception of breads that receive an egg wash prior to baking. Steaming bread that has been washed would remove the wash from the bread. Steam causes the starch on the crust of the bread to transform into sugars. This contributes not only to the color of the bread but also to the flavor.

Shortly after the bread is placed in the oven, the dough begins to heat up. The increased heat causes the fermentation process to speed up, increasing the production of carbon dioxide. Moisture in the dough begins to heat and expand. This initial expanding of the bread is referred to as *oven spring*. The steam adds to the bread's ability to rise, and the additional moisture in the oven prevents the crust from drying and setting. As the crust begins to gain color, the steam has served its purpose and the vents on the oven can be opened. When steaming bread, be careful to not oversteam it; too much moisture in the oven prevents crust formation, leading to a loaf of bread that will collapse.

As the baking process continues, dough temperature reaches 140°F (60°C) and the yeast begins to die. Starches begin to swell and gelatinize as the temperature reaches 140 to 158°F (60 to 70°C). The gelatinization of starches is the first sign the crumb of the bread is starting to set. The gluten protein begins to coagulate when the internal temperature reaches 158 to 176°F (70 to 80°C). At 194°F (90°C), starch gelatinization and protein coagulation is completed and internal baking is done. The bread remains in the oven until the proper crust color has been achieved.

Cooling

Once the bread has completed baking, carefully remove it from the oven using a peel or sheet pan. Baked bread should be placed on cooling racks to allow moisture to evaporate. Leaving the bread on a sheet pan or loaf pan will prevent the steam from escaping and create a soggy crust. Bread must cool completely to ensure that the proper texture and flavor have been developed.

Storing

Bread must be completely cooled before considering storage, wrapping a warm loaf of bread will cause condensation inside the wrap and make the loaf soggy. Using bread the same day it is baked does not require wrapping. The best wrapper for breads is paper, which allows the bread to breath and maintains the crust. While storing bread for long periods of time, it is necessary to wrap the bread in plastic and place in the freezer. Refrigeration is strongly discouraged. While refrigeration will prevent molding, the bread stales faster at refrigeration temperature. Starch retrogradation is the staling of baked goods. As baked goods age, they continue to develop structure, and some of the water is squeezed out of the starch and evaporates.

Troubleshooting for Breads

Issue	Cause
Dough splits on the side when baked.	1. Formula contained too much yeast; reduce yeast. 2. Dough was not proofed long enough. Give dough a longer proof. 3. Dough needed to expand more during baking. Score dough properly.
When bread cools, crust cracks and looks slightly collapsed.	The dough needed additional gluten development. Add a fold or two during fermentation.
When sliced, bread has a thick crust.	The bread was baked too long at too low a temperature. Reduce the amount of time the bread is baked.
Bread does not rise.	1. Ingredients scaled improperly; check formula for accuracy. 2. The incorrect yeast was used; check type of yeast. 3. The yeast is expired; check expiration date of yeast.

Recipes

Baguette Pâte Fermentée

Yield: 1 lb 3 oz (539 g)
Portions: 1
Portion size: 1 lb 3 oz (539 g)
Yield description: 1 at 1 lb 3 oz (539 g)

Ingredients	U.S.	Metric	%
Bread Flour	10.7 oz	312 g	100
Water	8 oz	218 g	70
Malt	0.05 oz	1.6 g	0.5
Instant Yeast	0.05 oz	1.6 g	0.5
Salt	0.2 oz	6.25 g	2

Procedure

1. Mix for 6 minutes on speed 2.
2. Ferment for 3 hours at room temperature; then place in refrigerator for 12 hours.

Baguette Final Dough

Yield: 4 lb 15 oz (2271 g)
Portions: 7 loaves
Portion size: 11.25 oz (324 g)
Yield description: 7 loaves at 11.25 oz (324 g)

Ingredients	U.S.	Metric	%
Bread Flour	2 lb 3 oz	1000 g	100
Pâte Fermentée, cut into pieces	1 lb 3 oz	539 g	54
Water	1 lb 8.7 oz	700 g	70
Malt	0.17 oz	5 g	0.5
Instant Yeast	0.13 oz	4 g	0.4
Salt	0.81 oz	23 g	2.3

Note: After mixing the final dough, remove 1 lb 3 oz (539 g) to replace the pâte fermentée used in the production of the baguette final dough. Ferment the dough covered for 3 hours at room temperature; then store in the refrigerator. The pâte fermentée can be made and stored for 3 days under refrigeration. Using this method, the pâte fermentée will continue developing flavor with each batch of baguette dough made. When using this method, the final dough will produce five baguettes.

Procedure

1. Use improved mix, DDT 78°F (25°C).
2. Allow bulk fermentation 90 minutes; fold once after 45 minutes.
3. Scale loaves at 11.25 oz (324 g).
4. Preshape and rest 30 minutes.
5. Final shape into a baguette procedure on page 40.
6. Proof for 90 minutes at 88°F (31°C).
7. Score dough with five to six cuts.
8. Bake at 450°F (232°C) with 10 seconds steam for 25 to 30 minutes.

Kalamata Thyme

Yield: 4 lb 9.2 oz (2086 g)
Portions: 4 loaves
Portion size: 1 lb 2 oz (520 g)
Yield description: 4 loaves at 1 lb 2 oz (520 g)

Ingredients	U.S.	Metric	%
Bread Flour	2 lb 10 oz	1200 g	100
Water	1 lb 11.5 oz	780 g	65
Kalamata Olives, chopped and dried	2.1 oz	60 g	5
Thyme, fresh, picked	0.17 oz	4.8 g	0.4
Instant Yeast	0.63 oz	18 g	1.5
Salt	0.84 oz	24 g	2

Procedure

1. Use improved mix; add kalamata olives and thyme at the end of mixing. Continue mixing until combined. DDT 78°F (25°C).
2. Allow bulk fermentation 90 minutes; fold once after 45 minutes.
3. Scale loaves at 1 lb 2 oz (520 g).
4. Preshape and rest 30 minutes.
5. Final shape into a boule procedure on page 40.
6. Proof for 45 minutes at 88°F (31°C).
7. Score with three cuts across the dough.
8. Bake at 450°F (232°C) with 10 seconds steam for 25 to 30 minutes.

Focaccia

Yield: 4 lbs 8 oz (2090 g)
Portions: 1
Portion size: 1 full sheet pan
Yield description: 1 full sheet pan at 4 lbs 8 oz (2090 g)

Ingredients	U.S.	Metric	%
Bread Flour	2 lb 9 oz	1162 g	100
Water	1 lb 7.75 oz	673 g	57.9
Sugar	2 oz	57 g	4.9
Olive Oil	0.8 oz	22.5 g	1.9
Instant Yeast	1.2 oz	34 g	2.9
Salt	1.2 oz	34 g	2.9
Sun-Dried Tomatoes, sliced	3.5 oz	100 g	8.6
Rosemary, fresh, chopped	0.3 oz	8 g	0.7

Procedure

1. Soak sun-dried tomatoes in water from recipe for 1 hour.
2. Use intense mix.
3. Allow bulk fermentation 90 minutes.
4. Brush a sheet pan with olive oil, roll dough to fit sheet pan.
5. Proof for 1 hour at 88°F (31°C).
6. Bake 450°F (230C), 3 seconds steam for 5 minutes.
7. Reduce oven temperature to 420°F (215°C) for 15 to 20 minutes.
8. Remove from oven and brush with olive oil.

FIGURE 2.15 Baguette, Kalamata Thyme, and Focaccia

Beer Bread Poolish

Yield: 1 lb 3.2 oz (544.2 g)

Portions: 1

Portion size: 1 lb 3.2 oz (544.2 g)

Yield description: 1 at 1 lb 3.2 oz (544.2 g)

Ingredients	U.S.	Metric	%
Bread Flour	9.6 oz	272 g	100
Water	9.6 oz	272 g	100
Instant Yeast	0.007 oz	0.2 g	0.0007

Procedure

1. Combine ingredients with a dough hook and mix for 8 minutes on second speed.
2. Ferment at room temperature, 72°F (22°C), for 12 hours.

Beer Bread Final Dough

Yield: 4 lb 3 oz (1904 g)

Portions: 4 loaves

Portion size: 1 lb 0.75 oz (476 g)

Yield description: 4 loaves at 1 lb 0.75 oz (476 g)

Ingredients	U.S.	Metric	%
Bread Flour	1 lb	454 g	71.4
Whole Wheat Flour	5 oz	142 g	22.3
Dark Rye Flour	1.4 oz	40 g	6.3
Beer Bread Poolish	1 lb 3.2 oz	544 g	85.5
Beer	10.9 oz	310 g	48.7
Water	1.3 oz	37 g	5.8
Instant Yeast	0.1 oz	2.8 g	0.4
Salt	0.65 oz	18.5 g	2.9
Bacon, sliced ⅛ in. and cooked until crispy	4 oz	113 g	17.8
Onion, brunoise	5 oz	141 g	22.2
Sauerkraut, rinsed and drained	3.5 oz	100 g	5.1
Caraway Seeds, toasted	0.08 oz	2.3 g	0.4

Procedure

1. Use improved mix DDT 78°F (25°C).
2. Allow bulk fermentation 90 minutes, fold once after 45 minutes.
3. Scale loaves at 1 lb 0.75 oz (476 g).
4. Preshape and rest 30 minutes.
5. Final shape into a boule procedure, page 40.
6. Brush dough with beer bread topping and dust heavily with rye flour.
7. Proof for 3 hours at 88°F (31°C).
8. Bake at 450°F (232°C) with 10 seconds steam for 10 minutes.
9. Reduce oven temperature to 420°F (215°C) for 22 to 24 minutes.

Beer Bread Topping

Yield: 11.29 oz (318.2 g)
Portions: 1
Portion size: 11.29 oz (318.2 g)
Yield description: 1 at 11.29 oz (318.2 g)

Ingredients	U.S.	Metric	%
Rye Flour	3.9 oz	110 g	100
Beer	7.1 oz	200 g	181.8
Salt	0.21 oz	6 g	5.5
Instant Yeast	0.08 oz	2.2 g	2

Note: Any additional Beer Bread Topping can be reserved in the refrigerator for 3 days.

Procedure

1. Combine all ingredients.
2. Reserve for beer bread.

Ciabatta Biga

Yield: 12.07 oz (341 g)
Portions: 1
Portion size: 12.07 oz (341 g)
Yield description: 1 at 12.07 oz (341 g)

Ingredients	U.S.	Metric	%
Bread Flour	6.6 oz	186 g	100
Water	5.4 oz	153 g	82
Yeast	0.07 oz	2 g	1.1

Procedure

1. Combine ingredients with a dough hook and mix for 8 minutes on second speed.
2. Ferment at room temperature, 72°F (22°C), for 12 hours.
3. Store in refrigerator for up to 3 days.

Ciabatta Final Dough

Yield: 4 lb 6.oz (1986 g)
Portions: 4 loaves
Portion size: 1 lb 1.5 oz (496 g)
Yield description: 4 loaves at 1 lb 1.5 oz (496 g)

Ingredients	U.S.	Metric	%
Bread Flour	1 lb 15.7 oz	900 g	100
Ciabatta Biga	12.07 oz	341 g	38
Water	1 lb 8.7 oz	700 g	77.8
Olive Oil	0.35 oz	10 g	1.1
Instant Yeast	0.35 oz	10 g	1.1
Salt	0.9 oz	25 g	2.8

Procedure

1. Use improved mix, double hydration, DDT 78°F (25°C).
2. Allow bulk fermentation 2 hours; fold once every 30 minutes.
3. Turn dough onto heavily floured table.
4. Fold in half and even out dough.
5. Cut into four equal pieces; dust cut ends in flour.
6. Place into floured couche.
7. Proof for 45 minutes at 88°F (31°C).
8. Bake at 450°F (232°C) with 10 seconds steam for 35 to 40 minutes.

FIGURE 2.16 Multigrain Bread and Ciabatta

Multigrain Soaker

Yield: 1 lb 13 oz (820 g)

Portions: 1

Portion size: 1 lb 13 oz (820 g)

Yield description: 1 at 1 lb 13 oz (820 g)

Ingredients	U.S.	Metric	%
Whole Wheat Flour	4.1 oz	116 g	100
Multigrain Mix	12.3 oz	348 g	300
Buttermilk	12.3 oz	348 g	300
Salt	0.3 oz	8 g	7

Note: Cornmeal, flax seed, oats, sunflower seeds, or other grains can be used in place of multigrain mix.

Procedure

1. Combine all ingredients with a paddle.
2. Store at room temperature 72°F (22°C) for 12 hours.

Multigrain Biga

Yield: 1 lb 13 oz (820 g)

Portions: 1

Portion size: 1 lb 13 oz (820 g)

Yield description: 1 at 1 lb 13 oz (820 g)

Ingredients	U.S.	Metric	%
Bread Flour	1 lb 0.5 oz	468 g	100
Water	12.4 oz	350 g	75
Instant Yeast	0.1 oz	2 g	0.4

Procedure

1. Combine ingredients with dough hook.
2. Mix for 5 minutes on second speed.
3. Ferment for 1 hour at 72°F (22°C).
4. Refrigerate for 12 hours before use.

Multigrain Final Dough

Yield: 4 lb 5.7 oz (1973 g)

Portions: 4

Portion size: 1 lb 1.4 oz (493 g)

Yield description: 4 loaves at 1 lb 1.4 oz (493 g)

Ingredients	U.S.	Metric	%
Bread Flour	5.6 oz	160 g	100
Multigrain Biga	1 lb 13 oz	820 g	513
Multigrain Soaker	1 lb 13 oz	820 g	513
Sugar	4.2 oz	118 g	74
Butter	1.1 oz	30 g	19
Instant Yeast	0.5 oz	14.5 g	9
Salt	0.37 oz	10.5 g	6.5

Procedure

1. Cut up soaker and biga, add to remaining ingredients.
2. Mix for 8 minutes on second speed, DDT 78°F (25°C).
3. Allow bulk fermentation 90 minutes; fold once after 60 minutes.
4. Scale loaves at 1 lb 1.4 oz (493 g).
5. Preshape and rest 30 minutes.
6. Final shape into batard.
7. Proof for 1 hour 15 minutes at 88°F (31°C).
8. Bake at 450°F (232°C) with 10 seconds steam for 5 minutes.
9. Reduce oven temperature to 420°F (215°C) for 15 to 20 additional minutes.

Pretzel Bread Poolish

Yield: 7.8 oz (220 g)

Portions: 1

Portion size: 7.8 oz (220 g)

Yield description: 1 at 7.8 oz (220 g)

Ingredients	U.S.	Metric	%
Bread Flour	3.89 oz	109.5 g	100
Water	3.89 oz	109.5 g	100
Instant Yeast	0.02 oz	1 g	0.9

Procedure

1. Combine ingredients thoroughly.
2. Ferment for 12 hours at 72°F (22°C).

Pretzel Bread Final Dough

Yield: 4 lb 7.8 oz (2036 g)

Portions: 35

Portion size: 2 oz (56.7g) rolls

Yield description: 36 rolls at 2 oz (56.7g) rolls

Ingredients	U.S.	Metric	%
Bread Flour	2 lb 6.8 oz	1100 g	100
Water	11.3 oz	319 g	29
Milk, scalded	11.3 oz	319 g	29
Pretzel Bread Poolish	7.8 oz	220 g	20
Butter	1.1 oz	32 g	2.9
Brown Sugar	0.5 oz	15.5 g	1.4
Instant Yeast	.27 oz	7.7 g	0.7
Salt	.8 oz	23.1 g	2.1
Pretzel Salt	As Needed	As Needed	

Procedure

1. Combine ingredients with poolish, improved mix, DDT 78°F (25°C).
2. Allow bulk fermentation 90 minutes; fold once after 45 minutes.
3. Divide the dough into 2 oz (56.7 g) round rolls.
4. Place rolls on a flour-dusted couche and proof for 30 minutes at 88°F (31°C).
5. At this point, the rolls can be dipped in the lye solution or placed in the poaching liquid. Follow the procedure listed next.

Lye Solution

Ingredients	U.S.	Metric
Water, room temperature	4 lbs	1800 g
Lye, food-grade	2 oz	57 g

Note: Dipping the dough in a lye solution gives the bread the characteristic soft dark crust and flavor. Gloves and safety glasses are recommended when using lye to prevent burns to skin and eyes.

Procedure

1. Add lye to water; stir to combine.
2. Place the roll in the lye solution for 20 seconds.
3. Drain and place on a silpain or silpat.
4. Sprinkle with pretzel salt and score.
5. Bake at 375°F (190°C) for 15 to 18 minutes.

Poaching Liquid

Ingredients	U.S.	Metric
Water	8 lb	3600 g
Baking Soda	4 oz	115 g
Sugar	2 oz	56.7 g

Procedure

1. Combine all ingredients and heat to 180°F (82°C).
2. Poach rolls for 1 minute, drain, and place on silpain or silpat.
3. Brush with egg whites, add pretzel salt, and score.
4. Bake at 375°F (190°C) for 15 to 18 minutes.

FIGURE 2.17 Honey Wheat, Pretzel, and Cottage Cheese Dill

Cottage Cheese Dill

Yield: 4 lb 12.8 oz (2204 g)

Portions: 38

Portion size: 2 oz (56.7g)

Yield description: 38 rolls at 2 oz (56.7g)

Ingredients	U.S.	Metric	%
Bread Flour	2 lb 6 oz	1100 g	100
Cottage Cheese	1 lb 6.1 oz	627 g	57
Milk	7.4 oz	210 g	19
Sugar	2.1 oz	60 g	5.4
Butter	2.7 oz	77 g	7
Fresh Dill, chopped	0.4 oz	11 g	1
Whole Egg	2.7 oz	77 g	7
Instant Yeast	0.7	20 g	1.8
Salt	0.75	22 g	2
Kosher Salt	As needed	As needed	

Procedure

1. Use intense mix, DDT 78°F (25°C).
2. Allow bulk fermentation 1 hour.
3. Scale rolls at 2 oz (56.7 g).
4. Preshape and rest 30 minutes.
5. Final shape into knots.
6. Proof for 45 minutes at 88°F (31°C).
7. Egg wash (p. XXX) and sprinkle with kosher salt.
8. Bake at 375°F (190°C) for 15 to 20 minutes.

Honey Wheat

Yield: 3 lb 14.4 oz (1800 g)

Portions: 31

Portion size: 2 oz (56.7 g)

Yield description: 31 rolls at 2 oz (56.7 g) rolls

Ingredients	U.S.	Metric	%
Bread Flour	1 lb 5.5 oz	610 g	61.3
Whole Wheat Flour	13.5 oz	385 g	38.7
Water	1 lb 3 oz	538 g	54.1
Honey	4.75 oz	135 g	13.6
Sugar	1.2 oz	34 g	3.4
Butter	1.2 oz	34 g	3.4
Instant Yeast	0.73 oz	21 g	2.1
Salt	0.9 oz	26 g	2.6

Procedure

1. Use intense mix.
2. Allow bulk fermentation 90 minutes.
3. Scale at 2 oz (56.7 g) and shape into rolls.
4. Proof for 1 hour at 88°F (31°C).
5. Egg wash (see below) and bake at 350°F (175°C).

Egg Wash

Yield: 10.6 oz (300 g)

Portions: 1

Portion size: 10.6 oz (300 g)

Yield description: 1 at 10.6 oz (300 g)

Ingredients	U.S.	Metric
Whole Eggs	7.1 oz	200 g
Egg Yolks	3.5 oz	100 g
Salt	Pinch	Pinch

Procedure

1. Combine all ingredients and whisk.
2. Strain through a chinois.

Sour Starter

Yield: 4 lb (916 g)
Portions: 1
Portion size: 3 lb 12 oz (803 g)
Yield description: 1 at 3 lb 12 oz (803 g)

Ingredients	U.S.	Metric	%
Day 1			
White Rye Flour	3 oz	85 g	50
Bread Flour	3 oz	85 g	50
Honey	0.3 oz	8.5 g	10
Water	3 oz	85 g	50
Days 2–4 Feed			
Sour from previous feed	5 oz	142 g	100
Bread Flour	5 oz	142 g	100
Water	3 oz	85 g	60
Day 5 Feed			
Sour from previous feed	4 oz	113.4 g	11.5
Bread Flour	2 lb	908 g	100
Whole Wheat Flour	4 oz	113.4 g	11.5
Water	1 lb 8 oz	680 g	69.4

Note: When starting the sour, a portion is discarded during days 2–5. Not discarding this portion would result in a very large amount of waste at the start of the fifth day. The remaining mature starter at the end of the day will not produce the desired results and should be discarded, leaving only enough to be fed for the following day. This will help to maintain a healthy and balanced environment for the wild yeast to naturally ferment. Working with a sour requires planning. Schedule the breads for production the following day and scale the day 5 feed to accommodate this.

Procedure Day 1

1. Combine ingredients and mix to a stiff dough consistency.
2. Store uncovered at room temperature, 72°F (22°C), for 24 hours.

Procedure Days 2–4

1. Scale 5 oz (142 g) of dough from previous day; discard remaining dough.
2. Combine ingredients and mix by hand.
3. Store covered at room temperature, 72°F (22°C), for 24 hours.
4. Repeat this process for days 2, 3, and 4.

Procedure Day 5

1. Scale 4 oz (113.4 g) of dough from previous day, discard remaining dough.
2. Combine ingredients and mix at second speed for 6 minutes.
3. Store covered at room temperature, 72°F (22°C), for 12 hours.
4. Refrigerate for up to 2 days, then repeat day 5 procedure.

Sour Dough

Yield: 4 lb 11 oz (2124 g)
Portions: 4
Portion size: 1 lb 2.75 oz (531 g)
Yield description: 4 loaves at 1 lb 2.75 oz (531 g)

Ingredients	U.S.	Metric	%
Bread Flour	2 lb 6 oz	1075 g	100
Water	1 lb 8.5 oz	695 g	65
Sour Starter (see this page)	11.5 oz	326 g	31.4
Salt	1 oz	28.3 g	2.7

Procedure

1. Use improved mix, DDT 78°F (25°C).
2. Allow bulk fermentation 90 minutes; fold once after 45 minutes.
3. Scale loaves at 1 lb 2.75 oz (531 g).
4. Preshape and rest 30 minutes.
5. Final shape into a boule.
6. Proof for 2 hours at 88°F (31°C).
7. Score with three deep cuts.
8. Bake at 450°F (232°C) with 10 seconds steam for 25 to 30 minutes.

Semolina

Yield: 4 lb 12 oz (2145 g)

Portions: 3

Portion size: 1 lb 9 oz (716 g)

Yield description: 3 loaves at 1 lb 9 oz (716 g)

Ingredients	U.S.	Metric	%
Bread Flour	1 lb 4.3 oz	578 g	55
Semolina	1 lb 1.6 oz	472 g	45
Sour Starter (p. 50)	12.3 oz	350 g	33
Water	1 lb 8 oz	685 g	65
Olive Oil	0.9 oz	24 g	2.3
Sugar	0.37 oz	10.5 g	1
Salt	0.93 oz	26.3 g	2.5
Sesame Seeds	As needed	As needed	

Procedure

1. Use improved mix, DDT 78°F (25°C).
2. Allow bulk fermentation 90 minutes; fold after 45 minutes.
3. Scale loaves at 1 lb 9 oz (716 g).
4. Preshape and rest 30 minutes.
5. Final shape and roll in sesame seeds; place into greased loaf pan.
6. Proof for 2 hours and 15 minutes at 88°F (31°C).
7. Bake at 450°F (232°C) with 10 seconds steam for 25 to 30 minutes.

Chocolate Cherry Bread

Yield: 4 lb 12 oz (2160 g)

Portions: 4

Portion size: 1 lb 3 oz (540 g)

Yield description: 4 loaves at 1 lb 3 oz (540 g)

Ingredients	U.S.	Metric	%
Bread Flour	1 lb 15.7 oz	900 g	100
Sour Starter (p. 50)	9.5 oz	270 g	30
Cocoa Powder	1.6 oz	45 g	5
Water	1 lb 3.4 oz	550 g	61.1
Dark Chocolate 55%, melted	2.1 oz	60 g	6.7
Salt	0.9 oz	25 g	2.8
Chocolate Chips	5.4 oz	155 g	17.2
Dried Cherries, rinsed in warm water	5.4 oz	155 g	17.2

Procedure

1. Combine first six ingredients and mix for 6 minutes at first speed.
2. Add Chocolate Chips and Dried Cherries; mix for 2 minutes second speed, DDT 78°F (25°C).
3. Allow bulk fermentation 90 minutes; fold once after 45 minutes.
4. Scale loaves at 1 lb 3 oz (540 g).
5. Preshape and rest 30 minutes.
6. Final shape into a bâtard.
7. Proof for 2 hours and 15 minutes at 88°F (31°C).
8. Score with three cuts.
9. Bake at 450°F (232°C) with 10 seconds steam for 5 minutes.
10. Reduce oven temperature to 420°F (215°C) for 22 to 24 minutes.

FIGURE 2.18 Semolina and Chocolate Cherry Bread

Potato Onion Bread

Yield: 4 lb 6.2 oz (1995 g)

Portions: 4

Portion size: 1 lb 1.5 oz (498 g)

Yield description: 4 loaves at 1 lb 1.5 oz (498 g)

Ingredients	U.S.	Metric	%
Bread Flour	1 lb 5.6 oz	615 g	78.3
Whole Wheat Flour	6 oz	170 g	21.7
Sour Starter (p. 50)	12.7 oz	360 g	45.9
Water	1 lb 2.7 oz	530 g	67.5
Yukon Gold Potato, small dice, roasted	9 oz	255 g	32.5
Yellow Onion, ⅛ in. sliced, caramelized	10.6 oz	300 g	38.2
Salt	0.9 oz	26.4 g	3.4
Black Pepper, ground	0.2 oz	6 g	0.7

Note: Potatoes and onions are cooked after scaling.

Procedure

1. Use improved mix, adding potatoes and onions at the end of mixing. Continue mixing until incorporated DDT 78°F (25°C).

2. Allow bulk fermentation 90 minutes; fold after 45 minutes.

3. Scale loaves at 1 lb 1.5 oz (498 g).

4. Preshape and rest 30 minutes.

5. Final shape into a boule.

6. Proof for 2 hours at 88°F (31°C).

7. Score in an X.

8. Bake at 450°F (232°C) with 10 seconds steam for 25 to 30 minutes.

Pizza Dough

Yield: 4 lb 8.4 oz (2054 g)

Portions: 8

Portion size: 9 oz (255 g)

Yield description: 8 pieces at 9 oz (255 g)

Ingredients	U.S.	Metric	%
00 Flour	2 lb 9.6 oz	1180 g	100
Sour Starter (p. 50)	4.2 oz	118 g	10
Water	1 lb 9 oz	708 g	60
Instant Yeast	0.04 oz	1 g	0.1
Salt	1.6 oz	47 g	4

Procedure

1. Combine half of the 00 Flour with the remaining ingredients.

2. Mix for 10 minutes on speed 2.

3. Add remaining flour and mix for 5 additional minutes.

4. Rest dough for 45 minutes.

5. Divide into 9 oz (255 g) pieces and round.

6. Retard for 12 hours in refrigerator.

7. Roll dough into 10-in. (25-cm) circles.

8. Top and bake at 500°F (260°C).

Raisin Walnut Sour

Yield: 4 lb 6.9 oz (2019 g)

Portions: 4

Portion size: 1 lb 1.7 oz (504 g)

Yield description: 4 loaves at 1 lb 1.7 oz (504 g)

Ingredients	U.S.	Metric	%
Bread Flour	15.5 oz	440 g	55
Whole Wheat Flour	12.7 oz	360 g	45
Sour Starter (p. 50)	12.7 oz	360 g	45
Water	1 lb 2 oz	512 g	64
Raisins, rinsed	6.3 oz	184 g	23
Walnuts, toasted and chopped	4.5 oz	128 g	16
Salt	1.2 oz	35 g	4.4

Procedure

1. Use improved mix; add raisins and walnuts at the end of mixing. Continue mixing until incorporated. DDT 78°F (25°C).

2. Allow bulk fermentation 90 minutes, fold once after 45 minutes.

3. Scale loaves at 1 lb 1.7 oz (504 g).

4. Preshape and rest 30 minutes.

5. Final shape into a bâtard.

6. Proof for 2½ hours at 88°F (31°C).

7. Score with three deep cuts.

8. Bake at 450°F (232°C) with 10 seconds steam for 5 minutes.

9. Reduce oven temperature to 420°F (215°C) for 22 to 24 minutes.

Rye Sour Starter

Yield: 3 lb 14 oz (1820 g)

Portions: 1

Portion size: 3 lb 14 oz (1820 g)

Yield description: 1 at 3 lb 14 oz (1820 g)

Ingredients	U.S.	Metric	%
Bread Flour	1 lb 10.4 oz	750 g	75
Dark Rye Flour	8.8 oz	250 g	25
Water	1 lb 6.6 oz	700 g	70
Sour Starter (p. 50)	4.2 oz	120 g	12

Procedure

1. Combine all ingredients in a mixer with a paddle to form a paste.

2. Store at room temperature 72°F (22°C) for 12 hours.

Sour Rye

Yield: 4 lb 6 oz (1995 g)

Portions: 4

Portion size: 1 lb 1.5 oz (498 g)

Yield description: 4 loaves at 1 lb 1.5 oz (498 g)

Ingredients	U.S.	Metric	%
Bread Flour	1 lb 1.6 oz	500 g	50
High-Gluten Flour	8.8 oz	250 g	25
Dark Rye Flour	8.8 oz	250 g	25
Water	1 lb 7 oz	650 g	65
Caraway Seeds, toasted and cooled	0.5 oz	15 g	1.5
Rye Sour Starter	10.5 oz	300 g	30
Salt	1 oz	30 g	3

Procedure

1. Use intense mix, DDT 78°F (25°C).
2. Allow bulk fermentation 2 hours; fold every 30 minutes.
3. Scale loaves at 1 lb 1 oz (495 g).
4. Preshape and rest 15 minutes.
5. Final shape into a batard.
6. Proof for 2½ hours at 88°F (31°C).
7. Bake at 450°F (232°C) with 10 seconds steam for 25 to 30 minutes.

FIGURE 2.19 Raisin Walnut Sour Bread and Sour Rye

Key Terms

Pericarp
Endosperm
Wheat germ
Soaker
Baker's percentage
Desired dough temperature (DDT)

Total temperature factor
Preferments
Straight mixing method
Sponge mixing method
Brioche mixing method
Double hydration

Minimal mixing
Autolyse
Short mix
Intense mix
Improved mix
Gluten

Questions for Review

1. Discuss the differences between short mix, intense mix, and improved mix.

2. Discuss how preferments benefit breads.

3. When is steam used, and how does it affect the crust of bread?

4. Why is bread scored?

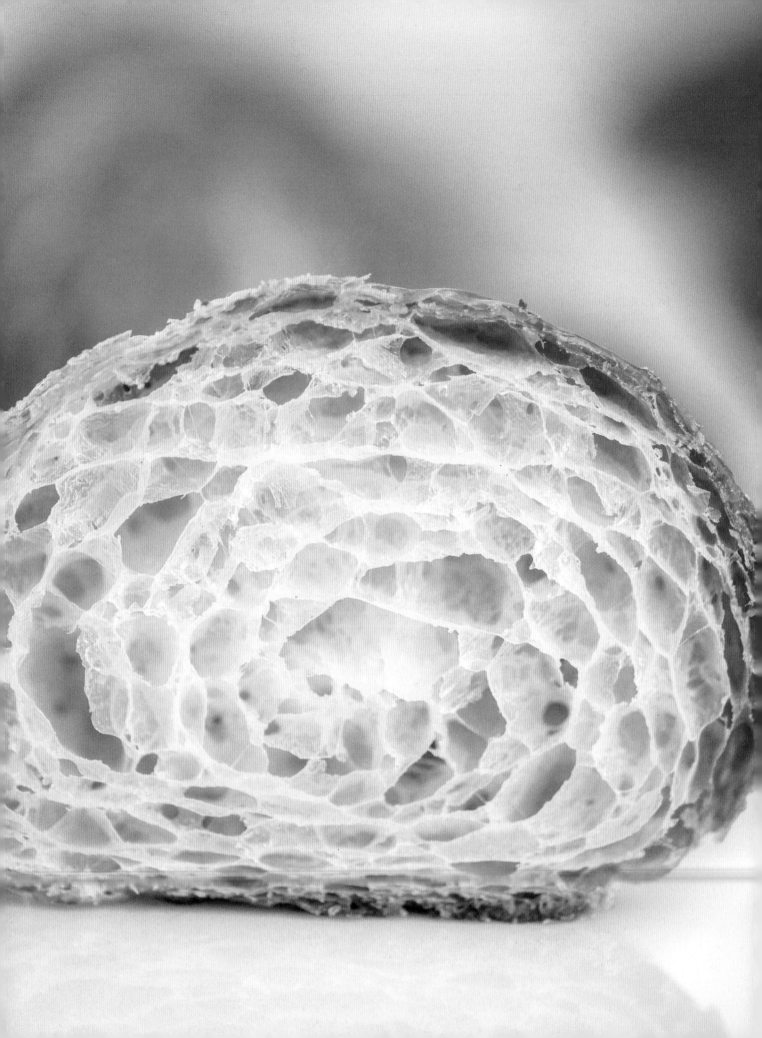

CHAPTER 3

Viennoiserie

Croissants, pain au chocolate, and brioche evoke memories of France—sitting in a small café with a freshly baked, flaky croissant and a cup of coffee. While the French are often credited with Viennoiserie, it originates in Austria. It was Marie Antoinette who brought the croissant to France. The French built on the popularity of the Viennoiserie, continuing to make and improve the techniques—much like pastry chefs do with all products in their kitchen.

LEARNING OBJECTIVES

After reading this chapter, you should be able to:

1. **Demonstrate** the single and book-fold methods for laminating dough.
2. **Identify** the ingredients used in Viennoiserie and their function.
3. **Prepare** a variety of laminated and enriched products.
4. **Prepare** puff pastry.
5. **Demonstrate** the technique for mixing and laminating doughs.

Introduction to Viennoiserie

Flaky, buttery, and *rich* are the words that best describe Viennoiserie. These yeast-raised products include more sugars, fats, milk, and eggs when compared to the lean doughs from Chapter 2. Viennoiserie can be broken down into two main groups: laminated and enriched doughs. **Lamination** is the process of layering dough and fat to produce a flaky pastry, such as those used for croissants and Danishes. An enriched dough incorporates additional fats or sugars during the mixing process. Examples include brioche, kugelhopf, and sweet roll dough.

Ingredients and Function

Liquid

Viennoiserie relies on water, milk, and eggs to hydrate the flour. Eggs will be addressed in the following section, as they provide more than just liquid to the recipe. Liquids are used to incorporate all ingredients to form a dough. If used alone, water will create a crispy crust; however, most Viennoiserie incorporates both water and milk. Milk provides fat, sugar, protein and vitamins to the bread. The small percentage of fat in milk helps to make the crumb more tender and produce a soft crust. The additional sugar assists in the browning of the crust when baking.

Milk contains enzymes that can weaken the bond of the gluten. Denaturing these enzymes is accomplished by **scalding** the milk. Sugar contributes to the browning of the dough, and the fat makes the baked bread soft.

When scalding milk, scale slightly more than needed and heat until a skin forms on the top of the milk or to a temperature of 190°F (88°C). During processing, pasteurized milk is heated to 161°F (72°C), but this is not sufficient to completely destroy all of the enzymes, which weaken gluten. After scalding the milk, cover tightly with plastic wrap and cool quickly on an ice bath; this helps to reduce any possible evaporation. Scale the milk after it has cooled to 80°F (17°C).

To save time and avoid the need of scalding the milk, powdered milk can be used. Powdered milk is available as whole milk powder and milk solids nonfat (MSNF). Powdered milk products are heated to 200°F (94°C), which destroys the gluten-weakening enzymes. MSNF has an increased shelf life due to defatting, and is easily available through most distributors.

To convert a recipe from whole milk to MSNF, use the following procedure.

In this example, the recipe calls for 32 oz of whole milk.

To calculate the amount of MSNF needed, multiply the amount of milk needed by 0.10.

32 oz × 0.10 = Amount of MSNF

3.2 oz = Amount of MSNF

In the next step, the amount of MSNF is subtracted from the amount of whole milk. This will yield the amount of water needed.

Whole milk − MSNF = Weight of water

32 oz − 3.2 oz = Weight of water

28.8 oz = Weight of water

Thus, to convert 32 oz whole milk in a recipe using MSNF, the recipe would need 28.8 oz of water and 3.2 oz of MSNF.

Eggs

Eggs are 76% water. Like milk and water, eggs also hydrate the flour. Brioche and Danish use eggs to give the dough flavor and a rich yellow color. Fats present in the yolk create a smooth and tender dough. At the same time, the yolk softens the crust of the bread and facilitates browning. During the baking process, the egg proteins coagulate, adding structure and strengthening the bread.

Flour

Viennoiserie products differ from yeast breads described in Chapter 2. Many of these doughs are mixed, laminated, shaped, and fermented. All of these steps contribute to the development of gluten. In some formulas, high-gluten flour is used to combat the shortening effects of fats. Some formulas may contain a blend of stronger flours (high-gluten and bread) and weaker flours (cake and pastry) to create a more tender dough. Flours vary a great deal, and adjustments to formulas may need to be made. The goal is to use the correct flour or blend of flours to support the extra ingredients in the dough.

Sugar

Sugar adds sweetness to the bread, provides food for the yeast, controls gluten development, and retains moisture. The amount of sugar in a formula can range from 12% to 30%. Additional sugar also creates a denser dough with a fine crumb. Granulated sugar is most frequently used in Viennoiserie formulas. However, honey, maple syrup, and even brown sugar can be used to add additional flavor. Since products that are higher in sugar will brown more easily than the breads produced in Chapter 2, be sure to adjust oven temperatures.

Yeast

The same guidelines discussed in Chapter 2 are used in production of Viennoiserie. Yeast provides flavor and leavening for the breads. **Osmotolerant yeast** is preferred for Viennoiserie because many of these products contain more than 10% of sugar and/or fat. Using osmotolerant yeast will provide more consistent results and increased volume in the final product. If osmotolerant yeast is not available, increase the amount of yeast in the recipe by up to 30%.

Salt

The flavor of salt helps to balance the sweetness often found in Viennoiserie. Salt also controls fermentation, and can range from 1% to 2.3%. Higher percentages of salt in the dough will retard fermentation.

Fat

Viennoiserie is identified by the yellow color of the doughs, soft rich dough, and flaky laminated doughs. This is done with the use of eggs and fat. The quality of the fat that goes into the dough will ultimately change the color and flavor of the dough. Butter is the preferred fat because it provides the best flavor, color, and mouth feel to the dough. In regards to laminated dough, butter can be very hard when cold and extremely soft at room temperature. This increases the difficulty when laminating the dough. Shortening is more workable at refrigerator temperature and at room temperature. It maintains a plastic consistency that is easy to roll in laminated dough, but it provides no flavor. Margarine has more yellow color than butter, and has some of the characteristics of shortenings, including ease of rolling. Margarine contains salt, so adjustments to the recipe need to be made when changing to margarine.

Most Viennoiserie products have all the fat added during the mixing process, while croissants and Danish have a majority of the fat added during the lamination process. Laminated doughs have a small amount of fat included in the dough to increase flexibility and extensibility. The amount of fat typically ranges from 5% for laminated dough, up to 70% for an enriched dough. Laminated doughs commonly have an additional 25% of butter added for the roll-in.

Croissant and Danish dough have a small percentage of fat, which can be added during the mixing process without any adverse effects. Enriched doughs contain much more fat. Once the percentage starts to reach 10% fat, it is added at the end of mixing, just as the dough reaches full development. Do not include the fat in the beginning of the mix because it will dramatically increase the amount of mixing time. During this extended mixing time (sometimes as much as double the time), the dough may become overoxidized and too warm. As a result, fermentation may occur too quickly. When mixing doughs with a fat percentage above 10%, follow the brioche method on pages 34–35 in Chapter 2.

Laminated Doughs

Laminated doughs have fat incorporated through a series of folding and turns to create thin layers of fat and dough. **Croissant** and **Danish** are two varieties of yeasted doughs. Croissants are made from a lean dough, low in fat and sugar, with a butter roll-in. Danish are made with a rich dough, higher in fat and sugar, with a butter roll-in. Danish doughs might also include spices. There are nine key steps to producing properly laminated dough: mixing, roll-in fat preparation, enclosing the fat, rolling and folding, shaping, proofing, filling and egg washing, baking, and finishing and storage.

Mixing the Dough

The mixing of the dough is one of the most important of the nine steps. When making laminated dough, the gluten does not need to be fully developed. Gluten development will continue during the rolling and folding process. A short mix is sufficient to develop the dough. The dough should be mixed to the point that it is not completely smooth and free of holes or tears. Refer to Figure 3.1. The dough on the left is croissant dough mixed for 5 minutes: It is not as smooth as the doughs prepared in Chapter 2. The dough on the right was mixed for 3 minutes: the holes and tears are easily identifiable. This dough does not have enough structure to hold the roll-in fat and will tear easily during rolling. The final product will not rise as high due to lack of structure. By contrast, using dough that has been fully developed, as discussed in Chapter 2, will result in tough final dough. This will require additional resting time between folds.

After mixing the dough it is rested under refrigeration for a minimum of 1 hour, or as long as 12 hours.

FIGURE 3.1 1. Properly mixed dough; 2. Undermixed dough

Roll-in Fat Preparation

The next step is shaping the butter into a slab in preparation of enclosing. To do this, slice a pound of cold butter slightly thicker than ½ in. (15 mm). A pound of butter will yield nine slices. Lay the butter slices out on a sheet of plastic wrap in three rows, three slices across, with the slices touching. This will form a 3 × 3 square. Cover the butter slices with another piece of plastic wrap. Gently press the butter with a rolling pin to maintain an even thickness of the butter.

The goal is to press the butter into one solid piece and begin to soften it. The final thickness of butter will be ½ in. (15 mm) and measure 8 in.² (21 cm²). Allow the butter slab to continue softening at room temperature until the dough has finished fermenting.

FIGURE 3.2 Left: Butter placed on plastic wrap; Right: Butter flattened into slab

FIGURE 3.3 1. Properly laminated croissant dough; 2. Improperly laminated croissant dough

Enclosing the Fat

Enclosing the fat in the dough is as important as the first step of mixing the dough. The consistency of the butter and dough must be the same. This step requires the pastry chef to understand what happens when the butter and dough are combined. The aim of lamination is to layer the fat evenly between the layers of dough.

Butter that is too cold will create lumps when added to the chilled dough. Rather than roll with the dough, the butter will break up, not spreading evenly between the layers. On the other hand, butter that is too warm will spread too easily, creating uneven layers of fat and dough. Since the butter spreads easier than the dough, this will cause the butter to push through the ends of the dough when rolling.

To check the consistency, feel both the butter and the dough. Separately, they should feel the same. If the dough is stiffer than the butter, place the butter in the cooler until it firms; this may take as little as 5 minutes. If the butter is too firm, allow it remain at room temperature until the butter softens to the consistency of the refrigerated dough. Since there can be range of temperatures for coolers and room temperature, these times are approximate and may require some adjustments to yield the optimal results. Be sure to check the consistency of dough and fat before proceeding. This step is the same when enclosing butter using the traditional or blunt cross method.

Traditional Method

When using the traditional method, roll the dough to 1.5 times the length of the butter. The dimensions of the dough will be 9 × 13 in. (23 × 33 cm). Place the butter slab on the left side of the dough, being sure to allow some dough to remain exposed on the sides of the butter. The seam will ensure the dough closes and the butter will remain inside while rolling. To enclose the butter, fold the dough on the uncovered dough on the right side over the butter. This will reach the center of the butter slab. Then fold the dough from the left over the center of the dough and gently close the ends.

FIGURE 3.4 1. Place the butter on the dough.

FIGURE 3.5 2. Fold the right side over the butter.

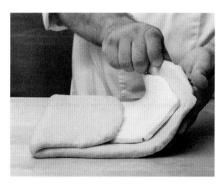

FIGURE 3.6 3. Fold the left side over the center.

This method gives the dough more layers of lamination than the blunt cross. After enclosing the butter there are five layers: two layers of butter and three layers of dough.

Blunt Cross Method

The **blunt cross** method involves rolling the dough into a cross shape and placing the butter into the center. Using this method the butter is fully enclosed in the dough and less likely to escape from the sides during rolling.

When preparing to enclose the fat, roll the dough into a cross with rounded edges. The dough in the center of the cross is slightly thicker and the arms are rolled so the edges are thinned. It is important to roll the dough with the varying thickness to ensure the butter has equal amounts of dough on each side. Measuring the blunt cross through the center, the distance from the tips of the arms will be 18 in. (45 cm). The arms are then folded over into the center and the dough is pinched to seam the pieces.

FIGURE 3.7 1. Place the butter on the dough.

FIGURE 3.8 2. Fold over the closest side.

FIGURE 3.9 3. Repeat, folding in the remaining sides.

Rolling and Folding

After enclosing the fat, the next step is to begin rolling and folding the dough. It is important to decrease the thickness of the dough gradually to create even layers of butter and dough. The dough is rolled to ¼ in. (6 mm) thick—be sure to brush any remaining dusting flour from the top of the dough. The extra flour left on the dough will not be absorbed by the dough. If too much flour is applied, it will be visible in the lamination of the final dough; additionally, this flour will not taste good when eaten. When it comes to folding, there are two options: **single fold** and **book fold**.

A single fold, or three-fold, is done by visually dividing the dough in thirds. The third on the right side is folded over the center portion, and the piece on the left is then brought over the center section. When using the three fold method, this process will need to be completed a total of three times.

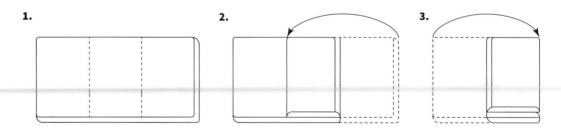

FIGURE 3.10 Single-fold procedure: 1. Already-rolled dough is marked with dotted lines for thirds. 2. Fold the dough from the right side. 3. Fold the dough from the left side.

To execute the book-fold procedure, or four-fold, fold the dough over from both the right and left side so they touch. It is best to offset the point where the two sides meet. Fold the right side in 75 percent and the left side 25 percent. This helps to evenly distribute the layers of dough. The dough is then folded in half. Yeast-leavened laminated doughs that use the book-fold procedure start with one single fold, followed by a book fold. There are only two rolling and folding steps in this process. This speeds up production but will result in less lamination. The types and amount of folds are strictly based on personal preference. The following table exams how many layers will be present in the final dough.

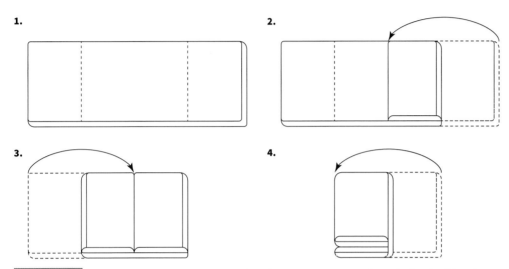

FIGURE 3.11 Book-fold procedure: 1. Already-rolled dough is marked on right and left side of dough ¼. 2. Right side is folded over 25%. 3. Left side is folded over 25%. 4. Dough is folded in half.

Layer Count for Laminated Dough Using Traditional Butter Lock in Procedure

Type of Fold	Lock in Layers	1st Fold	2nd Fold	3rd Fold
Single fold	5	15	45	135
1 single fold and 1 book fold	5	15	60	

Layer Count for Laminated Dough Using Blunt Cross Procedure

Type of Fold	Lock in Layers	1st Fold	2nd Fold	3rd Fold
Single fold	3	9	27	81
1 single fold and 1 book fold	3	9	36	

The dough will need to rest under refrigeration for a minimum of 20 minutes between folds when using a mechanical sheeter, and 45 minutes for hand rolling. This serves three purposes: it relaxes the gluten, retards fermentation, and solidifies the fat. After relaxing the dough, the additional rolling and folding can be done. When rolling the rested dough, be sure to turn 90 degrees, so that the gluten is developed equally in all directions. Once the desired folds are in place, rest the dough for 60 minutes in the refrigerator.

There are many steps in the production of laminated doughs. Following is a sample schedule to assist in the manufacturing of the dough. As each procedure is executed, enter the rest time on the sheet. This will help to make sure the correct number of folds are completed and that the dough has had a sufficient rest period before moving to the next step.

Schedule for Producing Croissant Dough

Step	Dough Resting Time	Start Time 7:00 AM
Mixing dough	60 minutes	8:00 AM
Butter lock-in and first fold	20 minutes	
Second fold	20 minutes	
Third fold	60 minutes	
Final rolling	15 minutes in freezer	
Cutting and shaping		

Shaping

The dough is now ready for final rolling. Roll the dough in the same direction as the previous roll until the desired width is reached. Then turn the dough and continue rolling to a thickness of ⅛ in. (3 mm). When using a dough sheeter, roll the dough through on the final thickness two times. At this point, the thickness of the dough will determine the final size of the products. In the next step the dough is cut to the desired size. Assuming the thickness of the dough is even, the cut and shaped pastries will be the same size.

After rolling the gluten needs a short rest to relax, which prevents the dough from shrinking after it is cut. Place the dough in the freezer for 15 to 20 minutes. Completely freezing the dough is not necessary. In the freezer, the dough will relax and the fat will harden, which will help to achieve a clean cut. If the dough is too warm, the fat and dough will compress and stick together, and lamination will not be visible on the edges of the dough.

While the dough is in the freezer, gather the tools needed for cutting and shaping. Many shapes are easily achievable with a sharp knife and ruler. Even though the dough is in the freezer, it is sheeted very thinly and will thaw quickly, so it is important to be organized and move quickly. The ruler is critical in measuring the dough and ensuring the pieces are the same size. Consistency in cutting and shaping will provide consistent products that proof and bake at the same rate.

After shaping the dough, there are two options: The dough can continue moving on the following steps or it can be retarded or frozen. If freezing a shaped product, place it on parchment-lined sheet pans and wrap tightly. It is recommended to not store the product in the freezer for longer than two weeks. When ready to use the frozen product, space the dough out on a parchment-lined sheet pan. Allow the items to thaw completely before placing in the proof box. This can also be done overnight in the refrigerator. Then continue with the following steps.

FIGURE 3.12a–d Croissant-shaping procedure:

1. Cut the dough. **2.** Stretch the length. **3.** Stretch the arms. **4.** Roll the croissant.

FIGURE 3.13a–c Pain Au Chocolate:

1. Cut the dough.

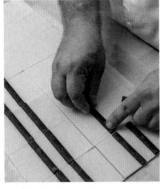

2. Fill with chocolate.

3. Roll the dough.

FIGURE 3.14a–b Pocket fold:

1. Cut the dough.

2. Fold and press the corners in the center.

FIGURE 3.15a–c Pinwheel fold:

1. Cut the dough.

2. Cut the "X"

3. Fold the corners.

FIGURE 3.16a–d Shaping snails:

1. Cut the strip.

2. Twist the dough.

3. Roll the dough out.

4. Wrap the dough.

FIGURE 3.17a–d Cinnamon rolls:

1. Coat the dough with cinnamon sugar mixture.

2. Roll the dough.

3. Cut the dough.

4. Tuck the end of the dough under the roll.

Proofing

After shaping the dough, apply a coat of egg wash. This coat will help to prevent a skin from forming while proofing. Proofing can be done covered at room temperature at 68–70°F (20–22°C) or in a proof box. When using a proof box, set temperature at 80°F (27°C) and humidity at 80%. The inclusion of butter in Viennoiserie requires the proofing temperature to be below 86°F (30°C) to prevent the butter from melting out of the dough. Due to the delicate nature of the dough, it cannot be fully proofed without risking the baked products collapsing, so proofing is completed at 75%. Remember that the additional sugar in the dough will slow down fermentation, and it may take as long as 90 minutes for the dough to be proofed properly.

Visually, it may be difficult to identify if the dough is properly proofed. Gently shake the pan: The movement of the dough can help determine if the dough is properly proofed. Under-proofed dough will look stiff and will not move when the sheet pan is moved. Properly proofed dough will jiggle slightly when the sheet pan is moved. Overproofed dough will jiggle, but may collapse and will be difficult to egg wash. Be careful, though, when testing: Shaking too hard or excessively will cause the dough to deflate.

Filling and Egg Washing

After the dough is finished proofing, it is prepared for baking. At this point, Danish and some croissants require fillings to be added. Fillings can include marmalade, cheese, spinach, sun-dried tomatoes, or pastry cream. Before applying the filling, gently degas the dough with your fingers where the filling will be deposited. Omitting this step may cause the filling to fall off the dough during baking.

The dough now undergoes a second egg washing. Remove the product from the proof box and allow it to sit at room temperature for 5 minutes. This step allows the dough to cool slightly, making it easier to egg wash. The moisture of the proof box can make the outer layer of the dough very soft. The short rest at room temperature will allow this layer to dry slightly, allowing the brush to slide over the dough, rather than sticking.

Egg wash gives the crust a deeper color and shine. When egg washing the dough, it is important to apply a thin coat and avoid the egg wash from pooling on or around the dough. Egg wash that pools on the dough will not only look unattractive, but it could also add a strong, undesirable egg flavor to the finished product. A soft brush works best, and a gentle touch will prevent deflating the proofed dough. Apply the egg wash to the dough in the same direction as the dough is laminated. For example, a croissant should be brushed following the same way it was rolled, not from end to end. Brushing over the cut edges of the dough will prevent the edges from fully expanding as the egg coagulates first.

Baking

Laminated dough relies on steam and yeast to leaven the dough. The correct oven temperature will ensure that enough steam is developed before the outer layer of the dough sets. The initial oven temperature of 375°F (190°C) will provide enough heat to quickly create steam and increase the volume of the Viennoiserie. To prevent the crust from forming too quickly, 2 to 3 seconds of steam can be injected in the oven. A small amount of steam will not rinse off the egg wash, just allow the dough a little more oven spring.

Once the dough has begun to color, vent the oven, allowing any extra steam to dissipate. It is possible to have a croissant that looks fully baked with an underbaked interior that will collapse. In order to prevent this, after 5 to 7 minutes, continue baking at 350°F (180°C) until done. To determine the doneness of Viennoiserie, the dough should be evenly colored a deep golden brown; the sides of croissants should be the same color as the top and bottoms. If too much browning is observed on the bottom of the product, double panning may be needed. Remember: All ovens have unique characteristics, so testing of oven settings will need to be conducted to achieve the best results.

Croissants and Danish are very fragile when warm, and care must be used when handling them right out of the oven. Allow them to cool before moving to the next step.

Finishing and Storing

After cooling, some croissants and Danish receive additional garnishes. They may be dusted with powdered sugar, brushed with apricot glaze, piped with chocolate, garnished with fresh fruit, or have a sugar glaze applied. Store the products uncovered at room temperature. Due to the delicate nature of the croissant and Danish, they are best consumed the same day they are produced.

Enriched Breads

Enriched breads cover a wide variety of yeasted doughs, sweet dough, brioche, coffee cakes, stollen, and donuts. The process of making enriched breads is similar to those used in Chapter 2. The main difference is that they include larger quantities of eggs, sugar, and fat.

Mixing

Due to the large quantity of fats and sugar, enriched breads benefit from using the sponge method and brioche method described in Chapter 2. Some enriched breads that contain lower percentages of sugar and fat can be mixed using the straight dough method. Formulas that contain over 10% sugar or fat benefit from developing the dough before adding the sugar or fat. Adding the sugar and fat early in the development of the dough increases the mixing time, resulting in an overoxidized, warm dough.

After mixing, refer to the 14 steps of bread production in Chapter 2. When working with enriched bread, consider temperature. These doughs will be softer due to the higher percentage of fat. Chilling the dough will make it easier to shape and handle. It will also slow down fermentation and provide a better flavor to the dough.

Proofing and Baking

Enriched breads, much like croissants and Danish, benefit from a lower proofing temperature. To prevent the butter in the dough from melting, a proof box temperature of 80°F (27°C) and humidity at 80%, work best. After proofing, all enriched breads must be egg washed. Remove the dough from the proof box and let it rest for 5 minutes at room temperature before egg washing.

Most enriched breads will be baked in a moderate oven at 350°F (180°C). Larger loaves may require the temperature of the oven to be lower, to finish baking the interior of the bread and avoid undesired overbrowning of the crust. Monitor the bread during the baking process to ensure the dough, especially the bottom, is not browning too quickly. If the bottom of the dough is taking on too much color, double panning may be necessary.

Products baked in pans will need to be unmolded to allow excess moisture to escape from the cooling product. The bread must cool slightly before unmolding, allowing the bread to stabilize. Unmolding too quickly will cause the bread to collapse under its own weight. Place the unmolded loaf on a cooling rack, preventing moisture from building up under the dough.

Puff Pastry

Puff pastry is a laminated dough that does not contain yeast or sugar. The richness of the dough comes from the butter used for lamination. The amount of butter for the roll-in can be up to 50% of the final dough. It is used in the production of turnovers, mille feuille, St Honoré, and arlettes. Because the dough does not contain sugar, it can be used for savory applications.

There are three different types of puff pastry: traditional, blitz, and reverse. **Traditional puff pastry** is made in a similar fashion as the laminated Viennoiserie. A dough is made and then laminated. The difference is that puff pastry uses four book folds to create the layers. Traditional puff pastry may contain as many as 1,000 layers of dough and fat. **Reverse puff pastry** has an equal amount of layers. **Blitz puff pastry** is comparable to a pie dough with an increased amount of fat. Blitz puff pastry gets its name from the fact that is quickly mixed, rested for a short period of time, and laminated quickly at one time. The layers are not as clearly defined and it will not be as flaky as the traditional or reverse puff pastry. It is an excellent option when the desire is for the buttery flavor and a flaky dough that does not need to rise as high. When traditional puff pastry is baked, it can rise almost eight times the original thickness. This is done by steam alone. It takes a considerable amount of time to produce puff pastry, but the end result is flaky, light dough.

Traditional puff pastry is laminated in the same way as croissant and Danish dough. Enclosing the fat can be done using the traditional or blunt cross methods, followed by four book folds. During folds, the dough is rolled to a thickness of ¼ in. (6 mm). Resting periods between folds remain at 20 minutes. The following schedule will provide a way to monitor the production of traditional puff pastry.

Baking Puff Pastry

Puff pastry requires steam to create the flakiness associated with the dough. To create the steam, the dough is started in a hot oven 425°F (220°C). Once the dough has risen and begun to set, baking is finished at 350°F (180°C) to bake through the center. Since puff pastry does not contain any sugar, it can withstand the higher temperature and longer baking time.

Schedule for Producing Puff Pastry Dough

Step	Amount of Dough Resting Time	Start Time 7:00 AM
Mixing dough	60 minutes	8:00 AM
Butter lock-in and first book fold	20 minutes	
Second book fold	20 minutes	
Third book fold	20 minutes	
Fourth book fold	60 minutes	
Final rolling	15 minutes in freezer	
Cutting and shaping		

Some products require a flaky dough, but not as flaky as traditional puff pastry. To create a flaky dough that can be made quickly, pastry chefs use Blitz Puff Pastry. This dough is similar to pie dough with a higher percentage of fat. The dough is mixed like a pie dough and then allowed to rest in the refrigerator for 15 minutes and then rolled. The dough is rolled to ⅛ in. (3 mm) and then given a book fold. The dough is turned 90 degrees, and this process is completed two more times without resting the dough. At this point, the dough is rested again for 30 minutes and then rolled to the desired thickness, ready for use.

Reverse puff pastry has the butter encasing the dough. It is difficult to imagine rolling butter with a rolling pin, and cannot be done without adding flour to the butter. This helps to make the butter more dough like, and absorb moisture in the butter so it does not stick to the rolling pin. The advantage of reverse puff pastry is that it does not shrink as much during the baking process.

Troubleshooting for Vienoisserie

Issue	Cause/Solution
When laminating dough the butter can be seen through the dough in chunks	1. Fat has hardened due to low refrigerator temperature or extended time in the refrigerator, reduce resting time in refrigerator 2. Fat is too cold, use butter that is the same consistency of the dough
When laminating the dough the fat breaks through the end of the dough	1. Fat is too soft, use butter that is the same consistency of the dough 2. The dough is rolled down too quickly, gradually reduce the thickness of the dough when rolling to ensure dough and fat roll at the same rate.
Laminated product is not flaky	The dough was rolled too thin, follow the thickness guidelines in the section rolling and folding. Rolling the dough too thin will compress the layers and reduce flakiness.
Butter runs out of the dough in the proof box	The proof box temperature was too high. Reduce the temperature of the proof box
Butter runs out of laminated dough when baking	The dough was not laminated properly; the fat is too thick in the dough and runs out.
Croissants unroll when baking	1. The dough is too tough, reduce mixing time for the next batch. 2. When shaping the croissant the dough was rolled too tightly, roll looser next time

Recipes

Croissant

Yield: 4 lb 1.9 oz (1871 g)
Portions: 24
Portion size: 2.7 oz (76 g)
Yield description: 24 croissants at 2.7 oz (76 g)

Ingredients	U.S.	Metric	%
Bread Flour	1 lb 12 oz	795 g	100
Milk, scalded and cooled	1 lb 0.8 oz	477 g	60
Butter, soft	2.5 oz	70 g	8.9
Sugar	1.5 oz	43 g	5.4
Instant Yeast	0.5 oz	14 g	1.8
Salt	0.65 oz	18 g	2.3
Butter for roll-in	1 lb	454 g	57.1

Procedure

1. Combine all ingredients with exception of the roll-in butter.
2. Mix for 5 minutes on second speed, DDT 76°F (24°C)
3. Allow bulk fermentation, 1 hour.
4. Refrigerate for 1 to 12 hours.
5. Follow rolling and folding procedure on page 65.

Whole Wheat Croissant

Yield: 3 lb 14.8 oz (1796 g)
Portions: 23
Portion size: 2.7 oz (78 g)
Yield description: 23 croissants at 2.7 oz (78 g)

Ingredients	U.S.	Metric	%
Bread Flour	1 lb 5.1 oz	600 g	75
Whole Wheat Flour	7 oz	200 g	25
Water	14.1 oz	400 g	50
Milk Powder	0.7 oz	20 g	2.5
Egg Yolk	2.25 oz	64 g	8
Salt	0.6 oz	16 g	2
Sugar	3.1 oz	88 g	11
Instant Yeast	0.28 oz	8 g	1
Butter, soft	1.1 oz	32 g	4
Butter for roll-in	12.9 oz	368 g	46

Procedure

1. Combine all ingredients with exception of the roll-in butter.
2. Mix for 5 minutes on second speed, DDT 76°F (24°C).
3. Allow bulk fermentation 1 hour.
4. Refrigerate for 1 to 12 hours.
5. Follow rolling and folding procedure on page 64.

FIGURE 3.18 Croissant and Whole Wheat Croissant

Danish Dough

Yield: 3 lb 14 oz (1761 g)

Portions: 25

Portion size: 2.25 (65 g)

Yield description: 25 Danish at 2.25 (65 g)

Ingredients	U.S.	Metric	%
Bread Flour	1 lb 10.4 oz	750 g	100
Water	11.9 oz	338 g	45
Sugar	4 oz	112 g	15
Eggs	2.9 oz	83 g	11
Butter, soft	1.3 oz	38 g	5
Milk Powder	1.3 oz	38 g	5
Cardamom	0.13 oz	3.8 g	0.5
Osmotolerant Yeast	0.31 oz	9 g	1.2
Salt	0.53 oz	15 g	2
Butter for roll-in	13.2 oz	375 g	50

Procedure

1. Combine all ingredients with exception of the roll-in butter.
2. Mix for 8 minutes on second speed, DDT 76°F (24°C).
3. Allow bulk fermentation, 1 hour.
4. Refrigerate for 8 to 12 hours.
5. Follow rolling and folding procedure on pages 65–66.

FIGURE 3.19 Assorted Danish: Blueberry Almond Cream Danish (top), Pain au Chocolate (right), Apricot Almond Cream (front)

FIGURE 3.20 Assorted Danish: Bear Claw (top), Cinnamon Cream Cheese (right), Fresh Fruit Pinwheel (front)

FIGURE 3.21 Assorted Rich Doughs (From top left going clockwise): Kugelhopf, Brioche Loaf, Stollen, Pain Au Lait with Poppyseeds

Kugelhopf Sponge

Yield: 11.35 oz (321 g)

Portions: 1

Portion size: 11.35 oz (321 g)

Yield description: 1 at 11.35 oz (321 g)

Ingredients	U.S.	Metric	%
Bread Flour	6.75 oz	191 g	100
Water	4 oz	113 g	59.1
Instant Yeast	0.6 oz	17 g	0.9

Procedure

1. Combine ingredients; mix for 6 minutes at second speed, DDT 76°F (24°C).
2. Ferment for 1 hour.

Kugelhopf-Soaked Raisins

Yield: 9.25 oz (263 g)

Portions: 1

Portion size: 9.25 oz (263 g)

Yield description: 1 at 9.25 oz (263 g)

Ingredients	U.S.	Metric
Raisins	7.75 oz	220 g
Rum	1.5 oz	43 g

Procedure

1. Rinse raisins to remove excess sugars.
2. Drain and dry on paper towels.
3. Pour rum over fruit and soak for 24 hours.

Kugelhopf

Yield: 3 lb 14.6 oz (1780 g)

Portions: 2

Portion size: 1 lb 15 oz (890 g)

Yield Description: 2 loaves at 1 lb 15 oz (890 g)

Ingredients	U.S.	Metric	%
Bread Flour	1 lb 2.75 oz	532 g	100
Milk, scalded and cooled	4 oz	169 g	31.8
Eggs	8 oz	169 g	31.8
Osmotolerant Yeast	0.05 oz	1.6 g	0.3
Salt	0.17 oz	5 g	0.9
Sugar	4 oz	113 g	21.2
Butter	7.25 oz	205 g	38.5
Soaked Raisins	9.25 oz	263 g	49.4
Kugelhopf Sponge	11.35 oz	321 g	60.3

Procedure

1. Use intense mix for all ingredients except raisins, DDT 76°F (24°C).
2. Add raisins and mix until combined.
3. Allow bulk fermentation 1 hour.
4. Refrigerate for 8 to 12 hours.
5. Scale loaves at 1 lb 15 oz (890 g).
6. Allow bench fermentation 30 minutes.
7. Degas and shape into a ring.
8. Place the dough into buttered fluted mold (9 in. × 4 in.; 22.8 cm × 10 cm).
9. Proof for 2 hours at 85°F (29°C).
10. Bake at 350°F (175°C) 40 to 45 minutes.
11. Remove from pans and place on cooling racks.
12. Once bread is completely cooled, dust with powdered sugar.

Pain au Lait

Yield: 4 lb 3 oz (1908 g)
Portions: 33
Portion size: 2 oz (57 g)
Yield description: 33 rolls at 2 oz (57 g)

Ingredients	U.S.	Metric	%
Bread Flour	2 lb 1.8 oz	960 g	100
Sugar	3.4 oz	96 g	10
Osmotolerant Yeast	0.27 oz	8 g	0.8
Salt	0.71 oz	20 g	2
Eggs	5.1 oz	144 g	15
Milk, scalded and cooled	1 lb 0.9 oz	480 g	50
Butter, soft	7.1 oz	200 g	20.8

Procedure

1. Use intense mix, DDT 76°F (24°C).
2. Allow bulk fermentation, 1 hour.
3. Refrigerate overnight.
4. Scale into 2 oz (56.7 g) rolls.
5. Proof for 90 minutes at 85°F (29°C).
6. Egg wash.
7. Bake 350°F (176°C).

Stollen Sponge

Yield: 10.25 oz (276 g)
Portions: 1
Portion size: 10.25 oz (276 g)
Yield description: 1 at 10.25 oz (276 g)

Ingredients	U.S.	Metric	%
Bread Flour	3 oz	80 g	100
Water	6 oz	160 g	200
Milk Powder	0.75 oz	20 g	25
Instant Yeast	0.5 oz	14 g	18
Honey	0.09 oz	2.4 g	3

Procedure

1. Combine ingredients with paddle and mix for 5 minutes.
2. Ferment for 1 hour at 72°F (22 C).

Stollen Fruit

Yield: 1 lb 3.5 oz (562 g)
Portions: 1
Portion size: 1 lb 3.5 oz (562 g)
Yield description: 1 at 1 lb 3.5 oz (562 g)

Ingredients	U.S.	Metric
Golden Raisins	8.25 oz	238 g
Raisins	8.25 oz	238 g
Candied Orange Peel	1.25 oz	36 g
Rum	1.75 oz	50 g

Procedure

1. Rinse all fruit to remove excess sugars.
2. Drain and dry on paper towels.
3. Pour rum over fruit and soak for 24 hours.

Stollen Almond Paste

Yield: 8 oz (240 g)

Portions: 5

Portion size: 1.5 oz (43 g)

Yield description: 5 pieces at 1.5 oz (43 g)

Ingredients	U.S.	Metric
Almond Paste	8 oz	225 g
Whole Eggs	0.5 oz	15 g

Procedure

1. Mix ingredients to combine.
2. Scale almond paste mixture at 1.5 oz (43 g) and roll into a cylinder 7 in. (17 cm) long.
3. Reserve in refrigerator for final bread shaping.

Stollen Final Dough

Yield: 4 lb 8 oz (2092 g)

Portions: 4

Portion size: 1 lb 2 oz (520 g)

Yield description: 4 loaves at 1 lb 2 oz (520 g)

Ingredients	U.S.	Metric	%
Bread Flour	1 lb 6 oz	635 g	100
Sponge	9.4 oz	273 g	43
Water	1.4 oz	40 g	6.3
Sugar	2.2 oz	63.5 g	10
Whole Eggs	4.1 oz	120 g	18.8
Butter	11 oz	317 g	50
Salt	0.4 oz	12.7 g	2
Stollen Fruit	1 lb 3.5 oz	562 g	88.5
Sliced Almonds	2 oz	57 g	9
Lemon Zest	0.2 oz	6 g	1
Spice Blend	0.2 oz	6 g	1

Note: Spice blend is equal parts nutmeg and mace by weight.

Procedure

1. Combine first seven ingredients using intense mix, DDT 76°F (24°C).
2. Add remaining ingredients and mix for an additional 2 minutes.
3. Allow bulk fermentation 90 minutes; fold once after 45 minutes.
4. Scale loaves at 1 lb 2 oz (520 g).
5. Allow bench fermentation 30 minutes.
6. Degas and flatten center of loaf with a rolling pin.
7. Enclose the almond paste mixture in the dough; fold the dough over.
8. Proof for 60 minutes at 85°F (29°C).
9. Bake at 350°F (175°C) 30 to 35 minutes.
10. While loaves are still warm, brush all surfaces including the bottom with 6 oz (170 g) of melted butter and dredge in sugar.
11. Once bread is completely cooled, dust with powdered sugar.

Brioche

Yield: 4 lb (1818 g)

Portions: 4

Portion size: 1 lb (454 g)

Yield description: 4 loaves at 1 lb (454 g)

Ingredients	U.S.	Metric	%
Bread Flour	1 lb 13.1 oz	825 g	100
Milk	7.1 oz	200 g	24.2
Eggs	10.9 oz	310 g	37.6
Sugar	1.8 oz	50 g	6.1
Salt	0.6 oz	16 g	1.9
Instant Yeast	0.26 oz	7.3 g	0.9
Butter, cold and cubed	14.5 oz	410 g	49.7

Procedure

1. Mix all ingredients except butter for 8 minutes on second speed, DDT 78°F (25°C).
2. Add the butter and continue mixing until it is incorporated.
3. Allow bulk fermentation 1 hour.
4. Refrigerate overnight.
5. Scale into 1 lb (454 g).
6. Shape into loaves and place into greased loaf pans.
7. Proof for 2 hours at 85°F (29°C).
8. Egg wash.
9. Bake at 350°F (175°C) for 35 to 40 minutes.

Sweet Dough

Yield: 3 lb 7 oz (1508 g)

Portions: 24

Portion size: 2.29 oz (60 g)

Yield description: 24 cinnamon rolls at 2.29 oz (60 g)

Ingredients	U.S.	Metric	%
Bread Flour	1 lb 12.2 oz	800 g	80
Milk, scalded and cooled	11.6 oz	330 g	41
Eggs	3.1 oz	88 g	11
Butter	4.8 oz	135 g	17
Sugar	4.8 oz	135 g	17
Osmotolerant Yeast	0.3 oz	9.5 g	1.1
Salt	0.2 oz	5.6 g	0.7
Vanilla Paste	0.2 oz	5.6 g	0.7

Procedure

1. Use straight dough method.
2. Mix for 8 minutes.
3. Ferment dough for 1 hour at room temperature, 72°F (22°C).
4. Refrigerate for 12 hours before using dough.
5. Roll dough to 12 in. (40 cm) wide and thickness of ⅛ in. (3 mm).
6. Spread a thin layer of cinnamon smear on dough and roll.
7. Cut into 0.75 in. (20 mm) thick pieces.
8. Proof for 2 hours at 85°F (29°C).
9. Bake at 350°F (175°C) for 15 to 20 minutes.

Cinnamon Smear for Cinnamon Rolls

Yield: 1 lb 10.5 oz (752 g)

Portions: 1

Portion size: 1.1 oz (31 g)

Yield description: 24 cinnamon rolls at 1.1 oz (31 g)

Ingredients	U.S.	Metric
Brown Sugar	1 lb	454 g
Butter, soft	8 oz	227 g
Cinnamon	1 oz	28 g
Egg Whites	1.5 oz	43 g

Procedure

1. Cream butter, brown sugar, and cinnamon on low.
2. Slowly add egg whites, scraping often.
3. Reserve in refrigerator.

Sticky Bun Smear

Yield: 1 lb 3.25 oz (577.5 g)

Portions: 3

Portion size: 10-in. (25-cm) cake pans

Yield description: Three 10-in. (25-cm) cake pans

Ingredients	U.S.	Metric
Brown Sugar	10 oz	300 g
Butter	4 oz	120 g
Honey	2.5 oz	75 g
Corn Syrup	2.5 oz	75 g
Vanilla Bean Paste	0.25 oz	7.5 g

Procedure

1. Cream butter and sugar.
2. Add honey and corn syrup on low speed.
3. Add vanilla on low speed.
4. Mix until combined.
5. Spread a thin layer into a 10-in. (25-cm) cake pan.
6. Top with 8 cinnamon rolls.
7. Follow proofing and baking directions for cinnamon rolls.

Almond Cream

Yield: 1 lb (452 g)

Portions: 1

Portion size: 1 lb (452 g)

Yield description: 1 at 1 lb (452 g)

Ingredients	U.S.	Metric
Almond Flour	4 oz	113 g
Sugar	4 oz	113 g
Butter, soft	4 oz	113 g
Whole Eggs	4 oz	113 g

Note: Observe mixing speeds when making almond cream. Incorporating air during mixing will cause the cream to collapse after baking.

Procedure

1. Combine almond flour, sugar, and butter.
2. Mix with paddle attachment on low speed until combined.
3. Slowly incorporate eggs in three additions, scraping thoroughly.
4. Reserve in refrigerator.

Bear Claw Filling

Yield: 1 lb 15 oz (878 g)

Portions: 1

Portion size: 1 lb 15 oz (878 g)

Yield description: 1 at 1 lb 15 oz (878 g)

Ingredients	U.S.	Metric
Almond Paste	4 oz	113 g
Sugar	4 oz	113 g
Butter, soft	4 oz	113 g
Cake Crumbs	1 lb	454 g
Eggs	3 oz	85 g

Procedure

1. Cream almond paste and sugar on low speed.
2. Add butter and cake crumbs.
3. Slowly add eggs, scraping often.
4. Reserve in refrigerator.

Oatmeal Streusel

Yield: 1 lb 14.85 oz (874 g)

Portions: 1

Portion size: 1 lb 14.85 oz (874 g)

Yield description: 1 at 1 lb 14.85 oz (874 g)

Ingredients	U.S.	Metric
All-Purpose Flour	8.75 oz	248 g
Oatmeal	6 oz	170 g
Brown Sugar	8 oz	227 g
Cinnamon	0.1 oz	2.8 g
Butter	8 oz	227 g

Procedure

1. Cube butter into ¼-in. cubes and place in the refrigerator
2. Place dry ingredients in a mixing bowl.
3. Blend dry ingredients.
4. Add cold fat and continue mixing until fat is a cornmeal consistency.
5. Top Danish or other pastries as desired before baking.
6. Refrigerate any additional Oatmeal Streusel for up to 7 days.

Cream Cheese Filling

Yield: 1 lb 9.4 oz (721 g)

Portions: 1

Portion size: 1 lb 9.4 oz (721 g)

Yield description: 1 at 1 lb 9.4 oz (721 g)

Ingredients	U.S.	Metric
Cream Cheese	1 lb	454 g
Sugar	8 oz	227 g
Salt	0.2 oz	5.6 g
Vanilla Paste	0.25 oz	7.1 g
Egg Yolk	1 oz	28 g

Procedure

1. Cream sugar and cream cheese on low speed, scraping often.
2. Add remaining ingredients and mix until smooth.
3. Shape Danish dough using the cinnamon roll procedure, p. 66.
4. After proofing, fill the Danish dough using the filling procedure, p. 66.
5. Pipe the cream cheese filling into the indention created in the Danish dough.
6. Top with Oatmeal Streusel and bake following the procedure on p. 67.
7. Cool completely and dust with powdered sugar.

Puff Pastry

Yield: 3 lb 1.75 oz (1414 g)

Portions: 1

Portion size: 3 lb 1.75 oz (1414 g)

Yield description: 1 at 3 lb 1.75 oz (1414 g)

Ingredients	U.S.	Metric	%
Bread Flour	1 lb	454 g	69.5
Water	7 oz	200 g	30.5
Butter, melted	5.3 oz	150 g	22.9
Salt	0.35 oz	10 g	1.5
Butter for roll-in, cubed	14.1 oz	400 g	61.2
Bread Flour for roll-in	7 oz	200 g	30.5

Procedure

1. Combine first four ingredients and mix for 5 minutes on second speed with dough hook.
2. Combine butter and flour for roll-in in a mixer.
3. Cover dough and rest under refrigeration for a minimum of 1 hour.
4. To complete laminating dough, follow the schedule for producing puff pastry on page 69.

Blitz Puff Pastry

Yield: 2 lb 8 oz (1143 g)

Portions: 1

Portion size: 2 lb 8 oz (1143 g)

Yield description: 1 at 2 lb 8 oz (1143 g)

Ingredients	U.S.	Metric	%
All-Purpose Flour	1 lb	454 g	100
Butter	1 lb	454 g	100
Water, ice cold	8 oz	227 g	50
Salt	0.3 oz	8.5 g	2

Procedure

1. Cut butter into ¼-in. cubes and place in refrigerator.
2. Cut cold butter into flour on low speed.
3. Dissolve salt in water.
4. When mixture is pea size, add ice-cold water and mix until a dough forms.
5. Place dough in the refrigerator for 1 hour.
6. Roll dough to ¼ in. and complete a three-fold.
7. Immediately turn the dough 90 degrees and repeat steps 6 and 7 two more times.
8. Refrigerate the dough for 30 minutes.
9. Roll dough to desired thickness.

Key Terms

Lamination
Scalding
Osmotolerant yeast
Croissant

Danish
Blunt cross
Single fold
Book fold

Enriched breads
Traditional puff pastry
Reverse puff pastry
Blitz puff pastry

Questions for Review

1. Discuss how fat is used in Viennoiserie and enriched doughs to produce different products.

2. What is osmotolerant yeast?

3. Identify the advantages and disadvantages associated with butter, shortening, and margarine in laminated doughs.

4. Why are laminated doughs rested between rolling and folding?

5. Each type of puff pastry has an advantage. Describe the benefits associated with all three.

6. Why is it important to scald milk?

CHAPTER 4

Modern Pastry Techniques

Pastry chefs are constantly looking for ways to enhance the experience of their guests through the use of new techniques and ingredients. A spoon of a flavorful gravity defying foam, adding something crunchy, or even a fruit flavored caviar added to a dish, all of this can be achieved through the use of modern cooking techniques. The use of these ingredients is nothing new, they have been used for years to improve the quality of products we eat every day. As these ingredients have become more easily available chefs and pastry chefs have a chance to experiment and create new experiences for their guests.

LEARNING OBJECTIVES

After reading this chapter, you should be able to:

1. **Prepare** foams using various hydrocolloids.
2. **Explain** bloom strength of gelatin.
3. **Describe** the difference between spherification and reverse spherification.
4. **Identify** how hydrocolloids can be used to improve existing recipes.

Modern Cuisine

Many of the top restaurants in the world have gained a reputation through a use of modern cooking techniques. ElBulli in Spain was first credited with using the ingredients and techniques in a full-service restaurant. The techniques used in ElBulli kitchens made them the top restaurant in the world a total of five times. There are many other restaurants around the world that build on the popularity of modern techniques, using ingredients that have been around for a long time and have only recently worked their way into the kitchen.

Originally, the manufacturing industry used these ingredients in foods that were readily available in the corner grocery store. Manufacturers used large quantities of the ingredients. Finding them in smaller quantities was a challenge to restaurant chefs. Acquiring these ingredients became easier due to the increase in popularity and smaller packaging made it possible for many smaller restaurants to experiment with the ingredients.

As more and more restaurants began using modern techniques and ingredients, the industry adopted the phrase *molecular gastronomy* to identify this style of cooking. This term conjures up thoughts of using chemicals in food, yet nothing could be further from the truth.

Modern cuisine is a better way to describe this style of cooking. It incorporates ingredients and different techniques to create food. There are no unnatural additives used; most of the ingredients used are plant-based, with the exception of gelatin, which is animal-based—and these ingredients are consumed every day.

Basics of Modern Pastry

Getting Started

The correct name for the group of ingredients used for creating modern cuisine is **hydrocolloids**, a substance that forms a gel in the presence of water. Hydrocolloids bind the water molecules and affect the texture and viscosity of foods. The most common uses include thickening, gelling, emulsifying, and stabilization. It is important to understand how the ingredients in the recipe interact with one another. The ability to gel or thicken a product is based on the type of hydrocolloid, the quantity, the pH of the ingredients, and the temperature of the ingredients.

Equipment

If precision were an ingredient in modern cuisine, it would be the most important part of the recipe. Many of the recipes throughout this book use small quantities of ingredients that would be extremely difficult to scale using ounces, and volume is not an accurate way to scale these ingredients. As a result, it is necessary to use a small gram scale that can measure to 1/100 of a gram. The more precision used in scaling will yield the most consistent results. The only other equipment needed is an immersion blender, blender, and probe thermometer. Immersion blenders and blenders are used to create powders and foams. Probe thermometers can give accurate readings of solutions and ingredients. Remember that modern cuisine relies greatly on science and precision to get the correct results.

Additional equipment associated with modern cuisine includes immersion circulators, vacuum sealers, ISI cream whippers, and dehydrators. An immersion circulator offers a precisely controlled temperature and is adjustable to 1/10°F (0.05°C). It can be precisely adjusted to the temperature and circulate the water around the food, ensuring quick and even cooking. A combi oven can be used in the same way, with very similar results. Set the oven to combi cooking mode with the temperature needed and 40% steam. Both of these methods provide accurate cooking temperatures. The precision at which they operate allows for the food to cook to the proper temperature without overcooking. Whichever of these methods are used, it is necessary to have a vacuum sealer. The food must be completely sealed in a vacuum bag. Cooking in this style is referred to as *sous vide,* which literally translates from French to "under vacuum." During the cooking process, this prevents moisture from getting into the food, and shortens the cooking time. The vacuum bag must be completely free of air. Air is a poor conductor of heat and prevents the warm water of the immersion circulate from coming into contact with the food in the vacuum bag. The bag must be sealed and completely vacuumed to allow the heat to penetrate the food equally from all sides. Vacuum sealers can also be used to compress fruits for plated desserts.

One of the easiest techniques to start with when beginning with modern techniques is making foams. They are a fun way to add flavor and visual texture to a plate. A **foam** is a frothed mixture; it can be fruit based, coffee, vanilla, or chocolate—the possibilities are endless. There are many different ways to create foams—one way is to use an ISI cream whipper with nitrous oxide (N_2O). N_2O creates a dense foam similar to shaving cream. Hot or cold foams can be made. The cream whipper can also be charged with carbon dioxide (CO_2). CO_2 does not produce a stable foam but can be used to create customs carbonated sodas for desserts. Fresh fruit, such

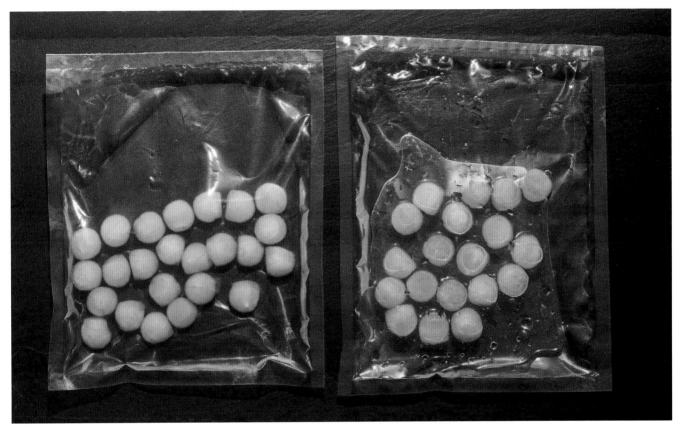

FIGURE 4.1 Properly sealed vacuum bag (left) and improperly sealed vacuum bag (right)

as cherries, can also be placed inside the cream whipper and charged with CO_2. This infuses the fruit with CO_2; as the fruit is eaten, it fizzes just like soda.

Dehydrators are used to dry out fruits and fruit leathers, and can be used to hold products at specific temperatures. While cooking cannot be accomplished in a dehydrator, some models reach high enough temperatures to hold food at safe temperatures. Most of the time, dehydrators are used strictly to dry products or even reduce liquids that do not need to be cooked. Low temperatures allow extra moisture to evaporate from a fruit purée without overheating and changing the flavor or color. If a dehydrator is not available, the same results can be achieved by using a low oven.

Animal-Based Hydrocolloids

Gelatin

It seems hard to believe that gelatin is a hydrocolloid, considering it is readily available in almost every pastry shop. Gelatin is used to stabilize mousse, create foams, and clarify liquids. As other hydrocolloids such as carrageenan and agar have become more readily available, the role of gelatin has decreased. These newer products create firmness in mousses and gels and provide a texture.

Gelatin is produced through chemically denaturing collagen from the bones, connective tissue, and skins of pork, beef, or fish. Pork is the primary source for gelatins used in the pastry kitchen. When processing pork products into gelatin an acid is added to the water to transform the collagen into gelatin. The gelatin is then filtered, purified, and reduced to a powder or sheet form.

Gelatin is easily usable and works in most applications, but there are some areas that need to be addressed when working with gelatin. One drawback to gelatin is that it is an animal-product base. Including gelatin in recipes means that a small percentage of the population, such as vegetarians and individuals with special dietary restrictions or religious beliefs, cannot eat these products.

There are not many ingredients that inhibit the setting of gelatin. Tannins in tea, salts, acids, alcohol, and bromelain cause gelatin to lose setting strength. **Bromelain** is an enzyme present in many tropical fruits such as pineapple, kiwi, mango, papaya, peach, and guava. However, if you heat the fruit to 185°F (85°C), it will denature the enzyme and allow the gelatin to set.

Blooming Gelatin

Gelatin must be bloomed prior to use. **Blooming** gelatin is the process of hydrating the gelatin in a liquid. Recipes using powder gelatin will also have the amount of liquid to bloom. Typically, this is 4 parts liquid to 1 part gelatin. Blooming powder gelatin in warm water may cause the gelatin to form clumps before hydrating fully, reducing the setting strength. When blooming sheet gelatin, it is completely covered with cold water until it softens. Some recipes will specify the amount of liquid to use when blooming sheet gelatin, amount of time, or the weight of the gelatin after blooming. It is critical to properly bloom the gelatin. Not following the procedure correctly can produce a product that is too soft and falls apart or is too stiff and unpleasant to eat.

After the gelatin is bloomed, it must be dissolved over a water bath or carefully in a microwave. Gelatin is **thermoreversible**, meaning it can be melted and set repeatedly without losing any strength. However, use caution when heating gelatin to not boil it, as this will reduce the setting strength.

When using gelatin, it is important to think about the temperature at which the gelatin will be served. Food containing gelatin will be firmer at cold temperatures—for example, a plated dessert served right out of the cooler. An item placed on the buffet will gradually warm to room temperature. As the temperature increases, the gelatin will begin to soften and lose some of the structure it had when cold. Consider a small increase in the amount of gelatin when preparing items that will be served on a buffet. Gelatin melts below body temperature. When eating the dessert the gelatin melts in the mouth, which adds a desirable mouth feel. The characteristics of gelatin are what make it great as a way to set desserts.

Bloom Strength

Oscar Bloom is credited with inventing a way to test the strength of gelatin. Bloom strength of gelatin varies; the higher the number, the stronger the gelatin will set. The bloom strength of powder gelatin is listed on the packaging or can be acquired through the distributor. The powder gelatin used in this book has a bloom strength of 225.

Sheet gelatin is available in different grades: bronze, silver, gold, or platinum. When sheet gelatin is used in a recipe it can be scaled by the sheet or by weight. Recipes in this text will specify sheet gelatin by the piece. Gelatin counted by the sheet can be interchanged between the different grades without making any quantity changes. The Gelatin Bloom Strengths chart below states the weights and bloom strength per sheet. Platinum gelatin contains fewer impurities than gold gelatin. A more refined gelatin will not impart any color, flavor, or odor in the final product. The difference in the sheet weight is mostly impurities. Removing these impurities from the platinum gelatin create a lighter sheet that still has the same setting strength as a sheet of gold gelatin. The recipes included in this text use gold sheet gelatin.

Gelatin Bloom Strengths

Name	Bloom Strength	Grams per Sheet
Bronze	140	3.3
Silver	160	2.5
Gold	200	2
Powder	225	
Platinum	250	1.7

Gelatin Conversion

It is important to work with both sheet and powder gelatin. The formula below can be used to adjust between powder and sheet gelatin.

For this example, we need to convert from 10 grams powder gelatin to platinum sheet gelatin. In the formula the powder will be GelatinA, and platinum sheet gelatin will be GelatinB.

GelatinB = GelatinA × (Bloom Strength GelatinA/Bloom Strength GelatinB)

The first step is to place the numbers into the formula:

GelatinB = 10 g × (225/250)

Now divide the bloom strengths.

Gelatin B = 10 grams × 0.9

Multiply the weight by 0.9 to get the answer.

GelatinB = 9 grams of platinum sheet gelatin

When calculating the replacement values from powder to sheet, be sure to remember the answer is in weight, not in sheet count.

Gelatin

Origin	Animal collagen
Thermoreversible	Yes
Texture	Soft gel, melts below body temperature
Clarity	Clear
Dispersion	Blooms in cold water
Melting Temperature	95°F (35°C)
Setting Temperature	69°F (20°C)
Setting Speed	Slow, hours
Promoters	Sugar, milk
Inhibitors	Alcohol, salt, acid, tannins

Plant-Based Hydrocolloids

Agar

Also referred to as agar-agar, the name originates from the Malay language for the red algae used to produce the agar. Agar has been used in Asia for over 400 years to produce jelly desserts. Its discovery was made when red algae was boiled with water. As the liquid cooled, it set into a firm gel. Today, the agar is extracted much in the same way. After extraction, the agar is filtered and then freeze-dried and ground into a powder.

Agar is also known as a vegetarian form of gelatin. It can be used to stabilize mousses, creams, and jellies. When using agar, the powder is added to a cold or hot liquid and heated to a boil. The gel will set at 105°F (40°C). This is a special property of agar—the high melting point and low setting point is known as **hysteresis**. Warming the agar gel back to 185°F (85°C) will return the jelly to a liquid, that will set again. Products made with agar can withstand higher temperatures without melting or weeping. They can even be served hot and still maintain a gelled consistency. When agar is set, it forms a brittle gel that will not melt in the mouth.

Agar

Origin	Red algae
Thermoreversible	Yes
Texture	Heat resistant, brittle
Clarity	Semi opaque
Dispersion	Cold or hot water
Melting Temperature	195°F (90°C)
Setting Temperature	105°F (40°C)
Setting Speed	Fast, minutes
Promoters	Sugar, sorbitol and glycerol
Inhibitors	Tannic acid

Carrageenan

Carrageenan, like agar, is extracted from red algae. Carrageenan can produce a thickening effect in a sauce to firm gels. A range of textures in the gels can be achieved from soft and elastic to firm and brittle. The name comes from the Gaelic term for moss, *carraigin*. Dating back more than 200 years, the red algae was boiled in milk, and this mixture thickened into a custard as it cooled. It wasn't until the 1930s that carrageenan became an ingredient used by manufacturers of food.

Carrageenan can be used to increase the viscosity of a liquid, set a custard, suspend particles, and substitute fat. Soy milk uses carrageenan to create a texture similar to milk; without this, the soy milk would have a watery consistency. It is also added to milkshakes to create a thicker mouthfeel. Italian dressing uses carrageenan to suspend particulate in the dressing. Chocolate milk also benefits from the carrageenan's ability to suspend particles—without it, the cocoa solids would settle out of the milk.

Carrageenan can be used as a vegetarian form of gelatin to stabilize mousse and creams. When using carrageenan, the powder is combined with sugar, then added to the cold liquid. The mixture is then brought to a boil, poured into molds, and allowed to set.

Carrageenan

	Iota	Kappa
Origin	Red seaweed	Red seaweed
Thermoreversible	Yes	Yes
Texture	Soft gel when used with calcium	Firm, brittle gel when used with potassium
Clarity	Opaque	Cloudy
Dispersion	Cold water, combine with sugar	Cold water, combine with sugar
Melting Temperature	176°F (80°C)	176°F (80°C)
Setting Temperature	158°F (70°C)	158°F (70°C)
Setting Speed	Fast, during cooling	Fast, during cooling
Promoters	Calcium	Potassium
Inhibitors	N/A	Salts

Gellan

Gellan is a unique gum produced by fermenting algae. It is available in two forms: low acyl and high acyl. Gellan is used to create gels, reduced-sugar jams, baked fillings, and spherifications. **Spherification** is the process of shaping liquids into spheres by adding drops of one liquid into a second solution. It is one of the most flexible hydrocolloids, and can be used with almost any ingredient regardless of the acidity. It sets quickly, can be easily molded, and does not impart any flavor.

Modern cuisine is not just about ingredients and procedures. It also incorporates textures in the experience. Gellan gum has many unique properties. For instance, the texture of the gel has a unique mouthfeel. Using gellan along with pectin in a fruit filling creates a filling that will not run when heated, reducing the possibility of running out and burning. The low acyl produces a firm gel similar to agar and kappa carrageenan, while the high produces a softer gel. As the gel is broken apart, it feels as if it is going from a solid back to a liquid. High acyl gellan has a short hysteresis, which makes it suitable for quickly setting products along with gelatin or other hydrocolloids for fast unmolding.

Gellan

	Low Acyl	High Acyl
Origin	Fermentation of Algae	Fermentation of Algae
Thermoreversible	No	Yes
Texture	Brittle gel	Elastic gel
Clarity	Transparent	Opaque
Dispersion	Cold water	Cold water
Melting Temperature	Does not melt	176°F (80°C)
Setting Temperature	140°F (60°C)	158°F (70°C)
Setting Speed	Quick set, minutes	Quick set, minutes
Promoters	Calcium, sodium, potassium, acids	N/A
Inhibitors	Sodium/calcium salts	N/A

Lecithin

Lecithin is not technically a hydrocolloid, but it is incorporated in many modern cuisine recipes. Increased flexibility of this ingredient is due to being a **phospholipid**—it is able to dissolve in fats and liquids. It is used primarily for creating foams, as an emulsifier, and to improve the elasticity of bread. Foams, a light airy soap-bubble-like type of sauce, are one of the most popular techniques and one of the easiest to test.

Lecithin dissolves best in cold solutions. Incorporating excessive quantities of lecithin in a recipe will not produce a stable foam. When testing, start with smaller quantities and then work up until the desired foam is achieved. Adding a few drops of fat to a foam will help to create a stronger foam.

Foams can be either a cold or hot preparation. To foam the mixture, use an immersion blender and start at the top of the liquid. This will help to incorporate air. As the mixture begins to foam, move the immersion blender down into the mixture. Allow the foam to rest for a minute before using. This will allow some of the liquid in the foam to settle down to the bottom of the foam and prevent the foam from bleeding on the plate. Carefully spoon the foam from the top and add to the dessert.

Lecithin

Origin	Soybeans
Thermoreversible	N/A
Texture	N/A
Clarity	N/A
Dispersion	Cold liquid or fat
Melting Temperature	N/A
Setting Temperature	N/A
Setting Speed	N/A
Promoters	N/A
Inhibitors	N/A

FIGURE 4.3a–e Foaming procedure

1. Passion Fruit Purée, lecithin, distilled water, sugar, and immersion blender

2. Sugar and lecithin are added to passion fruit purée and water

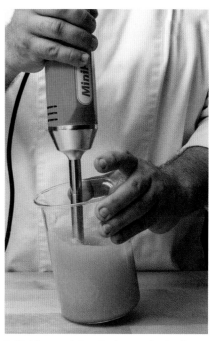

3. Holding container is at an angle starting to foam

4. Foam rests in the container for 3 to 5 minutes

5. Foam is applied to a dessert

Methylcellulose

Methylcellulose is derived from cellulose, the main component of cellulose-rich plant cell walls. When it is heated, it forms a solid gel—think of a warm panna cotta. As it cools, it returns to a liquid state, oftentimes referred to as *melting*. Think of the experience of serving a warm "ice cream" that turns into a liquid as it cools. This is the opposite of what is expected to happen. Normally, food softens as it warms, and in the case of ice cream, it melts when it warms.

Creating warm custards is a fun way to work with methylcellulose, but there are many practical applications as well. Many baked fillings lose shape as they bake. Methylcellulose can help to retain the shape of these items while they are heated. In a cold state, methylcellulose can increase the viscosity of sauces as well as create foams. The foam is prepared when the liquid is cool. After foaming, the foam is placed in a warm oven, setting the methylcellulose. Dried overnight, the results are a crisp, light foam.

Methylcellulose

Origin	Cellulose-rich plants
Thermoreversible	Yes
Texture	Cold—Foams Hot—Soft elastic gel
Clarity	Opaque
Dispersion	Hot or cold
Melting Temperature	Melts below 140°F (60°C)
Setting Temperature	Gels at 140°F (60°C)
Setting Speed	Quick, minutes
Promoters	Alcohol
Inhibitors	Salt

Pectin

Pectin is produced from many fruits—citrus, apples, apricots, and cherries. Apple pomace and citrus peels account for the majority of pectin used today. Marmalades and jellies are set with the use of pectin. They are classified into two groups: low methoxyl (LM) and high methoxyl (HM). Pectin requires additional ingredients, calcium or acid, to act as jellifiers. Be sure to check the pectin used in the recipe to ensure the desired results are achieved.

All LM pectins are thermoreversible, can gel in low sugar environments, and require calcium to set. NH, a subcategory under LM, is used for glazes and fillings. This pectin is a blend of LM pectin and calcium. HM Pectins are not reversible, need a high percentage of sugar, and need an acid to set the pectin. These pectins are used for jams, jellies, and pâte de fruit.

When adding pectin to a recipe, combine it with some of the granulated sugar to prevent encapsulation. **Encapsulation** occurs when a fine powdered ingredient is combined with a liquid. The liquid quickly forms a shell around the dry powder. Once this happens, it is extremely difficult to break the sphere of dry pectin. This creates lumps in the mixture and reduces the setting strength due to a reduction in the amount of pectin.

Pectin

	Low Methoxyl (LM)	High Methoxyl (HM)
Origin	Citrus peel and apple pomace	Citrus peel and apple pomace
Thermoreversible	Yes	No
Texture	Gel	Gel
Clarity	Transparent	Transparent
Dispersion	Cold or hot water	Cold or hot water
Melting	Yes	No
Setting Temperature	Varies	140°F (60°C)
Setting Speed	Slow	Slow
Promoters	Calcium	Acid, high sugar %
Inhibitors	High sugar %	N/A

Sodium Alginate

Sodium alginate, a product of brown algae, is used in the spherification process. Almost any liquid can be used to create spheres of "caviar." Sodium alginate is added to a flavored liquid and dropped into a solution of calcium chloride. As the spheres are dropped into the calcium chloride, the solutions interact and create a membrane around the droplet. For small drops, 30 seconds is adequate to form the membrane. Remove the spheres and rinse under cold running water to remove any excess calcium chloride. This process continues to transform the sphere into a solid. After removing from the calcium chloride and thoroughly rinsing, they must be served immediately to maintain a liquid center.

When working with acidic fruits with a pH lower than 4, sodium citrate can be added to neutralize the acid. The pH can be tested with paper test strips or a digital meter. Acidic fruit will cause the sodium alginate to gel prematurely, which makes it difficult to form droplets, as the mixture will be too thick.

Reverse spherification changes the way the solutions are combined. The flavored liquid is combined with the calcium chloride and placed into a sodium alginate bath. An immersion blender is used to combine the alginate and water. As the alginate hydrates, the liquid becomes viscous and traps small bubbles. To create a smooth, clear sphere, this solution needs to rest for several hours. Using reverse spherification, larger spheres with liquid center can be made. When the sphere is removed from the alginate bath, the reaction between the two solutions stops.

Sodium Alginate

Origin	Brown algae
Thermoreversible	No
Texture	Spherification—Firm, solid gel Reverse spherification—Firm gel with liquid center
Clarity	Clear
Dispersion	Cold water
Melting Temperature	No
Setting Temperature	Independent of temperature
Setting Speed	Depends on size; 30 seconds to 5 minutes
Promoters	Calcium for gelling
Inhibitors	pH less than 4

Tapioca Maltodextrin

Tapioca maltodextrin is a starch that has the ability to absorb oil. Flavorful powders can be created with any fat-based items. A ratio of 2 parts tapioca maltodextrin to 1 part fat is the recommended starting point. The liquid fat is streamed into a food processor containing tapioca maltodextrin. When combined at high speed, the fat is dispersed in small globules; mixing at a slower rate will cause larger lumps. When eaten, the powder dissolves when it comes in contact with water in the mouth, leaving the flavor of the fat behind. Tapioca maltodextrin can be used with olive oil, chocolates, Nutella, butter, caramel, and even bacon fat.

Tapioca Maltodextrin

Origin	Tapioca
Thermoreversible	no
Texture	Dry powder that absorbs fat
Clarity	Opaque
Dispersion	N/A
Melting Temperature	Melts on contact with water
Setting Temperature	N/A
Setting Speed	N/A
Promoters	N/A
Inhibitors	N/A

Xanthan

Xanthan is produced by the fermentation of glucose, sucrose, or lactose. It is most commonly used as a thickener, foam, and emulsifier. Gluten-free products that contain a large percentage of water can use Xanthan to help absorb the water. Since xanthan does not need to be heated, it is an excellent thickener for fruit sauces. It emulsifies the pulp of the fruit with the water and prevents the sauce from bleeding on the plate. Adding too much Xanthan can create a stringy texture that is not desirable.

Xanthan

Origin	Fermentation of Glucose, Sucrose, or Lactose
Thermoreversible	Yes
Texture	High viscosity
Clarity	Clear
Dispersion	Cold
Melting Temperature	N/A
Setting Temperature	N/A
Setting Speed	N/A
Promoters	N/A
Inhibitors	N/A

Gelatin Recipes

Strawberry Water (gelatin clarification)

Yield: 1 lb 1 oz (540 g)

Portions: 1

Portion size: 1 lb 1 oz (540 g)

Yield description: 1 at 1 lb 1 oz (540 g)

Ingredients	U.S.	Metric
Strawberry Juice	2 lb 3.3 oz	1000 g
Gelatin Powder	0.26 oz	7.5 g

Note: To make the strawberry juice, process fresh strawberries through a juicer. Any fruit juice can be clarified using this method.

Procedure

1. To bloom the gelatin, sprinkle the gelatin powder on top of the cold strawberry juice.

2. Allow gelatin to bloom for 15 minutes.

3. Warm to 85°F (30°C). Be careful to not overheat this mixture, as it will cause the color and flavor to change.

4. Place juice into a hotel pan and place in freezer overnight.

5. While still frozen, carefully cut frozen juice into 2 in. (5 cm) squares; this will yield more juice as the mixture thaws.

6. Line a chinois with rinsed cheesecloth and place the cut juice pieces inside the cheesecloth.

7. Place the chinois into a bain marie and cover with plastic wrap.

8. Allow mixture to thaw under refrigeration for 2 days.

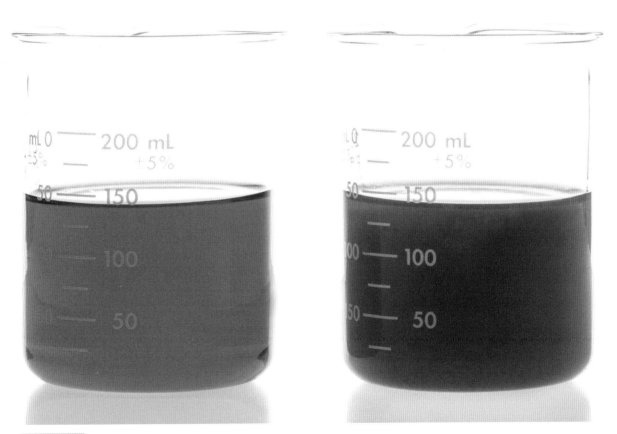

FIGURE 4.2 Gelatin clarification: clarified strawberry juice (left) and strawberry juice (right)

Vanilla Bean Vodka Foam

Yield: 14.1 oz (400 g)

Portions: 1

Portion size: 14.1 oz (400 g)

Yield description: 1 at 14.1 oz (400 g)

Ingredients	U.S.	Metric
Vodka	12 oz	340 g
Sugar	2.1 oz	60 g
Gelatin Sheets, bloomed	3 each	3 each
Vanilla Beans, split and scraped	2 each	2 each

Note: After charging the ISI siphon with the carbon dioxide, the container is under high pressure. Be sure to release all pressure before attempting to open the siphon.

Procedure

1. Combine all ingredients and warm to dissolve sugar.
2. Strain through a chinois.
3. Place into an ISI siphon and charge with 2 nitrous oxide charges, shaking between additions.
4. Place in refrigerator for 4 hours.
5. Dispense as needed.

Raspberry Cloud

Yield: 14.1 oz (400 g)

Portions: 1

Portion size: 14.1 oz (400 g)

Yield description: 1 at 14.1 oz (400 g)

Ingredients	U.S.	Metric
Raspberry Purée	11.8 oz	335 g
Sugar	2.3 oz	65 g
Gelatin Sheets, bloomed	4 each	4 each

Procedure

1. Heat 100 g of purée with sugar and gelatin to dissolve sugar.
2. Place remaining 235 g of cold purée in a mixer with a whip attachment.
3. Turn mixer to high speed and add warmed purée mixture.
4. As the gelatin begins to set, it will incorporate air.
5. Mixture can be used as a loose foam on top of a dessert or refrigerated for 4 hours and then shaped into a quenelle for service.

Agar Recipes

Dehydrated Curd

Yield: 2 lb 8.8 oz (1164 g)
Portions: 1
Portion size: 2 lb 8.8 oz (1164 g)
Yield description: 1 at 2 lb 8.8 oz (1164 g)

Ingredients	U.S.	Metric
Lemon Juice	9.5 oz	270 g
Whole Eggs	9.5 oz	270 g
Sugar	9.5 oz	270 g
Butter, cold and cubed	12.3 oz	350 g
Agar	0.14 oz	4 g

Procedure

1. Combine lemon juice, eggs, sugar, and agar in a heavy-bottom saucepan and bring to a boil.
2. Boil mixture for 1 minute while whisking constantly.
3. Pour mixture into a blender and add 2 cubes of butter at a time.
4. Strain through a chinois and refrigerate for 12 hours.
5. Mix the curd with a whisk to soften and smooth mixture.
6. Spread a thin layer on a silpat and dehydrate at 135°F (60°C) until completely dried.
7. Store in an airtight container.

Milk Chocolate Agar Mousse

Yield: 2 lb 5.2 oz (1058 g)
Portions: 9
Portion size: 4 oz (113 g)
Yield description: 9 portions at 4 oz (113 g)

Ingredients	U.S.	Metric
Milk Chocolate	10.5 oz	300 g
Milk	7 oz	200 g
Sugar	1.75 oz	50 g
Agar	0.28 oz	8 g
Heavy Cream, whipped to soft peaks	1 lb 1.7 oz	500 g

Procedure

1. Melt milk chocolate.
2. Mix agar with sugar and then whisk into milk.
3. Bring milk mixture to a boil and combine with melted chocolate to make a ganache.
4. Cool ganache to 105°F (40°C) and fold in whipped cream.
5. Pour into molds and refrigerate.

Bakeproof Raspberry Jam

Yield: 1 lb 13 oz (825 g)

Portions: 1

Portion size: 1 lb 13 oz (825 g)

Yield description: 1 at 1 lb 13 oz (825 g)

Ingredients	U.S.	Metric
IQF Raspberries	14.8 oz	420 g
Sugar	14.1 oz	400 g
Agar	0.18 oz	5 g

Procedure

1. Combine sugar and agar.
2. Add sugar mixture to IQF raspberries in a heavy-bottom saucepan.
3. Heat on low until raspberries start to break down.
4. Strain to remove seeds.
5. Return liquid to heat and bring to a boil.
6. Place in a container and cool; store in refrigerator.

Pliable Ganache

Yield: 2 lb 2 oz (977 g)

Portions: 16

Portion size: 2 oz (56 g)

Yield description: 16 portions at 2 oz (56 g)

Ingredients	U.S.	Metric
Heavy Cream	12.7 oz	360 g
Sheet Gelatin, bloomed	1.5 each	1.5 each
White Chocolate	15.9 oz	450 g
Distilled Water	1.97 oz	56 g
Sorbitol	3.5 oz	100 g
Agar	0.14 oz	4 g
Glucose	0.14 oz	4 g
Salt	0.11	3 g
Orange Blossom Water	20 drops	20 drops

Procedure

1. Combine heavy cream, distilled water, sorbitol, agar, glucose, and salt in a heavy-bottom saucepan.
2. Bring to a boil.
3. Pour liquid over chocolate and emulsify.
4. Add gelatin and orange blossom water.
5. Strain through a chinois directly into metal frame 12 × 12 in. (30 × 30 cm) placed on a silpat.
6. Allow to set at room temperature for 10 minutes; cover with plastic wrap touching the surface of the ganache.
7. Refrigerate for 4 hours.
8. Cut into desired shape.

Carrageenan Recipes

Olive Oil Gel

Yield: 14.2 oz (405 g)

Portions: 14

Portion size: 1 oz (28.3 g)

Yield Description: 14 portions at 1 oz (28.3 g)

Ingredients	U.S.	Metric
Extra Virgin Olive Oil	7.05 oz	200 g
Distilled Water	7.05 oz	200 g
Iota Carageenan	0.18 oz	5 g

Procedure

1. Bring distilled water to a boil.
2. Whisk in iota carageenan slowly.
3. Using an immersion blender, add oil to water mixture. This must be done on a low speed to maintain the emulsion.
4. Pour into silicone molds and refrigerate until set.

Peanut Butter Panna Cotta

Yield: 1 lb 14 oz (854 g)

Portions: 10

Portion size: 3 oz (85 g)

Yield Description: 10 portions at 3 oz (85 g)

Ingredients	U.S.	Metric
Heavy Cream	9.5 oz	270 g
Milk	9.5 oz	270 g
Peanut Butter	3.5 oz	100 g
Vanilla Bean Paste	0.35 oz	10 g
Sugar	7.1 oz	200 g
Salt	0.07 oz	2 g
Iota Carageenan	0.14 oz	4 g

Procedure

1. Combine milk, vanilla paste, sugar, and salt in a blender.
2. While blender is running, add iota carageenan.
3. In a saucepan, combine milk mixture with the cream and bring to a boil.
4. Use an immersion blender to incorporate peanut butter.
5. Mold immediately and place in the refrigerator for 2 hours.

Chocolate Gel

Yield: 2 lb 4 oz (976 g)

Portions: 17

Portion size: 2 oz (56 g)

Yield description: 17 portions at 2 oz (56 g)

Ingredients	U.S.	Metric
Heavy Cream	12.87 oz	365 g
64% Chocolate	8.82 oz	250 g
Sugar	2.1 oz	60 g
Distilled Water	10.58 oz	300 g
Iota Carageenan	0.028 oz	0.8 g
Kappa Carageenan	0.028 oz	0.8 g

Procedure

1. Bring cream to a simmer.
2. Pour over chocolate, mix to emulsify the ganache.
3. Using an immersion blender, add iota carageenan and kappa carageenan to distilled water.
4. Heat the water mixture to a boil.
5. Combine water mixture with ganache.
6. Mold into metal rings and refrigerate until set.

Gellan Recipes

Passion Fruit Cubes

Yield: 1 lb 2.9 oz (539 g)

Portions: 49

Portion size: 0.4 oz (11 g)

Yield description: 49 portions at 0.4 oz (11 g)

Ingredients	U.S.	Metric
Passion Fruit Purée	1 lb 1.6 oz	500 g
Lemon Juice	0.70 oz	20 g
Sugar	0.53 oz	15 g
Gellan, Hi-Acyl	0.07 oz	2 g
Gellan, Low-Acyl	0.07 oz	2 g

Procedure

1. Combine both hi-acyl and low-acyl gellans and sugar.
2. Heat purée to 115°F (45°C).
3. Whisk in sugar and gellan mixture; bring to a boil.
4. Add lemon juice.
5. Pour into mold and refrigerate for 2 hours.
6. Cut into desired shapes.

Reduced Sugar Strawberry Jam

Yield: 2 lb 4 oz (1000 g)

Portions: 1

Portion size: 2 lb 4 oz (1000 g)

Yield description: 1 at 2 lb 4 oz (1000 g)

Ingredients	U.S.	Metric
IQF Strawberries	1 lb 0.87 oz	450 g
Sugar	10.05 oz	285 g
Distilled Water	9.17 oz	260 g
Gellan, Hi-Acyl	0.088 oz	2.5 g
Citric Acid Solution	0.088 oz	2.5 g

Note: Citric acid solution is equal parts citric acid and water.

Procedure

1. Pulse frozen strawberries in a food processor to break into smaller pieces.
2. Combine sugar and hi-acyl gellan.
3. Whisk sugar and gellan mixture into distilled water.
4. Add the fruit and bring the mixture to a boil for 2 minutes while stirring.
5. Remove from heat, place in mason jars, and seal.

Yogurt Sphere

Yield: 14.1 oz (400 g)

Portions: 1

Portion size: 0.5 oz (14 g)

Yield description: 28 spheres at 0.5 oz (14 g)

Ingredients	U.S.	Metric
Yogurt Sphere		
Yogurt	14.1 oz	400 g
Milk	As needed	As needed
Yogurt Sphere Bath		
Distilled Water	1 lb 1.6 oz	500 g
Gellan, Low-Acyl	0.79 oz	2.25 g
Sodium Hexametaphosphate	0.0088 oz	0.25 g

Note: The amount of milk will vary, depending on the type of yogurt used. A thicker Greek yogurt will require more milk than a standard yogurt. The goal is to create a fluid that will flow when the sphere is broken.

Procedure

1. Adjust consistency of the yogurt using milk. If the yogurt is too stiff, the finished spheres will not flow. The thinner the consistency of the yogurt, the better the flow.

2. Dissolve sodium hexametaphosphate in distilled water, then add low-acyl gellan.

3. Using a teaspoon, place a spoon of the yogurt mixture into the yogurt sphere bath.

4. Allow the yogurt to remain in the yogurt sphere bath for 2 minutes.

5. Remove the yogurt and rinse in cold water.

6. Hold in a simple syrup bath (p. 109) for service.

Orange Veil

Yield: 8.8 oz (227 g)

Portions: 1

Portion size: 1 oz (28 g)

Yield description: 8 portions at 1 oz (28 g)

Ingredients	U.S.	Metric
Orange Juice	5.29 oz	150 g
Sugar	1.76 oz	50 g
Distilled Water	0.88 oz	25 g
Gellan, Low-Acyl	0.035 oz	1 g
Gellan, Hi-Acyl	0.035 oz	1 g
Vanilla Bean, split and scraped	2 each	2 each

Procedure

1. Combine dry ingredients.

2. Combine dry ingredients, distilled water, and orange juice in a saucepan using a whisk.

3. Warm ¼ sheet pan in the oven. The pan does not need to be hot. Warming the pan helps to ensure a thin veil when casting.

4. Bring the mixture to a boil and pour onto the warm ¼ sheet pan.

5. Refrigerate for 2 hours; cut into desired shapes.

Lecithin Recipe

Passion Fruit Foam

Yield: 1 lb 3.4 oz (601.5 g)

Portions: 1

Portion size: 0.25 oz (7 g)

Yield Description: 85 portions at 0.25 oz (7 g)

Ingredients	U.S.	Metric	%
Passion Fruit Purée	7.94 oz	225 g	37.4
Distilled Water	7.94 oz	275 g	45.7
Sugar	3.53 oz	100 g	16.6
Lecithin	0.053 oz	1.5 g	0.3

Procedure

1. Combine purée, distilled water, and sugar with an immersion blender.

2. Continue mixing with the immersion blender and sprinkle lecithin into the center of the container.

3. Once all lecithin is incorporated, begin lifting immersion blender.

4. After forming the foam, allow it to rest for 3 to 5 minutes (this will create a more stable foam).

5. Use a spoon to apply the foam to the dessert.

Methylcellulose Recipes

Crispy Raspberry Foam

Yield: 7 oz (200 g)
Portions: 14
Portion size: 0.5 oz (14 g)
Yield description: 14 portions at 0.5 oz (14 g)

Ingredients	U.S.	Metric
Raspberry Water, recipe on page 98	2.47 oz	70 g
Sugar	5.29 oz	150 g
Distilled Water	10.23 oz	290 g
Methylcellulose	0.56 oz	16 g

Procedure

1. Combine distilled water, raspberry water, and sugar in a bowl.
2. Whisk in methylcellulose.
3. Immediately transfer the mixture to a mixer fitted with a whip.
4. Whip on high speed to create the foam, which resembles a stiff meringue when done.
5. Spread on a silpat-lined sheet pan 0.75 in. (2 cm) thick.
6. Place in a 150°F (65°C) oven for 12 hours or until completely dry.
7. Store in an airtight container.
8. Break into desired size pieces.

Hot Ice Cream

Yield: 1 lb 0.9 oz (487 g)
Portions: 16
Portion size: 1 oz (28 g)
Yield description: 16 scoops at 1 oz (28 g)

Ingredients	U.S.	Metric
Hot Ice Cream Base		
Cream Cheese	7.05 oz	200 g
Butter	1.76 oz	50 g
Sugar	3.53 oz	100 g
Salt	0.07 oz	2 g
Vanilla Bean, split and scraped	1 each	1 each
Distilled Water	4.23 oz	120 g
Methylcellulose	0.52 oz	15 g
Hot Ice Cream Warming Bath		
Distilled Water	2 lb 3.3 oz	1000 g
Sugar	8.82 oz	250 g
Vanilla Bean, split and scraped	2 each	2 each

Procedure

1. In a blender, combine cream cheese, butter, sugar, salt, vanilla bean seeds, and salt.
2. Whisk methylcellulose into water and add to blender while running.
3. Refrigerate the base for 12 hours.
4. Combine distilled water, sugar, and vanilla bean.
5. Heat to dissolve.
6. Reserve for hot ice cream at a temperature of 193°F (90°C).
7. Scoop the Hot Ice Cream base with a #30 portioner.
8. Submerge the scoop into the Hot Ice Cream Warming Bath for 30 seconds. This will set the outside of the hot ice cream, to help hold its shape.
9. Release the hot ice cream into the warming bath and cook for an additional 2 minutes.
10. Remove with a perforated spoon and serve.

Pectin Recipes

Pectin Fruit Gelee

Yield: 12 oz (343 g)

Portions: 1

Portion size: 12 oz (343 g)

Yield description: 1 at 12 oz (343 g)

Ingredients	U.S.	Metric
Fruit Purée	8.8 oz	250 g
Glucose	1.94 oz	55 g
Pectin NH	0.12 oz	3.5 g
Sugar	1.23 oz	35 g

Procedure

1. Combine pectin and sugar.
2. Warm the purée and glucose.
3. While whisking the purée mixture and add in the sugar/pectin mixture.
4. Bring to a boil.
5. Pour into mold and freeze.

Nut Tuille

Yield: 1 lb 1.8 oz (506.5 g)

Portions: 1

Portion size: 0.5 oz (14 g)

Yield description: 32 tuilles at 0.5 oz (14 g)

Ingredients	U.S.	Metric
Sugar	5.29 oz	150 g
Butter	4.41 oz	125 g
Yellow Pectin	0.05 oz	1.5 g
Glucose	1.76 oz	50 g
Almonds, sliced	5.29 oz	150 g
Pecans, chopped	1.06 oz	30 g

Procedure

1. Combine sugar and yellow pectin.
2. Place the butter and glucose in a heavy-bottom saucepan and heat to melt.
3. Add the sugar/pectin mixture to the sauce pan and bring to a boil.
4. Add the nuts to the mixture and refrigerate.
5. Roll the mixture between two pieces of parchment paper to ⅛ in. (3 mm).
6. Remove the top piece of paper and bake at 375°F (190°C) until golden brown.
7. Cut into desired shape.
8. Store in an airtight container.

Apricot Glaze

Yield: 1 lb 8.4 oz (782 g)

Portions: 1

Portion size: 1 lb 8.4 oz (782 g)

Yield description: 1 at 1 lb 8.4 oz (782 g)

Ingredients	U.S.	Metric
Sugar	7.05 oz	200 g
Pectin NH	0.78 oz	22 g
Water	14.11 oz	400 g
Apricot Purée	0.35 oz	100 g
Lemon Juice	0.35 oz	10 g
Glucose	1.76 oz	50 g

Note: If glaze is not thick enough, continue boiling for an additional 1 to 2 minutes. If too thick, add water to achieve desired consistency.

Procedure

1. Combine sugar and pectin.
2. In a heavy-bottom saucepan, combine the water, apricot purée, and glucose.
3. While whisking the water mixture, add pectin/sugar mixture and boil for 10 minutes.
4. Add lemon juice and strain through a chinois.
5. Store in refrigerator.

Clear Glaze

Yield: 1 lb 11.7 oz (787 g)

Portions: 1

Portion size: 1 lb 11.7 oz (787 g)

Yield description: 1 at 1 lb 11.7 oz (787 g)

Ingredients	U.S.	Metric
Pectin NH	0.85 oz	24 g
Sugar	7.05 oz	200 g
Water	1 lb 1.6 oz	500 g
Glucose	1.76 oz	50 g
Vanilla Beans, used	2 each	2 each
Orange Zest	0.11 oz	3 g
Lemon Juice	0.35 oz	10 g

Note: If glaze is not thick enough, continue boiling for an additional 1 to 2 minutes. If too thick, add water to achieve desired consistency.

Procedure

1. Combine sugar and pectin.
2. In a heavy-bottom saucepan combine the water, glucose, zest, and vanilla bean.
3. While whisking the water mixture, add pectin/sugar mixture and boil for 10 minutes.
4. Add lemon juice and strain through a chinois.
5. Store in refrigerator.

Sodium Alginate Recipes

Coffee Caviar (spherification)

Yield: 1 lb 1.7 oz (502.5 g)

Portions: 1

Portion size: 1 lb 1.7 oz (502.5)

Yield description: 1 at 1 lb 1.7 oz (502.5)

Ingredients	U.S.	Metric
Coffee Caviar		
Coffee	1 lb 1.63 oz	500 g
Sodium Alginate	0.088 oz	2.5 g
Caviar Setting Bath		
Distilled Water	1 lb 1.63 oz	500 g
Calcium Chloride	0.088 oz	2.5 g

Procedure

1. Combine coffee with sodium alginate using an immersion blender; allow to set for 15 minutes.

2. Combine calcium chloride with distilled water, using a whisk.

3. Using a dropper, deposit small drops of the coffee caviar solution into the caviar setting bath.

4. After 30 seconds, remove the coffee caviar and rinse with cold water.

FIGURE 4.4a–c

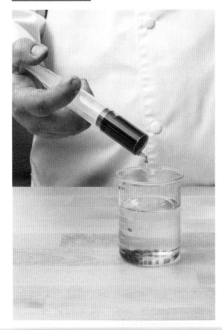

1. Drop the coffee solution into the setting bath (step 3)

2. Remove the caviar (step 4)

3. Finished caviar

Mango Sphere (reverse spherification)

Yield: 8.6 oz (245 g)

Portions: 1

Portion size: 0.5 oz (14 g)

Yield description: 16 spheres at 0.5 oz (14 g)

Ingredients	U.S.	Metric
Mango Sphere		
Mango Purée	8.47 oz	240 g
Calcium Gluconate	0.18 oz	5 g
Alginate Bath		
Distilled Water	2 lb 3.3 oz	1000 g
Sugar	1.76 oz	50 g
Sodium Alginate	0.18 oz	5 g
Simple Syrup Bath		
Distilled Water	1 lb 5.16 oz	600 g
Sugar	14.11 oz	400 g

Note: The purée used in the sphere can be thickened slightly with a small amount of xanthan gum. This will vary, depending on the selected purée or juice.

Procedure

1. Combine calcium gluconate with mango purée.
2. Deposit mango purée into desired shape flexipan and freeze.
3. Combine sodium alginate and sugar.
4. While slowly whisking distilled water, stir in algin mixture.
5. Allow this to set for 15 minutes and release any bubbles formed during mixing.
6. Combine distilled water and sugar to make the simple syrup bath.
7. Boil to dissolve sugar and cool on an ice bath.
8. Submerge frozen purée mixture into alginate bath for 30 seconds.
9. Carefully transfer the spherified mango from the alginate bath to a bowl with cold water to rinse.
10. After rinsing, the spheres can be held in a simple syrup bath.

1. Deposit purée into a mold (step 2)

2. Place frozen purée mixture into alginate bath (step 8)

3. Demonstrating the liquid center of the sphere (left); the finished sphere is on the right

Thin Film

Yield: 8.8 oz (254 g)

Portions: 4

Portion size: 2 oz (56 g)

Yield description: 4 at 2 oz (56 g)

Ingredients	U.S.	Metric
Thin Film		
Apple Juice	7.05 oz	200 g
Sodium Alginate	0.14 oz	4 g
Sugar	1.76 oz	50 g
Thin Film Spraying Solution		
Distilled Water	7.05 oz	200 g
Calcium Lactate	0.35 oz	10 g

Procedure

1. Combine sugar and align.

2. Using an immersion blender, combine the sugar/sodium alginate mixture and apple juice. Allow any bubbles to dissipate before use.

3. Combine calcium lactate and distilled water with whisk and place in a spray bottle.

4. Pour a thin layer of the apple juice mixture onto a plate.

5. Spray the thin film spraying solution mixture over the plate.

6. Allow 5 minutes for the thin film to set.

7. Microwave in 5-second intervals to evaporate the extra spray.

Tapioca Maltodextrin Recipes

Dry Caramel

Yield: 9.3 oz (265 g)
Portions: 1
Portion size: 9.3 oz (265 g)
Yield description: 1 at 9.3 oz (265 g)

Ingredients	U.S.	Metric
Caramel		
Sugar	2.10 oz	60 g
Glucose	1.96 oz	55 g
Heavy Cream	2.79 oz	79 g
Butter	0.56 oz	16 g
Dry Caramel Powder		
Caramel	7.41 oz	210 g
Tapioca Maltodextrin	2.30 oz	65 g

Procedure

1. Combine sugar, glucose, cream, and butter.
2. Over medium heat, cook to 257°F (125°C).
3. Pour onto a silpat and cool completely.
4. Break up caramel into small pieces.
5. Combine broken caramel and tapioca maltodextrin in food processor.
6. Mix until caramel mixture is absorbed by tapioca maltodextrin.
7. Store in an airtight container.

Nutella Powder

Yield: 7 oz (200 g)
Portions: 28
Portion size: 0.25 oz (7 g)
Yield description: 28 at 0.25 oz (7 g)

Ingredients	U.S.	Metric
Nutella	4.23 oz	120 g
Tapioca Maltodextrin	2.82 oz	80 g

Procedure

1. Combine Nutella and tapioca maltodextrin in a food processor.
2. Process until mixture resembles coarse cornmeal.
3. Store in an airtight container.

Brown Butter Nuggets

Yield: 11.6 oz (330 g)

Portions: 1

Portion size: As desired

Yield description: 1 at 11.6 oz (330 g)*

Ingredients	U.S.	Metric
Brown Butter	8.82 oz	250 g
Tapioca Maltodextrin	2.65 oz	75 g
Salt	0.18 oz	5 g

*Note: There is no true way to control the size of the balls; they are random and meant to be so. Maltodextrin is incredibly light, and even using an accurate microgram scale, the balls would be difficult to weigh.

Procedure

1. Strain brown butter of all solids, keep warm.
2. Place tapioca maltodextrin in a food processor.
3. Turn on the food processor and stream in brown butter.
4. When a paste forms stop adding the butter.
5. Using your hands, form the paste into small balls.
6. Place on a silpat-lined sheet pan and bake at 375°F (190°C) for 5 minutes.
7. After cooling, store in an airtight container.

Xanthan Recipes

Clear Strawberry Sauce

Yield: 10.9 oz (310.7 g)

Portions: 20

Portion size: 0.5 oz (14 g)

Yield description: 20 portions at 0.5 oz (14 g)

Ingredients	U.S.	Metric
Strawberry Water, recipe on p. 98	8.11 oz	230 g
Sugar	2.82 oz	80 g
Xanthan Gum	0.025 oz	0.7 g

Procedure

1. Combine xanthan and sugar.
2. Whisk into strawberry water.
3. Allow sauce to rest overnight to remove any bubbles.

Fruit Sauce

Yield: 11.6 oz (330.2 g)

Portions: 23

Portion size: 0.5 oz (14 g)

Yield description: 23 portions at 0.5 oz (14 g)

Ingredients	U.S.	Metric
Fruit Purée	10.58 oz	300 g
Trimoline	1.06 oz	30 g
Xanthan Gum	0.007 oz	0.2 g

Note: This sauce does not need to be cooked and maintains the fresh flavor of the fruit.

Procedure

1. Combine purée, xanthan, and trimoline with immersion blender.
2. Store in refrigerator.

Carbonated Coco

Yield: 9.9 oz (281 g)

Portions: 6

Portion size: 1.5 oz (42 g)

Yield Description: 6 portions at 1.5 oz (42 g)

Ingredients	U.S.	Metric
Coconut Water	7.05 oz	200 g
Coconut Rum	1.06 oz	30 g
Amaretto	0.71 oz	20 g
Sugar	1.06 oz	30 g
Xanthan Gum	0.035 oz	1 g

Note: After charging the ISI siphon with carbon dioxide, the container is under high pressure. Be sure to release all pressure before attempting to open the canister.

Procedure

1. Combine coconut water, coconut rum, amaretto, and sugar with an immersion blender.
2. While immersion blender is running, incorporate xanthan gum.
3. Place mixture into an ISI siphon.
4. Charge twice with carbon dioxide cartridges, shaking between each addition.
5. Dispense Coco-Cola into glasses and serve immediately.

Gluten-Free Flour Replacer

Yield: 4 lb 7.2 oz (2020 g)

Portions: 1

Portion size: 4 lb 7.2 oz (2020 g)

Yield Description: 1 at 4 lb 7.2 oz (2020 g)

Ingredients	U.S.	Metric
Potato Starch	1 lb 8.69 oz	700 g
Tapioca Starch	15.87 oz	450 g
White Rice Flour	15.87 oz	450 g
Brown Rice Flour	7.05 oz	200 g
Nonfat Milk Powder	7.05 oz	200 g
Xanthan Gum	0.71 oz	20 g

Note: This formula can be used in place of flour in many recipes. Some slight modifications to the recipe may be necessary, such as increasing leaveners.

Procedure

1. Combine all ingredients in a food processor and mix until combined.
2. Store covered at room temperature.

Summary

Many hydrocolloids are used in small percentages in the recipe. Great care must be taken to accurately scale all ingredients. Follow the procedures included with the recipes. When making adjustments to the recipes, be sure to test carefully, as changes in ingredients can impact the ability of the hydrocolloid to gel. An understanding of basic pastry techniques, ingredients, and procedure are necessary to produce successful results.

Key Terms

Hydrocolloids
Foam
Bromelain
Blooming

Thermoreversible
Hysteresis
Spherification
Phospholipid

Encapsulation
Reverse spherification

Questions for Review

1. How can pH affect spherification?

2. What does *thermoreversible* mean?

3. Discuss the difference between low-acyl and high-acyl gellan.

4. What is the enzyme in tropical fruits that destroys gelatin?

CHAPTER 5

Creams and Mousses

In 1755, French writer Menon described a drink containing chocolate, boiling water, and beaten egg as a favorite of King Louis XV. This is the earliest record of a mousse-like dessert being served. Technology and understanding of ingredients have changed a great deal in the last 400 years. Today, pastry chefs continue to build on these classical desserts and strive to impress their guests with their creations.

LEARNING OBJECTIVES

After reading this chapter, you should be able to:

1. **Identify** the temperatures at which egg proteins coagulate.
2. **Prepare** baked and stirred custards.
3. **Explain** the difference between a Bavarian, diplomat, mousse, and Chiboust.
4. **Describe** the three components of a mousse.
5. **Differentiate** between a pastry cream and crème anglaise.
6. **Demonstrate** how to temper gelatin for a warm and cold process.

Custard

Custards are one of the fundamental building blocks used in every kitchen. A simple crème anglaise can be used as a sauce on a plated dessert, as a part of a recipe to create a light and airy Bavarian, or baked with corn and leeks and served warm as part of an entrée. Custards provide the pastry chef a base recipe that can be flavored with spices, nuts, fruits, or chocolate; the possibilities are only limited by the imagination of the chef. Just as flavors are added, new creations based on these fundamental recipes are being invented.

The Custard Family Tree demonstrates how closely related all of the custards are. By changing one ingredient, the ratio of ingredients or the process in which they are mixed and cooked, a completely different product can be made. This chapter focuses on the ingredients, base recipes, and processes used in making them to further the understanding of the recipes. Custards are used in all aspects of the pastry kitchen. Mastering them and the versatility they offer will allow pastry chefs to expand their repertoire of recipes.

Custard is typically classified as a product thickened by the **coagulation** of egg proteins. Eggs are an excellent way to set the custard, and can be used to adjust the consistency of the finished product. Understanding the function of eggs in a recipe and how they interact with the other ingredients in the recipe will provide insight into how the recipe is executed. Additionally, having a working knowledge of the ingredients will ensure that the final product will be executed correctly.

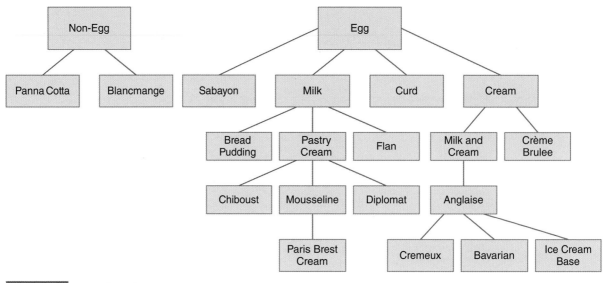

FIGURE 5.1 Custard Family Tree

Egg Tech

Eggs provide structure, color, and flavor to many types of custard. Eggs are a commodity that is readily available to the chef in a variety of forms, providing ease of use. In the pastry shop, the egg is used as a whole, as separate parts (white and yolk), or together in a variety of ratios. By making adjustments to the part(s) of the egg used in a formula, the final product can be changed.

An egg is composed of approximately 43% yolk and 57% egg white. The yolk is 50% water, 33% fat, and 16% protein; the remaining 1% is lecithin, iron, and color. Fat in the yolk provides flavor and color to the recipes. It is used when the desired set of the custard is creamy and soft. The white is 85% water; the remaining 15% is albumin and ovalbumin. The egg white is typically not used alone in custard recipes, but as part of the whole egg. Custards set with egg whites tend to be firmer.

Egg proteins coagulate at different temperature ranges. At the lower end of the temperature range the egg will begin to gel, and as the higher temperatures are reached the white and yolk will no longer flow. Specific temperatures can be found on the following Egg Coagulation Temperature table. Gentle cooking of custards will help to achieve the proper texture in the final product. Baked custards should be placed in a water bath in the oven at 300°F (149°C), while stirred custards should be cooked over low to medium direct heat or in a double boiler.

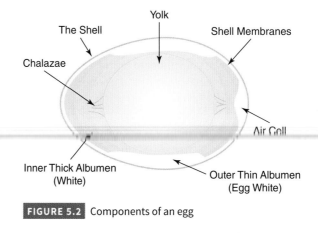

FIGURE 5.2 Components of an egg

FIGURE 5.3 Properly baked crème brûlée (left) and overbaked crème brûlée (right)

Reducing the intensity of the heat during the cooking process allows proteins to coagulate at a more even rate. Custards can be easily overcooked while being heated or through carry-over cooking.

Carryover cooking is not a typical topic discussed in the pastry shop. Custards can easily become overcooked if they remain in the pan they were cooked in for any additional time. To avoid overcooked custards, proper mise en place should be followed. Having all equipment in place and understanding the process will help to prevent this from happening.

When eggs cook for too long or are cooked to a temperature that is too high, syneresis occurs. **Syneresis** occurs when the liquid or moisture that is contained with protein molecules is expelled. As the custard begins to overcoagulate, the proteins begin to shrink as a result of overcooking and water is released. As the water is released, the final texture becomes coarse and grainy. The resulting curdled mixture develops a strong egg flavor as well as an unpleasant texture.

Egg Coagulation Temperatures

	Low	High
Whole Egg	140°F (60°C)	165°F (74°C)
Egg Yolk	149°F (65°C)	158°F (70°C)
Egg White	140°F (60°C)	149°F (65°C)

The temperatures in the Egg Coagulation Temperatures table are for eggs cooked alone. Several factors, at the control of the pastry chef, can change the coagulation temperature. As previously mentioned, the intensity of the heat and duration of cooking play a critical role in the procedure. The concentration of egg product in the recipe can change the coagulation temperature. The addition of ingredients to the eggs can help to lower or raise the coagulation temperatures Adding sugar, dairy products, or decreasing the amount of egg product results In an Increased temperature. Once dairy products are added, the coagulation temperature increases to 175°F (80°C). Conversely, increasing the amount of egg in the recipe, or by adding salt or acids result in coagulation occurring at a lower temperature.

When working with eggs, it is important to follow all local sanitation regulations. Keep in mind that salmonella is killed instantly when subjected to temperatures of 165°F (74°C) or higher. As a general rule, custards should be kept for no longer than 3 days under refrigeration.

Stirred Custards

Stirred custards provide a base for the pastry chef to work with; they can be used independently or as a part of a recipe. They can be broken down into two groups—those containing eggs and those without. One thing they all have in common is that they are cooked on the stove. The final texture of these products is a softer set than their baked counterparts. As the custard is stirred on the stove, the eggs coagulate. The stirring helps to disconnect the coagulated particles, and make sure the custard cooks evenly. It is recommended that these custards be cooked in heavy-bottom stainless steel pans to prevent scorching.

1. Egg-based custards rely on coagulated egg proteins to create the texture of the custard:
   - Pastry cream
   - Crème anglaise
   - Curd
2. Non–egg-based custards do not contain any egg product and set with the addition of gelatin, cornstarch, or agar.
   - Cornstarch-based (blancmange)
   - Gelatin-bound (panna cotta)

Egg-Based Custards

Eggs provide an excellent thickener for custards, adding to the smooth, creamy richness associated with these products. There are some guidelines that can be applied to all egg-based custards, regardless of the final product. Pans, whisks, and bowls need to be stainless steel. Using aluminum pans will cause the custard to become gray, due to the whisk scraping the pan and removing small amounts of aluminum.

Cooking custards properly will help to produce the proper final consistency; key steps make this easy to achieve. Before tempering, a small amount of the sugar is added to the eggs, which begins denaturing the egg proteins in preparation of the hot liquid that is to be added. **Tempering** is the process of gradually warming the eggs with a hot liquid, and then returning the warmed egg mixture to saucepan to continue cooking. Adding the eggs directly to the hot pan will cause them to curdle immediately. Once the tempering process is completed,

FIGURE 5.4 When combining eggs and sugar, make sure to properly stir the mixture. Otherwise, the sugar will begin to coagulate the egg proteins, creating a coarse texture in the custard and reducing the thickening power of the eggs.

the custard is returned to the heat. At this point, continue stirring the custard even after it is removed from the heat source. This will prevent overcooking the custard; there is still sufficient heat in the pan when it is removed from the heat to cause this. After cooking, all stirred custards need to be strained.

Pastry Cream

Pastry cream is used on a daily basis in the pastry shop. It is made from milk, egg, egg yolk, sugar, cornstarch, vanilla, and butter, one of the most delicious items and also an interesting one. A variety of ingredients can be used to flavor pastry cream, including vanilla, chocolate, liquor, nut pastes, and spices. Taking a look at the pastry cream recipe, two things are clear: The eggs cannot be cooked over 185°F (85°C), and the cornstarch must be boiled to 212°F (100°C) to cook out the starch. How can this be?

There is a dual purpose to boiling the pastry cream. In order to produce a smooth, creamy consistency with good mouthfeel and flavor, the starch must be boiled. Additionally, eggs contain an enzyme called amylase. Amylase will reduce the thickening power of the starch over time as it destroys the starch. By boiling the cream, the amylase is neutralized.

Pastry Cream Method

1. Combine milk, first sugar, and scraped vanilla bean in a heavy-bottom saucepan and bring to a boil.
2. In a stainless steel bowl, combine second sugar and cornstarch; mix to disperse cornstarch in sugar.
3. Add eggs and egg yolks to cornstarch mixture; whisk to combine.
4. Carefully whisk half of the boiling milk into the egg mixture.
5. Continue the tempering process by returning the warmed egg mixture to the saucepan.
6. Return the saucepan to the heat and bring pastry cream to a boil for 2 minutes while whisking constantly. At this point, the cream can be tasted to ensure all the starch has been cooked out.
7. Remove from the heat and incorporate the butter.
8. Press the pastry cream through a tamis.
9. Place the finished pastry cream into a shallow pan and cover with plastic wrap directly on the cream to prevent a skin from forming.
10. Place on an ice bath inside the refrigerator.

Crème Anglaise

Crème anglaise, also referred to as English cream, is used as a sauce, base for Bavarian Cream, crémeux, and ice cream. It can be flavored in many ways similar to pastry cream. One major difference must be remembered: Crème anglaise is not boiled when cooking. The final temperature of the cooked crème anglaise is 175°F (80°C). A properly cooked crème anglaise will have the correct viscosity due to fully coagulating the egg proteins.

An overcooked cream will present a curdled texture and strong egg flavor. Although this is not the desired final product, the cream can be returned to a smooth consistency with an immersion blender or food processor. In most cases, it is advised to cook the crème anglaise again, and carefully follow the procedure to avoid overcooking.

Keep in mind that using low to medium heat and constantly stirring will evenly cook the custard. A higher heat may bring the custard to the correct temperature quicker but as a result chance of curdling increases. Additionally, the use of thermal circulators and combi ovens provide another way to cook custards. These methods provide a more controlled cooking process through closely monitored temperature, ensuring that the cream is not overcooked.

Crème Anglaise Method

1. Combine milk, cream, and half the sugar in a saucepan and bring to a boil.
2. Whisk remaining sugar and egg yolks in a stainless steel bowl.
3. Temper half of the boiling mixture into the egg yolk mixture.
4. Continue the tempering process by returning the warmed egg mixture to the saucepan.
5. While stirring with a heat-resistant rubber spatula, return to a low to medium heat and cook to 175°F (80°C).
6. Immediately strain through a chinois and place in an ice bath to cool.

Curd

Curds are intensely flavored custards that contain a large percentage of butter, providing a smooth creamy texture. Typically, strong-flavored acidic fruits are used in curds. They can include lemon, lime, orange, passion fruit, or mango. The strong acidity of these fruits helps to balance out the large quantity of butter in the recipe.

Curd Method

1. Combine juice with half the amount of sugar in a saucepan and heat to a boil.
2. Whisk remaining sugar with eggs.
3. Temper all of the boiling juice mixture with eggs.
4. Finish cooking the custard over a double boiler to a temperature of 175°F (80°C).
5. Strain and cool the custard to a temperature of 96°F (36°C).
6. Add the softened butter.
7. Mix with an immersion blender on high for 5 minutes to completely emulsify the curd.
8. Cover with plastic wrap; it's important that the plastic wrap makes contact with the curd.

Non–Egg-Based Custards

While eggs contribute a great deal to custards, non–egg-based custards provide another recipe in the repertoire of the pastry chef. The textures of these custards are different from egg-based ones due to the fact they are set with gelatin, cornstarch, or carrageenan (see Chapter 4). In addition to differing textures, different flavors can be achieved. The richness of custard comes from the eggs; color and flavor change from the eggs. Custards without the addition of eggs tend to be white in color and have a stronger dairy flavor. They also tend to be lighter in mouthfeel as a result of decreased fat in the recipe. Non–egg-based custards also provide an alternative to customers with egg allergies or an increased sensitivity to eggs.

Blancmange

Blancmange is a custard set using cornstarch, and in some cases, carrageenan is used. The earliest record of blancmange was in the Middle Ages, and its origin is difficult to locate. It was served to royalty during festive occasions, colored with very intense colors. Served in today's restaurants, it would be left its original color and garnished with colorful berries. The flavor of the blancmange is lightly sweet with a mild dairy flavor.

Panna Cotta

The name translates from Italian to "cooked cream." In recent years, panna cotta has seen an increase in popularity on restaurant menus. It is a light dessert perfect for summer, as a layer inside an entremets or on a buffet. Milk, cream, sugar, vanilla bean, and gelatin are warmed just to dissolve the sugar and gelatin, strained, and chilled in the refrigerator.

Baked Custards

There are many items used in the pastry shop that can be included under baked custards: crème brûlèe, flan, bread pudding, and cheesecake. These items can prove challenging in determining doneness, it is through practice and understanding the process it can be simplified. Unlike stirred custards, baked custards eggs coagulate in the oven. As the egg coagulates, a firmer texture is created due to the fact they are not disturbed during coagulation.

Ingredients

Baked custards contain dairy products, egg, sugar, and flavorings. Some may contain other items such as large quantities of bread in bread pudding. Changing the ingredients will impact the consistency and flavor of the final product.

Crème brûlée is characterized by a soft, creamy texture. The use of heavy cream and egg yolks are used to achieve this. Adjusting the recipe to include whole eggs in place of some of the yolk will result in the crème brûlée having a firmer texture. The additional egg white will produce a firmer setting custard. In the same recipe if we remove a portion of the cream and replace it with milk, the final product will be firmer. The crème brûlée may almost start to represent the texture of flan, having the ability to be unmolded.

If the consistency of a custard is too firm or soft, refer to the Adjusting Custard Consistency table below. Slight changes in the quantity or type of ingredient used will change the final texture of the custard. Softening a custard can be done by decreasing the amount of egg, changing the type of egg product to egg yolk, or replacing milk with cream. The custard can be made firmer by increasing the quantity of egg, replacing the egg in the recipe with whole eggs or egg whites, or replacing heavy cream with milk. Slight changes in the ingredients will have a significant impact on the final product. When testing new formulations, only change one ingredient at a time. This will make it easier to identify what ingredient change provided the correct final result.

Adjusting Custard Consistency

Softer	Firmer
Decrease egg product	Increase egg product
Egg Yolks	Whole eggs
Heavy Cream	Egg whites
	Milk

Baking Procedure

Baked custards are delicate items that need the same care and attention that is given to stirred custards. A gentle cooking process is used to be certain that the custard is cooked evenly throughout. Baked custards should be baked at a temperature no higher than 300°F (149°C) in a water bath. A larger-size container may require a lower baking temperature. The water bath helps to insulate the custard; this slows down the heat transfer and prevents the custard from overcooking on the outer edges.

Tools available to the chef continue to improve, providing the pastry chef more control to save time and produce a consistent product. A combi oven is an excellent tool to assist in the baking of custards. These ovens are convection ovens that can cook in a dry, moist, or combination method. Custards baked in a combi oven can be baked faster and more evenly. A lower baking temperature and a small amount of steam is used to help transfer the heat in the oven into the custard. If using a combi oven to prepare baked custards, set the oven in combi mode and reduce fan speed. Bake the custard in a water bath as you would in a conventional oven at 250°F (121°C) and 20% steam with a reduced fan speed.

Testing for Doneness

Time can give us an estimate of when the custards will be done, but many other factors play into time. The best way to check a custard is by sight or feel. When using sight, consider how the heat transfers into the custard. The heat coagulates the eggs from the edge of the pan or ramekin and works in toward the center.

A gentle tap on the side of the container will show how set the custard is. The custard should wiggle slightly and stop, this is referred to as the wiggle test. A good way to think about this is a calm swimming pool. If the custard is not set, it will ripple in waves, similar to the way the water would move if a rock were thrown into it. When performing the wiggle test, the custard may appear to be solid on the edge and only ripple in the center. This indicates that the custard is baking and only the center needs to cook.

In some instances, such as a cheesecake or bread pudding, the test can be performed by touch or sight. By gently touching the cheesecake it should feel soft, but firm. If the cake has a liquid-like movement when pressed, the center is not baked. Use caution when testing using touch, as these products are hot. Sight is the preferred method for testing, while touch can be helpful along with the visual. Remember, during the baking process our ingredients undergo many changes. Sugars become liquids and fats become more fluid, as the custard cools the fats and sugars solidify and become firm again. A properly baked custard will still feel soft to the touch.

Overbaked custards provide some signs that something went wrong. When checking the custards, they should appear smooth. Bubbling along the edge and not set in the middle is an indication that the oven temperature was too high or the baking time was too long. The egg proteins are overcoagulated; the results will be a curdled watery custard. Cheesecakes differ slightly; normally, boiling is not noticed, as this custard is much thicker. The cheesecake will begin to rise as it bakes due to the creation of steam inside the cake. When the cake cools and the steam dissipates, the cake collapses. There is no structure inside the cake to hold it up; this will give the cake a grainy, dry texture and large cracks across the top.

Types of Baked Custards

Crème Brûlée

Crème brûlée translates from French to "burnt cream." Simple ingredients are combined with careful preparation to create this famous creamy, rich custard. After the custard is baked and cooled, a thin coating of sugar is placed on top and burned under a broiled or with a torch. A warm, crispy, caramelized sugar layer on top of a cold, creamy custard, providing textural and temperature contrasts in one dish.

Preparing the crème brûlée custard is almost identical to the crème anglaise method. In the crème brûlée method, the warmed cream is added to the eggs to start the cooking process and help the custard to cook more evenly when it is placed in the oven.

Crème Brûlée Method

1. Combine half the sugar with the heavy cream and scraped vanilla bean in a heavy-bottom saucepan and heat to a boil.
2. Add remaining sugar to the egg yolks and whisk to combine.
3. Temper all of the boiling cream mixture into the egg yolks.
4. Strain through a chinois and fill ramekins.
5. Bake in a water bath 300°F (149°C).
6. Store in refrigerator.

Flan

Flan, also referred to as crème caramel, is a firmer custard baked with caramelized sugar in the ramekin. The caramelized sugar adds color to the top of the custard when it is unmolded, as well as producing a sauce as the caramel dissolves in the ramekin. The traditional flavor of flan is vanilla. However, chocolate, spices, and even fruit purées can be added to the custard to customize the flavor. Flan or a closely related variety can be found in most every country throughout the world.

The use of evaporated milk and sweetened condensed milk in the formula produces a style of flan that is traditional in Latin American countries. Some formulas contain milk and sugar and produce an even firmer custard. In the case of a milk-based flan formula, the sugar and caramel can be removed to produce a savory custard or **royale**, which can be used to garnish consommé or an entrée.

Wet Caramel Method

1. Place water in saucepan; add sugar and corn syrup. Make sure the sugar is in the water but do not stir. Stirring causes sugar crystals to form on the side of the pan. If crystals do form, use a brush and cold water to clean the sides of the pan.
2. Heat over high heat until sugar caramelizes.
3. Immediately shock the pan in an ice bath.
4. Pour caramel into ramekins and allow to cool completely.

Flan Method

1. Combine evaporated milk, sweetened condensed milk, eggs, and flavorings in a bowl and mix until combined.
2. Strain through a chinois.
3. Fill ramekins in a hotel pan.
4. Bake in a water bath 300°F (149°C).
5. Store in refrigerator overnight.
6. Unmold for service.

Bread Pudding

Bread pudding is custard that many can identify with. Originally, it provided an excellent way to use old bread that would be otherwise thrown away. In an effort to find new ways to reinvent this classic dessert, pastry chefs have turned to using croissants, Danish, and even donuts to add a twist to the familiar flavor. Other ingredients such as chocolate chips, fruit, or toasted nuts can be used for additional flavors and textures. Reducing the sugar and adding cheese, dried fruits, vegetables, and even foie gras can be used to create savory applications for bread pudding.

Bread Pudding Method

1. Combine milk, sugar, eggs, and flavorings.
2. Strain through a chinois.
3. Combine with bread.
4. Allow this mixture to rest for 4 hours under refrigeration, allowing the bread to absorb the custard.
5. Fill containers and wrap in plastic wrap covered in foil; steam to a temperature of 175°F (80°C).
6. Remove plastic wrap and bake at 400°F (205°C) for 7 to 10 minutes to crisp top of pudding slightly.

Cheesecake

Cheesecake is found in bakeries and menus at restaurants around the world. In the United States, cheesecake is made with cream cheese, in France it is be made with fromage blanc, and ricotta is used in Italy. Each of these cheeses has a distinct flavor and texture. The flavor of cheesecake is easily recognizable; it can be served as simple as a slice of vanilla cheesecake or can be used as a layer in a dessert.

Technique can be used to make a good cheesecake great. Room temperature cream cheese mixes best. Avoiding lumps during mixing will also ensure a smooth consistency. Lumps in the cheesecake will be noticeable once the cake is baked a sliced, the lumps will not be mixed as evenly with the eggs. This will give them a lighter color compared to the rest of the custard. Be sure to mix the custard on low at all times to avoid incorporating air into the mix.

A dense, creamy cheesecake has an excellent mouthfeel. Additional air in the mix creates steam during the baking process and causes the cheesecake to rise. As the cake cools, the steam dissipates and the custard will shrink and possibly crack. This lighter airy texture also makes it more difficult to determine when the cheesecake is finished baking.

Cheesecake Method

1. Using a paddle attachment, mix cream cheese on low.
2. Add half the amount of sugar to the cream cheese.
3. Mix for 2 minutes and scrape the bowl and attachment.
4. Add remaining sugar mix for 2 more minutes and scrape.
5. Slowly add eggs, stopping to scrape the bowl three times while adding all the eggs.
6. Fill pans and bake in a water bath 300°F (149°C) until done.

Note: If batter is lumpy, a food processor or immersion blender can be used.

Mousse and Creams

The light and airy texture of a mousse is in direct contrast to the dense, creamy custards previously discussed. Building on a base recipe with the addition of an ingredient such as whipped cream, or another recipe such as an Italian meringue, simple pastry cream can be transformed into a diplomat cream or chiboust.

Bases

Bases are used as a starting point for assembling a mousse or cream. Crème anglaise, pastry cream, ganache, curd, and fruit purée can all be used as a base. These bases can be used alone or in a combination together. Ganache is an example of this. A **ganache** is a fat-in-water **emulsion** created when a liquid is combined with chocolate. In the most common form, ganache is cream and chocolate; for some mousse bases, an anglaise-based or fruit purée ganache can be used. More information can be found on ganache in Chapter 13, "Chocolate Work."

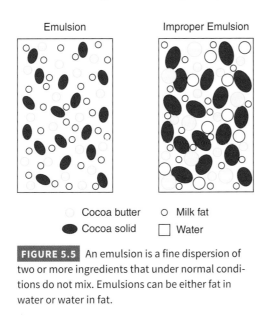

Emulsion   Improper Emulsion

○ Cocoa butter   ○ Milk fat
● Cocoa solid   □ Water

FIGURE 5.5 An emulsion is a fine dispersion of two or more ingredients that under normal conditions do not mix. Emulsions can be either fat in water or water in fat.

Aerators

The final texture of a mousse should be light and airy. This can be achieved through the use of egg foams and whipped cream. Some applications use both, while others use one. The aerators can impact the flavor, consistency, and stability of the mousse.

Whipped Cream

The most basic form of chocolate mousse can be made with sweetened whipped cream and chocolate. Whipped cream is the most common aerator and can be found in most mousses and creams. When whipping cream, air is trapped between fat particles. The optimal temperature for whipping cream is 40°F (5°C). Creams with lower fat percentage whip best; 30% fat is ideal. Higher-fat creams can whip to a stiffer consistency, but are more prone to overwhipping. The additional fat will also reduce the intensity of flavors, as the fat coats the mouth.

Properly whipped cream is doubled in volume with soft peaks. As the cream is whipped, the fat particles grow into larger clusters. Proceeding to whip the cream past stiff peaks will cause more of the fat particles to bind together; extremely overwhipped cream will result in a complete separation of fat from liquid.

FIGURE 5.6 Underwhipped cream (left), properly whipped cream (center), and overwhipped cream (right)

Continuing to whip the cream will produce a stiffer cream with no additional gain in volume. Cream that has very stiff peaks will be difficult to fold into the mousse, and it runs the risk of overmixing during the making of the mousse. Properly whipped cream will give the mousse a stable volume and correct final texture. If cream is whipped and left to sit before use, the fat and liquid will begin to separate. The heavier liquid will settle on the bottom, with the lighter fat on top. Be sure to whisk for a short time to make sure the cream is whipped properly before using.

Egg Foams

Egg foams are used in a similar way as cream to lighten the mousse. The part of the egg used and how we treat the eggs will impact the final texture. Eggs can add flavor, richness, volume, and texture to a mousse. Common egg foams found in mousse and creams are French meringue, Italian meringue, and pâte à bombe. A meringue is a mixture of egg white and sugar. Ovalbumin and albumin are proteins found in egg whites that are whipped and can be stabilized to maintain the volume they have gained during whipping. **Ovalbumin** is the protein in egg whites that coagulates when heated, making the meringue resistant to collapsing and creating a crispy texture. **Albumin** is the protein found in egg whites that creates a stable foam when whipped.

Mousse prepared using a meringue will have a lighter consistency compared to using the pâte à bombe. The albumin in the egg white allows the meringue to increase up to eight times the original volume. However, an uncooked meringue is extremely fragile. Cooking the meringue, creating a Swiss or Italian meringue, will produce a foam that is more stable and slightly denser due to the increased amount of sugar. Pâte à bombe will roughly double in size. **Pâte à bombe** is a mixture of whipped egg yolks and cooked sugar. The sugar is cooked to 248°F (120°C) and added to the whipped yolks, transforming the mixture into a creamy, airy mass.

These three foams not only affect texture and flavor but also how the mousse is going to be used and can also play a factor in which egg foam or recipe should be used. French meringue has the ability to add lightness to a mousse, but it is not a stable foam, nor has it been cooked. Salmonella and other microorganisms may be present in the uncooked egg whites. It is recommended to use pasteurized egg whites when making a French meringue that will not undergo any additional cooking to reduce this risk. Italian meringue and pâte à bombe are both fully cooked and provide the most stable forms of egg foams.

Italian meringue is mostly used in Chiboust and fruit mousses. The meringue provides lightness to the mousse, and gives a creamy mouthfeel. Fruit purées have a light flavor that is enhanced by the meringue. Pâte à bombe is occasionally used in fruit mousse. The egg yolks contribute a flavor and richness that does not work well with some lighter flavored fruits. Fruit purées also have a delicate color that the pâte à bombe may cover up or wash out. Some stronger flavored fruit mousses may benefit from the use of a pâte à bombe.

Pâte à bombe is typically used in chocolate mousse, the richness and flavor pair well with the chocolate. Color is not an issue due to the deep color of the chocolate. In some instances, a French meringue can be used in a chocolate mousse to lighten the mousse slightly. Due to the French meringue's lack of stability, it is best suited in applications where the mousse would be served in a glass or other dish.

Stabilizers

Mousses and creams are fragile recipes that need some sort of a stabilizer to maintain their structure. Whether they are served in a container or as cake on a buffet, the fat and waters inside must be stabilized. This can be done with the use of cocoa butter, gelatin, or agar. Additional information on gelatin and agar can be found in Chapter 4.

Tempering Gelatin

1. Bloom gelatin.
   - Sheet gelatin is bloomed in ice water for 15 minutes.
   - Powder gelatin is bloomed in liquid specified in recipe, if no liquid is specified, then use 4 times the weight of the gelatin in water for 5 minutes.
2. Dissolve gelatin.
   - Warm process such as Bavarian cream—add gelatin to warm anglaise.
   - Cold process such as fruit mousse—warm over a double boiler.
3. Add 10% of mousse mixture to dissolved gelatin.
4. Warm to 100–105°F (38–40°C).
5. Return warmed gelatin mixture to mousse.

Whether the mousse is stabilized with cocoa butter or gelatin there are visible signs that show the process was done correctly. The mousse should appear free of lumps and smooth. Chocolate mousse should be smooth, shiny, and elastic after the chocolate is added. This is evidence that the cocoa butter was the proper temperature and has not crystallized during the mixing process. When working with stabilizers, special attention must be paid to the temperatures of these products, the quantity in the recipe and the process of tempering them into the recipe.

FIGURE 5.7   Proper incorporated gelatin (left); improper incorporation (right)

Pâte à Bombe Method

1. Whip egg yolks on high speed for 5 minutes.

2. Combine water and sugar in a saucepan and cook to 248°F (120°C).

3. Carefully pour sugar syrup into whipping yolks and allow to cool.

4. Whip cream to soft peaks.

5. Fold whipped cream and pâte à bombe together.

6. Melt chocolate to 110°F (43°C).

7. Fold chocolate into whipped cream mixture.

FIGURE 5.8a–d

1. Adding the sugar to the water

2. Sugar boiling in the pan (note that the sides of the pan are clean)

3. Pan that has been stirred (crystals form on the side of the pan)

4. Washing the side of the pan with a clean brush and cold water

FIGURE 5.9 Final dark chocolate mousse with chocolate incorporated: too cool (left), just right (center), too warm (right)

Anglaise-Based Method

1. Prepare a crème anglaise and strain into half-melted chocolate.
2. Add purée or liquor to ganache and cool to 105°F (41°C).
3. Whip cream to soft peaks.
4. Fold cream into ganache.

Fruit Mousse Method

1. Bloom gelatin.
2. Prepare an Italian meringue.
3. Whip cream to soft peaks.
4. Fold cream, purée, and meringue together.
5. Temper gelatin into mousse.

Bavarian Method

1. Bloom gelatin.
2. Prepare a crème anglaise; add gelatin to dissolve.
3. Whip cream to soft peaks.
4. Cool crème anglaise to 75° to 85°F (24° to 29°C).
5. Fold in whipped cream.

Chiboust Method

1. Bloom gelatin.
2. Prepare a pastry cream.
3. Add gelatin to warm pastry cream base; cover and reserve.
4. Prepare an Italian meringue.
5. When meringue is cooled, fold into pastry cream base.

Diplomat Method

1. Prepare a pastry cream and cool completely.
2. Bloom gelatin.
3. Whip cream to soft peaks.
4. Soften pastry cream and fold in whipped cream.
5. Temper gelatin using the cold process.

Troubleshooting for Custards, Mousses, and Creams

Issue	Cause/Solution
Stirred custard is slightly curdled.	1. Heat of the stove was too high; reduce heat on stove and cook slower. 2. Thermometer is not calibrated; recalibrate thermometer.
Pastry cream appears curdled and greasy.	Cooked over too high of a heat or mixture boiled too long after eggs were added; reduce heat and cook less.
Baked custard is curdled on the edges.	1. Custard is overcooked; reduce oven temperature. 2. Water bath was not high enough or evaporated during baking; make sure that the water bath is high enough.
Only have a convection oven to work with and the custard is forming a skin.	The convection fan has dried out the top of the custard. Bake the custard in a hotel pan covered in foil; this will prevent the skin from forming.
Bavarian looks curdled and broken after folding in cream.	The mixture was overmixed; the gelatin structure that formed was broken by mixing.
Chocolate mousse has a gritty mouthfeel.	1. Chocolate was not at the correct temperature before folding in the cream. Melted chocolate needs to be warmed to temperature specified in the recipe. 2. Chocolate was not folded into the cream mixture fast enough. Incorporate the cream into the chocolate faster or increase chocolate temperature by a few degrees.
Gelatin stabilized mousse has lumps.	1. The gelatin powder was not completely hydrated; bloom gelatin properly. 2. The gelatin was not completely melted; dissolve gelatin properly. 3. The temperature of gelatin and 10% mousse base was not heated high enough; increase temperature by 2 degrees above the temperature in the recipe.

Recipes

Chocolate Mousse (Pâte à Bombe)

Yield: 3 lb 4 oz (1479 g)
Portions: 13
Portion size: 4 oz (113 g)
Yield description: 13 portions at 4 oz (113 g)

Ingredients	U.S.	Metric
Egg Yolks	5 oz	143 g
Sugar	5 oz	143 g
Water	1.3 oz	38 g
Dark Chocolate 58%, melted	1 lb 0.9 oz	480 g
Heavy Cream, whipped to soft peaks	1 lb 9.1 oz	713 g

Procedure

1. Pâte à bombe method on page 132.

Variation

Milk or White Chocolate Mousse
Milk and white chocolate can be substituted in place of the dark chocolate.

Ingredients	U.S.	Metric
Milk Chocolate or White Chocolate 33%, melted	1 lb 9.2 oz	715 g

Chocolate Mousse (Anglaise Based)

Yield: 4 lb (1840 g)
Portions: 16
Portion size: 4 oz (113 g)
Yield description: 16 portions at 4 oz (113 g)

Ingredients	U.S.	Metric
Milk	6.7 oz	190 g
Heavy Cream	6.7 oz	190 g
Sugar	1.4 oz	40 g
Egg Yolks	2.8 oz	80 g
Bittersweet Chocolate	1 lb 2 oz	510 g
Rum	1.8 oz	50 g
Heavy Cream, whipped to soft peaks	1 lb 11.5 oz	780 g

Note: The rum can be replaced with fruit purée or other liquor.

Procedure

1. Anglaise-based method, on page 133.

Fruit Mousse

Yield: 3 lb 2 oz (1418 g)

Portions: 12

Portion size: 4 oz (113 g)

Yield description: 12 portions at 4 oz (113 g)

Ingredients	U.S.	Metric
Fruit Purée (see note)	1 lb	454 g
Egg Whites	6 oz	170 g
Sugar	12 oz	340 g
Water	3 oz	85 g
Gelatin Sheets, bloomed	8 each	8 each
Heavy Cream, whipped to medium peaks	1 lb	454 g

Note: Use any fruit purées, excluding orange, blood orange, lemon, lime, or passion fruit.

Procedure

1. Fruit mousse method on page 133.

White Chocolate Coconut Mousse

Yield: 2 lb 15 oz (1274 g)

Portions: 11–19

Portion size: 4 oz (113 g)

Yield description: 11 portions at 4 oz (113 g)

Ingredients	U.S.	Metric
Coconut Purée	10.6 oz	300 g
White Chocolate	8.5 oz	240 g
Powder Gelatin	0.5 oz	15 g
Water #1, cold	2.1 oz	60 g
Egg Yolk	3.6 oz	102 g
Sugar	3.6 oz	102 g
Water #2	1 oz	27 g
Heavy Cream, whipped to soft peaks	1 lb 2.1 oz	515 g

Procedure

1. Bloom powder gelatin in cold water #1.
2. Make a pâte à bombe with egg yolks, sugar, and water #2.
3. Heat coconut purée and combine with white chocolate to make a ganache.
4. Add gelatin mixture to warm ganache and emulsify; reserve ganache at 90°F (32°C).
5. Fold cooled pâte à bombe and whipped heavy cream together.
6. Fold ganache mixture into whipped cream mixture.

Citrus Mousse

Yield: 4 lb 4.3 oz (1944 g)
Portions: 17
Portion size: 4 oz (113 g)
Yield description: 17 portions at 4 oz (113 g)

Ingredients	U.S.	Metric
Curd (p. 139)	1 lb 3.8 oz	560 g
Gelatin Sheets, bloomed	4 each	4 each
Egg Whites	4.5 oz	128 g
Sugar	9 oz	256 g
Water	2.3 oz	64 g
Heavy Cream, whipped to medium peaks	2 lb 3 oz	1000 g

Note: Orange, blood orange, passion fruit, lemon or lime curd can be used in this recipe.

Procedure

1. Fruit mousse method on page 133.

Vanilla Mousse

Yield: 4 lb 3.5 oz (1900 g)
Portions: 16
Portion size: 4 oz (113 g)
Yield Description: 16 portions at 4 oz (113 g)

Ingredients	U.S.	Metric
Egg Yolks	14.1 oz	400 g
Sugar	12.3 oz	350 g
Water	3.5 oz	100 g
Vanilla Beans, split and scraped	2 each	2 each
Heavy Cream, whipped to medium peaks	2 lb 8.6 oz	1150 g
Gelatin Sheets, bloomed	6 each	6 each

Note: Cook pâte à bombe syrup with vanilla beans; remove before adding sugar to the whipping yolks.

Procedure

1. Make a pâte à bombe with sugar, water, vanilla beans, and egg yolk.
2. Fold cooled pâte à bombe and whipped cream together.
3. Temper in gelatin.

Passion Fruit Chiboust

Yield: 2 lb 13.8 oz (1300 g)

Portions: 11

Portion size: 4 oz (113 g)

Yield description: 11 portions at 4 oz (113 g)

Ingredients	U.S.	Metric
Passion Fruit Purée	7 oz	200 g
Heavy Cream	8.8 oz	250 g
Egg Yolks	7 oz	200 g
Sugar	3.5 oz	100 g
Cornstarch	1.8 oz	50 g
Gelatin Sheets, bloomed	4 each	4 each
Egg Whites	7.1 oz	200 g
Sugar	10.6 oz	300 g
Water	2.8 oz	80 g

Note: The Italian meringue in this recipe has a lower percentage of sugar, which can lead to overwhipping the meringue. To prevent this after the sugar is added turn the mixer to the lowest setting to cool the meringue.

Procedure

1. Chiboust method on page 133.

Variation

Vanilla Chiboust

Replace passion fruit purée with milk and add vanilla bean.

Ingredients	U.S.	Metric
Milk	7 oz	200 g
Vanilla Bean, split and scraped	1 each	1 each

Diplomat Cream

Yield: 2 lb 2.5 oz (979 g)

Portions: 8

Portion size: 4 oz (113 g)

Yield description: 8 portions at 4 oz (113 g)

Ingredients	U.S.	Metric
Pastry Cream (p. 140)	1 lb	454 g
Heavy Cream, whipped to medium peaks	1 lb	454 g
Gelatin Powder	0.5 oz	14 g
Water, cold	2 oz	57 g

Procedure

1. Diplomat method on page 133.

Praline Mousseline

Yield: 3 lb 4 oz (1474 g)

Portions: 26

Portion size: 2 oz (56 g)

Yield description: 26 portions at 2 oz (56 g)

Ingredients	U.S.	Metric
Pastry Cream (p. 140)	1 lb	454 g
Praline Paste	12 oz	340 g
Butter, soft	1 lb 8 oz	680 g

Note: When the cold pastry cream is added to butter, it will cause the mixture to break. Continue mixing until the ingredients come back together.

Procedure

1. Whip butter and praline paste with a paddle attachment.
2. Slowly add pastry cream.
3. Mix until mixture is light and fluffy.

Vanilla Bavarian

Yield: 3 lb (1360 g)

Portions: 12

Portion size: 4 oz (113 g)

Yield Description: 12 portions at 4 oz (113 g)

Ingredients	U.S.	Metric
Milk	9.2 oz	260 g
Heavy Cream	9.2 oz	260 g
Vanilla Bean, split and scraped	2 each	2 each
Sugar	7.1 oz	200 g
Egg Yolks	3.5 oz	100 g
Gelatin Sheets, bloomed	7 each	7 each
Heavy Cream, whipped to medium peaks	1 lb 3 oz	540 g

Note: To make a fruit-flavored Bavarian, replace the milk with purée. Add the purée after the crème anglaise has been cooked to avoid altering the flavor of the purée.

Procedure

1. Bavarian method on page 133.
2. Pour into molds and freeze.

Citrus Curd

Yield: 1 lb 9 oz (734 g)

Portions: 12

Portion size: 2 oz (56 g)

Yield description: 12 portions at 2 oz (56 g)

Ingredients	U.S.	Metric
Eggs	5.8 oz	165 g
Sugar	6.7 oz	190 g
Citrus juice or purée	4.7 oz	132 g
Butter, soft	8.7 oz	247 g

Note: Mango, passion fruit, lemon, lime, or orange can be used to flavor the curd.

Procedure

1. Curd method on page 124.

Buttermilk Panna Cotta

Yield: 2 lb 7.5 oz (1119 g)

Portions: 13

Portion size: 3 oz (85 g)

Yield description: 13 portions at 3 oz (85 g)

Ingredients	U.S.	Metric
Heavy Cream	1 lb	454 g
Granulated Sugar	6 oz	170 g
Vanilla Bean, split and scraped	1 each	1 each
Gelatin Powder	0.5 oz	14 g
Water, cold	2 oz	56 g
Buttermilk	15 oz	425 g

Procedure

1. Bloom gelatin in water.
2. Combine heavy cream, sugar, and vanilla bean in a saucepan and heat to dissolve sugar.
3. Add gelatin mixture, and cool to 98°F (36°C).
4. Add buttermilk and strain through a chinois.
5. Pour into molds or glasses and refrigerate for 4 hours.

Flan

Yield: 3 lb 4 oz (1487 g)
Portions: 13
Portion size: 4 oz (113 g)
Yield description: 12 portions at 4 oz (113 g)

Ingredients	U.S.	Metric
Flan Custard		
Evaporated Milk	1 lb 10 oz	737 g
Sweetened Condensed Milk	14 oz	396 g
Eggs	12 oz	340 g
Vanilla Paste	0.5 oz	14 g
Flan Caramel		
Sugar	1 lb	454 g
Corn Syrup	2 oz	56 g
Water	4 oz	113 g

Procedure

1. Prepare Flan Caramel using the wet caramel method, p. 127.
2. Pour the caramel into 13 ramekins.
3. Prepare the Flan Custard using the flan method on p. 127.

Crème Brûlée

Yield: 3 lb 4 oz (1473 g)
Portions: 13
Portion size: 4 oz (113 g)
Yield description: 13 portions at 4 oz (113 g)

Ingredients	U.S.	Metric
Heavy Cream	2 lb	907 g
Egg Yolks	12 oz	340 g
Sugar	8 oz	226 g
Vanilla Bean, split and scraped	1 each	1 each

Procedure

1. Crème brûlée method on page 127.

Pastry Cream

Yield: 1 lb 9 oz (714 g)
Portions: 12
Portion size: 2 oz (56 g)
Yield Description: 12 portions at 2 oz (56 g)

Ingredients	U.S.	Metric
Milk	1 lb	454 g
Sugar #1	2 oz	56 g
Egg Yolks	1.25 oz	35.4 g
Whole Eggs	1.75 oz	50 g
Cornstarch	1.25 oz	35.4 g
Sugar #2	2 oz	56 g
Butter	1 oz	28 g
Vanilla Bean, split and scraped	1 each	1 each

Procedure

1. Pastry cream method on page 123.

Vanilla Cremeux

Yield: 1 lb 3 oz (551 g)
Portions: 9
Portion size: 2 oz (56 g)
Yield description: 9 portions at 2 oz (56 g)

Ingredients	U.S.	Metric
Milk	7 oz	198 g
Cream	7 oz	198 g
Egg Yolks	3.3 oz	93 g
Sugar	2.2 oz	62 g
Vanilla Beans, split and scraped	2 each	2 each
Gelatin, bloomed	3.5 sheets	3.5 sheets

Procedure

1. Crème anglaise method on page 124.
2. Add bloomed gelatin before straining.

Eggless White Chocolate Cremeux

Yield: 2 lb 1 oz (960 g)

Portions: 16

Portion size: 2 oz (56 g)

Yield description: 17 portions at 2 oz (56 g)

Ingredients	U.S.	Metric
Milk	7 oz	200 g
Lemon Zest	0.4 oz	10 g
Glucose	0.4 oz	10 g
Gelatin, bloomed	3 each	3 each
White Chocolate	12 oz	340 g
Heavy Cream	14.1 oz	400 g

Procedure

1. Melt white chocolate and add glucose.
2. Combine milk and zest; bring to a simmer.
3. Add milk to chocolate mixture.
4. Add heavy cream and emulsify with immersion blender.
5. Strain through a chinois and refrigerate for 6 hours before using.

Coconut Rice Pudding

Yield: 3 lb 8 oz (1587 g)

Portions: 14

Portion size: 4 oz (113 g)

Yield description: 14 portions at 4 oz (113 g)

Ingredients	U.S.	Metric
Jasmine Rice	6 oz	170 g
Milk	1 lb 8 oz	680 g
Coconut Purée	8 oz	227 g
Eggs	6 oz	170 g
Sugar	4 oz	113 g
Vanilla Bean, split and scraped	1 each	1 each
Heavy Cream	8 oz	227 g

Procedure

1. Combine milk and purée in a heavy-bottom saucepan and bring to a boil.
2. Add jasmine rice and cover.
3. Bake at 350°F (175°C) for 30 minutes, check rice for doneness.
4. Combine eggs and sugar.
5. Temper rice mixture into eggs, be careful to not break up the rice.
6. Return to a low-medium heat and cook to 175°F (80°C).
7. Add heavy cream.
8. Place in an ice bath to cool.

Ganache

Yield: 1 lb 9.5 oz (724 g)

Portions: 1

Portion size: 1 lb 9.5 oz (724 g)

Yield description: 1 lb 9.5 oz (724 g)

Ingredients	U.S.	Metric
Heavy Cream	12.75 oz	362 g
Semisweet Chocolate 58%	12.75 oz	362 g

Procedure

1. Bring heavy cream to a boil.
2. Add the chocolate in four additions; stir between additions to create an emulsion.
3. Emulsify ganache with an immersion blender.
4. Place plastic wrap directly on the surface of the ganache and refrigerate until needed.

Soft Ganache

Yield: 1 lb 11 oz (766 g)

Portions: 1

Portion size: 1 lb 11 oz (766 g)

Yield description: 1 lb 11 oz (766 g)

Ingredients	U.S.	Metric
Heavy Cream	12 oz	340 g
Milk	4 oz	114 g
Butter	1 oz	28 g
Semisweet Chocolate 58%	10 oz	284 g

Procedure

1. Combine milk and heavy cream in a heavy-bottom saucepan and bring to a boil.
2. Pour mixture over chocolate and stir to combine.
3. Add butter and emulsify with immersion blender.
4. Strain through a chinois.
5. Store refrigerated for 24 hours.
6. Whip until ganache forms stiff peaks.

Crème Anglaise

Yield: 1 lb 8 oz (680 g)
Portions: 48
Portion size: 0.5 oz (14 g)
Yield description: 48 portions at 0.5 oz (14 g)

Ingredients	U.S.	Metric
Milk	8 oz	227 g
Heavy Cream	8 oz	227 g
Sugar	4 oz	113 g
Egg Yolks	4 oz	113 g
Vanilla Bean, split and scraped	1 each	1 each

Procedure

1. Crème anglaise method on page 124.

Chocolate Pot de Crème

Yield: 3 lb 5 oz (1502 g)
Portions: 13
Portion size: 4 oz (113 g)
Yield description: 13 portions at 4 oz (113 g)

Ingredients	U.S.	Metric
Milk	2 lb	907 g
Chocolate 64%	6.5 oz	184 g
Egg Yolks	8 oz	227 g
Sugar	6.5 oz	184 g

Procedure

1. Combine half the sugar with the milk, place in a heavy-bottom saucepan, and heat to a boil.
2. Add remaining sugar to egg yolks mixture.
3. Temper all of the boiling milk mixture into the egg yolks.
4. Slowly add the hot custard to the chocolate.
5. Emulsify with an immersion blender.
6. Strain through a chinois and fill ramekins.
7. Bake in a water bath 300°F (149°C).
8. Store in the refrigerator.

Clafoutis

Yield: 2 lb 0.5 oz (979 g)

Portions: One 9-in. fluted tart pan

Portion size: 2 lb 0.5 oz (979 g)

Yield description: One 9-in. fluted tart pan at 2 lb 0.5 oz (979 g)

Ingredients	U.S.	Metric
Cream	8 oz	227 g
Milk	8 oz	227 g
Sugar	6 oz	170 g
Kirsch	4 oz	114 g
Eggs	5 oz	142 g
Cake Flour	3 oz	85 g
Vanilla Paste	0.5 oz	14 g

Procedure

1. Combine sugar and cake flour.
2. Combine cream, milk, eggs, kirsch, and vanilla paste.
3. Mix wet ingredients with dry ingredients.
4. Bake at 350°F (175°C).

Cheesecake

Yield: 3 lb 1 oz (1389 g)

Portions: One 10-in. cake, 12 portions

Portion size: 3 lb 1 oz (1389 g)

Yield description: One 10-in. cake at 3 lb 1 oz (1389 g)

Ingredients	U.S.	Metric
Cream Cheese	2 lb	907 g
Sugar	8 oz	227 g
Eggs	8 oz	227 g
Vanilla Paste	1 oz	28 g

Procedure

1. Cheesecake method on page 128.

Key Terms

Coagulation
Carryover cooking
Syneresis
Tempering

Royale
Ganache
Emulsion
Egg foams

Ovalbumin
Albumin
Pâte à bombe

Questions for Review

1. Describe the process for making a Chiboust.

2. Determine the proper cooking technique for a stirred custard that contains cornstarch.

3. What is the role of gelatin in a mousse?

4. Explain the process of tempering gelatin by using the cold process.

5. Discuss the advantages and disadvantages of using a French meringue in a mousse.

CHAPTER 6

Frozen Desserts

Nothing says comfort food like ice cream. In the United States, yearly consumption of frozen dessert products is just less than six gallons per person. Ice cream is a comfort food, something almost everyone can relate to. Building on this already-existing familiarity with frozen desserts gives the pastry chef a way to introduce new products to the customer. It is not as simple as mixing milk, cream, sugar, eggs, and vanilla anymore.

LEARNING OBJECTIVES

After reading this chapter, you should be able to:

1. **Explain** the function of sugars in frozen desserts.
2. **Calculate** overrun percentages of ice cream and sorbet.
3. **Calculate** the AFP of ice creams.
4. **Balance** sorbet and ice cream recipes.
5. **Make** a variety of churned and still frozen desserts.

Ingredients

Frozen desserts are created from basic ingredients: air, water, sugar, eggs, dairy products, and flavorings. In each group of ingredients, there are different types of products available, as well as different procedures to execute the recipe. Changing the ingredients, ratio, or sequence of the recipe will yield completely different results. All of these ingredients must be carefully balanced and the procedures followed to create a final product that demonstrates the craftsmanship of the pastry chef.

Air

Frozen desserts rely on air to create the light, creamy texture of a parfait, and the dense, soft texture of gelato. The amount of air incorporated in these items can create the correct mouthfeel. Frozen desserts fall under two main categories. **Churned** frozen desserts, such as ice cream, gelato, and sorbet, incorporate air during the freezing process. **Still frozen** desserts, such as parfaits and soufflé glacé, are aerated and then frozen. A frozen dessert that does not have any air incorporated will freeze into a solid block of ice that will be difficult to serve and eat.

In ice cream manufacturing, **overrun** is used to describe the amount of air incorporated into the final product. Understanding the ingredient functions in the recipe and how batch freezers work will help produce the correct amount of overrun. Sorbets typically have an overrun of 30%

to 40% while ice cream is 50% to 100%. The higher the percentage of overrun, the more airy the product becomes; Ice cream can almost take on an undesirable frozen mousse consistency if too much air is incorporated. High overrun is associated with economy ice creams. Calculating the overrun can be performed using the following formula:

$$\frac{(\text{Weight of 1L of mix before freezing} - \text{Weight of 1L of mix after freezing})}{\text{Weight of 1L of mix before freezing}} \times 100 = \% \, \text{Overrun}$$

When calculating the overrun, the first step is to weigh the unchurned ice cream base mixture in a container. It is best to use a volume measure container; quarts or pints are adequate. Fill the container and weigh the ice cream base; for this example, we will use a 1 L measure.

For example:

Weight of 1L of ice cream base before freezing = 1200 g

Next, process the base in an ice cream machine according to the manufacturer's instructions. Fill the machine to the recommended optimal level and process until the correct frozen consistency is achieved. Fill the same container with the churned ice cream. Weigh this container; the weight should be less than the original weight of the unchurned base.

Weight of 1L after freezing = 820 g

With this information, the overrun can be calculated using the formula above.

$$\frac{(1200 - 820)}{1200} \times 100 = \frac{380}{1200} \times 100 = 0.3166 \times 100 = 31.7\%$$

Be sure to use a container large enough to provide an accurately measurable sample. A measuring cup would be too small—too large of a container and it will not be filled to the top.

All ice cream machines vary a great deal in the way they operate, how quickly they churn, and how quickly they freeze. This will play a role in the final product; be sure to consult the user manual and follow all instructions as directed in the manual. Overfilling or underfilling an ice cream machine will change the amount of air the machine can incorporate into the mixture, or take too long to freeze. Recipes containing cream that are left in the machine too long can cause the cream to be overwhipped. Fat will separate from the base and create a coarse texture with a grainy mouthfeel. Undermixed bases will be grainy as a result of the water not being completely frozen while churning, as well as reduced final volume. After the ice cream is extracted from the machine, it is still very soft and needs to harden in the freezer. A blast chiller is the preferred method, with temperatures as low as –40°F (–40°C) preventing any air from escaping as the ice cream or sorbet continues freezing.

Water

Water impacts everything in the pastry shop. Oftentimes, it is overlooked as an ingredient because it is everywhere. Remember, a large percentage of a frozen dessert is water, yet water does not add any flavor. **Free water** is water that is not bound to any other part of the ingredients; this can lead to large ice crystals forming during the freezing process or in storage. Incorporating dry solids, sugar, glucose powder, dextrose, stabilizers, and emulsifiers into ice cream and sorbet helps to reduce the amount of free water. The water binds to the solids, creating a dense texture in the frozen dessert and assists in incorporating air during the churning process. The amount of nonfat dry solids in an ice cream should be in 24% to 32% and in sorbet 31% to 36%.

The balance of the recipe and use of ingredients not only changes the flavor, but also creates the proper texture. Water freezes at 32°F (0°C), but by adding other ingredients to a recipe, the freezing temperature can be reduced. Sugars and alcohol can also be added to reduce the temperature. When water is frozen in a solid block, large ice crystals form, and it would be difficult to eat. To prevent this, aerated eggs and cream are added to still frozen desserts, allowing the air to separate the water and lighten the mixture. Churned products are placed in an ice cream machine, where the intense agitation during the freezing process creates small ice crystals and incorporates air.

Sugars

Sugars provide many functions to a recipe: They allow ice cream to develop the proper texture, prevent sorbet from freezing too hard, and add flavor. In order to understand the function sugars perform, an evaluation of the recipe must be conducted. The most common association with sugars is sweetness. While this is true, think about what else the sugar is doing in the recipe.

In Chapter 5, sugar was used to denature egg proteins when preparing custards. Many frozen desserts are custard based and utilize the same cooking methods introduced in Chapter 5. Sugars also play a function in the final product by controlling the freezing temperature, maintaining the texture, preventing crystallization, and improving flavor. Not having enough sugars in a recipe creates a product that freezes too hard or can become grainy. At the opposite end of the spectrum, having excessive amounts of sugar in a recipe yields a product that is too soft, in addition to being too sweet.

Many types of sugars are available to the pastry chef, each having different properties and effects on the final product. Some common sugars found in the production of frozen desserts are granulated sugar (sucrose), lactose, honey, dextrose, glucose powder, glucose syrup, inverted sugar, and dextrose. Each of these contributes a different **sweetening power (SP)**, with sugar always being 100%, **antifreezing power (AFP)**, and percentage of solids.

The Power of Sugar chart below provides a list of sugars commonly used in the production of frozen desserts. Sugars can be used interchangeably in a recipe. Understanding the difference between sugars will help to select the amount and type correctly. When adjusting the sugars in the recipe, do not change the total quantity. If the recipe calls for 100 grams of sugar, adjustments can be made inside this total quantity. An example of this will follow in Guidelines to Formulating a Neutral Ice Cream Base.

The SP can easily be noted by tasting the base; if it's too sweet or not sweet enough, adjustments can be easily made by decreasing or increasing the amount of sugar. Understanding that the recipe is balanced based on the percentage of sugar, it would be better to adjust the type of sugar in the recipe. A high AFP means that the final product requires a lower temperature to freeze. Exchanging honey for granulated sugar not only impacts the sweetness, it affects the AFP. If honey is added, the ice cream would be noticeably softer than ice cream made with granulated sugar served at the same temperature. Invert sugar and dextrose will impact the AFP the same way. Balancing the FP and AFP will give the ice cream the correct flavor and texture.

Examples of Sugar Ratios in Ice Cream Base Using 1000 g of Total Sugar Served at 14°F (10°C)

	Base #1	Base #2	Base #3
Sugar	1000 g	900 g	250 g
Glucose Powder		100 g	
Honey			750 g

Traditionally, ice cream bases were made using granulated sugar, and a decent base can be produced using granulated sugar. The first example uses only granulated sugar. The second example incorporates glucose powder into the original quantity of 1000 grams. Base #2 will be slightly less sweet than Base #1 and will have a slightly denser texture due to the incorporation of the glucose powder. Base #3 uses honey. Honey is sweeter than sugar and the AFP is almost double. This product will be softer, sweeter, and have a different texture, almost gummy.

Solids in the sugars also play an important role in the production of ice cream. The more solids in the ice cream means there is less water. Solids absorb the water and interfere with the formation of large ice crystals in the finished ice cream, assisting in producing a smooth texture. The percentage of solids in ice cream should be no more than 32%. Exceeding this will cause the ice cream to have a coarse mouthfeel. Incorporating solids into the recipe will produce an ice cream that does not melt quickly when plated for service.

The amount of total solids in a recipe hinders the formation of ice crystals. A high AFP means the final product requires a lower temperature to freeze, and holding these products at a higher temperature will cause them to melt. Balancing the SP and AFP will give the frozen dessert the correct flavor and texture.

Power of Sugar

Sugars	Sweetening Power (SP)	Anti-Freezing Power (AFP)	Total Solids %
Granulated Sugar (sucrose)	100	1	100
Honey	130	1.9	75
Lactose	16	1	100
Invert Sugar	130	1.9	78
Dextrose	75	1.9	92
Glucose Powder 40 DE	50	0.9	95
Glucose Syrup 28 DE	50	0.5	78

DE is an abbreviation for **Dextrose Equivalent**. A higher DE will mean an increase in the SP and AFP. Glucose powder and syrup are available at different DE. The Power of Sugar table represents the most commonly available DE for these products. Be sure to check the DE with the distributor if it is not listed. All recipes in this book will utilize the products specified in the Power of Sugar table.

The AFP can be used to determine the serving temperature of the ice cream. The ideal temperature for ice cream and sorbet is 14°F (–10°C). An AFP between 241 and 260 will give the correct consistency at this temperature. The sugars in the recipe can be adjusted to achieve the needed AFP. For every 20 points the AFP increases, the temperature is reduced by 1.8°F (1°C). To calculate the total AFP of an ingredient, multiply the weight of the ingredient by the AFP and add each of the ingredients to get the total for the recipe. The AFP is based on 2.2 lb (1 kg) of ice cream base.

Ingredient weight × AFP = Total AFP

Calculating Antifreezing Point of French Vanilla Ice Cream

Sugars	Quantity	AFP	Total AFP
Granulated Sugar	140 g	1	140
Glucose Powder	32 g	0.9	28.8
MSNF (51.3% lactose)	50 g × 0.513 = 25.65 g	1	25.65
Milk (4.8% lactose)	500 g × 0.048 = 24 g	1	24
Cream 35% (3.5% lactose)	175 g × 0.035 = 6.125 g	1	6.125
		Total	**224.575**

Note: To calculate the AFP accurately, the lactose must be included. Refer to the Lactose in Dairy Products table below. Multiply the total weight of the ingredient by the percentage to determine the amount of lactose by ingredient.

The total AFP for the Vanilla Ice Cream is 225 (rounded up), which would equate to an ideal serving temperature of 15.8°F (–9°C). Sugars can be adjusted to correct the difference. Granulated sugar could be increased to 156 g (and thus, the total AFP for the sugar would be 156), and the total AFP for all ingredients would be adjusted to 241. It is important to remember when writing recipes that it is a process—there are many more variables to an ice cream recipe. The formulas can help to get you close to an accurate result; the best way to check a recipe is to compare the finished results with what was calculated on paper.

Types of Sweeteners

Granulated Sugar Granulated sugar is produced from either sugar cane or sugar beets. It is one of the most readily available sugars, and can come in a variety of forms, granulated and extra fine. Granulated sugar is used as the base for determining the SP and AFP of all other sugars.

Honey Honey is one of the sweetest sugars available, and has one advantage over the other sugars. Through the use of honey, the flavor of the sweetener can be changed. Orange blossom, lavender, buckwheat, clover, acacia, or chestnut nectar can all be used in the production of honey. These nectars flavor the honey and can enhance the flavor of a recipe. Honey has a high AFP, meaning it will not freeze as hard as the other sugars; care must be taken to not just replace the same amount of honey for another sugar in the recipe.

Lactose Lactose is found in products made from milk. It is naturally occurring in milk and cream, which are used in frozen desserts. Some recipes use additional milk powders to add flavor as well as absorb water. In order to accurately calculate the serving temperature and adjust recipes, lactose cannot be ignored. Lactose is not used as a sweetener in ice cream, however; it is a part of milk products. It does add sweetness and contributes to the overall AFP calculations.

Lactose in Dairy Products

Product	Lactose
Whole Milk	4.8%
Skim Milk	5.2%
Light Whipping Cream 30%	3.9%
Whipping Cream 35%	3.5%
Heavy Whipping Cream 40%	3.0%
Butter	0.9%
Milk Solids Nonfat (MSNF)	51.3%

Glucose Glucose, glucose powder, and dextrose are products closely related to each other, and they all contain dextrose. Dextrose can be made from many types of starches, including corn, potatoes, rice, barley, tapioca, and wheat. These starches are then converted into simple sugars. These products are referred to by their dextrose equivalent (DE).

Pure dextrose has a DE of 100, which means that all of the starch has been fully converted to dextrose. The DE of glucose syrup and glucose powder indicates that only the specified percentage, represented by the DE, of starch has been converted to dextrose. Glucose syrup 28 DE and glucose powder 40 DE are the most commonly used in the production of frozen desserts. Glucose powder is glucose that has had 95% of the water removed.

Glucose syrup can provide a desirable texture to frozen desserts, but its use is somewhat limited due to the large percentage of water remaining. The advantage of using glucose powder and dextrose is that they do not add water to the recipe and they prevent crystallization by inverting the sugar. While these three products will be used in this chapter, it is important to remember that careful attention must be paid when scaling the recipes and to use the correct product—while they are similar, each has a different SP.

Invert Sugar **Invert sugar**, also known by the brand name Trimoline, provides many of the same functions as glucose: It prevents crystallization, adds sweetness, and softens ice cream. Glucose syrup is a clear, thick liquid and invert sugar is an opaque, thick gel. Invert sugar contains an emulsifier, which helps to stabilize a recipe. It normally is not used in ice cream and sorbet production, as it leads to a gummy texture if too much is used. It can be useful in recipes that contain chocolate or praline paste to soften the texture and emulsify additional fats in the recipe.

Sugar Density

Sugar plays a critical role in the development and production of frozen desserts. **Brix** is a measure of the amount of dissolved solids in solution; the strength of the solution is reported as degrees Brix, or °Brix. Determining the Brix of a sugar solution using a refractometer provides a more precise way to measure the concentration, and adjustments can be made. In some instances, a thermometer can be used to determine the amount of sugar. However, this is not as accurate a method. A sugar solution that is 20 grams sugar in 100 grams of water is written as 20° Brix. Calculations can be made to determine the amount of sugar in a recipe with fairly accurate results. However, during the heating process evaporation of water will take place, causing a change to the balance of the recipe.

Degrees Brix Ranges for Frozen Desserts

Type	°Brix
Ice Cream	16–23
Sorbet	28–31
Granités	16–19

Sugar concentration can be checked through the use of a refractometer. A refractometer measures how light passes through a liquid—the more sugar in a solution, the more difficult it is for the light to pass through. An optical refractometer passes light through the solution and a prism. Figure 6.1 on the left is what would be seen with distilled water and Figure 6.2 shows what a 23° Brix would look like.

FIGURE 6.1 Optical refractometer image showing 0° Brix

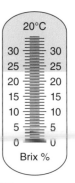

FIGURE 6.2 Optical refractometer image showing 23° Brix

Optical refractometers work best with natural light and sugar solutions; color found in purées or milk solids can give an inaccurate reading. To get a more accurate reading, use a digital refractometer; while they carry a higher cost, the accuracy is much better.

Sugar is one of the many factors needed to consider when evaluating a frozen dessert. The ingredients in a recipe interact with each other and with the sugar, which explains the ranges of °Brix. Not only is the final texture of the product important, flavor must be considered. In a sorbet recipe the acidity of the fruit will change the amount of sugar needed to provide sweetness; higher acidity fruits will require more sugar. In regards to ice cream, the fat content will impact flavor. A higher percentage of fat will require a greater quantity of sugar to create sweetness. The ranges throughout this chapter provide a guideline to allow the formulation of new recipes and the ability to make adjustments to existing recipes.

Eggs

The egg is an incredible and versatile ingredient used in many pastry recipes. They are used in both churned and still frozen dessert preparations. As discussed in Chapter 5, eggs can be used to create volume and lightness in a mousse or the thickened creamy texture of a crème anglaise.

Egg Yolk Components

Water	Fat	Protein	Lecithin	Total Solids
44%	30%	18%	8%	56%

Many churned frozen desserts rely on egg yolks in the custard to provide color, flavor, fat, thickening power, and emulsification. The white of the egg is rarely used in ice cream production due to the large amount of water contained in it. As a result, they provide no additional emulsifying properties. Egg whites also contain bacteria. It is recommended to use pasteurized egg whites if they are used in ice cream custard. Sanitation is critical when working with eggs and ice cream. The custard bases used for ice cream production need to be cooked to 175°F (80°C). At this point, the custard will be cooked to a **nappe** consistency and the custard is the proper thickness and is pasteurized.

Pasteurization is the process of heating food to a specific temperature for a set amount of time to reduce the number of pathogens. There are several different methods of pasteurization. **High temperature/Short time (HTST)** is the process used in this book. In compliance with U.S. Food and Drug Administration (FDA) Guidelines, HTST requires that ice cream bases be heated to 175°F (80°C) for 25 seconds or 180°F (82°C) for 15 seconds. After pasteurization, these products must be cooled quickly; an ice bath is recommended.

Still frozen desserts can use the yolk, white, or whole egg. The usage of eggs in still frozen desserts is very similar to the way they are used in making a mousse. In fact, the methods and ingredients are identical. What differs is the ratio; an increase in quantity of sugar or alcohol keeps the final texture soft when served from the freezer.

The fat contained in the egg yolk creates a rich, dense foam as well as adding color to the final product. Additional fat also can reduce the strength of flavors, due to the fat coating the mouth. Milder flavors, such as banana, would benefit from the use of a meringue. Meringues add lightness to still frozen desserts and do not impart any color to the final product.

Can I use pasteurized egg products for this recipe? This question is asked all too often, and the answer is yes. Unless a recipe specifies "fresh" next to the ingredient, pasteurized products can be substituted. Not only do they save labor, they are excellent products and at times can be better than their fresh counterparts. Still frozen desserts benefit from the use of pasteurized eggs; potential pathogens are destroyed through the pasteurization process.

Dairy Products

Vanilla is by far the most popular ice cream flavor. It is a common flavor but it is much more than vanilla. It's a combination of textures, sweetness, temperature, and flavor. While vanilla is the "flavor," there is a considerable amount of flavor that comes from the dairy used in the recipe. A simple recipe for vanilla ice cream might contain milk and cream, while others may have added milk solids. There are many good vanilla ice creams available, yet by understanding the important role dairy products play in the recipe, a great version could be made.

Dairy products, just like sugars and eggs, are used together to develop the flavor and texture desired in the final product. Understanding what is in dairy products will help to provide insight as to their function in the recipe.

Solids in Dairy Products

Product	Total Solids	Fat Solids	Nonfat Solids	Water
Whole Milk	12%	3.6%	8.4%	88%
Skim Milk	9.2%	0%	9.2%	91%
Light Whipping Cream 30%	36.5%	30%	6.5%	63.5%
Whipping Cream 35%	41%	35%	6%	59%
Heavy Whipping Cream 40%	45.5%	40%	5.5%	54.5%
Butter	84%	82%	2%	16%
Milk Solids Nonfat (MSNF)	97%	0%	97%	3%

Dairy products are composed of fat solids, nonfat solids, and water. The fat and nonfat solids are what give milk its flavor and body. Skim milk and whole milk look somewhat similar. When comparing taste and texture, the skim milk is thinner and has less flavor. Whole milk is the preferred milk used in the pastry kitchen; unless a recipe specifies skim milk, use whole milk. MSNF are combined with milk to increase the flavor and amount of solids in the recipe and absorb free water.

MSNF are used due to their low cost, shelf life, water-binding capability, and ability to stabilize the emulsion of the custard. Whole milk powders are available—due to the inclusion of fat, they have a shorter shelf life of 6 months compared to MSNF shelf life of 3 years. The emulsion is stabilized due to the high protein content of the MSNF and its ability to distribute the fat in the recipe; egg yolks also assist the emulsion. A broken emulsion in an ice cream cannot be visualized as with mayonnaise; it occurs on a minuscule level. The results of broken emulsion may present in a grainy texture or ice cream that melts too quickly. Stabilizing the emulsion and proper pasteurization contribute to the final texture of the ice cream.

Including too much MSNF will cause the ice cream to take on a grainy texture. The final product will take on a sandy texture due to the lactose crystalizing. Lactose crystals form a triangular shape and feel sharp on the tongue.

Just as the sugar in the recipe needs to be balanced, so does the amount of fat. Too high of a fat content will make the ice cream extremely heavy and mask the flavors. In addition, it makes the ice cream prone to overmixing during the churning process. Overmixing causes the fat to separate out from the cream in the same way that it happens to whipped cream. When brought to low temperatures, the fat is very firm and coarse; if this occurs, the ice cream should be discarded. To prevent this from happening, it is recommended to use a 35% fat cream. If further reduction in fat is needed, milk can be added.

Emulsifiers and Stabilizers

Creating and maintaining an emulsion in ice cream is an important factor in developing the proper texture of the final product. Emulsifiers assist in creating and holding the emulsion. There are two kinds of emulsifiers: diglycerides and monosterates. Although there is lecithin in egg yolks, it is not sufficient to fully emulsify the mixture. During the maturation phase of the ice cream making process. the emulsifiers "attach" to fat and water and permanently bond them.

There is no need to use emulsifiers in sorbets, since they do not contain any dairy. Sorbet benefits from the use of stabilizers. These stabilizers are made from plant-based materials: guar gum, xanthan gum, and iota carrageenan. The same benefits can be achieved in sorbets as in ice cream, with the only difference being that there are no emulsifiers in sorbet base due to no added fats.

Using emulsifiers and stabilizers offers five advantages:

1. Emulsifies fat and water
2. Better overrun
3. Improved texture
4. Absorbs free water to prevent crystals from forming (100% solids)
5. Stabilizes finished product from melting quickly after serving

There are many excellent stabilizers and emulsifiers commercially available to the pastry chef. Purchasing these products already done saves time, provides a consistent product, and can include multiple stabilizers and emulsifiers to yield excellent results. Care must be taken when scaling these products; they should not exceed 1% of the total recipe. During the pasteurization of the mix, the stabilizers hydrate and continue developing during the maturation process. Adding too much stabilizer creates a gummy texture after churning. Egg yolks contain lecithin, a natural emulsifier. Depending on the quantity of yolks in the recipe, the amount of stabilizer can be reduced or omitted completely. Slight adjustments may be needed based on the brand used—check with the supplier for recommended quantities.

Some chefs prefer to not add these products, while others add them to every recipe. There is no right or wrong answer, although there has been a great deal of discussion about the use of stabilizers and emulsifiers over the years. They are natural products extracted from plant-based materials (seeds, seaweed, or plants)—they are not chemicals. One question constantly asked: Are emulsifiers and stabilizers necessary to use in a recipe that includes them? The simple answer is no. Recipes can be made without them and the recipe will work, but the results may be slightly different.

Churned Frozen Desserts

Churned frozen desserts go by many names, but they all have one thing in common. During the freezing process, they are churned mechanically or, in some instances, by hand. Agitation prevents large ice crystals from forming and incorporates air. Freezing these products without churning would result in a solid block of ice that would be extremely difficult to eat. There are many different styles of churned frozen desserts, which can be broken down into two main groups: dairy and nondairy.

Ice Cream Machines

Batch Freezer

Batch freezers are used to churn ice cream, sorbet, gelato, and sherbet. The machine contains a compressor that freezes a metal cylinder. The base mixture is added to the machine in a liquid form. Although the base is being frozen, the dasher spins quickly, incorporating air into the mixture and forming small ice crystals.

When producing churned frozen desserts using a batch freezer, refer to the user's manual associated with the machine. The time needed to freeze an ice cream or sorbet base will vary. This depends on the makeup of the recipe, the amount of mixture in the machine, and even how often the machine is used. A machine filled to maximum capacity will take longer to freeze than a machine that is only half full. The first batch of ice cream that is run will take longer than the following batches. This is due to the ice cream cylinder being cooled from the previous batch. Be sure to carefully observe the ice cream or sorbet during the churning process to ensure the proper consistency of the final product.

FIGURE 6.3 Batch Freezer
(Photo courtesy of Advanced Gourmet Equipment & Design)

Paco Jet

A Paco Jet uses a high-speed blade to transform frozen bases into ice cream, sorbet, gelato, and sherbet. The main difference between a Paco Jet and batch freezer is that the base is frozen before processing. A Paco Jet can also be used to produce nut pastes.

FIGURE 6.4 Sorbet: an unprocessed beaker (left); a processed beaker (right)

Dairy-Based Churned Frozen Desserts

Ice Cream

Ice cream is a term that can be used to describe several different styles of ice cream. The FDA regulates what can be called ice cream. The regulations state that the product must contain a minimum 10% milk fat and 10% milk solids. If the milk fat percentage is higher than 10%, the total of the fat and solids must be a minimum 20%. Egg yolks can also be added to ice cream at a maximum amount of 1.4%. An ice cream that has no egg yolk added is often referred to as Philadelphia-style ice cream, or crème glacée.

French Style Ice Cream

Most ice creams produced in restaurants and pastry shops are custard based or French-style ice cream. What sets it apart from ice cream is the addition of egg yolks. A minimum of 1.4% egg yolk is required. Although there is additional cost associated with using egg yolks, the ice cream benefits through additional richness, flavor, texture, and color, as well as increased stability during storage.

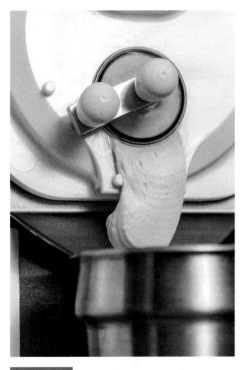

FIGURE 6.5 Front of ice cream machine extruding properly churned ice cream

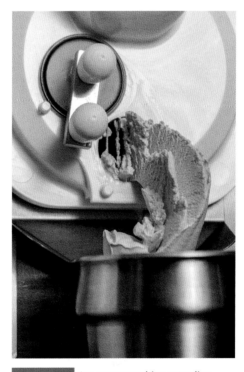

FIGURE 6.6 Ice cream machine extruding overchurned ice cream

Gelato

Gelato is Italian for ice cream. In the United States, it is used in many establishments to refer to anything, including ice cream. The FDA does not regulate the use of this term. However, gelato has a different texture and flavor than ice creams or frozen custards. A gelato recipe is similar to a custard-based ice cream. It contains egg yolk, lower milk fat percentage (3% to 10%), and higher sugar percentage (up to 24%). Gelato has less overrun, 30% to 40%, and is served at a slightly warmer temperature than ice cream. Less overrun and additional sugar help to keep the gelato soft and creamy in light of the fact the fat content is lower.

Sherbet

Sherbet base is composed of sugar, water, flavoring, and dairy ingredients. Milk fat percentage in sherbet is 1% to 2%. Chocolate, coffee, tea, alcohol, and fruit can all be used to flavor sherbet. Since sherbet typically contains fruit purée, it is often confused with sorbet. In addition, the name is often misspelled (or mispronounced) as *sherbert*, adding further confusion.

Frozen Yogurt

Frozen yogurt is certainly not a new concept; it is most often associated with soft-serve yogurt shops that continue to grow in popularity. In the pastry shop, frozen yogurt is a unique product that does not fit into any of the other categories. It is made from yogurt, sugars, flavorings, and sometimes additional milk. Increased access to Greek yogurt has given this product an increased flavor profile in comparison to the traditional yogurts found in the United States. Greek yogurt is thicker and more flavorful, and can provide an enjoyable tart flavor.

Method

The process of pasteurizing an ice cream recipe is just as important as the balance of the recipe. Through this process, the ice cream mix is heated to a high temperature to kill any pathogenic microorganisms, dissolve solids, and emulsify the mixture. Final texture, reduced overrun, and length of service time can all be negatively affected by not carefully monitoring this process.

There are many recipes with different pasteurization procedures; the following is the process that will be used in many of the recipes included in this chapter.

Ice Cream Base Process

1. Combine the stabilizer with 10 times its weight in granulated sugar.
2. Combine the egg yolks with some of the sugar.
3. Combine the milk, cream, and MSNF; continue stirring to make sure the solids do not burn on the bottom of the pan.
4. Temper the egg yolks into the mixture, followed by the stabilizer mixture and remaining sugars (granulated sugar, glucose powder, dextrose, honey).
5. Continue cooking over low heat to 175°F (80°C) for 15 seconds.
6. Quickly cool the mixture to 40°F (4°C).
7. Allow the mixture to mature under refrigeration for 6 to 12 hours. This step allows the dry ingredients to fully hydrate and fat globules to crystallize and collect around air cells, increasing the ability to trap air during churning.
8. Using an immersion blender, homogenize the mixture.
9. Freeze in an ice cream machine following the manufacturer's instructions.
10. Extract ice cream from the machine into prefrozen containers; cover and freeze to −22°F (−30°C) to stabilize the ice cream. Store at this temperature until needed for service.
11. Temper to 10°F (−12°C) for service.

Guidelines for Formulating Basic Ice Cream Custard

Each ingredient has a function in the recipe: sweetening, providing solids, removing free water—all these come together to create the perfect texture. The recipe is not based solely on one ingredient and the function of that ingredient, but how all the ingredients interact with each other. Understanding the function of the ingredients and the guidelines for formulating a basic custard will provide a starting point for modifying existing recipes or creating a new customized product. Some ingredients provide a range, while others have set percentages to follow.

Ingredient Percentage Ranges for a Neutral Ice Cream Base for 1000 g Yield

Ingredients	% Range	Grams
Fat	6–10%	80–100 g
Sugars (includes max 4% glucose powder)	17–22%	170–220 g
Egg Yolk	3–10%	30–100 g
Stabilizer	0.1–1%	
MSNF	0–10%	0–100 g

To manufacture 1000 grams of base, identify the percentages of each ingredient needed. For this recipe the following percentages were selected:

Fat	10%
Sugar	20%
Egg Yolk	5%
Stabilizer	0.5%
MSNF	5%

The first step in the process is calculating the stabilizer, egg yolks, and MSNF. (For this recipe, we will be using a premade stabilizer.) To do this, multiply each of these ingredients by 1000 grams.

Stabilizer 1000 g × 0.005 = 5 grams

Egg yolk   1000 g × 0.05   = 50 grams

MSNF   1000 g × 0.05   = 50 grams

Sugars are calculated in the same way. However, we have different sugars that can be used and provide different sweetness, textures, and AFP. For this recipe, we will use the maximum 4% glucose powder, with the remaining 16% being granulated sugar. It is recommended that you calculate the AFP for this recipe, once all ingredients are finalized, prior to testing in the kitchen.

Glucose   1000 g × 0.04 = 40 grams

Granulated Sugar 1000 g × 0.16 = 160 grams

One more step and the recipe will be ready for testing. The fat percentage for the recipe was determined at the beginning of the process to be 10%. Now that all the other ingredients are calculated, the remaining weight of the recipe would be composed from the milk and the whipping cream. The total for the sweeteners, egg yolks, MSNF, and stabilizer is 305 grams. To yield a total of 1000 grams, 695 grams of milk and whipping cream is needed. But how much of each is needed?

Vanilla Ice Cream Recipe

Ingredient	Weight	Percentage
Milk		
Whipping Cream		
Granulated Sugar	160 g	20% Total
Glucose Powder DE 40	40 g	
Egg Yolks	50 g	5%
MSNF	50 g	5%
Stabilizer	5 g	0.5%

The following formula is used to calculate the weight of the whipping cream. Once this is calculated, the amount of milk can be determined. This formula takes into account how many grams of total fat are needed and how much total weight is needed to complete the formula. Practice will be needed in using this formula. However, it will yield precise results to assist in balancing ice cream formulas.

When calculating the whipping cream and milk, the fat percentages for the dairy products must be converted to the decimal form.

Converting Fat Percentages to Decimals

Product	Fat Solids Percent	Fat Solids Decimal Form
Whole Milk	3.6%	0.036
Skim Milk	0%	0.0
Light Whipping Cream 30%	30%	0.30
Whipping Cream 35%	35%	0.35
Heavy Whipping Cream 40%	40%	0.40
Butter	82%	0.82

$$\left[F - (M \times D) \right] = \text{Total grams of cream} (W - M)$$

Note: This formula is presented in two ways. The formula above can be entered into a scientific calculator. The following formulas break the formula into smaller components, either way will provide the same answer.

F = Total grams of fat needed in recipe = 100 g

M = Percentage of fat in milk in decimal form = 0.036

W = Percentage of fat in whipping cream in decimal form = 0.35

D = Total dairy weight = 695 g

The first line is calculated by multiplying the milk fat in decimal form by the total dairy weight:

Line 1 = M × D

Line 1 = 0.036 × 695 g

Line 1 = 25.02 g

Next, subtract the total grams of fat needed in the recipe by the answer from Line 1:

Line 2 = F − Line 1
Line 2 = 100 g − 25.02 g
Line 2 = 74.98 g

For the next portion of the formula, subtract the milk fat from the whipping cream fat; remember to use these in decimal form:

Line 3 = W − M
Line 3 = 0.35 − 0.036
Line 3 = 0.314

To complete the problem, divide the answer from line 2 by the answer from line 3:

Grams of whipping cream = Line 2/Line 3
Grams of whipping cream = 74.98 g/0.314
Grams of whipping cream = 238.789

This answer can be rounded to 239 g

The weight of milk is calculated by subtracting the whipping cream weight from the remaining ingredient weight of 695 g:

695 g − 239 g = 456 g milk

The final calculated recipe is:

Vanilla Ice Cream Recipe

Ingredient	Weight	Percentage
Milk	456 g	10% Fat
Whipping Cream	239 g	
Granulated Sugar	160 g	20% Sugar
Glucose Powder DE 40	40 g	
Egg Yolks	50 g	5%
MSNF	50 g	5%
Stabilizer	5 g	0.5%
Total Weight	**1000 g**	

The percentages used to calculate the recipe are not intended to equal 100% the way it is written. The percentages represent the ingredients that are used to create the desired texture. By adjusting these ingredients, the last ingredient, water, is controlled. Remember that the ingredient that was of concern was the fat percentage. A large component of milk and whipping cream is water. By balancing the recipe and following the percentage ranges, a balanced recipe can be created. The only ingredient that changes based on adjusting the percentages is the water. In ice cream making, the goal is to control the water, creating the proper consistency, flavor, and serving temperature.

Non–Dairy-Based Churned Frozen Desserts

Sorbet

Sorbet is created through a balanced recipe of fruit purée, water, sugars, and stabilizers. Although the FDA does not regulate sorbet, it should not contain any dairy products. The general perception of the public is that sorbet is dairy free, making it an option to vegan and lactose-intolerant customers. In some recipes, however, MSNF may be used to trap free water and create a creamy texture in the final product. Since there is no regulation as to what can be called a sorbet, some chefs use their creativity to create buttermilk or sour cream sorbets.

Sorbet: 28–31° Brix, Granité: 16–19° Brix, are the recommend sugar percentages for sorbet and granité syrups. They indicate a point of reference for calculating new recipes. Each fruit has a unique sugar percentage. The sugar percentage present in the fruit will need be included when calculating the total amount of sugar present in the recipe. Too high of a sugar content and the sugar will separate from the recipe when stored in the freezer.

Granités

Sorbet and granités have a common use of ingredients with different ratios. The reduced amount of sugar indicates the final product will freeze harder and create larger crystals. Granités are not churned in a machine; instead, they are stirred by hand during the freezing process. This creates more of a coarse, shaved-ice type consistency with large, flaky ice crystals.

Methods

When cooking ice cream bases, there is a focus on the temperature to prevent over coagulation of the egg proteins. While sorbet does not contain eggs the same attention must be given during the cooking process. If the syrup solution is cooked too high or for too long of a time, water will begin to evaporate and change the recipe. Only the syrup is cooked for a sorbet. Almost all fruits have a pH that is acidic enough that bacteria cannot survive. Additionally the fresh flavor of the fruit and bright colors are lost when heating.

Sorbet Method

1. Combine all dry ingredients and mix thoroughly.
2. Place water in saucepan and begin heating.
3. When the temperature reaches 104°F (40°C), add the dry ingredients to the water.
4. Heat the syrup to 185°F (85°C), while covered.
5. Quickly cool the mixture to 40°F (4°C).
6. Allow the mixture to mature under refrigeration for 6 to 12 hours.
7. Using an immersion blender combine the purée and syrup.
8. Freeze in an ice cream machine according to the manufacturer's instructions.
9. Extract sorbet from the machine into prefrozen containers, cover and freeze to –22°F (–30°C) to stabilize the sorbet. Store at this temperature until needed for service.
10. Temper to 10°F (–12°C) for service.

Guidelines for Formulating a Sorbet

Sorbet can be created with as few as three ingredients: fruit purée or other flavor, granulated sugar, and water. Increases in technology and availability of products have changed the way sorbets are made. While there are not many components, the ingredient of the fruit alone contains water, solids, and sugar. Each fruit requires its own formulation to create a balanced recipe. If using fresh fruit, adjustments may need to be made throughout the season to accommodate different sugar and solid levels. In order to maintain consistent results, it is recommended to use fruit purées for sorbets. Understanding how the ingredients and fruit work together make it possible to create a sorbet recipe.

Ingredient Percentages for Sorbet Base of 1000 g Yield

Ingredient	Range	Grams
Fruit Purée (sweet)	40–60%	400–600 g
Fruit Purée (acidic)	25–40%	250–400 g
Solids	31–36%	310–360 g
Sugar (includes maximum 6% glucose powder)	28–33%	280–330 g
Stabilizer	0–1%	0–10 g
Lemon Juice	0–5%	0–50 g
Water		

Solids in the recipe can range from 31% to 36%; this is a total of the solids in the fruit purées, additional sugars, and stabilizer. The following table provides a reference for sugar and solids percentage of fruits commonly used for sorbets. If the fruit is not listed on the chart, a refractometer can easily identify the percentage of solids in a purée.

Sugar and Solid Percentages in Fresh Fruit

Fruit	Sugar	Solids	Fruit	Sugar	Solids
Apple	10%	14%	Mango	14%	16%
Apricot	9%	12%	Orange	10%	12%
Banana	15%	24%	Papaya	8%	14%
Black Currant	7%	18%	Passion Fruit	11%	16%
Blackberry	7%	14%	Peach	9%	10%
Blueberry	11%	15%	Pear	10%	16%
Cherry	12%	18%	Pineapple	9%	12%
Guava	9%	19%	Raspberry	5%	14%
Lemon	3%	9%	Strawberry	6%	11%
Lime	1%	10%	Watermelon	7%	8%

To manufacture 1000 grams of fresh blueberry sorbet base identify the percentages of each ingredient needed. For this recipe the following percentages were selected, with a target of 35% solids. The sum of the solids from the purée, glucose powder, and stabilizer are used to determine how much sugar is needed to meet the solid percentages. The quantity of lemon juice in this recipe is negligible and will not have an impact on the final percentages; it is used to enhance the flavor of the fruit. Once this is calculated the only remaining ingredient is the water.

Ingredient	Weight	Percentage
Fresh Blueberry Purée	400 g	40%
Sugar		
Glucose Powder DE 40	30 g	3%
Stabilizer	5 g	0.5%
Lemon Juice	20 g	2%
Water		

Calculating solids:

Blueberry Purée 400 g × 0.15 = 60 g

Glucose Powder   30 g × 0.95 = 28.5 g

Stabilizer   5 g × 1.00 = 5 g

Total solids   = 93.5 g

Note: The 0.95 reference in the glucose line is derived from the Power of Sugar table on p. 150.

The total solids needed for the blueberry sorbet were determined to be 30% or 350 grams. To determine how much granulated sugar to add, subtract the total solids from 350. In some instances, when the solids are required and sweetness does not need to be increased up to 2% dextrose can be added to the recipe.

Granulated sugar = 350 g – 93.5 g = 256.5 g

Ingredient	Weight	Percentage
Fresh Blueberry Purée	400 g	40%
Sugar	256.5 g	25.65%
Glucose Powder DE 40	30 g	3%
Stabilizer	5 g	0.5%
Lemon Juice	20 g	2%
Water		

Calculating the amount of water is done in a similar fashion. The total of all ingredients, 711 grams is subtracted from the original required total of 1000 g.

Water needed = 1000 g – 711 g = 289 g water.

Final Blueberry Sorbet Recipe

Ingredient	Weight	Percentage
Fresh Blueberry Purée	400 g	40%
Sugar	256.5 g	25.65%
Glucose Powder DE 40	30 g	3%
Stabilizer	5 g	0.5%
Lemon Juice	20 g	2%
Water	289 g	28.9%
Total	1000.5 g	100%

It is recommended to calculate the AFP of the sorbet before proceeding to the next step. After testing in the kitchen and evaluating the final product adjustments can be made to the ingredients to achieve the desired texture.

Granita Method

1. Combine sugar and water.
2. Heat to dissolve sugar, cool syrup over an ice bath.
3. Combine syrup with flavorings.
4. Place mixture in a shallow pan in freezer and begin freezing.
5. Scrape mixture every 30 minutes until frozen.

Serving Churned Desserts

The process of making churned desserts requires careful detail to attention and an understanding of the processes and ingredients involved. This can also be extended to include serving these items. An ice cream served at too cold of a temperature will be difficult to scoop and too cold to reveal the full flavor. A service temperature that is too warm will not provide an attractive presentation. The ideal serving temperature for ice cream and sorbet is 10°F (−12°C).

A properly balanced recipe will give the ice cream and sorbet a soft texture making them easy to present as a round scoop or quenelle. A quenelle is an oval-shaped scoop created using a spoon. When scooping ice cream and sorbet the scoop or spoon should be placed in warm water between scoops. This will help the scoop to pass through the ice cream as well as release from the scoop when finished.

Still Frozen Desserts

Still frozen desserts are known by many names: parfait, soufflé glacé, bombe glacé, semi-freddo, or mousse glacé. Some of these names have the same meaning just in a different language: French, Italian, and even English. They all contain an egg product, and it may even come down to the procedure of assembling the ingredients to set them apart. In the United States, there are no regulations specifying the differences in these products. Each of these products has unique textural differences as well as flavor profiles. This provides the pastry chef the opportunity to use different frozen items to maximize the flavor of their desserts.

Parfait

In the United States, a **parfait** is often thought of as a layered item served in a glass. A parfait is composed of pâte à bombe, whipped cream, and flavorings. It Is very similar to a mousse recipe, but to maintain the semi-frozen texture there is additional granulated sugar, around 30% more. The use of egg yolks in this recipe adds texture and richness; it is best paired with strong flavors. The additional fat can make the mouthfeel slightly heavier than the mousse glacé. Subtle flavors like banana or peach may be difficult to use, but strong flavors like chocolate or even vanilla work well with a parfait.

Mousse Glacé or Semifreddo

In French the name **mousse glacé** literally translates to "frozen mousse"; in Italian, it is known as **semifreddo** or "semi frozen." This product tends to be lighter in texture and flavor. The lightness comes from the use of a meringue, whipped cream, and flavorings. It is recommended to use an Italian meringue, due to the egg whites being fully cooked and removing any possible pathogens. A traditional Italian meringue uses 2 parts sugar to 1 part egg whites. This amount of sugar makes it difficult to freeze. Reducing the amount of sugar will create a product that will freeze and be the correct texture. The same process for making an Italian meringue is followed. Using ingredients with less fat gives a light texture and does not mask lighter flavors.

Soufflé Glacé

Soufflé glacé means "frozen soufflé." There are many variations for this product. One constant throughout all versions is that they contain alcohol, most commonly Grand Marnier. The base recipes can be as simple as a meringue, cream, and flavorings, just like the mousse glacé but containing more whipped cream. Other versions are made using a sabayon base, whipped cream, and flavorings. Following the literal translation, the soufflé glacé is served in a style to mimic that of the hot soufflé, rising out of a ramekin.

Bombe

Ice cream cakes are a popular item served in upscale pastry shops in the United States and Europe. The name **bombe** translates to "bomb" in English, and it refers to the traditional domed shape of ice cream cakes, also called *entremet glacé*. Baked Alaska would be an example of a bombe. More elaborate versions could contain several frozen components: ice cream, sorbet, coulis, and parfait. It is as much of an art to combine these techniques and balance the flavors of all the recipes inside the bombe, just as much as it is to have the correct balance of sugar to ensure when tempered the consistency of the cake is the same from one layer to the next.

Recipes

Vanilla Ice Cream

Yield: 2 lb 2.9 oz (990 g)
Portions: 34
Portion size: 1 oz (28.35 g)
Yield description: 34 scoops at 1 oz (28.35 g)

Ingredients	U.S.	Metric
Milk	1 lb 1.64 oz	500 g
Heavy Cream	6.17 oz	175 g
Sugar	4.94 oz	140 g
Glucose Powder DE 40	1.13 oz	32 g
Milk Solids Nonfat	1.76 oz	50 g
Ice Cream Stabilizer	0.11 oz	3 g
Egg Yolk	3.17 oz	90 g
Vanilla Bean, split and scraped	1 each	1 each

Procedure

1. Ice cream base process on page 158.

Chocolate Ice Cream (Philadelphia Style)

Yield: 2 lb 3 oz (993 g)
Portions: 35
Portion size: 1 oz (28.35 g)
Yield description: 35 scoops at 1 oz (28.35 g)

Ingredients	U.S.	Metric
Milk	1 lb 7.14 oz	656 g
Milk Solids Nonfat	0.99 oz	28 g
Sugar	1.98 oz	56 g
Inverted Sugar	1.98 oz	56 g
Ice Cream Stabilizer	0.14 oz	4 g
Chocolate 64%	6.77 oz	193 g

Procedure

1. Combine, nonfat milk powder, sugar, and ice cream stabilizer.
2. In a heavy-bottom saucepan, combine milk and inverted sugar.
3. Whisk dry ingredients into milk.
4. Heat to 185°F (85°C), while whisking.
5. Add chocolate and heat again to 189°F (87°C).
6. Emulsify and strain through a chinois and place on an ice bath.
7. Allow to mature for a minimum 6 hours under refrigeration.

Gianduja Gelato

Yield: 2 lb 3.3 oz (1002 g)
Portions: 35
Portion size: 1 oz (28.35 g)
Yield description: 35 scoops at 1 oz (28.35 g)

Ingredients	U.S.	Metric
Milk	1 lb 5.8 oz	618 g
Heavy Cream	2.05 oz	58 g
Sugar	5.5 oz	156 g
Egg Yolks	2.4 oz	68 g
Gianduja Chocolate	3.53 oz	100 g
Ice Cream Stabilizer	0.07 oz	2 g

Procedure

1. Ice cream base process on page 158.
2. After pasteurizing add chocolate.
3. Strain through a chinois and place on an ice bath.
4. Mature for a minimum 6 hours under refrigeration.

Pistachio Gelato

Yield: 2 lb 3 oz (1002 g)
Portions: 35
Portion size: 1 oz (28.35 g)
Yield description: 35 scoops at 1 oz (28.35 g)

Ingredients	U.S.	Metric
Milk	1 lb 3.75 oz	560 g
Cream	3.17 oz	90 g
Sugar	5.64 oz	160 g
Glucose Powder DE 40	1.41 oz	40 g
Egg Yolks	1.76 oz	50 g
Pistachio Paste, unsweetened	3.53 oz	100 g
Ice Cream Stabilizer	0.07 oz	2 g

Procedure

1. Ice cream base process on page 158.
2. Add pistachio paste after pasteurizing.
3. Strain through a chinois and mature for a minimum 6 hours under refrigeration.

Roasted Corn Ice Cream

Yield: 2 lb 3.4 oz (1005 g)

Portions: 35

Portion size: 1 oz (28.35 g)

Yield description: 35 scoops at 1 oz (28.35 g)

Ingredients	U.S.	Metric
Sweet Corn, roasted and scraped	4 oz	113 g
Milk	12 oz	340 g
Heavy Cream	8.4 oz	238 g
Egg Yolks	5 oz	142 g
Sugar	6 oz	170 g
Ice Cream Stabilizer	0.09 oz	2.5 g

Note: The roasted corn can be puréed into the ice cream base to increase the flavor.

Procedure

1. Remove the husk from corn and roast at 425°F (220°C) until the corn begins to gain color.
2. Allow the corn to cool and cut the kernels off the cob. Using the back of a knife scrape the cob to remove the milk.
3. Scale 13 g of the roasted kernels and milk from the cob for the recipe. Reserve the cob for the recipe.
4. Heat milk, cream, half the sugar, corn cobs, and roasted corn kernels and corn milk to a simmer.
5. Cover with plastic wrap and allow to steep overnight in the refrigerator.
6. Strain corn solids from milk and scrape cobs again to remove the milk and cream mixture. Press milk from corn kernels.
7. To finish follow the ice cream base process.

Brown Butter Ice Cream

Yield: 2 lb 2 oz (991 g)

Portions: 34

Portion size: 1 oz (28.35 g)

Yield description: 34 scoops at 1 oz (28.35 g)

Ingredients	U.S.	Metric
Unsalted Butter	6 oz	170 g
Milk	1 lb 1.64 oz	500 g
Heavy Cream	6.17 oz	175 g
Sugar	4.9 oz	140 g
Glucose Powder DE 40	1.13 oz	32 g
Milk Solids Nonfat	1.76 oz	50 g
Ice Cream Stabilizer	0.11 oz	3 g
Egg Yolks	3.17 oz	90 g
Salt	0.04 oz	1 g

Note: The flavor of the brown butter is steeped into the milk and cream.

Procedure

1. Brown butter in a saucepan.
2. Cool slightly; add milk and cream.
3. Steep overnight under refrigeration.
4. Strain off butter and return milk and cream mixture to the pan the butter was browned in.
5. To finish follow the ice cream base process.

Mango Ice Cream

Yield: 2 lb 3.3 oz (1002 g)

Portions: 35

Portion size: 1 oz (28.35 g)

Yield description: 35 scoops at 1 oz (28.35 g)

Ingredients	U.S.	Metric
Milk	11.53 oz	327 g
Heavy Cream	6.07 oz	172 g
Sugar	3.09 oz	87 g
Glucose Powder DE 40	1.41 oz	40 g
Milk Solids Nonfat	1.38 oz	39 g
Ice Cream Stabilizer	0.14 oz	4 g
Mango Purée	8.64 oz	245 g
Passion Fruit Purée	3.1 oz	88 g

Procedure

1. Ice cream base process on page 158.
2. After cooling, blend in purées.
3. Mature for a minimum 6 hours under refrigeration.

Strawberry Ice Cream

Yield: 2 lb 3 oz (1004 g)

Portions: 35

Portion size: 1 oz (28.35 g)

Yield description: 35 scoops at 1 oz (28.35 g)

Ingredients	U.S.	Metric
Milk	1 lb 4.1 oz	570 g
Heavy Cream	2.82 oz	80 g
Sugar	6.35 oz	180 g
Egg Yolks	2.47 oz	70 g
Ice Cream Stabilizer	0.14 oz	4 g
Strawberry Purée	3.53 oz	100 g

Procedure

1. Ice cream base process on page 158.
2. After cooling blend in purée.
3. Mature for a minimum 6 hours under refrigeration.

Pineapple Sherbet

Yield: 2 lb 5 oz (1068 g)

Portions: 37

Portion size: 1 oz (28.35 g)

Yield description: 37 scoops at 1 oz (28.35 g)

Ingredients	U.S.	Metric
Water	4.13 oz	117 g
Sugar	4.44 oz	126 g
Glucose Powder DE 40	1.9 oz	54 g
Ice Cream Stabilizer	0.13 oz	3.6 g
Milk	7.83 oz	222 g
Heavy Cream	1.16 oz	33 g
Pineapple Purée	1 lb 1.78 oz	504 g
Lemon juice	0.32 oz	9 g

Procedure

1. Combine sugar, glucose powder, and stabilizer.
2. Whisk the dry ingredients into to water and heat to 185°F (85°C).
3. Cool syrup on an ice bath.
4. Add syrup to milk, cream, pineapple and lemon purée, emulsify.
5. Allow mixture to mature a minimum 6 hours under refrigeration.

Frozen Yogurt

Yield: 2 lb 2.7 oz (995.7 g)

Portions: 35

Portion size: 1 oz (28.35 g)

Yield description: 35 portions at 1 oz (28.35 g)

Ingredients	U.S.	Metric
Greek Yogurt 2% fat	1 lb 14 oz	860 g
Sugar	1.83 oz	52 g
Glucose Syrup	1.98 oz	56 g
Inverted Sugar	0.92 oz	26 g
Ice Cream Stabilizer	0.06 oz	1.7 g

Procedure

1. Combine sugar and ice cream stabilizer.
2. In a heavy-bottom saucepan, combine yogurt and sugar mixture with a whisk.
3. Add glucose and inverted to saucepan.
4. Heat to 150°F (65°C).
5. Mix with immersion blender.
6. Allow mixture to mature for a minimum 6 hours under refrigeration.

Lemon Mosto Olive Oil Ice Cream

Yield: 2 lb 3 oz (1017.5 g)

Portions: 35

Portion size: 1 oz (28.35 g)

Yield description: 35 scoops at 1 oz (28.35 g)

Ingredients	U.S.	Metric
Milk	1 lb 0.93 oz	480 g
Cream	4.94 oz	140 g
Sugar	4.94 oz	140 g
Egg Yolks	5.64 oz	160 g
Lemon Mosto Olive Oil	3.35 oz	95 g
Ice Cream Stabilizer	0.09 oz	2.5 g

Procedure

1. Ice cream base process on page 158.
2. After cooling the base incorporate the lemon mosto olive oil using an immersion blender. Slowly stream the oil while mixing to emulsify.
3. Allow mixture to mature for a minimum 6 hours under refrigeration.

Vanilla Parfait

Yield: 2 lb 6 oz (1090 g)

Portions: 13

Portion size: 3 oz (85 g)

Yield description: 13 portions at 3 oz (85 g)

Ingredients	U.S.	Metric
Water	2.5 oz	70 g
Sugar	8.8 oz	250 g
Yolks	6.7 oz	190 g
Heavy Cream, whipped to medium peaks	1 lb 6.9 oz	650 g
Vanilla Bean, split and scraped	2 each	2 each

Note: Cook pâte à bombe syrup with vanilla beans; remove before adding sugar to the whipping yolks.

Procedure

1. Combine water, sugar, and vanilla beans in a saucepan.
2. Make a pâte à bombe with the egg yolks and sugar mixture.
3. When pâte à bombe is completely cooled, fold in cream.
4. Place in molds and freeze immediately.

Chocolate Parfait

Yield: 2 lb 7 oz (1116 g)

Portions: 13

Portion size: 3 oz (85 g)

Yield description: 13 portions at 3 oz (85 g)

Ingredients	U.S.	Metric
Water	1.1 oz	30 g
Sugar	4.7 oz	132 g
Egg Yolks	3.2 oz	90 g
Whole Eggs	4.7 oz	132 g
Heavy Cream, whipped to medium peaks	15.9 oz	450 g
Chocolate 63%, melted	11 oz	312 g

Procedure

1. Pâte à bombe mousse method on page 130.
2. Fill molds and freeze immediately.

Banana Mousse Glacé

Yield: 2 lb 10 oz (1207 g)
Portions: 14
Portion size: 3 oz (85 g)
Yield description: 14 portions at 3 oz (85 g)

Ingredients	U.S.	Metric
Heavy Cream, whipped to soft peaks	14.8 oz	420 g
Egg White	6.8 oz	192 g
Sugar	6.8 oz	192 g
Water	2.8 oz	80 g
Banana Purée	14.1 oz	400 g
Lime Zest	0.1 oz	3 g

Procedure

1. Make an Italian meringue with sugar, water, and egg whites (procedure on page 253).
2. Fold banana purée into meringue.
3. Fold cream and lime zest into meringue mixture.
4. Fill mold and freeze immediately.

Cappuccino Semifreddo

Yield: 2 lb 9 oz (1150 g)
Portions: 13
Portion size: 3 oz (85 g)
Yield description: 13 portions at 3 oz (85 g)

Ingredients	U.S.	Metric
Semifreddo Pastry Cream		
Milk	7.9 oz	224 g
Sugar	2.2 oz	63 g
Egg Yolks	0.74 oz	21 g
Eggs	0.74 oz	21 g
Regular Clear Gel	0.74 oz	21 g
Vanilla Bean, split and scraped	1 each	1 each
Cappuccino Semifreddo		
Pastry Cream	12.3 oz	350 g
Egg Whites	1.8 oz	50 g
Sugar	3.5 oz	100 g
Water	0.9 oz	25 g
Coffee Extract	3.5 oz	100 g
Coffee Liquor	1.8 oz	50 g
Heavy Cream, whipped to medium peaks	1 lb 1.6 oz	500 g

Procedure

1. Prepare the Semifreddo Pastry Cream using the pastry cream method on page 123.
2. Make an Italian meringue with sugar, water, and egg whites.
3. Mix pastry cream with a whisk to loosen consistency; add coffee extract.
4. Fold whipped cream into pastry cream.
5. Fold meringue into pastry cream mixture.
6. Fill molds and freeze immediately.

Soufflé Glacé

Yield: 2 lb 9 oz (1177 g)

Portions: 13

Portion size: 3 oz (85 g)

Yield description: 13 portions at 3 oz (85 g)

Ingredients	U.S.	Metric
Whole Eggs	6.3 oz	180 g
Egg Yolks	5.1 oz	145 g
Sugar	10.6 oz	300 g
Heavy Cream, whipped to medium stiff peaks	14.8 oz	420 g
Candied Orange Peel (p. 312), chopped fine	2.5 oz	72 g
Grand Marnier	2.1 oz	60 g

Procedure

1. Rinse candied peel in cold water and macerate in Grand Marnier overnight.
2. Combine eggs, egg yolks, and sugar; whisk over a bain marie.
3. Cook to 160°F (70°C).
4. Place in a mixer with a whisk and mix on high until cooled completely.
5. Fold in cream, zest, and remaining Grand Marnier.
6. Mold and freeze immediately.

Lemon Sorbet

Yield: 2 lb 2 oz (983 g)

Portions: 34

Portion size: 1 oz (28.35 g)

Yield description: 34 scoops at 1 oz (28.35 g)

Ingredients	U.S.	Metric
Lemon Purée	8.82 oz	250 g
Water	15.87 oz	450 g
Sugar	7.05 oz	200 g
Glucose Powder DE 40	1.41 oz	40 g
Trimoline	0.71 oz	20 g
Milk Solids Nonfat	0.71 oz	20 g
Sorbet Stabilizer	0.11 oz	3 g

Procedure

1. Sorbet method on page 162.

Raspberry Sorbet

Yield: 2 lb 6 oz (1078 g)

Portions: 38

Portion size: 1 oz (28.35 g)

Yield description: 38 scoops at 1 oz (28.35 g)

Ingredients	U.S.	Metric
Raspberry Purée	1 lb 5.16 oz	600 g
Sugar	5.08 oz	144 g
Glucose Powder DE 40	1.27 oz	36 g
Sorbet Stabilizer	0.04 oz	1.2 g
Water	10.48 oz	297 g

Procedure

1. Sorbet method on page 162.

Strawberry Sorbet

Yield: 2 lb 4 oz (1038 g)

Portions: 36

Portion size: 1 oz (28.35 g)

Yield description: 36 scoops at 1 oz (28.35 g)

Ingredients	U.S.	Metric
Strawberry Purée	1 lb 6.93 oz	650 g
Sugar	4.59 oz	130 g
Glucose Powder DE 40	1.16 oz	33 g
Sorbet Stabilizer	0.05 oz	1.3 g
Water	7.9 oz	224 g

Procedure

1. Sorbet method on page 162.

Green Apple Sorbet

Yield: 2 lb 4 oz (1030 g)

Portions: 36

Portion size: 1 oz (28 g)

Yield description: 36 scoops at 1 oz (28 g)

Ingredients	U.S.	Metric
Green Apple Purée	1 lb 5.16 oz	600 g
Sugar	4.66 oz	132 g
Glucose Powder DE 40	1.09 oz	30 g
Sorbet Stabilizer	0.04 oz	1.2 g
Water	9.42 oz	267 g

Procedure

1. Sorbet method on page 162.

Passion Fruit Sorbet

Yield: 2 lb 3.6 oz (1010 g)

Portions: 35

Portion size: 1 oz (28.35 g)

Yield description: 35 scoops at 1 oz (28.35 g)

Ingredients	U.S.	Metric
Passion Fruit Purée	14.28 oz	405 g
Sugar	7.44 oz	211 g
Glucose Powder DE 40	1.86 oz	53 g
Sorbet Stabilizer	0.06 oz	1.6 g
Water	11.99 oz	340 g

Procedure

1. Sorbet method on page 162.

Mango Sorbet

Yield: 2 lb 3 oz (996 g)

Portions: 35

Portion size: 1 oz (28.35 g)

Yield description: 35 scoops at 1 oz (28.35 g)

Ingredients	U.S.	Metric
Mango Purée	1 lb 1.63 oz	500 g
Sugar	7.05 oz	200 g
Glucose Powder DE 40	1.76 oz	50 g
Sorbet Stabilizer	0.04 oz	1 g
Water	8.64 oz	245 g

Procedure

1. Sorbet method on page 162.

Coconut Sorbet

Yield: 2 lb 3.2 oz (999.6 g)

Portions: 35

Portion size: 1 oz (28.35 g)

Yield description: 35 scoops at 1 oz (28.35 g)

Ingredients	U.S.	Metric
Coconut Purée	14.28 oz	405 g
Sugar	6.35 oz	180 g
Glucose Powder DE 40	1.76 oz	50 g
Sorbet Stabilizer	0.06 oz	1.6 g
Water	12.8 oz	363 g

Procedure

1. Sorbet method on page 162.

Apricot Sorbet

Yield: 2 lb 3 oz (993 g)

Portions: 35

Portion size: 1 oz (28.35 g)

Yield description: 35 scoops at 1 oz (28.35 g)

Ingredients	U.S.	Metric
Apricot Purée	1 lb 4.6 oz	585 g
Sugar	4.13 oz	117 g
Glucose Powder DE 40	1.02 oz	29 g
Sorbet Stabilize	0.04 oz	1.2 g
Water	9.21 oz	261 g

Procedure

1. Sorbet method on page 162.

Roasted Banana Sorbet

Yield: 2 lb 6 oz (1096 g)

Portions: 39

Portion size: 1 oz (28.35 g)

Yield description: 39 scoops at 1 oz (28.35 g)

Ingredients	U.S.	Metric
Roasted Banana Purée		
Bananas, ripe	2 lb 3.2 oz	1000 g
Cinnamon Sticks	2 each	2 each
Star Anise	2 each	2 each
Vanilla Bean, used	4 each	4 each
Roasted Banana Sorbet		
Roasted Banana Purée	1 lb 1.64 oz	500 g
Sugar	6.35 oz	180 g
Glucose Powder DE 40	1.59 oz	45 g
Sorbet Stabilizer	0.04 oz	1 g
Water	13.05 oz	370 g

Procedure

1. Break spices into pieces and stud bananas through the skin.

2. Roast on a paper-lined sheet pan at 375°F (190°C) until peels become dark brown, almost black.

3. Cool and remove peels and spices, purée.

4. Sorbet method on page 162.

Cherry Sorbet

Yield: 2 lb 4 oz (1046 g)

Portions: 36

Portion size: 1 oz (28.35 g)

Yield description: 36 scoops at 1 oz (28.35 g)

Ingredients	U.S.	Metric
Cherry Purée	1 lb 8.69 oz	700 g
Sugar	6.91 oz	196 g
Glucose Powder DE 40	1.73 oz	49 g
Sorbet Stabilizer	0.02 oz	0.7 g
Water	3.56 oz	101 g

Procedure

1. Sorbet method on page 162.

Tea Granita

Yield: 2 lb 5 oz (1058 g)

Portions: 18

Portion size: 2 oz (56 oz)

Yield description: 18 servings at 2 oz (56 oz)

Ingredients	U.S.	Metric
Water	1 lb 13.6 oz	840 g
Tea	0.3 oz	8.5 g
Sugar	6.3 oz	180 g
Lemon Juice	1.1 oz	30 g

Procedure

1. Combine water, sugar, lemon, and tea.
2. Heat to a simmer and allow to steep for 15 minutes.
3. Strain and cool.
4. Place in freezer and stir every 30 minutes until frozen.

Cherry Granita

Yield: 2 lb 1 oz (960 g)

Portions: 16

Portion size: 2 oz (56 oz)

Yield description: 16 servings at 2 oz (56 oz)

Ingredients	U.S.	Metric
Sour Cherry Purée	1 lb 0.9 oz	480 g
White Wine	8.5 oz	240 g
Honey	4.2 oz	120 g
Sugar	4.2 oz	120 g

Procedure

1. Warm 25% of the puree with the sugar to dissolve the sugar.
2. Follow the Granita method on page 165 to finish.

Apple Cider Granita

Yield: 2 lb 3 oz (1010 g)
Portions: 17
Portion size: 2 oz (56 g)
Yield description: 17 servings at 2 oz (56 g)

Ingredients	U.S.	Metric
Water	6.3 oz	180 g
Sugar	4.2 oz	120 g
Apple Cider	1 lb 8.7 oz	700 g
Calvados	0.35 oz	10 g

Procedure

1. Granita method on page 165.

Lemon Granita

Yield: 2 lb 6 oz (1100 g)
Portions: 19
Portion size: 2 oz (56 g)
Yield Description: 19 servings at 2 oz (56 g)

Ingredients	U.S.	Metric
Water	1 lb 10.5 oz	750 g
Sugar	3.5 oz	100 g
Lemon Juice	8.8 oz	250 g

Procedure

1. Granita method on page 165.

Summary

Formulating frozen desserts is no easy task. However, offering customized products with great flavor and textures will set the establishment apart from the rest. Understanding the processes and balance of the recipes is critical to producing an excellent product. Offering a wide variety of frozen desserts from still frozen to churned will showcase the knowledge of the pastry chef. Frozen desserts give us a way to serve a little nostalgia while helping to create new experiences.

Troubleshooting for Frozen Desserts

Issue	Cause/Solution
Cooked ice cream base is lumpy and curdled.	Thermometer is not correct; recalibrate thermometer and cook over lower heat.
Ice cream has a coarse texture when extracted from machine.	Product was overchurned, and fat has separated from the mix.
Ice cream has a mousse like airy texture.	Too much fat is in the recipe.
Ice cream melts too quickly.	1. Base was not cooked properly. 2. Not enough stabilizer. 3. Not enough total solids. 4. Freezer temperature is not low enough.
Ice cream/sorbet is too hard.	1. Freezer temperature is too low. 2. Not enough sugar/solids in the recipe.
Ice cream/sorbet Is icy.	1. Freezer temperature fluctuates. 2. Ice cream machine does not freeze fast enough or turn fast enough. 3. There is not enough sugar in the recipe.
Ice cream/sorbet has a gummy texture.	Too much stabilizer.
Frozen sorbet has a syrupy liquid in the bottom of the container.	Too much sugar; the water remains frozen and the sugar does not.

Key Terms

Churned
Still frozen
Overrun
Free water
Sweetening power (SP)
Antifreezing power (AFP)

Dextrose equivalent
Invert sugar
Brix
Nappe
Pasteurization
High temperature/Short time (HTST)

Parfait
Mousse glacé
Semifreddo
Soufflé glacé
Bombe

Questions for Review

1. Describe the process for cooking an ice cream base.
2. Explain the difference between dextrose and powdered glucose.
3. What are the benefits of using stabilizers and emulsifiers in frozen desserts?
4. Why is it important to know the different sweetening powers of sugars?
5. Why is air a critical ingredient in the production of frozen desserts?

CHAPTER 7

Cake Mixing and Baking

The Primrose Path by Ogden Nash goes so far as to say, ". . . piece of cake." This implies that cake is easy to make and conjures pleasant thoughts, and part of this is true. All throughout our lives, cake is served at celebrations. It is the centerpiece at weddings and birthdays. Oftentimes, the focus of the cake is the look—flavor and texture must be created and designed to enhance the exterior. Proficiency in cake mixing and baking will make certain the cake tastes as good as it looks.

LEARNING OBJECTIVES

After reading this chapter, you should be able to:

1. **Understand** the function of ingredients in cakes.
2. **Produce** a variety of high-fat and low-fat cakes.
3. **Demonstrate** the creaming and egg foam methods.
4. **Identify** cake defects and how to resolve them.
5. **Determine** the doneness of cakes.

Introduction to Cakes

There are many varieties of cakes; some are light while others can be dense and chewy. No matter what the final texture is, common ingredients are used throughout the production of cakes: eggs, flour, sugar, leaveners, and fats. Cakes are also used in many finished products in the pastry kitchen. This chapter will help provide a thorough understanding of ingredient functions, mixing methods, and proper baking skills that the pastry chef needs to develop the proper texture when baking cakes.

Ingredients

Cakes can be made from as few as four ingredients: fat, sugar, flour, and eggs. While others may contain 12 or more ingredients, this does not mean it will be a better cake—sometimes simple is better. The key is to understand how the ingredients function in the recipe, and know what the function of the cake is in the pastry. In some applications, the cake is a thin layer on the bottom of a dessert so it can be easily transferred without sticking. Other instances may require a tender layer inserted into an entremet that can be cut cleanly for service and provide texture. Knowledge of cake ingredients will help to make the proper selection.

Fats

Cakes utilize many different fats, including butter, shortening, high-ratio shortening, liquid shortenings, and oil. One of the main functions of the fats is to tenderize the cake by shortening the gluten and providing moisture. Fats are responsible for incorporating air, creating the smooth fluffy texture desired in high-fat cakes. Flavor can also be impacted by the type of fat used; for example, butter will provide excellent flavor (but carries a higher price).

When scaling a recipe, be sure to use the fat required. While butter and shortening can be easily exchanged, the flavor and feel of the cake will be different. Shortenings melt at 120°F (49°C), and since this is higher than body temperature, they can coat the mouth with fat. High-ratio shortening is typically used in cakes that contain a higher quantity of sugar and liquids in relation to the flour. The **two-stage method** commonly uses high-ratio shortening to assist in the emulsification of the additional ingredients. **Liquid shortenings** (Fluid Flex, Jilk, etc.) are specifically designed for cake production. These products contain additional emulsifiers and produce a light, fluffy cake. The recipes were designed to use these fats, and mixing times and speeds must be observed. Regardless of personal preferences, the fat specified in a recipe is the fat that must be used.

Sugars

There are many different forms of sugars available, and each one has its own individual properties. Sugars add sweetness, color, and moisture to the cake and help with maintaining a tender final product. The benefits of sugar begin during the mixing stage.

In the **creaming method**, the crystalline structure of the sugar helps to create air cells in the fat. As the fat and granulated sugar are mixed together, the grains cut the fat and create air cells. Up to 25% of the leavening in a cake can come from the properly formed air cells. During the mixing of foamed cakes, sugars begin to denature the eggs, ensuring that a stable foam is formed. Sugars also increase the temperature that egg proteins coagulate. This increase allows the cake additional time to rise, adding to the light texture of the cake.

The most commonly used sugar in the production of cakes is granulated sugar. Corn syrup, glucose syrup, Trimoline, and honey are used in some recipes along with or in place of granulated sugar. All sugars are **hygroscopic**; they have the ability to attract and hold water during the baking process and continue to attract moisture after baking. **Inverted sugars** have increased hydroscopicity, which prevents the cake from becoming dry. Moisture is lost during the baking process—keeping more moisture in the cake will help to extend shelf life. Increased shelf life is not the only advantage; absorbing water means that it is not available to the flour. This reduces the flour's ability to form gluten.

When substituting sugars, refer to the Power of Sugar table on page 150 in Chapter 6 to determine the sweetening power of the different sugars. It is not recommended to substitute liquid sweeteners for dry sweeteners, as this will change the balance of the recipe.

Flours (Driers)

Flours, or driers, are any ingredients added to a recipe that absorb water. A wide range of ingredients are covered under this group: flours, cocoa powder, corn starch, potato starch, milk powder, and nut flours. This is a wide range of ingredients; careful consideration must go into substituting one ingredient for another. Each flour has a different protein content and particle size. Smaller particles have increased surface area. Flours aid in the absorption of liquids and creating the final crumb texture of the cake. Higher-protein flours are not typically used in the production of cakes, as they tend to create a tough final product.

In most cases, flours are added toward the end of the mixing process to absorb liquids and prevent developing gluten. It is the goal of cake making to control the amount of gluten developed; while some gluten is needed it is the starch that will provide structure to the cake. During the baking process, as temperatures approach 120 to 140°F (50 to 60°C), starches begin to swell. Water absorption continues until the starches begin to set at 170°F (70°C). At this point, the shape of the cake will not change as the starches coagulate.

In recent years, there has been an increase in people diagnosed with **celiac disease**, which is an intolerance to gluten. In addition, others are choosing to live gluten free. The combination of these has increased the need and desire for products that are gluten free. There are commercially available flour replacers. However, they can easily be made with starches, nut flours, and rice flours. Some adjustment to the fat and sugars in the recipe may be needed to achieve the proper texture. Chapter 4 includes a recipe for a flour replacer that is flexible and works in many recipes.

Eggs

The role of eggs in cakes is multifaceted—color, flavor, emulsifier, structure, or leavener can all be achieved with an egg. The type of cake and recipe determine which part of the egg is used and how the egg is prepared for the cake. Creamed cakes normally call for whole eggs, while foamed cakes can use whole eggs, whites, yolks, or any combination of these.

A cake is an emulsion of fat and water. Creamed cakes start with fat and sugar. In the next step, eggs are added to the fat mixture, creating an emulsion. Eggs are mostly water, and the fat surrounds the water. When the eggs are added, air cells are formed in the emulsion that expand during baking. If this water-in-fat emulsion is broken, the water surrounds the fat. A broken emulsion will reduce the final volume and the cake will have a greasy feel to the touch. Warming the eggs slightly will help prevent this from happening. When incorporating eggs into a recipe, it is important to warm the eggs to 72°F (22°C).

Warmed eggs will also produce a more stable foam for low-fat cakes. In low-fat cakes, the air cells incorporated during the mixing process perform all of the leavening. Developing the proper structure in the egg foam is done slowly, creating small stable bubbles.

The process of making a genoise starts with whipping eggs and sugar. Start by whipping the eggs on a lower speed to begin denaturing the proteins. Similar to mixing bread, the proteins of an egg are tightly coiled and need to be relaxed and uncoil. Once the egg proteins transition into long strands, they are capable of trapping more air, which results in a lighter texture. Once the mixture has reached **ribbon stage**, mix at a lower speed to further stabilize the mixture. This will also remove any large bubbles that may have formed. The stability of the foam is critical in developing the final texture and volume in the cake.

Leaveners

In high-fat cakes, an extra boost of leavening is needed to produce a light cake. This is achieved through the use of chemical **leaveners**. Baking soda and baking powder are the most common leaveners for cakes. Both of these products release carbon dioxide into the cake mix, but how they do it is different.

Baking soda reacts with acids in the recipe to release carbon dioxide—heat is not needed to produce the reaction. Once the recipe is combined, the acid and baking soda start a chemical reaction that cannot be stopped. The carbon dioxide is released, and because there is not an endless supply, the product must be baked immediately. Proper mise en place is important when working with baking soda leavened products to maximize the volume of these products.

The result of combining baking soda with a dry acid is baking powder. Baking powder is available in several forms, with double acting being most common. Products made with double-acting baking powder require heat to activate the leavening. A small amount of carbon dioxide is produced when mixed; the remainder is released during the baking process. This reduces the need to quickly pan and bake the cakes, while still providing the same leavening.

Substitution of baking soda and baking powder at the same quantities will not yield the same results. When substituting baking powder for baking soda, increase the quantity by three. If the recipe originally calls for 1 oz (28 g) baking soda, the correct amount of baking powder would be 3 oz (84 g). When replacing baking powder with baking soda, combine 2 parts cream of tartar with 1 part baking soda. At this point, scale the same quantity of the homemade baking powder, as specified in the recipe.

Main Categories

Cakes can be broken down into two main categories: high fat and low fat. Cakes that are higher in fat are the preferred cake for the American palate. The high percentage of fat and sugar in these cakes creates a soft texture and sweet flavor. In some instances, high-fat cakes are too tender for slicing into thin layers—this is where low-fat cakes come in. Low-fat cakes are a more durable and resilient cake and can be sliced thin. Traditionally, low-fat cakes are brushed with flavored syrups to sweeten and add moisture.

There are many decisions to make when selecting a cake for particular job. While a low-fat cake can be sliced thin and layered, the same can be done with a high-fat cake such as devil's food cake. The high fat content of the devil's food cake may not make it ideal for slicing into thin layers, but it is possible. Deciding which cake is the correct selection should not be an issue of what is easier to work with but rather, which tastes best with the flavor combinations. You also must consider if the cake will hold up to its intended use.

Guidelines

Considering that there is a wide variety of cakes, with basic mixing methods, here are some key points to remember when making cakes:

1. The batter should be a smooth, **homogenous** mixture. Proper **emulsification** and dry ingredient distribution will help to ensure the proper final texture.

2. When mixing, all ingredients should be 72°F (22°C). At this temperature, eggs are more stable, develop more volume, and emulsify better with fats. One cold ingredient added to the rest of the ingredients will cool the recipe down and may make it difficult to mix together and achieve the correct volume.

3. Proper mise en place of ingredients, equipment and oven temperature must be done at the start of the process. Refer to individual recipes for pan preparation and oven temperature. Some cakes need to go directly into the oven; waiting for an oven to come to temperature will reduce the final volume of the cakes.

4. Moving cakes too soon in the baking process may cause the cake to collapse. There is no need to move a baking cake unless it needs to be turned to develop even color. Moving a cake too early in the baking process may disturb the proteins and starches that have not baked and cause the cake to collapse.

5. Thin cakes need to be baked at higher temperatures. Baking these cakes at low temperatures increases the moisture loss, resulting in a dry cake. Larger cakes bake at lower temperatures, allowing the cake to bake to the center while properly coloring the outside of the cake.

6. When testing for doneness, high-fat cakes pull away from the sides of the pans. Sponge cakes should feel soft and push back against the hand when gently pressed. Cake testers that remove cleanly from the cake can be used, although sight and touch are the preferred

methods. Testing of thin cakes is done by carefully lifting the parchment paper with an off-set pallet knife; browning on the bottom of the cake is an indication of doneness.

7. Properly baked cakes need to remain on cooling racks to completely cool. Wrapping warm cakes traps too much moisture and causes a sticky cake.

High-Fat Cake

High-fat cakes provide a soft texture that many U.S. customers think of when they think of cake. The texture of a high-fat cake may bring back memories of birthday celebrations or weddings. These cakes are characterized as having a soft texture and being tender, sweet, moist, and flavorful. Primarily, high-fat cakes are mixed using the creaming method, although some procedures use the whip.

Creaming Method

1. Prepare pans: Grease pan bottoms and sides. Line the bottom of the pan with parchment paper and lightly grease the paper.
2. Scale ingredients and allow them to warm to 72°F (22°C).
3. Mix fat and sugar with a paddle attachment until light and fluffy at medium high speed.
4. Add the eggs in three additions. Between each addition, scrape the bowl and paddle thoroughly.
5. Add the sifted dry ingredients in four parts, alternating with the wet ingredients in three parts. Be sure to end with the last addition of dry ingredients. Alternating between wet and dry ingredients allows the flour to absorb the additional quantity of wet ingredients, while not overdeveloping the gluten.

Two-Stage Method

1. Prepare pans: Grease pan bottoms and sides. Line the bottom of the pan with parchment paper and lightly grease the paper.
2. Scale ingredients and allow them to warm to 72°F (22°C).
3. Sift flour, leaveners, and salt, and combine with emulsified shortening.
4. Mix with a paddle attachment 2 minutes on low speed, and scrape.
5. Mix for 2 more minutes on low speed.
6. Add the sugar and mix for 4 minutes on low speed.
7. Combine remaining liquid ingredients in three additions, scraping the bowl between additions. This stage mixes for a total of 5 minutes.

Liquid Shortenings

1. Prepare pans: Grease pan bottoms and sides. Line the bottom of the pan with parchment paper and lightly grease the paper. Preheat oven to 325°F (165°C).
2. Scale ingredients and allow them to warm to 72°F (22°C).
3. Place wet ingredients in bowl with whip and add sifted dry ingredients.
4. Mix to combine and scrape bowl and attachments.
5. Whip on high for 4 minutes and scrape.
6. Continue mixing for 3 minutes on medium.

Low-Fat Cakes

Low-fat cakes (for example, cakes prepared using the **sponge method**, the **separation foam method**, the **jaconde method**, the **chiffon method**, or the **angel food method**) utilize egg foam to leaven the cake and create the final texture. The high percentage of eggs in these cakes results in a final product that is drier and firmer than a high-fat cake. While this may be viewed as a negative, since most people are used to the soft, moist high-fat cakes, it is actually a benefit and allows the cake to be used in different ways. Egg-foam-based cakes also have an eggy flavor associated with them when eaten alone. Since the cake is drier, additional flavoring can be added in the form of flavored syrups. Alcohol, fruit, and even aromatic herbs can be added to the simple syrup to infuse another layer of flavor into the cake. The texture of the cake makes it ideal for slicing thin layers to use as a base for a dessert, an internal layer and even a decorative sponge to wrap around the outside of a cake.

When preparing low-fat cakes, all preparations must be done before mixing begins. Due to the fact that these cakes do not contain chemical leaveners, they must be mixed, panned, and baked immediately to obtain the correct volume. Any delays between the stages will result in lost volume and dense cakes.

When preparing pans, take care to not grease the sides of the pans. Low-fat cakes are very fragile during the baking and cooling stages. As the cake bakes and rises, it sticks to the sides of the pan. Sticking to the side provides support to the delicate cake structure. Many low-fat cakes are turned upside down during cooling to allow the cake to hang in the pan. Additional moisture evaporates, and sugars and fats become solids as the cake cools and give the cake structure. Greasing the sides of the pan would cause the cake to fall out of the pan and collapse under its own weight.

Sponge Method

1. Prepare pans by lining with parchment paper; a small amount of fat may be used to prevent the paper from moving in the bottom of the pan.
2. Sift dry ingredients and begin melting butter.
3. Combine eggs and sugar; warm over a bain marie to 110 to 120°F (43 to 50°C) while stirring constantly.
4. Transfer warmed egg mixture to stand mixer and mix on high for 7 minutes.
5. Reduce speed to medium for 3 minutes.
6. Whip on speed one for 1 minute.
7. Remove from mixer and fold in dry ingredients in four additions.
8. Add a small amount of the batter to the hot melted butter; mix with a whisk to emulsify.
9. Fold the butter mixture into the cake batter.
10. Fill cake pans three-fourths of the way and bake immediately.

Note: When adding butter to the cake batter, it must be hot. The eggs cool during whipping, and the remaining ingredients are room temperature; this is enough to cool the butter too quickly. If the butter is not hot, it will not be evenly distributed inside the batter and may cause the cake to have a greasy feel.

Note also: Combining the butter with some of the cake batter and emulsifying prevents the butter from sinking to the bottom of the mixing bowl. Additional folding is necessary if the butter is not added properly, resulting in lost volume.

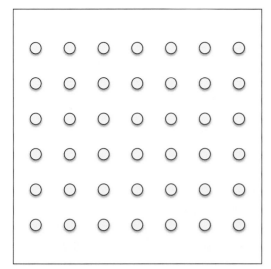

FIGURE 7.1 Butter properly distributed in cake batter: Melting the butter completely will properly distribute the butter evenly through the cake batter.

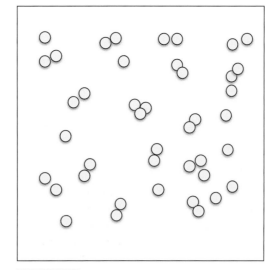

FIGURE 7.2 Butter not properly incorporated in cake batter: Butter that is not heated enough will cool quickly and become solid. This can lead to poor cake structure and a greasy cake.

Separation Foam

1. Prepare pans by lining with parchment paper; a small amount of fat may be used to prevent the paper from moving in the bottom of the pan.
2. Sift dry ingredients and begin melting butter.
3. Whip egg yolks and sugar on high speed to ribbon stage, approximately 10 minutes.
4. Make a common meringue with remaining sugar and egg whites.
5. Fold meringue into yolk mixture in three additions.
6. Fold in sifted dry ingredients in four additions.
7. Add a small amount of the batter to the hot melted butter; mix with a whisk to emulsify.
8. Fold the butter mixture into the cake batter.
9. Fill cake pans three-fourths of the way and bake immediately.

Note: Cakes made using the separation foaming method have increased volume and flexibility over the sponge method. The egg whites are allowed to reach maximum volume due to whipping without the yolk.

Jaconde Method

1. Prepare sheet pans by lining with silpat.
2. Scale ingredients and allow them to warm to 72°F (22°C).
3. Combine eggs, powdered sugar, flour, and almond flour, and whip on high speed for 10 minutes.
4. Make a common meringue with sugar and egg whites.
5. Fold meringue into egg mixture.
6. Add a small amount of the batter to the hot melted butter; mix with a whisk to emulsify.
7. Fold the butter mixture into the cake batter.
8. Spread into prepared cake pans and bake immediately.

FIGURE 7.3 Properly whipped meringue (left) and overwhipped meringue (right)

Chiffon Method

1. Prepare pans by lining with parchment paper.
2. Scale ingredients and allow them to warm to 72°F (22°C).
3. Sift flour, baking powder, salt, and half the sugar.
4. Combine oil, egg yolks, water, and flavorings; add the sifted dry ingredients and mix until smooth.
5. Make a common meringue with egg whites and remaining sugar.
6. Fold meringue into flour mixture in three additions.
7. Pan and bake immediately.

Angel Food Method

1. Scale ingredients and allow them to warm to 72°F (22°C).
2. Sift flour, salt, and first quantity of sugar.
3. Combine cream of tartar and a small amount of the second sugar with egg white; mix on low for 3 minutes to break down egg whites.
4. Turn the mixer speed up; add the remaining sugar when the egg whites have increased four times the original volume.
5. Continue whipping at medium high until whites become the consistency of shaving cream.
6. Fold dry ingredients in four additions.
7. Pan and bake immediately.

Troubleshooting for Cakes

Issue	Cause/Solution
Butter curdles during mixing.	1. Ingredients are too cold. Ingredients warmed to room temperature will incorporate better. 2. Liquids added too quickly. Add liquids more slowly.
Cake crust is too dark.	1. Oven temperature was too high. Reduce oven temperature. 2. Cake baked for too long of a time. Reduce baking time. 3. Too much sugar in the recipe. Check that all ingredients are scaled accurately.
Crust color is too light.	1. Oven temperature is too low. Increase oven temperature. 2. Cake did not bake long enough. Increase baking time.
Cake top cracks during baking.	Oven temperature was too high. Reduce oven temperature.
Cake is heavy.	1. Oven temperature was not high enough. Increase oven temperature 2. There was not enough leavener. Check that all ingredients are scaled accurately. 3. Cake was improperly mixed. Review mixing procedure.
Irregular crumb, large holes are apparent.	Cake is overmixed. Reduce mixing time.
Cake collapses while baking or cooling.	1. May have been moved before structure was set. Do not move the cake during the initial stages of baking. 2. There was too much chemical leavener. Check that all ingredients are scaled accurately.
Cake has poor flavor.	1. Check quality of ingredients. Make sure you are using good ingredients and they are scaled accurately. 2. Improper formula. Check formula if increasing the yield to make sure all ingredients are converted accurately.
Cake has uneven shape.	1. The oven is not level. Check if oven or racks are level. 2. Batter was not spread evenly. Make sure batter is spread evenly before baking. 3. Improperly distributed leavener. Sift the leavener(s) with the dry ingredients to evenly disperse through the final recipe.

Recipes

Yellow Cake (Liquid Shortening)

Yield: 5 lb (2264 g)

Portions: 2

Portion size: One 10-in. cake

Yield description: Two 10-in. cakes

Ingredients	U.S.	Metric	%
Sugar	1 lb 4.5 oz	580 g	117.1
Cake Flour	1 lb 1.5 oz	495 g	100
Baking Powder	0.75 oz	21 g	4.3
Salt	0.5 oz	14 g	2.8
Whole Eggs	1 lb 8 oz	680 g	137.3
Milk	7.5 oz	212 g	42.8
Liquid Shortening	9 oz	255 g	51.5
Vanilla Paste	0.25 oz	7 g	1.4

Procedure

1. Combine all ingredients in a mixer with whip attachment, and scrape bowl.
2. Whip on high for 4 minutes; scrape bowl.
3. Whip on medium for 3 minutes; scrape bowl.
4. Place the batter into two prepared 10-in. cake pans.
5. Bake at 325°F (160°C) for 25 to 30 minutes.

Chocolate Cake (Liquid Shortening)

Yield: 4 lb 12 oz (2179 g)

Portions: 2

Portion size: One 10-in. cake

Yield description: Two 10-in. cakes

Ingredients	U.S.	Metric	%
Sugar	1 lb 2.75 oz	531 g	144.2
Cake Flour	13 oz	369 g	100
Baking Powder	0.9 oz	25.5 g	6.9
Salt	0.38 oz	10.7 g	2.9
Whole Eggs	1 lb 8 oz	680 g	184.6
Milk	7.5 oz	213 g	57.7
Liquid Shortening	9.4 oz	266 g	72.3
Cocoa Powder	2.8 oz	79 g	21.5
Baking Soda	0.2 oz	5.6 g	1.5

Procedure

1. Combine all ingredients in a mixer with whip attachment, and scrape bowl.
2. Whip on high for 4 minutes; scrape bowl.
3. Whip on medium for 3 minutes; scrape bowl.
4. Place the batter into two prepared 10-in. cake pans.
5. Bake at 325°F (160°C) for 25 to 30 minutes.

High Ratio Cake

Yield: 4 lb 4 oz (1955 g)
Portions: 2
Portion size: One 10-in. cake
Yield description: Two 10-in. cakes

Ingredients	U.S.	Metric	%
Sugar	1 lb 3.9 oz	565 g	100
Salt	0.5 oz	15 g	2.7
High-Ratio Shortening	9.5 oz	270 g	47.8
Baking Powder	1.1 oz	30 g	5.3
Cake Flour	1 lb 3.9 oz	565 g	100
Milk	8.1 oz	230 g	40.7
Egg Yolks	1.9 oz	55 g	9.7
Eggs	7.9 oz	225 g	39.8

Procedure

1. Combine and sift dry ingredients.
2. Combine whole eggs, egg whites, and milk.
3. With the paddle attachment, combine the shortening, dry ingredients, and one-third of milk and egg mixture for 4 minutes on medium speed. At the end of the mixing time, scrape the bowl and paddle.
4. Add another third of the milk and egg mixture; mix for two minutes on medium speed. Scrape well.
5. Add the remaining milk and egg mixture; continue mixing for 2 more minutes.
6. Place the batter into two prepared 10-in. cake pans.
7. Bake at 350°F (180°C) 25 to 30 minutes.

Devil's Food Cake

Yield: 4 lb 1 oz (1865 g)
Portions: 2
Portion size: One 10-in. cake
Yield description: Two 10-in. cakes

Ingredients	U.S.	Metric	%
Cocoa Powder	2.9 oz	82 g	23.4
Boiling Water	12.5 oz	354 g	101.1
Whole Eggs	7.1 oz	200 g	57.1
Vanilla Paste	0.4 oz	12 g	3.4
Cake Flour	12.3 oz	350 g	100
Sugar	15.8 oz	450 g	128.6
Baking Soda	0.2 oz	5 g	1.4
Salt	0.2 oz	7 g	2
Butter, softened	12 oz	340 g	97.1
Bittersweet Chocolate 64%	2.3 oz	65 g	18.8

Procedure

1. Bring water to a boil.
2. Whisk water into cocoa powder and allow to cool.
3. Combine eggs and 3 oz (85 g) of cocoa powder mixture.
4. In a mixing bowl fitted with a paddle attachment, combine remaining dry ingredients and remaining cocoa powder mixture; mix until combined.
5. Add butter.
6. Mix on medium speed for 90 seconds.
7. Gradually add egg and cocoa powder mixture, scraping between additions.
8. Add melted chocolate.
9. Mix on medium for 1 minute.
10. Place the batter into two prepared 10-in. cake pans.
11. Bake at 350°F (180°C) for 35 minutes.

Carrot Cake

Yield: 7 lb 2 oz (3257 g)
Portions: 2
Portion size: One 10-in. cake
Yield description: Two 10-in. cakes

Ingredients	U.S.	Metric	%
Carrots, peeled, finely grated	1 lb 15 oz	880 g	295.3
Salt	0.5 oz	14 g	4.7
Brown Sugar	1 lb 5 oz	595 g	2
Cinnamon	0.16 oz	4.5 g	1.5
Egg Yolks	7.2 oz	205 g	68.8
Baking Powder	0.3 oz	8.5 g	2.9
Vegetable Oil	1 lb 3.5 oz	553 g	185.6
Walnuts, toasted and chopped	10.5 oz	298 g	100
Baking Soda	0.65 oz	18.4 g	6.2
All-Purpose Flour	8 oz	227 g	76.2
Cake Flour	10.5 oz	298 g	100
Raisins	5 oz	142 g	47.7
Vanilla Paste	0.5 oz	14 g	4.7

Procedure

1. Combine all ingredients.
2. Mix for 10 minutes on high with the whip attachment.
3. Place the batter into two prepared 10-in. cake pans.
4. Bake at 350°F (180°C) for 35 to 40 minutes.

Genoise

Yield: 2 lb 13 oz (1295 g)
Portions: 2
Portion size: One 10-in. cake
Yield description: Two 10-in. cakes

Ingredients	U.S.	Metric	%
Eggs	1 lb 4 oz	567 g	208.3
Sugar	11 oz	312 g	114.5
Honey	1.5 oz	42.5 g	15.6
Pastry Flour	9.6 oz	272 g	100
Potato Starch	2.6 oz	74 g	27.1
Butter, melted	1 oz	28 g	10.4

Procedure

1. Sponge method.
2. Bake at 350°F (180°C) for 25 to 30 minutes.

Chocolate Genoise

Yield: 2 lb 14 oz (1310 g)
Portions: 2
Portion size: One 10-in. cake
Yield description: Two 10-in. cakes

Ingredients	U.S.	Metric	%
Eggs	1 lb 4 oz	567 g	232.6
Sugar	11 oz	312 g	127.9
Honey	1.5 oz	42.5 g	17.4
Pastry Flour	8.6 oz	244 g	100
Potato Starch	2.6 oz	74 g	30.2
Cocoa Powder	1.5 oz	43 g	17.4
Butter, melted	1 oz	28 g	11.6

Procedure

1. Sponge method
2. Bake at 350°F (180°C) for 25 to 30 minutes.

Lady Finger Biscuit

Yield: 1 lb 1.3 oz (490 g)

Portions: 50

Portion size: 1 lady finger

Yield description: 50 lady fingers

Ingredients	U.S.	Metric	%
Egg Yolks	3.2 oz	90 g	90
Whole Eggs	0.9 oz	25 g	25
Sugar #1	3.5 oz	100 g	100
Egg Whites	4.8 oz	135 g	135
Sugar #2	1.4 oz	40 g	40
All-Purpose Flour	3.5 oz	100 g	100

Procedure

1. Separation foam method, page 187.
2. Pipe with a 0.5-in. (13-mm) plain tip, 3 in. (7.5 mm) long, onto a silpat.
3. Dredge with granulated sugar; let stand for 5 minutes.
4. Dust with powdered sugar.
5. Bake at 375°F (190°C) 7 to 9 minutes.

Roulade

Yield: 2 lb 5 oz (1077 g)

Portions: 3

Portion size: half sheet pan

Yield description: 3 half sheet pans

Ingredients	U.S.	Metric	%
Egg Yolk	8.8 oz	250 g	166.7
Sugar #1	1.2 oz	35 g	23.3
Honey	2.2 oz	62 g	41.3
Water	0.4 oz	11 g	7.3
Egg Whites	11.9 oz	338 g	225.3
Sugar #2	4.4 oz	125 g	83.3
Butter	1.1 oz	31 g	20.7
Milk	2.6 oz	75 g	50
All-Purpose Flour	5.3 oz	150 g	100

Procedure

1. Separation foam method; note sugar #1, water, and honey are boiled together and added to the egg yolk mixture.
2. Combine milk and butter; bring to a boil.
3. Fold butter/milk mixture into egg mixture.
4. Fold in sifted flour.
5. Scale 11.1 oz (315 g) per half sheet pan.
6. Bake at 400°F (200°C) for 10 to 12 minutes.

Angel Food Cake

Yield: 3 lb 7.4 oz (1569 g)
Portions: 2
Portion size: One 10-in. angel food cake pan
Yield description: Two 10-in. angel food cake pans

Ingredients	U.S.	Metric	%
Egg Whites	1 lb 8 oz	680 g	244.9
Sugar	10.6 oz	300 g	108.2
Cream of Tartar	0.2 oz	5.7 g	2
Salt	0.2 oz	5.7 g	2
Cake Flour	9.8 oz	278 g	100
Sugar	10.6 oz	300 g	108.2

Procedure

1. Angel food method.
2. Bake at 350°F (180°C) for 25 to 30 minutes.

Japonaise

Yield: 1 lb 7 oz (666 g)
Portions: 4
Portion size: 8-in. (20-cm) rounds
Yield description: 4

Ingredients	U.S.	Metric
Egg Whites	6.9 oz	195 g
Egg White Powder	0.2 oz	6.8 g
Sugar	6.9 oz	195 g
Almond Flour	2.6 oz	75 g
Powdered Sugar	6.9 oz	195 g

Note: Almond flour can be replaced with any nut flour, desiccated coconut, or seeds.

Procedure

1. Make a common meringue with first sugar and egg whites.
2. Combine second sugar and almond flour.
3. Fold dry ingredients into meringue.
4. Pipe with a 0.5-in. (13-mm) plain tip.
5. Bake at 185°F (85°C) for 45 to 50 minutes.

Pain de Genes

Yield: 2 lb 10 oz (1205 g)
Portions: 1
Portion size: 1 sheet pan
Yield description: 1 sheet pan

Ingredients	U.S.	Metric	%
Almond Paste	1 lb 0.9 oz	480 g	436.4
Whole Eggs	1 lb	454 g	412.7
Pastry Flour	3.9 oz	110 g	100
Baking Powder	0.2 oz	6 g	5.5
Butter, melted	5.5 oz	155 g	140.9

Procedure

1. Soften the almond paste with some of the eggs using a paddle attachment.
2. Add remaining eggs in several additions, cleaning the paddle and bowl often.
3. Sift together dry ingredients and fold into almond egg mixture.
4. Melt butter and incorporate into batter.
5. Spread in a 0.25-in. (6-mm) thick layer on a silpat-lined sheet pan.
6. Bake at 350°F (175°C) for 12 to 15 minutes.

Chocolate Pain de Genes

Yield: 2 lb 14 oz (1313 g)

Portions: 1

Portion size: 1 sheet pan

Yield description: 1 sheet pan

Ingredients	U.S.	Metric	%
Almond Paste	1 lb 2.3 oz	520 g	495.2
Powdered Sugar	3.7 oz	105 g	100
Whole Eggs	11.4 oz	325 g	309.5
All-Purpose Flour	3.7 oz	105 g	100
Baking Powder	0.28 oz	8 g	7.6
Butter	5.5 oz	155 g	147.6
Semisweet Chocolate 58%	3.4 oz	95 g	90.5

Procedure

1. Using the paddle attachment, combine almond paste and powdered sugar.

2. Melt chocolate and butter.

3. Slowly add eggs to almond paste mixture, scraping often.

4. Add chocolate and butter mixture to mixer.

5. Sift dry ingredients and add; mix until combined.

6. Spread in a 0.25-in. (6-mm) thick layer on a silpat-lined sheet pan.

7. Bake at 350°F (175°C) for 12 to 15 minutes.

Sacher Biscuit

Yield: 5 lb (2305 g)

Portions: 3

Portion size: 1 sheet pan

Yield description: 3 sheet pans

Ingredients	U.S.	Metric
Almond Paste	1 lb 3 oz	540 g
Powdered Sugar	7.1 oz	200 g
Egg Yolks	12.3 oz	350 g
Eggs	6.5 oz	185 g
Cocoa Powder	5.8 oz	165 g
Egg Whites	1 lb 1.6 oz	500 g
Sugar	7.1 oz	200 g
Butter, melted	5.8 oz	165 g

Procedure

1. Cream almond paste, powdered sugar, and cocoa powder in a mixer with the paddle attachment; mix until combined on low speed.

2. Slowly add eggs and egg yolks, scraping often.

3. Once all eggs are incorporated, mix on medium speed for 5 minutes.

4. Make a common meringue with sugar and egg whites.

5. Fold meringue into creamed almond paste mixture in three additions.

6. Incorporate a small amount of the cake batter with the melted butter.

7. Return the butter mixture back to the cake batter and fold to combine.

8. Spread 1 lb 8.5 oz (700 g) on one sheet pan, prepared with sprayed parchment paper.

9. Bake at 450°F (230°C) for 4 to 5 minutes.

10. Allow cakes to cool to 105°F (230°C) and wrap with plastic wrap; store in the freezer.

Orange Chiffon

Yield: 4 lb 15 oz (2196 g)

Portions: 2

Portion size: One 10-in. angel food cake pan

Yield description: Two 10-in. angel food cake pans

Ingredients	U.S.	Metric	%
Cake Flour	12.7 oz	360 g	100
Baking Powder	0.7 oz	20.6 g	5.7
Salt	0.4 oz	9.4 g	2.6
Sugar	1 lb 3.6 oz	555 g	154
Vegetable Oil	7.4 oz	210 g	58
Egg Yolks	7.4 oz	210 g	58
Water	8.5 oz	240 g	66
Orange Juice	1.7 oz	48 g	13
Orange Zest	1.5 each	1.5 each	
Egg Whites	14.8 oz	420 g	117
Sugar	4.2 oz	120 g	33
Cream of Tartar	0.13 oz	3.75 g	1

Procedure

1. Chiffon method.
2. Bake at 350°F (176°C) for 25 to 30 minutes.

Jaconde

Yield: 1 lb 11.6 oz (825 g)

Portions: 1

Portion size: 1 full sheet pan

Yield description: 1 sheet pan

Ingredients	U.S.	Metric	%
Eggs	6.2 oz	175 g	516.7
All-Purpose Flour	1.2 oz	34 g	100
Almond Flour	4.5 oz	128 g	375
Powdered Sugar	4.5 oz	128 g	375
Butter, melted	1 oz	28 g	83.3
Egg Whites	8.2 oz	232 g	683.3
Sugar	2 oz	57 g	166.7

Procedure

1. Jaconde method.
2. Prepare Jaconde and spread onto silpat or décor paste stencil.
3. Bake at 400°F (205°C) for 5 to 7 minutes. The cake should not develop any color.

Décor Paste for Jaconde Ribbon Sponge

Yield: 1 lb 12.75 oz (820 g)

Portions: 1

Portion size: 1 lb 12.75 oz (820 g)

Yield description: 1 lb 12.75 oz (820 g)

Ingredients	U.S.	Metric	%
Butter	7 oz	200 g	516.7
Powder Sugar	7 oz	200 g	100
Egg Whites	7 oz	200 g	375
Cake Flour	7.75 oz	220 g	375
Food Coloring	As needed	As needed	

Procedure

1. Creaming method.
2. Add color as needed.
3. Spread colored décor paste through a stencil onto a silpat.
4. Remove the stencil and freeze for 30 minutes.
5. Prepare the jaconde and spread immediately onto the frozen décor paste.
6. Bake according to the jaconde method.
7. After cake has cooled, wrap and freeze.
8. Carefully unmold cake from silpat after freezing.

FIGURE 7.4a–d Ribbon sponge method:

Spreading the color through the stencil (step 3)

Removing the stencil (step 4)

Spreading the jaconde on the stenciled décor paste (step 5)

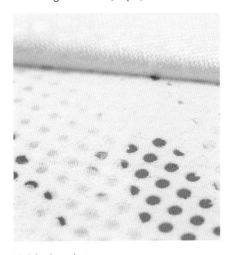

Finished product

Almond Dacquoise

Yield: 8 lb 2 oz (3690 g)

Portions: 3

Portion size: 1 full sheet pan

Yield description: 3 full sheet pans

Ingredients	U.S.	Metric	%
Almond Flour	2 lb 7.7 oz	1125 g	1250
Powdered Sugar	1 lb 15.7 oz	900 g	1000
All-Purpose Flour	3.2 oz	90 g	100
Egg Whites	2 lb 15.6 oz	1350 g	1500
Sugar	7.9 oz	225 g	250

Procedure

1. Sift almond flour, powdered sugar, and all-purpose flour.

2. Make a common meringue with egg whites and sugar.

3. Fold almond flour mixture into meringue.

4. Spread 2 lb 10 oz (1200 g) on one sheet pan prepared with sprayed parchment paper.

5. Bake at 400°F (200°C) for 12 to 13 minutes. To check for doneness, carefully lift the parchment paper to look under the cake. The bottom of the cake should be golden brown.

6. Allow cakes to cool completely and wrap with plastic wrap; store in the freezer.

FIGURE 7.5a-d Dacquoise procedure:

1. Sifting the dry ingredients

2. Preparing the meringue

3. Folding in the dry ingredients

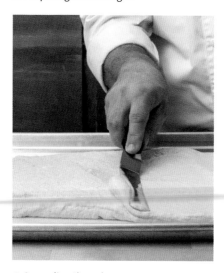

4. Spreading the cake

Coconut Dacquoise

Yield: 3 lb 6 oz (1635 g)

Portions: 1

Portion size: 1 full sheet pan

Yield Description: 1 full sheet pan

Ingredients	U.S.	Metric	%
Almond Flour	4.1 oz	115 g	54.8
All-Purpose Flour	7.4 oz	210 g	100
Desiccated Coconut, toasted	4.6 oz	130 g	61.9
Sugar	14.1 oz	400 g	190.4
Egg White	1 lb 3.8 oz	560 g	266.7
Egg White Powder	0.7 oz	20 g	9.5
Sugar	7.1 oz	200 g	95.2

Procedure

1. Combine almond flour, all-purpose flour, desiccated coconut, and sugar.

2. Add egg white powder to egg whites and make a common meringue with the sugar.

3. Fold dry ingredients into meringue.

4. Spread 3 lb 6 oz (1200 g) on one sheet pan prepared with sprayed parchment paper.

5. Bake at 400°F (200°C) for 12 to 13 minutes. To check for doneness, carefully lift the parchment paper to look under the cake. The bottom of the cake should be golden brown.

6. Allow cakes to cool completely and wrap with plastic wrap; store in the freezer.

Buttercream

Yield: 3 lb 9 oz (1640 g)

Portions: 1

Portion size: 3 lb 9 oz (1640 g)

Yield description: 1 portion at 3 lb 9 oz (1640 g)

Ingredients	U.S.	Metric
Egg White	4.4 oz	125 g
Sugar #1	0.5 oz	15 g
Sugar #2	8.8 oz	250 g
Water	2.6 oz	75 g
Milk	6.3 oz	180 g
Egg Yolk	4.9 oz	140 g
Sugar #3	6.3 oz	180 g
Vanilla Bean	1 each	1 each
Butter, softened	1 lb 10.4 oz	750 g

Procedure

1. Combine sugar #1 0.5 oz (15 g) with the egg whites.

2. Sugar #2 8.8 oz (250 g) and water are combined; prepare an Italian meringue, page 153.

3. Make a crème anglaise with the milk, sugar #3 6.3 oz (180 g), egg yolks, and vanilla bean.

4. Whip the creme anglaise on high speed until cooled.

5. Cream the butter and add the crème anglaise; fold in the meringue.

Cream Cheese Frosting

Yield: 2 lb 8 oz (1130 g)

Portions: 1

Portion size: 2 lb 8 oz (1130 g)

Yield description: 1 portion at 2 lb 8 oz (1130 g)

Ingredients	U.S.	Metric
Buttercream	1 lb	454 g
Cream Cheese	1 lb 8 oz	680 g

Procedure

1. Using the paddle attachment, soften the cream cheese.

2. Add the buttercream; mix until combined.

Chocolate Buttercream

Yield: 4 lb 1.2 oz (2401 g)

Portions: 1

Portion size: 4 lb 1.2 oz (2401 g)

Yield description: 1 portion at 4 lb 1.2 oz (2401 g)

Ingredients	U.S.	Metric
Whole Eggs	8 oz	227 g
Egg Whites	2 oz	57 g
Salt	0.2 oz	5.7 g
Vanilla Paste	0.5	14 g
Sugar	14 oz	397 g
Corn Syrup	0.5 oz	14 g
Water	3.5 oz	100 g
Butter, softened	2 lb	907 g
Chocolate 64%, melted	1 lb 8 oz	680 g

Procedure

1. Whip whole eggs, egg whites, salt, and vanilla paste on high speed.

2. Combine water, sugar, and corn syrup; cook on high heat to 248°F (120°C).

3. Add cooked syrup whipping egg mixture; continue mixing until completely cooled.

4. Add butter to egg mixture.

5. Add chocolate to the mixer; scrape and mix until combined.

Tres Leches Syrup

Yield: 4 lb 8 oz (2141 g)

Portions: 1

Portion size: 4 lb 8 oz (2141 g)

Yield description: 1 portion at 4 lb 8 oz (2141 g)

Ingredients	U.S.	Metric
Sweetened Condensed Milk	1 lb 12 oz	894 g
Evaporated Milk	1 lb 8 oz	680 g
Milk	1 lb	454 g
Brandy	4 oz	113 g

Procedure

1. Combine all ingredients in a heavy-bottom saucepan.

2. Warm syrup but do not boil.

3. For better absorption, the syrup should be warm when applied to the cake.

Key Terms

Two-stage method
Liquid shortenings
Creaming method
Hygroscopic
Inverted sugars
Celiac disease

Ribbon stage
Leaveners
Homogenous
Emulsification
High-fat cakes
Low-fat cakes

Sponge method
Separation foam method
Jaconde method
Chiffon method
Angel food method

Questions for Review

1. Describe the difference between high-fat and low-fat cakes.

2. Why is it important to have all ingredients at room temperature?

3. What is the advantage of using the separation foam method instead of the sponge method?

4. Discuss the methods for testing cake doneness.

5. Identify the five main ingredients in cakes and describe the function they perform in the recipe.

CHAPTER 8

Assembling Cakes

This is the first of four chapters that will build on the foundation of recipes and procedures from custards, frozen desserts, and cake mixing. These basic recipes are combined into delicious and creative works of art, to be shared with others for special occasions.

LEARNING OBJECTIVES

After reading this chapter, you should be able to:

1. **Split**, fill, and decorate a classic cake.
2. **Assemble** contemporary cakes.
3. **Prepare** a variety of glazes.
4. **Demonstrate** entremets assembly.
5. **Design** and assemble a glacé.

Classic Cakes

Traditionally used for celebrations like birthdays and weddings, cakes are a pastry that is easily identifiable to most customers. When thinking about cakes, it is important to consider the different varieties, including classic, wedding, contemporary, and glacé. The variety doesn't end there: Shapes, sizes, and flavors can be changed to create new varieties and an interesting assortment for a display case.

This section covers classic cakes; other cakes are discussed in the following sections.

Classic cakes, also referred to as layer cakes, are composed of cake, filling, icing, and garnish. These cakes can be as simple as yellow cake with butter cream frosting or as elaborate as a Black Forest Torte, containing chocolate cake, cherry filling, kirsch, whipped cream, brandied cherries, and chocolate shavings. Whether using a simple or more complex combination of components, the resulting cake must taste good.

Cake

The primary focus of most decorated cakes is the cake itself. The cake should be moist and flavorful. In the United States, the preferred style of cake is a high fat. These cakes have a tender texture and retain moisture well. Low-fat cakes may also be used and they are an excellent option to provide variety to the mix of flavors and textures offered. When using low-fat cakes, it is important to generously brush all layers with a flavored syrup composed of equal parts sugar and water.

Filling

A classic cake is split and reassembled with layers of cream between the cake layers. In some instances the filling for the cake may be the same as the icing on the outside of the cake. A wide variety of mousses and creams from Chapter 5 can also be used as fillings for cakes. While the filling is often thought of as strictly providing flavor, it also provides much-needed moisture to the cake. The amount of filling used between the layers can vary. A cake with even layers of cake and cream can have a very attractive appearance. If the flavor of the filling is strong or high in fat, a thinner layer may be used.

Icing

The icing on a cake is used to convey the flavor of the cake and enrobe the cake to protect it from drying out. As previously mentioned, although the filling and icing may be the same product, most icings are whipped cream or buttercream. When using an icing that is different from the filling, the flavors should complement each other. A smooth layer of the icing on the cake can help to convey the skill of the pastry chef that assembled the cake. When the cake is sliced, the thickness of the icing should be the same on the sides and the top of the cake, perfectly enrobing the cake inside.

Garnishes

The last of the four components is the garnish. It is often the smallest component of the cake, but it has a large impact. Garnishes can convey the flavor inside the cake. Similar to the approach of garnishing a dessert, the flavor displayed in the garnish should be a flavor in the cake. It would not make sense to garnish a carrot cake with a mint leaf, as this cake does not contain mint. A better garnish would be marzipan carrots or piped buttercream carrots.

Assembling

Splitting

The first step in assembling a classic cake is to split the cake layers. After baking the cake, it must be cooled thoroughly to facilitate slicing. Slicing cake layers can be done using a turntable or on a wood table with a cardboard round and a serrated knife.

If the cake is not level, trim the top of the cake to square up the edges. Holding the knife level, place it on the side of the cake at the desired thickness and proceed to score the side of the cake. Without moving the knife, turn the cake one full revolution. The knife should be at the same place it started and slightly cut into the cake. It is important to not use the knife to cut through the cake as you would a loaf of bread. At this point, use the turntable and knife together to cut through the cake. Turn the cake ¼ turn and pull the knife back toward you, leaving it still in the cake. Turn another ¼ turn and pull the knife back again. Continue to follow this procedure until the knife passes through the middle of the cake. This will take some practice, but it is the best way to quickly cut an even layer. Carefully place the sliced layers on cake boards and reserve for assembly.

Filling

The filling needs to be prepared and ready for application after the layers are split. If the split layers are not filled quickly, the exposure to the air will cause them to dry. If the layers are not going to be filled immediately, cover them with plastic wrap.

FIGURE 8.1a-c Cake splitting:

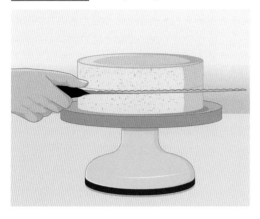

1. Marking the cake once around

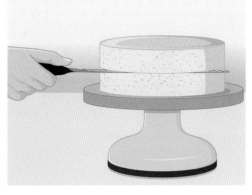

2. Slicing through the cake about halfway

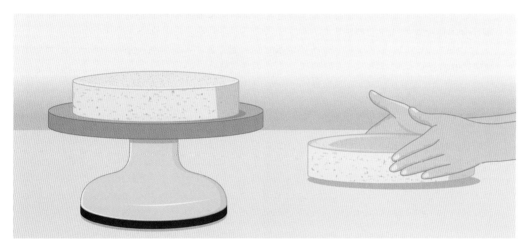

3. Removing the sliced layer

Place the cake layer on a cake board slightly larger than the cake. If decorating a 10-in. cake, use a 12-in. board to allow room for the border. Before applying the filling to the first layer, brush the cake with simple syrup. Place the filling in the center of the cake. Using an offset pallet knife, spread the icing. Work the icing from the center out while turning the turntable at the same time. Learning to use the turntable and pallet knife together will speed up the process. Work the filling to the edges of the cake. Creating a flat surface with the filling will prepare the cake for the next level. At this point, a small dome in the surface of the filling will continue to dome with the following layers, producing a cake that does not have a flat top. Continue stacking, applying syrup and filling the cake.

Icing and Garnishing

Icing and garnishing are the final steps of decorating a classic cake. The final icing of the cake should be smooth and free of crumbs. At this point, be sure to clean all work areas to remove any crumbs that may have resulted from filling the layers.

To prevent incorporating crumbs into the outer icing, a **crumb coat** can be used. This is a thin layer of icing applied to the cake that helps to trap crumbs. After the cake is coated, it is placed in the freezer for 10 minutes to freeze the icing. The crumb coat provides the foundation for the final icing. Pay close attention to this layer and make sure it is smooth.

FIGURE 8.2a–c

1. Cake layer with icing in the center

2. Using the turntable and pallet knife together to spread the icing

3. The finished smooth, flat filling

FIGURE 8.3a–d Icing a cake:

1. Spreading the icing on the top

2. Icing the sides

3. Smoothing the sides

4. Cleaning the top of the cake

FIGURE 8.4a–c Decorating a cake:

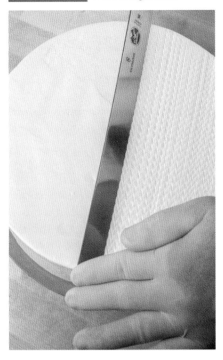

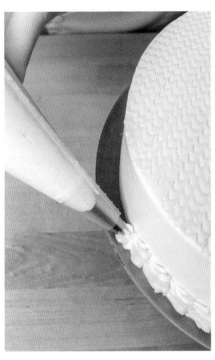

1. Using a serrated knife to comb the top of the cake

2. Piping the bottom border

3. Piping the top border

After removing the cake from the freezer, begin spreading icing on the top of the cake in the same manner as the filling. Spread this top layer so it extends past the sides of the cake. Next, ice the sides of the cake, which will push the overhanging icing from the top back up. After coating the sides of the cake, use a bench scraper to smooth the sides of the cake while spinning the turntable. The last step is to remove the icing that has built up on the top corners of the cake.

Dip the pallet knife in warm water and wipe dry with a clean towel. Holding the knife even with the top of the cake, pull the pallet knife straight toward you. As the pallet knife passes the center of the cake, lift it up to the back edge of the knife and lift off the cake. This will prevent the icing from sticking to the knife. Pulling the pallet knife straight across the top of the cake will ensure that clean square edges are present on the cake.

The iced blank cake is ready for decorating. A shell boarder piped along the bottom of the cake will help to clean the bottom edge where the cake meets the cake board. Some cakes require a boarder on the top as well. After piping the border, mark the top of the cake into the desired number of pieces. A 10-in. cake can be divided into 12 to 16 portions. Once the cake is marked, place a rosette of icing on each slice and apply the garnish.

Wedding Cakes

When most people think of cakes, two types come to mind: birthday and wedding cakes. Wedding cakes can be simplistic or extremely elaborate; either way, they are often the center-piece of many wedding celebrations. There is a considerable amount of planning that goes into selling and producing wedding cakes.

Meeting the Client

A wedding cake is different from other custom orders. The order might be placed as much as a year before the wedding. The first step in the process is to meet with the couple. At this meeting, a tasting may be arranged, presenting the client with a sampling of cakes, fillings, icings, and decorations. Many times, the customers know what flavor and design of cake they would like. A photo portfolio can also be used to showcase previous cakes that have been made.

Communication with the client must be open and honest. They must notify the pastry shop if there are any changes, and the pastry shop must do the same. During this meeting, flavor, design, date, location, number of servings, and price will be discussed. If the customer knows the flavor and design of the cake, confirm that the tasting you have presented is what they want and the design is possible, based on the size of the cake.

Historically, weddings were held in early spring or summer, although trends have changed over the years and weddings are held year round. Summer and spring still tend to be the busier time of year for weddings, and, as a result, scheduling of orders must be considered. The pastry shop has a limited amount of space and delivery options for wedding cakes, and the design of the cakes ordered for a particular day will impact how many orders can be taken and filled successfully.

Guiding the customer through the process is critical. There are many variables to consider when selling a cake, and sometimes the bride and groom may not be aware of what can and cannot be done. Location not only refers to where the cake will ultimately be delivered, but where the cake will be presented. A cake made using buttercream icing will not hold up well for an extended period of time at an outdoor summer wedding. The buttercream will melt as the cake begins to warm. Working together with the wedding planner or caterer will ensure that the cake is stored and presented properly.

Just like the flavors and design, the customer has an idea of what they would like to pay for the cake. It is important to remember that a wedding cake is a custom item prepared for a specific order. When pricing the cake, consider the ingredients that are used and the time spent on assembling and decorating the cake. Wedding cake prices are based on the number of servings. The diagrams below demonstrate portioning of different size cake layers to provide a guide for how many slices each round can yield.

Slices per Tier, 4 in. Tall Layers

Size	Round	Square
6 in. (15 cm)	12	18
8 in. (20 cm)	24	32
10 in. (25 cm)	38	50
12 in. (30 cm)	56	72
14 in. (35 cm)	78	98
16 in. (40 cm)	100	128

Cake Design

Wedding cakes can come in many shapes and designs. One constant between all of them is that they are stacked. Cakes placed on cakeboards can be stacked one tier directly on another or using columns to create spaces between the layers. Cakes and the fillings are fragile and need to be supported to prevent the tiers from compressing or sliding. Dowels or columns can provide the support needed to carry the weight of the upper tiers. The dowels are placed in the finished cake layer equal to the height of the icing on the cake. The next cake is placed on top and the procedure is repeated. Using this system, the weight of the cake is supported by the dowels and not by the cake layers.

Decorating Materials

Traditionally, the color of wedding cakes has been white. This is easily achieved through the use of buttercreams. Italian buttercream provides the best flavor and mouthfeel. However, the use of butter requires this cake to be served in an air-conditioned area. The use of butter also gives a yellow tint to the icing. When a white icing is needed, use a simple buttercream that is made with shortening. This will give the cake a pure white color and is more resistant to warmer temperatures than the Italian buttercream. These icings offer the flexibility of not only enrobing the cake but also creating borders, flowers, vines, and leaves. Royal icing, made from powdered sugar and egg whites, is used for string work and attaching pastillage. Royal icing can be piped, assembled, and dried in advance.

Rolled fondant has increased in popularity due to its ability to enrobe a cake in a completely smooth layer. After filling the cake layer, it is coated in a smooth layer of buttercream, then the fondant is applied. Fondant can be used to create a smooth covered cake, ruffles, swags, and flowers. Cakes enrobed in rolled fondant require more work and skill and carry a higher price than those coated in buttercream.

Decorations on wedding cakes can range from fresh flowers to blown sugar swans. Fresh flowers are an excellent option for decorating the cake, but be sure to use pesticide-free flowers. Gum paste can be used to create flowers that look real but are made of edible material. Gum paste is made of sugar, glucose and gums. This paste can rolled very thin, shaped, and dried. A realistic appearance can be achieved through the use of edible colors to give the flower a lifelike appearance. Dried gum paste flowers also store well and can be made in advance.

Modeling chocolate, marzipan, pastillage, pulled and blown sugar can also be used as decorations for wedding cakes. Modeling chocolate, marzipan and pastillage all hold up well under refrigeration and can be used to create flowers and other decorations. Pulled and blown sugar can add a truly elegant touch to any cake. They are both extremely fragile and do not tolerate humidity well. Many of the decorating techniques found in Chapters 13 and 14 can be used to create decorations for wedding cakes.

Contemporary Cakes

Contemporary cakes, often referred to as **entremets**, are cakes that contain layers of mousse, creams, and cake that are coated in a glaze. Entremets have many elements that are found in classic cakes, with higher percentage of creams to cake. They utilize a variety of flavors, textures, and garnishes. Shape can vary, based on the creativity of the chef—almost any shape can be made from stainless steel or silicone. The flavors and textures can be combined to create different portion sizes from whole cakes and individual pastries to petits fours.

Components

Entremets can have as few as five components: base, cake, cream, coating, and garnish. The base of the cake can be used to introduce texture into the entremets. There are many different variations of quantity of components and types of components. The goal is to create a cake that has an excellent flavor and attractive look. In some cases, too many layers can be placed inside the cake, making it difficult to cut a clean slice.

Base

Bases can be made from rolled-out streusel or tart dough. Some bases use a process that involves taking the baked dough and cutting or breaking the dough into small pieces and combining it with chocolate, nut pastes and butter to bind the base. Reconstructed bases add a different texture to the cake. If a soft texture for the cake is desired, the base can be a layer of cake. The base layer not only provides flavor and texture, it helps to make the cake servable.

Insert

Mise en place is very important when assembling entremets. Equipment and recipes must be gathered and ready to assemble. In some instances, the entremets contain an insert. The **insert** is a combination of cake layers and creams assembled together and placed into the center of the entremets. The insert may have cake on the bottom with a layer of cream on top or cream sandwiched between two layers of cake. Precision in layering the insert will add to the visual appeal of the sliced entremet.

Cake

The other baked layer found in an entremet is the cake. Even if cake is used as the base, another layer or two will be used inside the cake. Sponge, pain de genes, and even a thin layer of brownies can be used as the cake. The cake layer needs to contribute flavor to the cake as well as lighten the cake. The higher percentage of cream in the cake means a high percentage of fat. This can make the cake feel too rich and heavy.

Creams

The next components are the creams. Many times, two or more will be used. To lighten the texture of the cake, an aerated cream, such as chocolate mousse, fruit mousse, or Bavarian will be used. These can be combined with a heavier cream, like a creméux, panna cotta or gelée to introduce another texture or color. Much of the flavor will come from the creams.

Changing the ratios of the components or changing the recipes can adjust the flavor of the cake. It is easier to change the amount of creméux in the cake rather than reformulate the recipe. When building the entremets, it is best to scale the amount of each layer by weight to ensure each cake looks the same when cut and the flavors will be consistent between batches.

Coating

In the same way the classic cakes are covered with icing to protect the cake from drying out, entremets are sprayed with a coating of chocolate, giving the cake a velvet appearance, or the cake can be glazed. Glazing the cake will provide more protection from drying out and it also gives a mirror-like finish.

Garnish

After the glaze has set, the cake can be garnished. Garnishes used on the outside of the cake should clearly reflect the flavors inside the cake. A cake containing strawberry and pistachios can be garnished with pink macarons sprinkled with pistachios and fresh strawberries. Garnishes need to be edible and able to withstand the humidity encountered in a refrigerator. A light and wispy sugar twist may look beautiful, but it will quickly become dull and melt in the refrigerator.

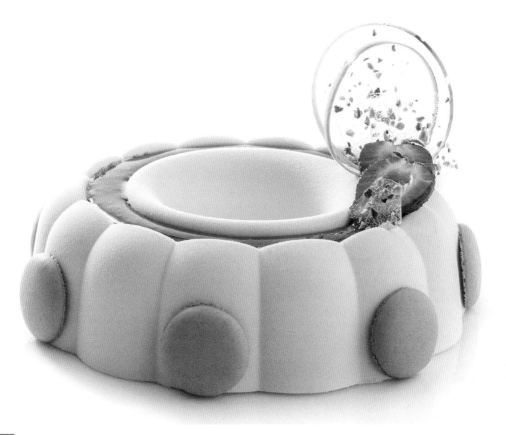

FIGURE 8.5 Garnished pistachio strawberry entremets

Assembly

Entremets can be assembled in two ways: top to bottom or bottom to top. Most cakes can be built either way, and much of the decision comes down to personal preference. The bottom-to-top method allows for a more tender base layer. The base is in place at the start of assembling and the rest of the cake is built on top. During the freezing of a bottom-to-top cake, the cream recesses slightly. This leaves the cake with a top that is not flat. When using the top-to-bottom method, the cake is built upside down, and the top of the cake will remain completely flat, making glazing easier. This method is used when assembling individual portions in flexipans.

Bottom-to-Top Method

In the **bottom-to-top method** the cake is assembled right side up. Place the baked base layer on a silpat-lined sheet pan, followed by the metal cake ring. Proceed to make the chocolate mousse. The mousse needs to be made à la minute and the insert should be stacked in the freezer ready for assembly. Pour some of the mousse into the prepared cake ring. Using a plastic bowl scraper, bring the mousse up the sides of the ring. Smoothing the mousse up the sides of the ring will prevent large air bubbles from being trapped in the mousse. Large pockets of air can become trapped when additional mousse is piped in the mold. These are difficult to fix once the cake is unmolded. The additional step of smoothing the mousse will guarantee a smooth surface ready for glazing. Firmly press the insert into the mousse, making sure it is centered in the ring. Add enough mousse to fill the ring and smooth the top with a pallet knife; immediately place in the freezer.

FIGURE 8.6a–e Bottom-to-top method:

1. Placing the ring over the base on the silpat

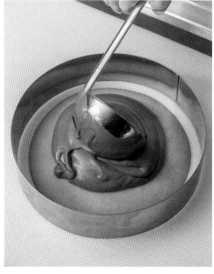

2. Placing mousse into the ring

3. Placing the insert

4. Filling the remainder of the mousse

5. Cleaning the top of the cake

Top-to-Bottom Method

The **top-to-bottom method** assembles the cake upside down, and is essentially the same procedure. The base is baked and cooled, insert is assembled and in the freezer, and mousse is scaled. Place a metal cake ring onto a piece of plastic wrap and place onto a flat sheet pan. Once the mousse is mixed, deposit enough to fill the ring slightly more than one-third. Using a plastic bowl scraper, bring the mousse up the sides of the ring. Press the insert into the mousse, being careful to not press the mousse all the way to the bottom of the ring. Add more of the mousse to almost fill the mold completely; smooth if necessary. Place the base onto the cake and press down with a cake cardboard. Clean any extra mousse from the base side of the mold with an offset pallet knife, and immediately freeze the cake.

FIGURE 8.7a–e Upside down cake assembly:

1. Filling with the mousse

2. Placing the insert

3. Adding more mousse and smoothing

4. Placing the base on top

5. Cleaning the cake before freezing

Unmolding

After the cake has had sufficient time to freeze through to the center, 1 hour in a blast chiller or 4 hours in a standard freezer, the cake can be unmolded. To unmold the cake, place it on a ring that is 1 in. (2.5 cm) smaller than the mold used for the cake. In this example, the cake is assembled in an 8-in. (20-cm) mold, so a 7-in. (18-cm) cake ring will be used. Place the smaller ring on a turntable and place the frozen cake on top of the ring. While slowly turning the table, use a blowtorch or heat gun to warm the metal ring. After turning and warming the cake ring for two turns, check to see if the ring will slide down. If not, apply more heat, being careful to not completely melt the chocolate mousse. Slide the ring down and place the unmolded entremets in the freezer. The cake can now be stored or glazed, thawed, and served.

FIGURE 8.8a–c Proper glazing technique:

1. Cake on rack, glaze in sauce gun

2. Glazing sides

3. Glazing top

Glazing

When applying glaze to the cake, the cake must be frozen. A frozen cake will maintain a clean edge and allow a pallet knife to be passed over the top of the cake to remove extra glaze. The temperature is critical to properly applying a thin coating to the entremets. Glaze that is to cool will not flow evenly across the top and down the side of the cake, due to the gelatin setting. A temperature that is too hot will melt the mousse layer and release fat into the glaze, creating fat streaks. A glaze that is too thin will expose the corners of the cream underneath and run down the sides of the cake. This will not sufficiently cover the sides, and any irregularities in the layer underneath will show through the glaze. Each glaze recipe will specify the optimal temperature for applying the glaze.

To apply the glaze to the cake, make sure it is at the correct temperature. Glaze can be poured directly from a measure with a pouring spout or using a sauce gun. Using a sauce gun will reduce the amount of air bubbles in the glaze. When the glaze is placed in the gun, any air in the glaze will rise to the top; the sauce gun releases the glaze from the bottom of the container.

Place the frozen cake on a metal glazing rack and apply the glaze to the edges of the cake. Be sure to completely cover the side of the cake—there is only one chance to do this. Going back and applying another layer of glaze will create a rough surface and a thick layer of glaze. After coating the sides, immediately glaze the top of the cake. With an offset pallet knife as wide as the cake, quickly pass over the top of the cake to remove any excess glaze. Place the glazed cake in the refrigerator for 10 minutes to set the glaze before moving off of the glazing rack.

Glacé

Another style of contemporary cake is **glacé**, a cake made using churned or still frozen components. Glacé also contain a coulis, base layer, glaze, and garnish. There are many similarities between entremets and glacé; the base serves the functions of flavor, ability to transfer the cake, and texture. Enrobing the cake in a glaze will protect the cake in the freezer, add flavor, and give the cake a glossy shine.

Base

The base of the glacé can be made from the same components used in entremets production, baked tart dough, sponge cakes, or reconstructed base. Recipes will vary slightly from those used in entremets production to account for being served frozen. The colder temperature of the base or cake may not be suitable for cutting or eating. The base provides flavor and texture to the cake and needs to taste good as well as be edible when frozen. Increasing the sugar or adding vegetable oils to cakes and doughs will help create a tender frozen base. While increasing the sugar will make the base sweeter, the sweetness will not be easily detected due to the low temperature of the cake. The cold temperature of the cake will reduce the intensity of the flavors.

Coulis

The coulis is a thin fruit-flavored layer inside the cake that has a large percentage of sugar to prevent the layer from freezing. Because the coulis is a thin layer, it needs to be flavorful and a contrasting color to the layers of the glacé. The higher percentage of sugar and the addition of alcohol prevents coulis from freezing. A frozen coulis layer that does not contain enough sugar or alcohol will not cut clean and will have an unpleasant icy mouthfeel.

Frozen Components

Glacé can be made using any of the components from Chapter 6. Ice creams, sorbets, gelato, parfaits, and semifreddos are used together to create different textures inside the cake. It is not necessary to use more than one frozen component. Baked Alaska is a simple form of a glacé. It is composed of cake and ice cream, coated in meringue. The use of multiple frozen components allows the introduction of different flavors and contrasting colors.

Coating

The coating on the cake protects the glacé from drying out in the freezer, and adds flavor and color to the cake. Meringue and glaze provide the best protection to the interior components. Airbrushed designs can also be placed on the cake before glazing. The glacé can also be sprayed with cocoa butter spray giving the cake a velvet-like appearance.

Garnish

Frozen cakes have a longer shelf life than the other cakes discussed in this chapter. The garnish will need to withstand being frozen, and it is important to think about what will happen to the garnish as the cake is thawing. The garnishes are small and delicate. They will thaw quickly when the cake is removed from the freezer and served. Chocolate decorations, dried meringues, or cookies are recommended for garnishing glacé.

Assembly

Glacé are built in metal or silicone molds. A bombe mold is often used for glacé. It is a stainless steel metal mold shaped like a half dome. Different size domes can be used in a system to create the layers inside the cake. The number of components, flavors, and colors will dictate the order the cake is assembled.

Working with the flavors of pistachio, yogurt, and strawberry, we can design how the glacé will be assembled. The components for this glacé will be strawberry sorbet, pistachio parfait, frozen yogurt, and strawberry coulis. The colors will work well together in any combination. Even though the coulis is red and the sorbet is red, the coulis will have a different shade and will contrast nicely against the sorbet.

Glacés are typically built using the top-to-bottom assembly method. Mise en place for glacé assembly includes freezing all molds, spatulas, and bowls. Due to the high sugar percentage in still frozen desserts, it is recommended to use the parfait as the inner layer of the cake. Using the smallest of the three molds, fill it with the parfait mixture and freeze. A blast chiller is best to thoroughly freeze the layers. This will also allow additional handling time for assembly due to the hardness of the layers.

After the parfait is completely frozen, it must be unmolded. To unmold the parfait, use 100°F (38°C) water—the temperature of the water is important to prevent melting the parfait too much. After unmolding, place the layer back in the freezer for 10 minutes. Frozen yogurt will be the next layer. Once the parfait is back in the freezer, process the yogurt in an ice cream machine. Remove the next size mold and spread the churned yogurt into the mold. Press the parfait into the yogurt, finish this layer with thin coating of the yogurt, and return to the blast chiller or freezer.

Unmold the bombe using the same process used for the parfait and place it back in the freezer. The next layer will be the strawberry coulis. This layer is applied the same as a glaze. After 10 minutes in the freezer, place the glacé on a glazing rack and pour a layer of strawberry coulis over the top. Transfer the glacé back to the freezer to set the coulis.

While the coulis is freezing, process the strawberry sorbet. Repeat the process used for placing the frozen yogurt layer. Before placing the mold back in the freezer, press the base into the bottom of the cake. Return the cake to the blast chiller and allow it to freeze completely.

The final step is to prepare the glacé for glazing. Remove the cake from the mold. Place the cake on a glazing rack and return it to the freezer for 10 minutes. When using a glaze, refer to the glaze recipe to determine the proper temperature for use. Pour the glaze over the cake and be sure to cover the entire cake in one pass. The half sphere shape of the cake makes glazing easy, and there is no need to use an offset pallet knife to remove extra glaze. Allow the glaze to set in the refrigerator for 5 minutes and then transfer the finished cake to a gold cardboard.

Troubleshooting for Cake Assembly

Issue	Cause/Solution
Entremets glaze is too thick.	1. The glaze was too cold. Check temperature of glaze. 2. The recipe was not scaled correctly or the glaze was cooked for too long. Make sure recipe was scaled correctly and the procedure was followed.
Entremets layers separate when cut.	The insert layers were too cold when assembled. Make sure the layers are firm and set in the refrigerator before stacking. If the layers are frozen, allow them to temper so they will adhere to each other before inserting into the cake.
Top of entremets is concave.	1. The mousse or bavarian slightly deflated before freezing, this is a normal occurrence. Use the top-to-bottom method. 2. The bavarian or mousse deflated due to an extended time at room temperature. Transfer the cake to the freezer quickly after assembling.
There are crumbs in final coat of icing.	1. The work station was not cleaned prior to starting the final coat. Clean work area before applying final coat. 2. A crumb coat was not used. Use a crumb coat.
Buttercream is difficult to spread on cake.	The buttercream is not properly aerated before use. Mix on low speed with a paddle to soften the buttercream.
Air pockets form in the outside of glacé and entremets.	1. Line molds carefully with a thin layer before filling. 2. Reserve some of the mixture used to fill the mold and fill in the air pockets.

Recipes

Chocolate Peanut Glacé

Portions: 1

Portion size: 7.9-in. (20-cm) hemisphere

Yield description: One 7.9-in. (20-cm) hemisphere

Ingredients	U.S.	Metric
Caramel Peanut Ice Cream, page 218	2 lb 3 oz	981 g
Chocolate Parfait, page 172	2 lb 7 oz	1116 g
Chocolate Glaze (glacé), page 219	2 lb 6 oz	1082 g
Chocolate Brioche Base, page 219	11.5 oz	325 g
Chocolate Decor		

Procedure

1. Churn the caramel peanut ice cream and fill a 6.3-in. (16-cm) hemisphere mold.
2. Freeze and unmold, place back into freezer.
3. Prepare the chocolate parfait and spread a layer inside of a 7.9-in. (20-cm) hemisphere mold.
4. Insert the caramel peanut ice cream into the chocolate parfait.
5. Spread a layer of the parfait on top of the ice cream insert.
6. Place the base in the bottom of the mold, freeze.
7. Unmold the finished cake and apply the glaze.
8. Apply chocolate decorations.

FIGURE 8.9 Chocolate Peanut Glacé

Caramel Peanut Ice Cream

Yield: 2 lb 3 oz (981 g)
Portions: 1
Portion size: 6.3-in. (16-cm) hemisphere
Yield description: One 6.3-in. (16-cm) hemisphere

Ingredients	U.S.	Metric
Sugar	1.8 oz	50 g
Water #1	0.5 oz	15 g
Milk	8.47 oz	240 g
Water #2	12.35 oz	350 g
Nonfat Milk Solids	2.82 oz	80 g
Ice Cream Stabilizer	0.21 oz	6 g
Inverted Sugar	4.59 oz	130 g
Egg Yolks	0.88 oz	25 g
Peanuts, toasted	3.53 oz	100 g

Procedure

1. Caramelize the sugar with water #1; once a deep caramel is reached pour onto a silpat.
2. After the caramel cools, grind in a food processor.
3. Use the ice cream base process (page 158). Use the caramel made in the previous step in place of the granulated sugar in the process.
4. Place the peanuts in Vitamix; pour enough of the hot ice cream base to cover the nuts.
5. Blend until smooth.
6. Strain through a chinois.
7. Quickly cool the mixture to 40°F (4°C).
8. Mature for 6 to 12 hours before churning.

Chocolate Brioche Base

Yield: 11.5 oz (325 g)
Portions: 1
Portion size: 7.1-in. (18-cm) layer
Yield description: One 7.1-in. (18-cm) layer

Ingredients	U.S.	Metric
Brioche, page 75	5.3 oz	150 g
Dark Chocolate	1.8 oz	50 g
Peanut Butter	3.5 oz	100 g
Butter	0.9 oz	25 g

Procedure

1. Cube the brioche into ¼-in. (6-mm) pieces. Toast until golden brown.
2. Melt the dark chocolate, peanut butter and butter.
3. Gently fold the cooled brioche into the melted chocolate mixture.
4. Press into a 7.1-in. (18-cm) disc and freeze.
5. Reserve for assembly.

Chocolate Glaze (glacé)

Yield: 2 lb 6 oz (1082 g)

Portions: 1

Portion size: 2 lb 6 oz (1082 g)

Yield description: 1 portion at 2 lb 6 oz (1082 g)

Ingredients	U.S.	Metric
Water	6 oz	170 g
Sugar	10 oz	284 g
Glucose	10 oz	284 g
Cocoa Powder	3.4 oz	96 g
Vodka	2 oz	57 g
Gelatin Sheets, bloomed	5.5 each	5.5 each
Sweetened Condensed Milk	6.75 oz	191 g

Procedure

1. Combine water, glucose, vodka, and sugar in a saucepan, heat to a boil.
2. Add gelatin and sweetened condensed milk.
3. Add cocoa powder and strain through a chinois, do not push through the chinois.
4. Cool to 82°F (27°C) for glazing.

Strawberry Pistachio Glacé

Portions: 1

Portion size: 7 in. (17.8 cm) × 2 in. (5.5 cm) high square

Yield description: One 7 in. (17.8 cm) × 2 in. (5.5 cm) high square

Ingredients	U.S.	Metric
Strawberry Sorbet, page 175	2 lb 4 oz	1038 g
Frozen Yogurt, page 171	2 lb 2.7 oz	995.7 g
Pistachio Gelato, page 168	2 lb 3 oz	1002 g
Pistachio Parfait, page 221	2 lb 7.6 oz	1135 g
Cocoa Butter Spray, White Chocolate, page 397		
Strawberry Glaze, page 224, Tropical Glaze Variation	1 lb 8 oz	695 g
French Macaron, page 314	2 lb 10 oz	1122 g

Procedure

1. Prepare macarons. Add red food color to make the macarons pink.

2. Prepare the strawberry sorbet. Mold in a 6.25 in. (16.8 cm) square frame × 0.5 in (12 mm) thick square frame and freeze.

3. Prepare the pistachio parfait and freeze in a 6.25 in. (16.8 cm) square frame × 0.75 in (1.9 cm) thick square frame.

4. Prepare the Strawberry glaze using the tropical glaze recipe; replace all purée with strawberry purée. Reserve for cake assembly.

5. Cut the pistachio dacquoise 6.25 in. (16.8 cm) square and place on the pistachio parfait.

6. Prepare the frozen yogurt and line a 7 in. (17.8 cm) × 2 in. (5.5 cm) high square mold.

7. Insert the pistachio parfait and pistachio dacquoise (assembling using the upside down method). Place in the freezer to set.

8. Unmold the strawberry sorbet and apply the strawberry glaze.

9. Spray the frozen yogurt with a white cocoa butter spray.

10. Place the strawberry sorbet on top of the frozen yogurt.

11. Place the pink macarons around the side of the cake.

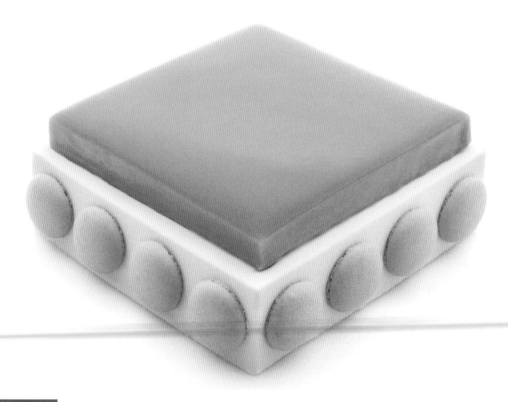

FIGURE 8.10 Strawberry Pistachio Glacé

Pistachio Parfait

Yield: 2 lb 7.6 oz (1135 g)

Portions: 1

Portion size: 2 lb 7.6 oz (1135 g)

Yield description: 1 portion at 2 lb 7.6 oz (1135 g)

Ingredients	U.S.	Metric
Sugar	8.8 oz	250 g
Water	2.5 oz	70 g
Egg Yolks	6.3 oz	190 g
Heavy Cream, whipped	1 lb 6.9 oz	650 g
Pistachio Paste	1.6 oz	45 g

Procedure

1. Combine water and sugar in a saucepan.
2. Make a pâte à bombe with the egg yolks and sugar mixture.
3. When pâte à bombe is completely cooled, add the pistachio paste.
4. Fold the cream into the pâte à bombe.
5. Mold and freeze.

Pistachio Dacquoise

Yield: 1 lb 13 oz (845 g)

Portions: 1

Portion size: Half sheet pan

Yield description: 1 half sheet pan

Ingredients	U.S.	Metric
Egg Whites	10.1 oz	285 g
Sugar	2.5 oz	70 g
Powdered Sugar	7.4 oz	210 g
Almond Flour	4.9 oz	140 g
Pistachio Flour	4.9 oz	140 g

Procedure

1. Sift almond flour, pistachio flour, and powdered sugar.
2. Make a common meringue with egg whites and sugar.
3. Fold sifted flour mixture into meringue.
4. Spread batter onto a silpat-lined half sheet pan.
5. Bake at 400°F (200°C) for 12 to 13 minutes.
6. Allow cake to cool completely and wrap with plastic wrap; store in the freezer.

Bird of Paradise

Portions: 1

Portion size: 7-in. (17.8-cm) ring

Yield description: One 7-in. (17.8-cm) ring

Ingredients	U.S.	Metric
Mango Ice Cream, page 170	2 lb 3.3 oz	1002 g
Banana Mousse Glacé, page 173	2 lb 10 oz	1207 g
Coconut Sorbet, page 176	2 lb 3.2 oz	999.6 g
Cherry Coulis, page 224	9.9 oz	282 g
Tropical Glaze, page 224	1 lb 8 oz	695 g
Coconut Dacquoise, page 199	3 lb 6 oz	1635 g

Procedure

1. Prepare the coconut dacquoise and pipe an 8-in. (20-cm) diameter circle with a 0.4-in. (1-cm) plain tip.

2. Prepare cherry coulis.

3. Fill a 6.5-in. (16.5-cm) ring mold halfway with the banana mousse glacé and freeze.

4. Fill the remaining space in the mold with the coconut sorbet and freeze.

5. Unmold and pour the cherry coulis over the insert and return to the freezer.

6. Line a 7-in. (17.8-cm) mold with the mango ice cream; press the insert into the mold and freeze.

7. Unmold and apply the tropical glaze.

8. Place the glazed ice cream cake on the coconut dacquoise.

FIGURE 8.11 Bird of Paradise

Tropical Glaze

Yield: 1 lb 8 oz (695 g)

Portions: 1

Portion size: 1 lb 8 oz (695 g)

Yield description: 1 portion at 1 lb 8 oz (695 g)

Ingredients	U.S.	Metric
Sugar	3 oz	85 g
Glucose	7.4 oz	210 g
Gelatin Sheets	5 each	5 each
Water, ice cold	1.4 oz	40 g
Mango Purée	8.8 oz	250 g
Passion Fruit Purée	1.8 oz	50 g
Neutral Glaze	2.1 oz	60 g

Procedure

1. Bloom gelatin in 1.4 oz (40 g) water.
2. Combine water, sugar, and glucose in a saucepan; melt over low heat.
3. Add purées to warmed sugar solution.
4. Add gelatin to saucepan and dissolve.
5. Using an immersion blender, incorporate neutral glaze.
6. Strain and cool to room temperature.

Variation

The purées in this recipe can be changed to any flavor.

Cherry Coulis

Yield: 9.9 oz (282 g)

Portions: 1

Portion size: 9.9 oz (282 g)

Yield description: 1 portion at 9.9 oz (282 g)

Ingredients	U.S.	Metric
Cherry Purée	8.6 oz	245 g
Trimoline	1.1 oz	30 g
Pectin NH	0.04 oz	1 g
Sugar	0.2 oz	6 g

Procedure

1. Combine purée with Trimoline in a saucepan and warm.
2. Mix pectin with sugar and add to purée.
3. Bring the mixture to a boil, whisking constantly.
4. Cool completely before using.

Carrot Cake

Portions: 1

Portion size: 8-in. (20-cm) round

Yield description: One 8-in. (20-cm) round

Ingredients	U.S.	Metric
Carrot Cake, one 8-in. round	7 lb 2 oz	3257 g
Cream Cheese Frosting	2 lb 8 oz	1130 g
Walnuts, toasted		
Marzipan	4 lb 12 oz	2180 g

Procedure

1. Split the carrot cake into two equal layers.

2. Spread a layer of the cream cheese icing and place the second layer on top.

3. Continue icing the cake using the method on page 206.

4. Apply the toasted walnuts on the side of the cake.

5. Roll the marzipan to ⅛ in. (3 mm) thick; cut and apply to the top of the cake.

6. Pipe a border around the bottom and the top of the cake.

FIGURE 8.12 Carrot cake

Strawberry Lemon

Portions: 1

Portion size: 8-in. (20-cm) round

Yield description: One 8-in. (20-cm) round

Ingredients	U.S.	Metric
Décor Sponge, page 197		
Honey Genoise, page 192	2 lb 13 oz	1295 g
Clear Glaze, page 106	1 lb 11.7 oz	787 g
Strawberry Marmalade		
Lemon Mousse, page 136	3 lb 2 oz	1418 g
Strawberry Mousse, page 136	3 lb 2 oz	1418 g
Lemon Simple Syrup, page 292	14 oz	410 g

Procedure

1. Slice two layers of the honey genoise ¼ in. (6 mm) thick; brush with lemon simple syrup and spread a thin layer of strawberry marmalade on each layer.
2. Trim the décor sponge 1.25 in. (3.2 cm) tall and line the 8-in. (20-cm) cake ring.
3. Place a layer of the honey genoise in the bottom.
4. Pipe two rings of lemon mousse; alternate with strawberry mousse.
5. Place the second layer of genoise in the cake ring and repeat piping the lemon and strawberry mousse.
6. Fill the mold to the top with the strawberry mousse and freeze.
7. Glaze the top of the cake with a clear glaze.

FIGURE 8.13 Strawberry Lemon

Peach Melba Charlotte

Portions: 1

Portion size: 7-in. (18-cm) square mold

Yield description: One 7-in. (18-cm) square mold

Ingredients	U.S.	Metric
Pain de Genes	2 lb 10 oz	1205 g
Raspberry Marmalade		
Poached Peaches, page 267		
Fresh Raspberries		
Vanilla Bavaria, page 139	3 lb	1360 g
Clear Glaze, page 106	1 lb 11.7 oz	787 g

Procedure

1. Peel the peaches and remove the pit; cut into ½-in. (12-mm) cubes.
2. Prepare the poaching liquid (page 267); add two sprigs of mint.
3. Poach the peaches until tender; chill on an ice bath.
4. Spread a very thin layer of raspberry marmalade on the pain de genes and stack to create four layers and freeze.
5. Slice ¼-in. (6-mm) thick layers of the pain de genes and arrange in 7-in. (18-cm) mold.
6. Prepare the vanilla Bavarian, fill the mold halfway.
7. Place the poached peaches into the mold and cover with remaining Bavarian.
8. Lastly, place another layer of pain de genes on the mold and freeze.
9. Unmold the cake and brush the top with clear glaze.
10. Apply white chocolate plaquettes with raspberry powder to the sides of the cake.

FIGURE 8.14 Peach Melba Charlotte

Mango Chocolate Entremets

Yield: 0.0 lb (00 g)

Portions: 1

Portion size: 8-in. (20-cm) hexagon

Yield description: One 8-in. (20-cm) hexagon

Ingredients	U.S.	Metric
Reconstructed Hazelnut Base, page 229	8.5 oz	240 g
Devil's Food, page 191	4 lb 1 oz	1865 g
Chocolate Mango Creméux, page 230	8 oz	230 g
Mango Curd, page 230	4 oz	115 g
Anglaise-Based Chocolate Mousse, page 135, replace the rum with mango purée		
Chocolate Mirror Glaze, page 231	2 lb	920 g

Procedure

1. Assemble the insert by filling a 7.5-in. (19-cm) round mold with 8 oz (230 g) chocolate mango creméux and 4 oz (115 g) mango curd, freeze.

2. Slice the devil's food cake into ¼-in. (6-mm) thick layers and place one layer on top of the frozen creméux and curd mixture.

3. Prepare the 8-in. (20-cm) hexagon mold and mousse; assemble using the upside-down method.

4. Freeze.

5. After unmolding, glaze the cake while frozen.

FIGURE 8.15 Mango Chocolate Entremets

Hazelnut Dough

Yield: 1 lb 8 oz (698.7 g)

Portions: 1

Portion size: 1 lb 8 oz (698.7 g)

Yield description: 1 portion at 1 lb 8 oz (698.7 g)

Ingredients	U.S.	Metric
Butter	6 oz	170 g
Sugar	4.6 oz	130 g
Hazelnut Flour	3.2 oz	90 g
Cake Crumbs	1.1 oz	30 g
Egg Yolks	2.1 oz	60 g
All-Purpose Flour	7.6 oz	215 g
Baking Powder	0.13 oz	3.7 g

Procedure

1. Creaming method.
2. Refrigerate dough for 2 to 3 hours.
3. Roll 8 oz (240 g) to ⅛ in. (3 mm) and bake.
4. While the dough is still warm, cut into 1/4-in. (6-mm) squares and cool.
5. Reserve for reconstructed hazelnut dough.

Reconstructed Hazelnut Dough

Yield: 1 lb 1 oz (480 g)

Portions: 1

Portion size: 1 lb 1 oz (480 g)

Yield description: 1 portion at 1 lb 1 oz (480 g)

Ingredients	U.S.	Metric
Hazelnut Dough	8.5 oz	240 g
Cassonade	1.8 oz	50 g
Butter	2.5 oz	70 g
Semisweet Chocolate 64%	4.2 oz	120 g

Note: Pâte Sablée, Chocolate Pâte Sablée, Short Dough, Chocolate Short Dough or Graham Cracker Dough can be used in place of the Hazelnut Dough.

Procedure

1. Combine cassonade and hazelnut dough in a bowl.
2. Melt chocolate and butter.
3. Fold melted chocolate mixture into hazelnut dough.
4. Press gently into cake ring.

Chocolate Mango Creméux

Yield: 1 lb 7 oz (670 g)

Portions: 1

Portion size: 1 lb 7 oz (670 g)

Yield description: 1 portion at 1 lb 7 oz (670 g)

Ingredients	U.S.	Metric
Heavy Cream	6.7 oz	190 g
Passion Fruit Purée	1.6 oz	45 g
Mango Purée	5.1 oz	145 g
Cassonade	1.2 oz	35 g
Egg Yolks	2.6 oz	75 g
Semisweet Chocolate 64%	6.3 oz	180 g

Procedure

1. Crème anglaise method using the heavy cream, passion fruit purée, mango purée, cassonade, and egg yolks.
2. Emulsify creméux with chocolate.
3. Pour into mold and freeze.

Mango Curd

Yield: 12.2 oz (350 g)

Portions: 1

Portion size: 12.2 oz (350 g)

Yield description: 1 portion at 12.2 oz (350 g)

Ingredients	U.S.	Metric
Passion Fruit Purée	2.6 oz	75 g
Mango Purée	2.6 oz	75 g
Egg Yolks	1.6 oz	45 g
Eggs	1.9 oz	55 g
Sugar	1.6 oz	45 g
Butter	1.9 oz	55 g
Gelatin Sheets, bloomed	1.25 each	1.25 each

Procedure

1. Curd method, page 124.
2. Mold and freeze for entremets assembly.

Chocolate Mirror Glaze

Yield: 2 lb (920 g)

Portions: 1

Portion size: 2 lb (920 g)

Yield description: 1 portion at 2 lb (920 g)

Ingredients	U.S.	Metric
Water	3.5 oz	100 g
Heavy Cream	8.5 oz	240 g
Sugar	9.2 oz	260 g
Glucose	7.1 oz	200 g
Cocoa Powder	4.2 oz	120 g
Gelatin Sheets, bloomed	7 each	7 each

Procedure

1. Combine water, heavy cream, sugar, and glucose in a saucepan.

2. Cook to 215°F (102°C).

3. Whisk in cocoa powder and gelatin.

4. Strain through a chinois; do not press glaze through the chinois. This will cause the glaze to be too thick and have a coarse texture from the cocoa powder.

5. Cool and use glaze at 95°F (35°C).

Milk Chocolate Blood Orange Entremets

Portions: 1

Portion size: 7-in. (18-cm) ring

Yield description: One 7-in. (18-cm) ring

Ingredients	U.S.	Metric
Crispy Hazelnut Base, page 234	13 oz	380 g
Flourless Chocolate Cake, page 234	5.3 oz	150 g
Caramel Creméux, page 235	4 oz	120 g
Blood Orange Pectin Gel, Page XXX, using blood orange purée		
Milk Chocolate Mousse, page 235		
Caramel Glaze, page 236		

Procedure

1. Assemble the insert by pouring 3.5 oz (100 g) of blood orange pectin gel into a 6.5-in. (16.5-cm) ring mold and refrigerate until set.

2. Next fill the mold with 4 oz (120 g) of caramel creméux.

3. Place the flourless chocolate cake cut to fit the bottom of the ring mold on the creméux and freeze.

4. Once the insert is completely frozen, prepare the milk chocolate mousse.

5. Fill the 7-in. (18-cm) ring mold and press the insert into the mousse.

6. Assemble the crispy hazelnut base and cut to fit the 7-in. (18-cm) ring mold.

7. Place the crispy hazelnut base even with the top of the mold.

8. Freeze until completely set.

9. Unmold and finish with the caramel glaze.

FIGURE 8.16 Milk Chocolate Blood Orange

Flourless Chocolate Cake

Yield: 1 lb 1 oz (495 g)

Portions: 1

Portion size: half sheet pan

Yield description: 1 half sheet pan

Ingredients	U.S.	Metric
Egg Whites	5.3 oz	150 g
Sugar	6.3 oz	180 g
Egg Yolks	3.9 oz	110 g
Cocoa Powder	1.9 oz	55 g

Procedure

1. Make a French meringue with the sugar and egg whites.
2. Once the egg whites are whipped to stiff peaks, add the yolks.
3. Fold the cocoa powder into the whipped egg mixture.
4. Spread onto silpat-lined half sheet pan.
5. Bake at 350°F (176°C) for 10 to 15 minutes.

Crispy Hazelnut Base

Yield: 13 oz (380 g)

Portions: 1

Portion size: 13 oz (380 g)

Yield description: 1 portion at 13 oz (380 g)

Ingredients	U.S.	Metric
Butter	1.9 oz	55 g
Glucose	1.6 oz	45 g
Powder Sugar	4.6 oz	130 g
Hazelnut Flour	5.3 oz	150 g

Procedure

1. Combine butter and glucose in a saucepan and bring to a boil.
2. Add powdered sugar and hazelnut flour to saucepan; stir to combine.
3. Roll between two silpats to a thickness of ⅛ in. (3 mm).
4. Bake at 350°F (176°C) until golden brown.
5. Cut into desired shape while warm; reserve for assembly.

Caramel Creméux

Yield: 1 lb 2 oz (526 g)
Portions: 1
Portion size: 1 lb 2 oz (526 g)
Yield description: 1 portion at 1 lb 2 oz (526 g)

Ingredients	U.S.	Metric
Sugar #1	2.1 oz	60 g
Glucose	1.4 oz	40 g
Water	0.5 oz	15 g
Milk	5.5 oz	155 g
Heavy Cream	5.6 oz	160 g
Vanilla Bean, split and scraped	1 each	1 each
Sugar #2	0.7 oz	20 g
Egg Yolks	3.2 oz	90 g
Gelatin Sheets, bloomed	2.25 each	2.25 each
Salt	0.05 oz	1.5 g

Procedure

1. Make a caramel with sugar #1, water, and glucose.
2. Deglaze the pan with the heavy cream and milk; add the vanilla bean.
3. Over a low heat, warm the mixture until all the caramel has dissolved.
4. Combine the egg yolks with sugar #2
5. Finish cooking using the crème anglaise method (page 124).
6. Add the gelatin and salt, strain through a chinois.

Milk Chocolate Mousse

Yield: 1 lb 7 oz (655 g)
Portions: 1
Portion size: 1 lb 7 oz (655 g)
Yield description: 1 portion at 1 lb 7 oz (655 g)

Ingredients	U.S.	Metric
Milk	2.6 oz	75 g
Heavy Cream	2.6 oz	75 g
Egg Yolks	1.1 oz	30 g
Gelatin Sheets, bloomed	1 each	1 each
Milk Chocolate	5.3 oz	150 g
Semisweet Chocolate 62%	1.8 oz	50 g
Heavy Cream, whipped to soft peaks	9.7 oz	275 g

Procedure

1. Prepare a crème anglaise (page 143) with the milk, heavy cream, and egg yolks.
2. Add the gelatin and strain.
3. Emulsify the crème anglaise with the milk and dark chocolate.
4. Cool to 86°F (30°C).
5. Fold in the whipped cream.

Caramel Glaze

Yield: 1 lb 12 oz (796.5 g)

Portions: 1

Portion size: 1 lb 15 oz (796.5 g)

Yield description: 1 portion at 1 lb 15 oz (796.5 g)

Ingredients	U.S.	Metric
Sugar	11.1 oz	315 g
Water #1	3 oz	85 g
Heavy Cream	9.3 oz	265 g
Water #2	4.6 oz	130 g
Tapioca Starch	0.6 oz	16.5 g
Gelatin Sheets, bloomed	3.5 each	3.5 each
Sweetened Condensed Milk	2.5 oz	70 g

Procedure

1. Combine the first water—3 oz (85 g)—and sugar in a saucepan and caramelize.
2. Deglaze the caramel with the heavy cream.
3. Cook over low heat to dissolve any solid caramel.
4. Make a slurry with the second water—4.6 oz (130 g)—and tapioca starch.
5. Whisk the slurry into the saucepan and bring to a boil.
6. Add the gelatin and sweetened condensed milk.
7. Blend with an immersion blender and strain through a chinois.
8. Reserve for assembly; glaze at 86°F (30°C).

Apricot Milk Chocolate Entremets

Portions: 1

Portion size: 7 in. (18 cm)

Yield description: 1 portion at 7 in. (18 cm)

Ingredients	U.S.	Metric
Chocolate Streusel, page 238	14 oz	400 g
Yogurt Panna Cotta, page 239	10 oz	306 g
Pectin Gel, page 105, using black currant purée		
Milk Chocolate Mousse, page 235		
Roasted Apricots, page 238	14 apricot halves	
Pistachio Dacquoise, page 221		
Milk Chocolate Spray, page 397		

Procedure

1. Prepare the black currant gel; pour a thin layer into 5.75-in. (14-cm) round silicone mold and freeze.
2. Arrange the roasted apricots on black currant gel.
3. Fill the mold with 7 oz (200 g) of yogurt panna cotta and freeze.
4. Cut the pistachio dacquoise to 5.75 in. (14 cm) round.
5. Unmold the panna cotta insert and place onto the pistachio dacquoise; reserve in freezer for assembly.
6. Prepare the milk chocolate mousse.
7. Assemble the entremets using the upside-down method.
8. Fill the mold halfway with the chocolate mousse; place the insert so it is even with the bottom of the mold.
9. Place the assembled cake in the freezer.
10. Unmold and spray with milk chocolate spray.
11. Place the sprayed cake on the Chocolate Streusel base.

FIGURE 8.17 Apricot Milk Chocolate

Chocolate Streusel

Yield: 14 oz (400 g)

Portions: 1

Portion size: 14 oz (400 g)

Yield description: 1 portion at 14 oz (400 g)

Ingredients	U.S.	Metric
Butter, soft	3.5 oz	100 g
Sugar	3.5 oz	100 g
All-Purpose Flour	2.5 oz	70 g
Cocoa Powder	1.1 oz	30 g
Almond Flour	3.5 oz	100 g

Procedure

1. Combine all ingredients with a paddle attachment mix until combined.
2. Roll into tubes and freeze.
3. Process the frozen tubes through a meat grinder; return to the freezer.
4. Place the frozen dough into a 7-in. (18-cm) metal ring and bake at 300°F (150°C) for 12 to 15 minutes.

Roasted Apricots

Portions: 1

Portion size: 14 apricot halves

Yield description: 1 portion at 14 apricot halves

Ingredients	U.S.	Metric
Apricots, cut in half, pit removed	7 each	7 each
Butter	1 oz	28 g
Vanilla Sugar	1 oz	28 g

Procedure

1. Melt the butter and pour over the apricot halves.
2. Add the sugar and mix to combine.
3. Place on a silpat-lined sheet pan.
4. Bake at 450°F (230°C) for 5 to 7 minutes.
5. Cool and slice the apricots; reserve for assembly.

Yogurt Panna Cotta

Yield: 10 oz (306 g)

Portions: 1

Portion size: 10 oz (306 g)

Yield description: 1 portion at 10 oz (306 g)

Ingredients	U.S.	Metric
Heavy Cream	4.2 oz	120 g
Sugar	1.6 oz	45 g
Vanilla Bean, split and scraped	½ each	½ each
Gelatin Powder	0.13 oz	3.8 g
Water	0.5 oz	15 g
Greek Yogurt 2%	4.1 oz	115 g
Yogurt Powder	0.25 oz	7.5 g

Procedure

1. Bloom gelatin in water.
2. Combine heavy cream, sugar, and vanilla bean in a saucepan.
3. Heat to dissolve sugar.
4. Add bloomed gelatin to warm cream mixture; cool to 95°F (35°C).
5. Add yogurt powder and Greek yogurt; remove vanilla bean.
6. Mix with an immersion blender.
7. Strain through a chinois.
8. Reserve for assembly.

Banana Lime Entremets

Portions: 1

Portion size: 9.8 in x 3.5 in (25 cm x 9 cm)

Yield description: 1 portion at 9.8 in x 3.5 in (25 cm x 9 cm)

Ingredients	U.S.	Metric
Reconstructed Lime Streusel Base, page 242	9 oz	255 g
Coconut Biscuit, page 242	1 lb 3 oz	555 g
Banana Creméux, page 243	8 oz	225 g
Lime Curd, page 243	8 oz	225 g
White Chocolate Coconut Mousse, page 136		
Banana Glaze, page 244		

Procedure

1. Assemble the insert by pouring lime curd in a 3.5 × 10 in. (8.9 × 25 cm) rectangular mold, place in the refrigerator to set.
2. Top the lime curd with banana creméux and freeze.
3. Cut the coconut biscuit to the same size as the curd mold; reserve for assembly.
4. Assemble the reconstructed lime struessel base; reserve in the freezer for assembly.
5. Prepare the coconut white chocolate mousse.
6. Spread a thin layer of mousse on the coconut biscuit and attach the curd to the cake.
7. Assemble the cake using the upside-down method; fill the mold with coconut white chocolate mousse.
8. Press the insert into the mold.
9. Spread a thin layer of the mousse.
10. Insert the reconstructed lime streusel base and freeze.
11. Unmold the entremets and apply banana glaze.

FIGURE 8.18 Banana Lime

Lime Streusel

Yield: 12 oz (362 g)
Portions: 1
Portion size: 12 oz (362 g)
Yield description: 1 portion at 12 oz (362 g)

Ingredients	U.S.	Metric
Butter, cold, cubed	2.8 oz	80 g
Brown Sugar	2.8 oz	80 g
Lime Zest	2 each	2 each
Dessicated Coconut	2.8 oz	80 g
All-Purpose Flour	4.2 oz	120 g
Salt	0.07 oz	2 g

Procedure

1. Combine all ingredients with a paddle attachment.
2. Spread onto a silpat-lined sheet pan and bake at 350°F (180°C).

Reconstructed Lime Streusel Base

Yield: 9 oz (255 g)
Portions: 1
Portion size: 9 oz (255 g)
Yield description: 1 portion at 9 oz (255 g)

Ingredients	U.S.	Metric
Lime Streusel, above	5.1 oz	145 g
White Chocolate	2.1 oz	60 g
Butter	1.1 oz	30 g
Rice Krispies	0.7 oz	20 g

Procedure

1. Combine lime streusel and rice krispies.
2. Melt white chocolate and butter over a water bath.
3. Fold melted white chocolate mixture into streusel mixture.
4. Press into a 3.5 × 10 x 0.25 in. (8.9 × 25 × 0.6 cm) mold and refrigerate until set.

Coconut Biscuit

Yield: 1 lb 3 oz (555 g)
Portions: 1
Portion size: half sheet pan
Yield Description: 1 half sheet pan

Ingredients	U.S.	Metric
Eggs	4.4 oz	125 g
Coconut Flour	0.7 oz	20 g
Powder Sugar	1.8 oz	50 g
Coconut Purée	3.2 oz	90 g
Sugar	1.7 oz	48 g
Cake Flour	2.1 oz	60 g
Salt	0.06 oz	2 g
Desiccated Coconut	0.9 oz	25 g
Egg Whites	4.8 oz	135 g

Procedure

1. Combine eggs, coconut flour, powder sugar, and coconut purée with a rubber spatula.
2. Make a French meringue with the egg whites and sugar.
3. Fold the meringue into the first mixture.
4. Fold in the cake flour.
5. Spread onto a silpat-lined half sheet pan.
6. Bake at 350°F (180°C) for 15 to 18 minutes.

Banana Creméux

Yield: 9.9 oz (280 g)

Portions: 1

Portion size: 9.9 oz (280 g)

Yield description: 1 portion at 9.9 oz (280 g)

Ingredients	U.S.	Metric
Banana Purée	4.1 oz	115 g
Heavy Cream	2.8 oz	80 g
Egg Yolks	1.2 oz	35 g
Sugar	1.8 oz	50 g
Gelatin Sheets, bloomed	1.5 each	1.5 each

Procedure

1. Prepare a crème anglaise (page 143) with the banana purée, heavy cream, egg yolks, and sugar.
2. Add the gelatin and strain through a chinois.

Lime Curd

Yield: 12 oz (350 g)

Portions: 1

Portion size: 12 oz (350 g)

Yield description: 1 portion at 12 oz (350 g)

Ingredients	U.S.	Metric
Lime Purée	5.3 oz	150 g
Egg Yolks	1.6 oz	45 g
Whole Eggs	1.9 oz	55 g
Sugar	1.6 oz	45 g
Butter	1.9 oz	55 g
Gelatin Sheets, bloomed	1.25 each	1.25 each
Green Food Coloring	As needed	As needed

Procedure

1. Curd method, page 124.
2. Reserve for assembly.

Banana Glaze

Yield: 1 lb 9 oz (718 g)

Portions: 1

Portion size: 1 lb 9 oz (718 g)

Yield description: 1 portion at 1 lb 9 oz (718 g)

Ingredients	U.S.	Metric
Powder Gelatin	0.2 oz	5.5 g
Water #1	1 oz	30 g
Cornstarch	1 oz	28 g
Water #2	3.2 oz	90 g
Sugar	4.9 oz	140 g
Banana Purée	4.9 oz	140 g
Mango Purée	1.8 oz	50 g
Passion Purée	0.7 oz	20 g
Glucose	1.8 oz	50 g
Yellow Food Coloring	As needed	As needed
Neutral Glaze	5.8 oz	165 g

Note: This glaze can be used to create a wide variety of fruit glazes, replace the purée with the desired flavor and the food color with a complimentary color.

Procedure

1. Bloom gelatin in first water 1 oz (30 g).
2. Make a slurry with the cornstarch and second water 3.2 oz (90 g).
3. Warm sugar, purées, and glucose to 104°F (40°C); whisk in the slurry.
4. Continue whisking and bring mixture to boil; add neutral glaze and yellow food coloring as needed.
5. Mix with an immersion blender and strain through chinois.
6. Glaze at 85°F (30°C).

Key Terms

Crumb coats   Insert   Top-to-bottom method
Entremets   Bottom-to-top method   Glacé

Questions for Review

1. Describe the similarities and differences between classic and contemporary cakes.

2. What are the functions of the base in a contemporary cake?

3. Why is it important to freeze the molds and equipment necessary for producing a glacé?

4. Identify the two methods of assembling a contemporary cake and describe the benefits of each.

CHAPTER **9**

Tarts and Pies

It's hard to imagine life without pie. Long before the centuries-old phrase, "Necessity is the mother of invention," pie dough answered the call, allowing sweet and savory fillings to be wrapped in dough, making transportation easier. Today, these delicate crusts still help to transport and deliver flavorful fillings while providing a crisp texture.

LEARNING OBJECTIVES

After reading this chapter, you should be able to:

1. **Prepare** a variety of pie and tart doughs.
2. **Fill** and assemble single- and double-crusted pies and tarts.
3. **Assemble** pies and tarts using various doughs and fillings.

Pies and Tarts

Whether it is a casual restaurant, bakery, or fine-dining restaurant, you can be sure there will be a pie or tart on the menu. So, what is the difference between a pie and a tart? The answer to this question is: not much. Both can be made sweet or savory, they can be made in large pans and cut for serving or in an individual size—either way, they are delicious. The main difference between a pie and tart is shape. Pies are made in pans that have sloping sides. Tarts are made in fluted tart pans or straight-sided flan rings. There is no rule that says you must use pie dough in a pie tin—doughs can be used interchangeably to create a wide variety of products (including the **galette**, an open-faced version of a pie, usually baked on a flat sheet pan). One other area remains true, making a great pie or tart starts with selecting the correct ingredients, recipes, and flavors.

Ingredients

Ingredients can be broken down into the crust and the fillings. Classic pies, like apple, pumpkin and cherry, are easily recognizable. All three have a crust and filling, and when we look toward creating newer versions of the classics, additional recipes can be added. This chapter takes a brief look at the classics and then gives them an updated twist. The new interpretations of these items need to use the flavors from the classics as well as an understanding of the ingredients and techniques used to create the doughs and fillings.

Doughs

The crust is the carrier for the filling, but it is much more than this, adding flavor and texture to the tart or pie. It should be delicate enough that it can be cut through easily—even if using a plastic fork—yet sturdy enough to hold up. Using the proper ingredients and understanding their function in the recipe will help to determine which ingredients will provide the desired results.

Types of Doughs

Dough	Ingredients
Pie	Flour, Fat, Water
Short Dough	Butter, Sugar, Egg, Flour
Chocolate Short Dough	Butter, Sugar, Egg, Flour, Cocoa Powder
Pâte Brisée	Flour, Butter, Egg, Water
Almond Sugar Dough	Butter, Sugar, Almond Flour, Flour, Egg

Flour

The key to creating a great pie or tart is in the crust. It is easy to make a crust that looks good and holds up—at the same time, it might be difficult to break and have poor flavor. Creating a tender crust is achieved through the use of low-protein-content flours. Using cake or pastry flour will yield a tender product.

Fat

Different doughs will call for different fats. For example, pie dough may use hydrogenated shortening, lard, or a mixture of butter and shortening while short doughs and pâte brisée benefit from butter. Regardless of which fat is used in a recipe, they all perform the same function in the dough and shorten the gluten. The fat coats the gluten and prevents it from forming long chains. For more on gluten development, see Chapter 2. Fat is also responsible for creating flakiness in the dough.

Hydrogenated shortening is primarily used in pie dough and has an excellent consistency for mixing. It is also inexpensive. Drawbacks are the high melting point, 120°F (49°C), which coats the mouth with a greasy feeling. Recent trends and legislation (trans fats have been banned in California and New York City and the FDA has given food manufacturers until June of 2018 to phase out use) have led to the development of trans fat–free, fully hydrogenated fats. During this process the consumer became aware of the negative health impacts of hydrogenated fats.

Rendering fat from pork produces lard. It is then deodorized to remove any flavor that may remain. Lard melts at 115°F (45°C); while this is close to the melting point of hydrogenated shortening, lard does not coat the mouth in the same way. Lard is softer at room temperature, which can make it somewhat more difficult to work with. It is also an animal-based product that is not suitable for vegetarian applications. An excellent, flaky pie dough can be made using lard.

Liquid

Pie dough needs a liquid to pull the dough together. Water works very well, and it is inexpensive and contributes to the texture of the crust. Milk can also be used, although it contains lactose (sugar) and fat. The lactose will cause the dough to take on more color and brown more easily, and the fat will keep the dough softer. These are not necessarily negatives, but keep in mind that changing the ingredients will impact the final product. Regardless of whether milk or water is used, great care must be taken to not overmix the dough once the liquid is added.

Sugar

Sugar contributes to the dough's sweetness and crust color. It also plays a role in controlling gluten development. The hygroscopic properties of sugar pull moisture away from flour, preventing the flour from properly hydrating. While powdered sugar and granulated sugar both provide the same sweetening power, they react differently in the dough. Doughs made with powdered sugar will not spread as much as those made with granulated sugar. Grinding the sugar into a very fine powder will increase the ability of the sugar to absorb liquid due to the larger surface area of the granules. Reducing the amount of liquid that is free in the dough will also prevent spread.

Eggs

Eggs can change the color, flavor, and texture of a tart shell. The majority of an egg white is water. All the water creates a dough that is firm, almost tough. The yolk of the egg is mostly fat. The rich yellow yolk adds flavor, color, and tenderizes the dough. But if using egg yolk creates a wonderful dough, why aren't all doughs just made with egg yolk? Because the intended use of the dough must be considered before just changing the ingredients. Although most recipes will function as expected when changing yolks for whole eggs and vice versa, dough is different. For example, a shell that needs to maintain its strength to support the filling when cut and served on a buffet would benefit from the use of whole eggs. The water in the egg white will give it strength. In contrast, desserts served à la carte can easily use the more tender dough made with only egg yolks.

Fruits

Incorporating fruit into pies and tarts adds texture and freshness to the final product. Fruits come in a variety of forms; fresh, frozen, dried, canned, and puréed. Fresh fruit provides the best flavor and texture, plus the benefit of using produce during the peak of freshness. But weather and insects can destroy crops and increase prices. At other times, the fruit may grow but not produce the ideal crop. Frozen, canned, dried, and puréed fruits can offer an option when fresh produce is not at its peak.

This is not to say that processed fruits are substandard either. In some cases they can be superior to fresh because the pastry chef is not limited to the seasonal availability of produce. Processed fruits are harvested when the fruits are in season and handled in a way to preserve the integrity of the fruit. Larger production batches of pies can be made with frozen or canned apples, while smaller quantities for restaurant service can use fresh apples.

Mixing Dough

When making dough for a pie or tart, minimal mixing will ensure the gluten is not overdeveloped, creating a tough crust. There are two mixing methods used for doughs, creaming and cutting in fat. The creaming method adds the flour at the end of the mixing procedure, while the cutting in fat method reserves the liquid until the last step. Both effectively minimize the gluten development of the dough. There are many variations for each of these methods; however, the procedures below are the most commonly used methods.

Creaming

1. Scale all ingredients and warm to 70°F (21°C).
2. Combine butter and sugar with a paddle on low speed.
3. Slowly add eggs in three additions and scrape the bowl and paddle often.

4. Lastly, add the flour in one addition, mix until combined.

5. Scrape the bowl and paddle again, mix briefly.

6. Flatten dough out to 1 in. (2.5 cm) thick using bread flour if necessary. Wrap in plastic wrap and refrigerate for at least 4 hours.

When using the creaming method, be sure to mix on low speed. Higher mixing speeds or prolonged mixing time will result in incorporating air into the dough. The extra air in the dough will expand during the baking process, thus causing changes to the shape of the dough. Room temperature ingredients will assist in reducing mixing time and creating the proper emulsion between the ingredients.

Cutting in Fat—Mealy Method

1. Scale ingredients.

2. Cube fat into ½ in. (15 mm) cubes, place in refrigerator to keep fat cold.

3. Combine fat and dry ingredients in mixer with paddle attachment.

4. Mix on low speed until mixture resembles cornmeal.

5. Add cold liquid in one addition mix until combined.

6. Flatten dough out to 1 in. (2.5 cm) thick, using bread flour if necessary. Wrap in plastic wrap and refrigerate for at least 4 hours.

Cutting in Fat—Flaky Method

1. Scale ingredients.

2. Cube fat into ½ in. (15 mm) cubes, place in refrigerator to keep fat cold.

3. Combine fat and dry ingredients in mixer with paddle attachment.

4. Mix on low speed until fat reaches "pea-sized particles."

5. Add cold liquid in one addition mix until combined.

6. Flatten dough out to 1 in. (2.5 cm) thick, using bread flour if necessary. Wrap in plastic wrap and refrigerate for at least 4 hours.

It is possible to make flaky and mealy dough from the same exact recipe. The use of the dough determines which method must be used when making the dough. **Mealy pie dough** is used for lining the bottoms of pies. Pie fillings, such as fruit fillings and custards, are not as easily absorbed into the mealy dough. **Flaky pie dough** is reserved for tops of double-crusted pies.

Traditionally, graham cracker crumbs are also used to line pie shells. The crumbs are combined with melted butter and pressed into the pan and baked briefly to toast the crumbs and set the crust. This same process can be done with almost any cookie or short dough. Biscotti, almond short dough, and even linzer dough can be used in place of the graham crackers to create a **crumb crust**; the flavor of the dough used for the crust can add additional flavor and show the creativity of the pastry chef.

Rolling and Lining Shell

Rolling

After the dough has been mixed, it must be allowed to cool; this is a critical step that is often overlooked. The resting period allows the flour to fully hydrate. Additionally, cooling allows the fats to solidify and create a dough that is firm enough to roll without having it become too soft and sticky.

Whether rolling the dough with a mechanical sheeter or by hand with a rolling pin, the process is the same. Always use bread flour when dusting the work surface; weaker flours, such as cake or pastry, can be easily absorbed by the dough.

Lightly dust the work surface with bread flour. Place 8 oz (230 g) chilled dough onto the table and dust the top of the dough. When using a rolling pin, gently roll the dough down and out. As the dough begins to expand, turn and move the dough to ensure it is not sticking to the table. Waiting until the end of rolling to check this typically results in dough that needs be rolled again. During the rolling process the dough should appear to float on top of the table as it is rolled. Roll the dough to ⅛ in. (3 mm) thick. At this point any additional dusting flour can be brushed off the dough. Place on a parchment paper-lined sheet pan and refrigerate for 10 to 20 minutes to allow the dough to become firm before lining the shells.

Lining a Shell

When lining a shell, the goal is to place the dough in the pan without stretching the dough. If at any point during the lining process the dough is stretched, it will shrink during the baking, leading to cracks or shells that do not fill the pan properly.

To limit the amount of stretching when transferring the dough, place a rolling pin on the dough and roll the dough around the pin. Lift the rolling pin and unroll the dough onto the shell. The second method involves folding the dough. Carefully fold the dough in half, work your hands underneath the dough, and lift it into the pan and unfold the dough.

Once the dough is transferred, begin to work the dough down into the pan. Gently lift the dough using your fingers and tuck it down into the corners of the pan while turning the pan. This is a gradual process, it may take two or three times around the pan work the dough down into the corners. Trying to do this step too quickly will cause the dough to be stretched in some areas and bunched up and overlapped in others.

A word of caution: Dough that has been stretched is thinner than originally rolled and dough that is overlapped will be thicker. Due to the differences in thickness the shell will not bake evenly, some spots will burn and others will be underbaked.

FIGURE 9.1A–C Process of rolling dough:

1. Dusting dough and table

2. Rolling the dough out

3. Turning the dough

Classic Pies and Tarts

Baked

Baked pies and tarts can be either **single crusted** or **double crusted**. A single-crusted pie may be referred to as open-faced. In the case of double-crusted pie, the filling is enclosed in the dough. Regardless of this, there is one constant for both varieties—they are baked. The filling and shell go into the oven assembled and bake together.

A single-crusted shell is placed in the pan following the lining procedure described in the previous section. When using the double-crusted method there some additional steps that must be followed. The filling used in the pie must be cool before placing in the shell. A warm filling will begin to melt the fat in the dough and create a soggy bottom. Be careful to not drip any of the filling on the edge of the crust that is to be sealed. This will prevent the doughs from adhering properly.

Brush the edges of the bottom shell with cold water, just enough to moisten the dough. Too much water at this point will cause the top dough to slide, rather than stick. Roll out another 8 oz (230 g) of dough following the rolling procedure. Carefully transfer the dough to the pie using a rolling pin, and unroll the dough onto the pie. There may be dough overhanging the sides of the pie: this dough can be rerolled and used in a future pie so it is not wasted. Trim the dough against the pie tin and crimp the edges. Then brush the top with egg wash, and vent if needed. Vents are small slits placed in the top of the dough that allow steam to escape from inside the pie. Be sure to brush the egg wash on the top before venting to prevent the egg wash from dripping inside the pie.

Baking

Baking a double-crusted pie requires some knowledge of the product and the oven. Different ovens bake at different rates. Since the pie is filled when it is placed in the oven, the pastry chef must make sure the filling is cooked at the same time the crust is baked. The temperatures provided in the recipes are a guide; adjustments may need to be made to the time and/or oven temperature to properly bake the pie. Pie dough may contain small amounts of sugar; therefore, it can withstand higher baking temperatures. Indications of doneness in a double-crusted pie can be observed through crust coloration. If at any point during baking the filling comes through the seam between the top and bottom crust, remove it from the oven immediately. If this occurs, the pie is overbaked, the filling is boiling, and fruits will lose their texture.

Whether the pie or tart is double crusted or a single crusted, it is important to use a hot oven—375°F (190°C) or in some cases higher. Higher baking temperatures set the crust of the pie quickly, preventing the bottom from becoming soggy. In some instances, the pie may be baked at 425°F (220°C) for the first 10 to 15 minutes of baking. Then the temperature is reduced to continue baking the filling.

Unbaked

Unbaked pies and tarts have a shell that is baked first and then filled. Banana cream pie, fresh fruit tarts, and lemon tarts are examples of unbaked pies. The fillings for these pies tend to be lighter than baked pies.

Baking

The dough for unbaked pies and tarts are **blind baked**, which means that the shells are completely baked and cooled before adding the filling. There are two methods for this: Shells may be blind baked using parchment paper and weights or using a second tin. The same results are obtained from each method, so it's a matter of personal preference as to which is selected. In both methods, the dough is **docked** after lining the pans. Rest the lined pans in the cooler to allow the dough to firm after lining.

After approximately 20 minutes in the cooler, the dough is lined with cut parchment paper rounds. The paper needs to be pressed firmly into the corners of the dough and against the sides, and then filled with weights. Weights can be rice, beans, or purchased pie weights. The shell is then placed in the oven and baked until golden brown. After the dough and weights have cooled, remove them from the shell and deposit the filling.

The second tin method works best with products baked in pie tins as they easily fit together when lined. The dough is lined, trimmed, and docked, and then a second tin is placed inside the dough. At this point, the pie shells can be stacked and placed in the freezer for later use. Invert the shell onto a sheet pan and place another sheet pan on top of the tins. This prevents the aluminum pie tin from moving. The dough is held firmly in place and baked until golden brown. Once cooled turn the shells over and remove the second pie tin.

Modern Tarts and Pies

Pies and tarts have been around for a long time. Many successful pastry items rely on familiar flavors presented in a new way. Consider using the flavors of a classical torte like Black Forest in a tart. Start with the flavors: chocolate, whipped cream, dark cherries, and kirsch. Transitioning these flavors to a tart can be done by using chocolate short dough, chocolate creméux, a thin layer of chocolate sponge cake soaked with the kirsch syrup, and dark cherry mousse, and then topped with vanilla whipped cream. Adding the layer of cake lightens the tart and allows the introduction of different flavors.

Changing the shape and size of the tart can also impact the visual perception. Pies and tarts are typically round, but that is basic. To create an interesting buffet or display case item, use different shapes, like ovals, squares, and rectangles. Different-sized products can also create an attractive display. For example, petits-fours, individual and whole tarts of different flavors, will break up the display.

Troubleshooting for Tarts and Pies

Issue	Cause
Dough shrinks.	**1.** Dough was mixed too long and gluten was developed. Mix for less time.
	2. The flour used had too much protein. Use weaker flour.
	3. The dough did not have enough fat. Increase fat.
Crust is soggy.	**1.** The dough did not bake during the initial stages of baking. Use a higher oven temperature for first 10 to 15 minutes.
	2. The heat on the bottom of the shell was not intense enough. Place on lowest rack in the oven.
	3. The dough is under baked. Bake dough longer.
Pie dough is too soft before baking.	The fat was mixed too long before adding the wet ingredients. When cutting the fat, reduce the mixing time.
Creamed doughs are greasy.	The emulsion of the butter and eggs was done too quickly. When mixing, gradually add eggs to maintain emulsion.
Dough is tough.	**1.** The dough is overmixed. Reduce mixing time.
	2. The flour used contained too much protein. Use a weaker flour.

Recipes

Pie Dough

Yield: 1 lb 9 oz (721 g)

Portions: 3

Portion size: 8 oz (227 g)

Yield description: Three 9-in. (23-cm) pie shells

Ingredients	U.S.	Metric	%
Pastry Flour	12.5 oz	354 g	100
Shortening, cold, cut into ½-in. (15-mm) cubes	8 oz	227 g	64.1
Water, ice cold	4 oz	113 g	31.9
Sugar	0.8 oz	23 g	6.5
Salt	0.15 oz	4.3 g	1.2

Procedure

1. Cutting in fat method, page 250.

Pâte Sablée

Yield: 1 lb 11 oz (772 g)

Portions: 3

Portion size: 8 oz (227 g)

Yield description: Three 9-in. (23-cm) tart shells

Ingredients	U.S.	Metric	%
Butter	7 oz	198 g	60.2
Almond Flour	1.4 oz	40 g	12.2
Powder Sugar	4.4 oz	125 g	38
Eggs	2.8 oz	79 g	24
Salt	0.04 oz	1.1 g	0.3
All-Purpose Flour	11.6 oz	329 g	100

Procedure

1. Creaming method, pages 249–250.

Variation

Chocolate Pâte Sablée

Ingredients	U.S.	Metric
All-Purpose Flour	9.3 oz	264 g
Cocoa Powder	2.3 oz	65 g

Short Dough

Yield: 1 lb 12 oz (793 g)
Portions: 3
Portion size: 8 oz (227 g)
Yield description: Three 9-in. (23-cm) tart shells

Ingredients	U.S.	Metric	%
Butter	6 oz	170 g	50
Powdered Sugar	6 oz	170 g	50
Egg Yolks	4 oz	113 g	33.3
Cake Flour, sifted	12 oz	340 g	100

Procedure

1. Cream butter and powder sugar on low speed.
2. Slowly add egg yolks in four additions, scraping between each addition.
3. Add cake flour; mix until combined.
4. Scrape and mix again briefly.
5. Refrigerate for 4 hours before use.

Variation

Chocolate Short Dough

Ingredients	U.S.	Metric	%
Cake Flour	1 lb 4 oz	600 g	36.9
Cocoa Powder	2 oz	60 g	3.8

Graham Cracker Dough

Yield: 1 lb 15 oz (904 g)
Portions: 1
Portion size: 8 oz (227 g)
Yield description: Three 9-in. (23-cm) tart shells

Ingredients	U.S.	Metric	%
Butter	3.5 oz	100 g	11.1
Powdered Sugar	3.1 oz	88 g	9.7
Brown Sugar	3.1 oz	88 g	9.7
Salt	0.1 oz	4 g	0.4
All-Purpose Flour	15 oz	425 g	47
Honey	1.8 oz	50 g	5.5
Egg Yolks	4.4 oz	125 g	13.8
Vanilla Paste	0.9 oz	25 g	2.8

Procedure

1. Cream butter, brown sugar, and salt.
2. Sift dry ingredients.
3. Slowly add liquids, scraping often.
4. Add dry ingredients and mix until combined.
5. Chill dough for 4 hours.
6. Roll to ⅛ in. (3 mm) thick.
7. Bake at 350°F (175°C).

Cream Cheese Dough

Yield: 1 lb 10 oz (749 g)

Portions: 3

Portion size: 8 oz (227 g)

Yield description: Three 9-in. (23-cm) tart shells

Ingredients	U.S.	Metric	%
Pastry Flour	12 oz	340 g	100
Salt	0.06 oz	1.7 g	0.5
Butter, cold, cubed ¼ in. (6 mm)	7.2 oz	204 g	60
Cream Cheese, cold, cubed ¼ in. (6 mm)	5.4 oz	153 g	45
Water, ice cold	1.2 oz	34 g	10
Cider Vinegar	0.6 oz	17 g	5

Procedure

1. Sift pastry flour and salt.
2. Cut in cream cheese and butter.
3. Add water and cider vinegar; mix until dough is formed.
4. Refrigerate for 4 hours.

Sablé Breton

Yield: 1 lb 12 oz (830 g)

Portions: 3

Portion size: 8 oz (227 g)

Yield description: Three 9-in. (23-cm) rings

Ingredients	U.S.	Metric	%
Butter	7.8 oz	220 g	78.6
Sugar	7.1 oz	200 g	71.4
Egg Yolks	3.5 oz	100 g	35.7
All-Purpose Flour	9.9 oz	280 g	100
Baking Powder	0.35 oz	10 g	3.6

Procedure

1. Cream butter and sugar.
2. Add yolks in four additions, scraping between each addition.
3. Sift dry ingredients.
4. Add dry ingredients to creamed mixture to form a dough.
5. Scrape and mix again briefly.
6. Refrigerate for 4 hours.
7. Roll dough to desired thickness cut and place inside of ring molds.
8. Bake at 330°F (165°C).

Pâte Brisée

Yield: 1 lb 10 oz (749 g)

Portions: 3

Portion size: 8 oz (227 g)

Yield description: Three 9-in. (23-cm) tart rings

Ingredients	U.S.	Metric	%
Pastry Flour	14.4 oz	408 g	100
Butter, cold, cut into ½ in. (15 mm) cubes	7.2 oz	204 g	50
Egg Yolk	1.2 oz	34 g	83.3
Water, cold	3.6 oz	102 g	25
Salt	0.06 oz	1.7 g	0.4

Procedure

1. Cut butter into flour, using the paddle attachment until mixture resembles coarse cornmeal.

2. Add salt, water, and yolks; mix to combine.

3. Refrigerate.

Old-Fashioned Apple Pie

Yield: 2 lb 13.75 oz (1300 g)

Portions: 1

Portion size: 9-in. (23-cm) pie

Yield description: One 9-in. (23-cm) pie

Ingredients	U.S.	Metric
Granny Smith Apples, whole	2 lb 8 oz	1134 g
Brown Sugar	1.8 oz	51 g
Sugar	1.8 oz	51 g
Lemon Juice	0.5 oz	14 g
Cinnamon	0.2 oz	5.7 g
Nutmeg	0.02 oz	0.6 g
Salt	0.07 oz	2 g
Butter	1 oz	28 g
Cornstarch	0.5 oz	14 g

Procedure

1. Peel and core apples, slice into ⅛ in. (3 mm) thick slices.

2. Combine apples, brown sugar, sugar, lemon juice, cinnamon, nutmeg, and salt.

3. Toss together; cover and refrigerate for 45 minutes.

4. Drain apples to remove any liquid.

5. Add the butter to the drained liquid and reduce to a thick syrup.

6. Toss apples with cornstarch.

7. Pour reduction over apples and toss.

Cherry Pie

Yield: 2 lb 7 oz (1102 g)

Portions: 1

Portion size: 9-in. (23-cm) pie

Yield description: One 9-in. (23-cm) pie

Ingredients	U.S.	Metric
IQF Cherries, thawed and drained	1 lb 8 oz	680 g
Water, cold	2 oz	57 g
Cornstarch	1 oz	28 g
Drained Juice from Cherries	6 oz	170 g
Sugar #1	2 oz	57 g
Vanilla Bean, split and scraped	1 each	1 each
Sugar #2	3.5 oz	99 g
Salt	0.25 oz	5.7 g
Lime Juice	0.25 oz	5.7 g

Procedure

1. Drain juice from cherries; reserve juice.
2. Combine cold water and cornstarch to make a slurry.
3. Add first amount of sugar, vanilla bean, and cherry juice and bring to boil.
4. Whisk in slurry and bring to a boil.
5. Add second sugar, salt, and lime juice.
6. Fold in cherries.
7. Cool completely before use.

Peanut Butter Tart

Yield: 1 lb 9.6 oz (769 g)

Portions: 1

Portion size: 9-in. (23-cm) tart

Yield description: One 9-in. (23-cm) tart

Ingredients	U.S.	Metric
Peanut Butter	8 oz	227 g
Cream Cheese	8 oz	227 g
Powdered Sugar	4 oz	113 g
Butter	1 oz	28 g
Salt	0.1 oz	2.8 g
Heavy Cream	4 oz	113 g
Powdered Sugar	0.5 oz	14 g
Chocolate Short Dough, page 255		

Procedure

1. Cream peanut butter, cream cheese, powdered sugar, butter, and salt on medium high speed until lightened.
2. Whip cream and second powdered sugar to soft peaks.
3. Fold whipped cream into cream cheese mixture.
4. Fill baked and cooled chocolate short dough shell and refrigerate for 2 hours.

Chantilly (Stabilized)

Yield: 2 lb 6.8 oz (1102 g)

Portions: 1

Portion size: 2 lb 6.8 oz (1102 g)

Yield description: 1 portion at 2 lb 6.8 oz (1102 g)

Ingredients	U.S.	Metric
Heavy Cream	2 lb	907 g
Sugar	4.75 oz	135 g
Vanilla Bean, split and scraped, seeds only	2 each	2 each
Gelatin Powder	0.125 oz	3.5 g
Water, cold	2 oz	57 g

Procedure

1. Bloom gelatin in cold water.
2. Whip heavy cream, vanilla bean seeds, and sugar to medium peaks.
3. Dissolve gelatin over a water bath to 110°F (43°C).
4. Add 10% of the whipped cream to the gelatin and warm to 105°F (40°C).
5. Stream warm gelatin mixture into whipping cream.
6. Quickly fold to evenly distribute gelatin mixture.
7. Reserve in refrigerator.

Whiskey Pecan Pie

Yield: 1 lb 12.9 oz (819 g)

Portions: 1

Portion size: 9-in. (23-cm) pie

Yield description: One 9-in. (23-cm) pie

Ingredients	U.S.	Metric
Whiskey	1.2 oz	34 g
Vanilla Paste	0.5 oz	14 g
Eggs	6 oz	170 g
Sugar	4.8 oz	136 g
Light Corn Syrup	6.4 oz	181 g
Pecans	6.7 oz	190 g
Dark Chocolate Chips	3.3 oz	94 g
Chocolate Pâte Sablée, page 254		

Procedure

1. Combine whiskey, vanilla paste, eggs, corn syrup, and sugar with a whisk to form a custard mixture.
2. Strain mixture through a chinois.
3. Line a pie shell with chocolate pâte sablée.
4. Place pecans and chocolate chips.
5. Pour custard mixture over chips.
6. Bake at 350°F (175°C).

Fresh Fruit Tart, Classic

Portions: 1

Portion size: 9-in. (23-cm) tart

Yield description: One 9-in. (23-cm) tart

Components	U.S.	Metric
Pâte Sablée, page 254		
Raspberry Marmalade		
Almond Cream, page 78	12 oz	360 g
Pastry Cream, page 140	6 oz	180 g
Fresh Seasonal Fruit		
Apricot Glaze, page 106		

Procedure

1. Roll pâte sablée to ⅛ in. (3 mm) and line a 9-in. (23-cm) tart pan.

2. Spread a thin layer of raspberry marmalade in the bottom of the tart shell.

3. Pipe a layer of almond cream into the tart shell.

4. Bake at 350°F (175°C) for 25 minutes or until shell is golden brown.

5. After shell has cooled completely, fill with pastry cream.

6. Arrange fruit on top of pastry cream. Be sure to cover all of the pastry cream with the fruit.

7. Brush the fruit with apricot glaze.

FIGURE 9.2 Fresh Fruit Tart

Fresh Fruit Tart, Contemporary

Portions: 1

Portion size: 9-in. (23-cm) tart

Yield description: One 9-in. (23-cm) tart

Components	U.S.	Metric
Pâte Sablée, page 254		
Raspberry Marmalade		
Almond Cream, page 78	12 oz	360 g
Pastry Cream, page 140	6 oz	180 g
Vanilla Creaméux, page 140		
Poached Pear		
Fresh Fruit		
Macarons, page 314		
Apricot Glaze, page 106		
Chocolate Decor		

Procedure

1. Follow steps 1–5 in the fresh fruit tart procedure.
2. Prepare the vanilla creméux and freeze in 7-in. (180-mm) round mold.
3. Unmold the vanilla creméux and place on top of the pastry cream.
4. Place the macarons on the tart so they are leaning on the creméux.
5. Arrange the fresh fruit and poached pear and glaze with apricot glaze.

FIGURE 9.3 Contemporary Fruit Tart

Lemon Tart

Portions: 1

Portion size: 9-in. (23-cm) tart

Yield description: One 9-in. (23-cm) tart

Components

Short Dough, page 255

Lemon Curd, page 139

Italian Meringue, page 266

Powdered Sugar

Procedure

1. Roll short dough to ⅛ in. (3 mm) and blind bake in a 9-in. (23-cm) tart shell.
2. Cool shell completely and fill with prepared curd.
3. Pipe Italian meringue on top of curd.
4. Dust meringue with powdered sugar.
5. Brown meringue in 425°F (220°C) oven for 3 to 5 minutes.

FIGURE 9.4 Lemon Tart

Italian Meringue

Yield: 1 lb 2 oz (510 g)

Portions: 1

Portion size: 1 lb 2 oz (510 g)

Yield description: 1 portion at 1 lb 2 oz (510 g)

Ingredients	U.S.	Metric
Egg Whites	6 oz	170 g
Sugar	12 oz	340 g
Water	3 oz	85 g

Procedure

1. Italian meringue procedure (page XXX).

Raspberry Pistachio Tart

Portions: 1

Portion size: 8.5-in. (22-cm) square tart shell

Yield description: One 8.5-in. (22-cm) square tart shell

Ingredients	U.S.	Metric
Pâte Sablée, page 254		
Raspberry Diplomat, page 138		
Raspberry Pastry Cream, page 268		
Pistachio Creaméux, page 268		
Pistachio Dacquoise, page 269		
White Chocolate, melted	3.3 oz	100 g
Clear Glazing Gel, page 106		
Raspberry Pistachio Crumble, page 269		
Fresh Raspberries		
Powdered Sugar		

Procedure

1. Roll pâte sablée to ⅛ in. (3 mm) and blind bake in an 8.5-in. (22-cm) square tart shell.
2. While shell is still warm, brush with melted chocolate.
3. Prepare a half batch of diplomat from raspberry pastry cream.
4. Spread a layer of the diplomat in the tart shell.
5. Cut the pistachio dacquoise to 7.5 in. (19 cm) and place on top of the raspberry diplomat.
6. Spread a layer of the raspberry diplomat on top of the pistachio dacquoise to level the tart shell.
7. Unmold the pistachio creméux and glaze with clear glaze.
8. Place the pistachio creméux on top of the tart.
9. Cover the exposed raspberry cream with the raspberry pistachio crumble.
10. Dust the crumble with powdered sugar.
11. Place the raspberries on the edge of the creméux.

FIGURE 9.5 Raspberry Pistachio Tart

Pistachio Creméux

Yield: 10 oz (297 g)

Portions: 1

Portion size: 10 oz (297 g)

Yield description: 1 portion at 10 oz (297 g)

Ingredients	U.S.	Metric
Heavy Cream	3.6 oz	102 g
Milk	3.4 oz	96 g
Vanilla Bean, split and scraped	1 each	2 each
Egg Yolks	1.7 oz	48 g
Sugar	1.1 oz	31 g
Gelatin Sheets, bloomed for 15 minutes	1.25 each	1.25 each
Pistachio Paste	0.7 oz	20 g

Procedure

1. Crème anglaise method (page 124).
2. Add gelatin sheets and pistachio paste to crème anglaise before straining.
3. Pour into 7-in. (180-mm) mold and freeze.

Raspberry Pastry Cream

Yield: 14 oz (415 g)

Portions: 1

Portion size: 14 oz (415 g)

Yield description: 1 portion at 14 oz (415 g)

Ingredients	U.S.	Metric
Raspberry Purée	8.8 oz	250 g
Sugar #1	1.1 oz	31 g
Egg Yolk	0.88 oz	25 g
Whole Egg	0.88 oz	25 g
Sugar #2	1.1 oz	31 g
Cornstarch	0.8 oz	22.5 g
Butter	1.1 oz	30 g

Procedure

1. Combine raspberry purée and first sugar in a saucepan and bring to a boil.
2. Combine second sugar and cornstarch in a stainless steel bowl.
3. Add eggs and egg yolks to cornstarch mixture.
4. Whisk half of the raspberry purée into the egg mixture.
5. Return this mixture back to the saucepan.
6. Bring the cream to a boil for 2 minutes.
7. Remove from the heat and incorporate the butter.
8. Press the cream through a tamis.
9. Place the finished cream into a shallow pan and cover directly with plastic wrap.
10. Place on an ice bath and refrigerate.

Raspberry Pistachio Crumble

Yield: 4 oz (126.5 g)

Portions: 1

Portion size: 4 oz (126.5 g)

Yield description: 1 portion at 4 oz (126.5 g)

Ingredients	U.S.	Metric
Pistachios, lightly toasted	1.1 oz	30 g
Corn Flakes	1.1 oz	30 g
White Chocolate	1.1 oz	30 g
Cocoa Butter	1.1 oz	30 g
Freeze Dried Raspberries	0.2 oz	6 g
Salt	0.02 oz	0.5 g

Procedure

1. Melt cocoa butter and white chocolate.
2. Combine corn flakes, raspberries, salt, and pistachios in a food processor; pulse to grind mixture.
3. Fold melted chocolate mixture into the corn flake mixture.
4. Roll out between two sheets of parchment paper and allow to crystallize.
5. Break the hardened mixture into pieces and pulse again in a food processor to a coarse consistency.

Pistachio Dacquoise

Yield: 1 lb 11 oz (840 g)

Portions: 1

Portion size: half sheet pan

Yield description: 1 half sheet pan

Ingredients	U.S.	Metric
Pistachio Flour	4.9 oz	140 g
Almond Flour	4.9 oz	140 g
Powdered Sugar	7.4 oz	210 g
Egg Whites	9.9 oz	280 g
Sugar	2.5 oz	70 g

Procedure

1. Sift pistachio flour, almond flour, and powdered sugar.
2. Make a common meringue with egg whites and sugar.
3. Fold dry ingredients into meringue.
4. Spread onto silpat-lined half sheet pan.
5. Bake at 400°F (200°C) for 12 to 13 minutes.

Peach Galette

Portions: 1

Portion size: 8-in. (20-cm) gallete

Yield description: One 8-in. (20-cm) gallete

Components

Cream Cheese Dough, page 256

Peach Galette Filling, page 271

Egg Wash

Oatmeal Streusel, page 79

Coarse White Sugar

Egg Wash

Powdered Sugar

Procedure

1. Roll cream cheese dough to ⅛ in. (3 mm) thick to a diameter of 11.5 in. (30 cm).

2. Place prepared peach galette filling in the center of the dough.

3. Fold the sides of the dough over the peaches, leaving the center uncovered.

4. Egg wash the sides of the dough and sprinkle with coarse sugar.

5. Top the galette with the oatmeal streusel.

6. Bake at 400°F (205°C) for 30 minutes.

7. After the galette has cooled, dust with powdered sugar.

FIGURE 9.6 Peach Galette

Peach Galette Filling

Yield: 1 lb 13 oz (843 g)

Portions: 1

Portion size: 1 lb 13 oz (843 g)

Yield description: 1 portion at 1 lb 13 oz (843 g)

Ingredients	U.S.	Metric
Peaches, sliced, ¼ in. (6 mm) thick	1 lb 8 oz	680 g
Sugar	3.3 oz	94 g
Salt	0.1 oz	2.8 g
Cinnamon	0.03 oz	0.9 g
Cornstarch	0.3 oz	8.5 g
Sliced Almonds, lightly toasted	2 oz	57 g

Procedure

1. Combine peaches, sugar, salt, and cinnamon. Let sit for 30 minutes.
2. Strain the juice from the peaches and reduce to a thick syrup.
3. Combine peaches, cornstarch, and sliced almonds.
4. Pour reduced syrup over peaches.

Tiramisu Tart

Portions: 1

Portion size: 13.75 × 4.5 in. (35 × 11.5 cm) tart

Yield description: One 13.75 × 4.5 in. (35 × 11.5 cm) tart

Components

Chocolate Short Dough, page 255

Mascarpone Cream, page 274

Dark Chocolate Ganache, page 351

Chocolate Genoise, page 192

Coffee Marsala Syrup, page 275

Cocoa Powder (as needed)

Procedure

1. Roll chocolate short dough to ⅛ in. (3 mm) thick and line 13.75 × 4.5 in. (35 × 11.5 cm) tart shell and blind bake.

2. Spread a layer of ganache in the bottom of the tart.

3. Place a ¼ in. (6 mm) thick layer of the chocolate genoise on top of the ganache.

4. Soak the genoise with the coffee marsala syrup.

5. Spread a layer of mascarpone cream to the top of the tart shell.

6. Pipe the remaining mascarpone cream with a St Honoré tip.

7. Lightly dust the top of the mascarpone cream with cocoa powder.

FIGURE 9.7 Tiramisu Tart

English Cream

Yield: 1 lb 9 oz (725 g)

Portions: 1

Portion size: 1 lb 9 oz (725 g)

Yield description: 1 portion at 1 lb 9 oz (725 g)

Ingredients	U.S.	Metric
Heavy Cream	1 lb 1.6 oz	500 g
Egg Yolk	3.5 oz	100 g
Sugar	4.4 oz	125 g
Gelatin Sheets, bloomed	3.5 each	3.5 each
Vanilla Bean, split and scraped	3 each	3 each

Procedure

1. Make a crème anglaise (page 143).

2. Add gelatin after cooking and strain through a chinois.

3. Refrigerate overnight.

Mascarpone Cream

Yield: 2 lb 8 oz (1160 g)

Portions: 1

Portion size: 2 lb 8 oz (1160 g)

Yield description: 1 portion at 2 lb 8 oz (1160 g)

Ingredients	U.S.	Metric
English Cream, from previous recipe	1 lb 8.7 oz	700 g
Mascarpone Cheese	1 lb 0.2 oz	460 g

Note: If overwhipped, mascarpone cheese will break.

Procedure

1. Mix English Cream in a mixer with a whip on high speed for 10 minutes.

2. Add mascarpone cheese and mix until the mixture resembles a mousse.

3. Fill molds or pipe immediately.

4. Refrigerate for 2 hours to set the cream.

Coffee Marsala Syrup

Yield: 7 oz (210 g)
Portions: 1
Portion size: 7 oz (210 g)
Yield description: 1 portion at 7 oz (210 g)

Ingredients	U.S.	Metric
Water	1.8 oz	50 g
Sugar	1.8 oz	50 g
Coffee Extract	3.5 oz	100 g
Marsala Wine	0.4 oz	10 g

Procedure

1. Combine water and sugar; heat to dissolve.
2. Cool syrup on an ice bath.
3. Add coffee extract and marsala wine.

Hazelnut Cream

Yield: 1 lb 11.75 oz (787 g)
Portions: 1
Portion size: 1 lb 11.75 oz (787 g)
Yield description: 1 portion at 1 lb 11.75 oz (787 g)

Ingredients	U.S.	Metric
Heavy Cream	8 oz	227 g
Milk	7.5 oz	213 g
Sugar	3 oz	85 g
Gelatin Powder	0.25 oz	7 g
Water	1 oz	28 g
Hazelnut Paste	8 oz	227 g

Procedure

1. Bloom gelatin in water.
2. Heat heavy cream, milk, and sugar to a simmer.
3. Add gelatin to dissolve.
4. Add hazelnut paste, emulsify, and strain through chinois.
5. Pour into molds and freeze.

Banana Tart

Portions: 1

Portion size: 9-in. (23-cm) tart

Yield description: One 9-in. (23-cm) tart

Components	U.S.	Metric
Pâte Sablée, page 254		
Milk Chocolate, melted	3.3 oz	100 g
Banana Mousse, page 173		
Bananas in Lime Juice, page 277		
Milk Chocolate Banana Ganache, page 277		
Stabilized Whipped Cream, page 259		
Chocolate Mirror Glaze, page 231		
White Chocolate Spray, page 397		

Procedure

1. Prepare the banana mousse and freeze in an 8-in. (20-cm) ring mold; freeze additional mousse in assorted half sphere molds.

2. Roll pâte sablée to ⅛ in. (3 mm) thick and blind bake in a 9-in. (23-cm) tart shell.

3. While the shell is slightly warm, brush with melted milk chocolate.

4. After the chocolate has crystallized, place the banana slices in the shell.

5. Pour the milk chocolate banana ganache over the bananas; refrigerate.

6. Unmold the ring mold of banana mousse and glaze with the chocolate mirror glaze, place onto the ganache.

7. Spray the half spheres of banana mousse with white cocoa butter spray tinted yellow; use these to garnish the tart.

8. Pipe Stabilized Whipped Cream around the tart.

FIGURE 9.8 Banana Tart

Milk Chocolate Banana Ganache

Yield: 15 oz (435 g)

Portions: 1

Portion size: 15 oz (435 g)

Yield description: 1 portion at 15 oz (435 g)

Ingredients	U.S.	Metric
Heavy Cream	6.3 oz	180 g
Milk Chocolate	7.2 oz	205 g
Banana Purée	1.8 oz	50 g

Procedure

1. Heat heavy cream to a boil.
2. Pour cream over chocolate and emulsify with an immersion blender.
3. Add banana purée and emulsify.
4. Pour into tart shell while warm.

Bananas in Lime Juice

Yield: 7 oz (200 g)

Portions: 1

Portion size: 7 oz (200 g)

Yield description: 1 portion at 7 oz (200 g)

Ingredients	U.S.	Metric
Bananas	7 oz	200 g
Lime Juice	1.1 oz	30 g

Procedure

1. Slice bananas into ⅛ in. (3 mm) thick slices.
2. Toss bananas in lime juice.
3. Drain to remove excess lime juice.

Chocolate Mousse Tart

Portions: 1

Portion size: 8.5-in. (22-cm) square tart

Yield description: One 8.5-in. (22-cm) square tart

Components

Chocolate Short Dough, page 255

Dark Chocolate Mousse, page 135

Caramel Glaze, page 236

Hazelnut Cream, page 275

Dark Chocolate Spray, page 397

Procedure

1. Roll chocolate short dough to ⅛ in. (3 mm) and blind bake in an 8.5-in. (22-cm) square tart shell.

2. Place two rings of the hazelnut cream in the bottom of the shell.

3. Fill to the top of the tart shell with dark chocolate mousse.

4. Pipe a border around the edge of the shell.

5. Freeze the tart and spray with dark chocolate spray for a velvet texture.

6. Glaze the center of the tart with caramel glaze.

FIGURE 9.9 Chocolate Mousse Tart

Cranberry Orange Tart

Portions: 1

Portion size: 9-in. (23-cm) tart

Yield description: One 9-in. (23-cm) tart

Components

Short Dough, page 255

Crème Brûlée, page 140

Poached Cranberries, page 281

Clafoutis, page 144, half batch

Orange Supremes

Clear Glaze, page 106

Procedure

1. Roll short dough to ⅛ in. (3 mm) thick and blind bake halfway in a 9-in. (23-cm) tart shell.

2. Cool shell and fill with poached cranberries and clafoutis custard bake at 350°F (175°C).

3. Unmold frozen brûlée, sprinkle with sugar and brûlée with a blowtorch while still frozen.

4. Transfer caramelized custard to cooled clafoutis tart shell.

5. Place orange supremes around the edge of the brûlée and apply clear glaze.

FIGURE 9.10 Cranberry Orange Tart

Poached Cranberries

Yield: 6 oz (185 g)
Portions: 1
Portion size: 6 oz (185 g)
Yield description: 1 portion at 6 oz (185 g)

Ingredients	U.S.	Metric
Water	1 lb 10 oz	800 g
Sugar	6.7 oz	200 g
Cranberry	6.2 oz	185 g

Procedure

1. Combine water and sugar; bring to a boil.
2. Reduce to a simmer and add cranberries.
3. Cook until cranberries are tender.
4. Strain and cool.

Cranberry Orange Tart Brûlée

Yield: 1 lb 9 oz (718 g)
Portions: 1
Portion size: 1 lb 9 oz (718 g)
Yield description: 1 portion at 1 lb 9 oz (718 g)

Ingredients	U.S.	Metric
Milk	4.8 oz	135 g
Cream	11.8 oz	335 g
Sugar	2.8 oz	80 g
Agar	0.06 oz	1.6 g
Egg Yolks	5.8 oz	165 g
Vanilla Bean, split and scraped	½ each	½ each
Gelatin Powder	0.02 oz	0.5 g
Water	0.07 oz	2 g

Procedure

1. Combine agar with half the sugar.
2. Bloom gelatin in water.
3. Add remaining sugar to egg yolks and whisk to combine.
4. Bring milk, cream, vanilla bean, and agar/sugar mixture to a boil; simmer for 5 minutes.
5. Temper milk and cream mixture into egg yolks; continue cooking like a crème anglaise.
6. Add gelatin mixture stir to dissolve.
7. Strain through a chinois.
8. Pour custard into a 7-in. (180-mm) mold and freeze.

Tea Tart

Portions: 1

Portion size: 9-in. (23-cm) tart

Yield description: One 9-in. (23-cm) tart

Components

Pâte Sablée, page 254

Tea Tart Ganache, page 283

Stabilized Chantilly, page 259

Chocolate Decoration

Procedure

1. Roll pâte sablée to ⅛ in. (3 mm) thick and blind bake halfway in a 9-in. (23-cm) tart shell.

2. Pipe stabilized Chantilly on top of crystallized ganache with a ¼-in. (6-mm) plain pastry tip.

3. Place chocolate decoration on top of stabilized Chantilly.

FIGURE 9.11 Tea Tart

Tea Tart Ganache

Yield: 1 lb 12 oz (815 g)

Portions: 1

Portion size: 1 lb 12 oz (815 g)

Yield description: 1 portion at 1 lb 12 oz (815 g)

Ingredients	U.S.	Metric
Heavy Cream	14.1 oz	400 g
Earl Grey Tea	0.4 oz	10 g
Honey	2.6 oz	75 g
64% Dark Chocolate	6.3 oz	180 g
Milk Chocolate	1.8 oz	50 g
Butter, softened	2.1 oz	60 g
Trimoline	1.4 oz	40 g

Procedure

1. Combine heavy cream and Earl Grey tea; heat, cover, and steep for 15 minutes. While steeping, add the honey.

2. Strain heavy cream to remove tea.

3. Return heavy cream to simmer and emulsify with dark and milk chocolate to create ganache.

4. Combine Trimoline and butter with ganache and emulsify.

5. Pour ganache into prebaked tart shell and allow ganache to crystallize for 4 hours before serving. Do not refrigerate tart.

Apple Tart

Portions: 1

Portion size: 8-in. (20-cm) tart

Yield description: One 8-in. (20-cm) tart

Components

Sablé Breton, page 256

Caramel Creméux, page 285

Apple Pectin Gel, page 285

Procedure

1. Roll sablée breton to ¼ in. (6 mm); cut and bake in a 8-in. (20-cm) metal ring.

2. Whip caramel creméux for 5 minutes and pipe onto cooled sablée breton.

3. Place apple pectin gel on top of caramel creméux.

FIGURE 9.12 Apple Tart

Apple Pectin Gel

Yield: 1 lb 7 oz (662 g)

Portions: 1

Portion size: 1 lb 7 oz (662 g)

Yield description: 1 portion at 1 lb 7 oz (662 g)

Ingredients	U.S.	Metric
Granny Smith Apples, peeled and sliced	14.1 oz	400 g
Sugar	5.3 oz	150 g
Glucose	2.3 oz	65 g
Water	1.4 oz	40 g
Pectin NH	0.2 oz	7 g

Procedure

1. Combine water, sugar, and glucose.
2. Heat to an amber caramel; pour onto a silpat to cool.
3. Grind caramel with pectin in a food processor.
4. Layer apples and caramel mixture in an 8-in. (20-cm) metal cake ring; place a weight on top of the apples to compress during baking.
5. Bake at 180°F (82°C) for 1 hour 45 minutes.
6. Place in the freezer to unmold apples.

Caramel Creméux

Yield: 2 lb 3 oz (1000 g)

Portions: 1

Portion size: 2 lb 3 oz (1000 g)

Yield description: 1 portion at 2 lb 3 oz (1000 g)

Ingredients	U.S.	Metric
Sugar	7.1 oz	200 g
Water	1.8 oz	50 g
Heavy Cream	1 lb 0.9 oz	480 g
Vanilla Beans, split and scraped	2 each	2 each
Egg Yolks	4.6 oz	130 g
Cocoa Butter	2.8 oz	80 g
Caramelia Chocolate	2.1 oz	60 g
Gelatin Sheets, bloomed	4 each	4 each

Procedure

1. Combine water and sugar; caramelize.
2. Deglaze with heavy cream and add vanilla beans.
3. Cook on low to dissolve any remaining caramel.
4. Bring cream mixture to simmer and temper into egg yolks; cook like a crème anglaise.
5. Pour caramel anglaise mixture over caramelia and cocoa butter; emulsify.
6. Add gelatin and strain through a chinois.
7. Place on an ice bath and reserve in the cooler.

Pear Almond Cream Tart

Portions: 1
Portion size: 9-in. (23-cm) tart
Yield description: One 9-in. (23-cm) tart

Components

Short Dough, page 255

Poached Pears, page 286

Almond Cream, page 78

Apricot Glaze, page 106

Procedure

1. Roll short dough to ⅛ in. (3 mm) thick and blind bake halfway in a 9-in. (23-cm) tart shell.

2. Pipe the almond cream into the tart shell.

3. Drain pears from poaching liquid; cut in half and slice.

4. Fan pears on top of almond cream.

5. Bake at 350°F (175°C) until short dough is a golden brown color.

6. After cooling brush the top of the tart with apricot glaze.

Poached Pears

Portions: 1
Portion size: 6 poached pears
Yield description: 1 portion at 6 poached pears

Ingredients	U.S.	Metric
Bosc Pears	6 each	6 each
Water	2 lb 3 oz	1000 g
Sugar	8.8 oz	250 g
Cinnamon Stick	1 each	1 each
Star Anise	1 each	1 each
Vanilla Bean, split and scraped	2 each	2 each

Procedure

1. Combine water, sugar, cinnamon stick, star anise, and vanilla bean and bring to a boil.

2. Peel pears and use a parisienne scoop to remove the seeds.

3. Add the pears to the liquid and reduce to a low simmer; cover the pears with a cartouche.

4. The size and ripeness of the pear will determine the cooking time. The more ripe the pear, the shorter the cooking time. Test the pears with a knife. When the knife is inserted without any resistance, the pears are cooked through.

5. Cover the pan with plastic wrap and cool over an ice bath.

6. To intensify the flavor, store the pears in the poaching liquid overnight before using.

Pumpkin Tart

Portions: 8

Portion size: 3.25 in. (9 cm)

Yield description: 8 tarts at 3.25 in. (9 cm)

Components

Graham Cracker Dough, page 255

Pumpkin Bavarian, page 288

White Chocolate Mousse, page 135

White Chocolate Spray, page 397

Procedure

1. Roll graham cracker dough to ⅛ in. (3 mm) and blind bake in 3.25-in. (9-cm) tart shells.

2. Prepare white chocolate mousse and freeze in 2.75-in. (7-cm) round molds.

3. After cooling tart shells, prepare pumpkin Bavarian and fill shells.

4. Unmold white chocolate mousse onto a parchment-lined sheet pan.

5. Spray white chocolate spray onto unmolded mousse to achieve a velvet texture (page 397).

6. Place the white chocolate mousse onto the pumpkin Bavarian.

FIGURE 9.13 Individual Pumpkin Tart

Pumpkin Bavarian

Yield: 1 lb 8 oz (668.5 g)

Portions: 1

Portion size: 1 lb 8 oz (668.5 g)

Yield description: 1 portion at 1 lb 8 oz (668.5 g)

Ingredients	U.S.	Metric
Pumpkin Purée	4.6 oz	130 g
Heavy Cream	4.6 oz	130 g
Vanilla Bean	1 each	1 each
Brown Sugar	3.7 oz	105 g
Egg Yolks	1.9 oz	53 g
Heavy Cream	9.5 oz	270 g
Gelatin Sheets	3 each	3 each
Pumpkin Pie Spice	0.04 oz	1 g

Procedure

1. Bavarian procedure (page 133).

Key Terms

Galette

Mealy pie dough

Flaky pie dough

Crumb crust

Single crusted

Double crusted

Blind baked

Docked

Questions for Review

1. Describe the difference between a pie and tart.

2. Identify two fats used in pie and tart doughs and discuss the advantages and disadvantages of each.

3. Why is it important to not stretch dough when lining a shell?

4. There are two methods used to blind bake dough: Select one and describe the process.

CHAPTER 10

Plated Desserts

The old saying goes, "You never get a second chance to make a first impression." When it comes to plated desserts, you never get a second chance to make a last impression. Throughout the years, the role of the pastry chef has become more important to restaurants, hotels, and country clubs. The last course that goes to the diner is the dessert; a great dessert can make a memorable experience even better.

LEARNING OBJECTIVES

After reading this chapter, you should be able to:

1. **Design** desserts utilizing familiar flavor combinations in a refined way.
2. **Create** plated desserts for a variety of restaurant styles.
3. **Explain** the importance of flavor, texture, temperature, and presentation.
4. **Identify** the components needed for a balanced dessert.
5. **Describe** the process for designing a plated dessert.

Presentation Approach

Plated desserts provide the pastry chef a way to create something both artistic and delicious for their guests. Originally, sugar showpieces were placed in the front windows of pastry shops to show the skill and mastery of the chef, as well as to market the shop's products. Restaurants have used different approaches—from dessert carts to printed menus, to social media—to promote its pastry chef and his or her creations. While these marketing approaches continue to transform and adapt, desserts continue to evolve, allowing the pastry chef to develop a signature "style."

Over the years, trends and techniques have changed—whether it is the combination of flavors used or the style in which the dessert is presented. Recent years have seen an increase in the use of savory items, such as bacon or beets in desserts. Along with introducing new flavors, plating styles change as well. The 1990s brought a wave of desserts that were over engineered and made the desserts difficult to eat. Ten years later, almost anything that could be "deconstructed," was. This trend brought classical items that were broken down into the different components and assembled in a way that did not resemble the original in any way except flavors.

Current plating style is a "**scattered**" appearance that at first looks like several items tossed on the plate. However, it is exactly the opposite. This style takes a considerable amount of effort to prepare and execute. No matter which style fits you best, new combinations can always be created; a major part of the job of the chef is to create a memorable experience for the guest. One thing that remains constant, though, is that *flavor is the single most important element on the plate.*

FIGURE 10.1a–c Three ways to plate a pineapple upside-down cake:

classical   fine dining   scattered dessert plating

Design

Plated desserts not only need to taste good, they also need to be appealing to the eye. As desserts are designed, a great deal of thought needs to be used to incorporate flavors that complement and contrast each other while producing an attractive design. A beautiful dessert that lacks in flavor will be easily forgotten. At the same time, a delicious dessert that is not presented in an attractive way will be difficult to sell. Unlike most art forms, which only focus on one of the senses, the pastry chef must construct desserts with a harmony between the elements of flavor and visual design.

The pastry chef has many tools to use to create a memorable experience. From a simple rustic tart to an elaborate à la minute dessert served in a high-end restaurant, there is a place for all styles. It is important to have a thorough understanding of what creates a balanced plate, in regards to both visual and flavor components. There are five key components to achieve this:

1. Flavor
2. Texture
3. Temperature
4. Color
5. Shape

Flavor

Flavor needs to be addressed first. You can create the most elaborate dessert, but without flavor the design will be forgotten. The dessert menu should harmonize with the previous courses and reflect continuity through the progression of the meal. In a restaurant that serves a classical French menu, a tropical dessert would not be a good fit for the end of the meal. A better selection to consider would be a more traditional French pastry such as a vanilla crème brûlée.

It is important to consider not only which flavors will be utilized but how many. A hard lesson to learn, but one of the greatest techniques that can be taught in the kitchen is editing—less can sometimes be more. While many different flavors can work on the plate, it can become confusing. When selecting flavor, decide what the "main" flavor of the plate will be and provide additional complementing and contrasting flavors. All too often, when a new component is added to a plate, a new flavor is introduced. Using the same flavor can build complexity on the plate, while keeping the "main" flavor. *The plate should be composed of no more than three flavors.*

There are some flavors that can be used on the plate that are not that different and can be treated as the same flavor; these flavors are in the same **flavor families**.

Flavor Families

Main Flavor	Similar Flavors		
Chocolate	Dark	Milk	White
Berry	Strawberry	Blueberry	Raspberry
Citrus	Lemon	Lime	Orange
Nut	Pistachio	Hazelnut	Peanut

The term *rich* is often used to describe desserts. The overall flavor profile tends to be on the sweet side for many desserts. This can be overcome by using a combination of the basic tastes: sweet, sour, salty, bitter, and umami. The term **umami** literally translates to "pleasant savory taste." Sometimes confused with the flavor of salt, it is different and refers to an earthy flavor. Mushrooms, meat, seafood, vegetables, cheese, and fermented products are some of the more common foods that have the umami flavor. However, many items ranging from classic to modern desserts use this flavor to add complexity. Sweet potato, green tea, cheeses, green peas, carrots, bacon, and even foie gras can be found on desserts in a wide variety of restaurants. These elements can be successfully added into a dessert menu. Many desserts focus on sweet, sour, salty, and bitter.

Successful flavor combinations can be developed easily from existing flavor combinations. Flavor is something experienced by more than just the palate. Familiar flavors like apple pie, chocolate chip cookies, or even peanut butter and jelly remind us of past events. Looking toward these combinations for inspiration will provide flavors that are proven to work together, and a familiarity for the guest.

Texture

Texture can make the difference between good and great. Utilizing contrasting components in a dessert creates an interesting experience. An experienced pastry chef works soft, crunchy, fatty, dry, and smooth textures into many desserts. These components can be obvious in the dessert's composition or hidden inside a component of the dessert. There are benefits to using both of these techniques. Having the different textures visible shows the complexity of the dessert. Providing a hidden crunchy layer inside a cake gives a surprise when eaten. When considering the dessert menu as a whole, implementing both of these techniques will provide a visual appeal to the desserts and ensure that there is something appealing to a variety of diners.

This helps to draw the guest in; something smooth and shiny provides a sleek look, leaving the imagination to guess what is inside. When the dessert is cut into, a surprise of colors, flavors, and textures elevates the already mysterious item. Placing textured items such as granola, nougatine, or finely chopped nuts directly on the plate provides eye appeal and helps identify the flavors that are on the plate. Additionally, they provide the crunchy element that is often missing from desserts. Smooth components add concentrated flavor to the dessert—they can be light and airy or dense. Cakes can provide a variety of textural elements, covering a wide range: dense, light, moist, dry, crispy, or chewy.

Temperature

Temperature differences not only change the eating experience but also the way the flavors come through. Consider a warm slice of apple pie à la mode. It consists of such simple combinations, yet there are many things happening on the plate. The warm pie creates a cool sauce out of the melted ice cream both on the plate and inside your mouth. Incorporating any combination of items ranging from frozen to hot allows the pastry chef the opportunity to introduce another element to the diner. Something unexpected will continue to build on the experience of the meal.

Color

This is one of the most difficult areas for a plate. The main challenge is understanding when there is enough color on a plate, and not adding color just for the sake of adding color. A vibrant, colorful plate can look very attractive to some diners, while others may not be concerned with this and will base their selection on other factors. This leaves the chef many options when creating plates; utilizing a range of color schemes and variety across the menu will produce a variety of options for the guest to choose from.

Just like the guest, some chefs may want a wide range of colors while others are not as concerned. The chef has many elements to work with when creating a plate, and color is only one of these. Color may be the first hint at what is on the plate, and start guiding the diner through the flavors they may experience. There are the four other plate design elements—flavor, temperature, texture, and shape—that chefs can use in their creations. Not all desserts need a variety of colors: **monochromatic** plates can be just as attractive and taste equally as good. The plate can be composed of one color and use the shades of that color to create interest. A dessert that is brown also can have yellow, orange, and burgundy.

Considering the seasonality of items will also influence the colors used in a dessert. Currently, restaurants are utilizing local ingredients and advertising this on the menu. The availability of seasonal and local ingredients will help to determine the flavors offered on the menu, and encourage menu changes throughout the year. Of course, many fruits such as strawberries, raspberries, and apples are available year round. However, berries tend to be a summer fruit and apples a fall fruit. There is no written rule against using berries in the fall, but having knowledge of seasonality will help your desserts taste and look the best they can be. It is important to remember that fruit in season not only looks better and tastes better, it tends to be less

FIGURE 10.2 Shades of brown

FIGURE 10.3 Plated dessert showing shades of brown

expensive. Researching new options for a red fruit that can replace a strawberry on a winter menu will show creativity and continue to help you expand your knowledge of the products available and new uses for them.

Back to the apple pie example: What are the colors on that plate? The pie and filling are both brown, with an off-white ice cream, creating an attractive yet monochromatic presentation. Adding color to the plate means revising the flavor component. Adding a strawberry garnish to the apple pie would add a pop of red to the plate (color) and strawberry could go with apple (flavor component). However, a sliced or fanned strawberry really does not do much more than add color. Thinking of the seasonality of these two items, apples are fall and strawberries are summer. There needs to be some logic behind the selection of all components to a plate. Sure the strawberry looks good and it doesn't taste bad with the apple pie, but why is it there? When thinking of apples, a fall crop, cranberry also comes to mind. It provides a deep red color that is in the same season that apples typically are harvested and eaten. Additions to the plate for any component should be well thought out and not just done to ensure all components are met.

While colorful desserts can be interesting and help convey the flavors, it is important to remember that too much color can be confusing. There is no rule limiting the amount of colors on the plate. The color wheel introduced to us in art class can provide some assistance in deciding on color usage. The color wheel provides an example of complementary and contrasting colors. Color is something that should be experimented with when creating a dessert. Remember to use colors that are available and occur in nature. In most cases, adding food color should not be necessary. Respecting the ingredients and handling them properly will help to provide the color desired.

Shape

The visual component of shape works together with color and textures present in a dessert. Shapes are to the eye what flavors are to the palate. A variety of shapes will present an attractive selection to the guest. This is not only on each individual plate, but also the dessert menu as a whole. The plate can have complementary and contrasting shapes to create interest and flow on the plate. These shapes can be used to move the diner's eye around the plate and ultimately visually lead them to the main component of the dish. A swoosh of sauce or an elegantly twisted tuile will catch the eye and bring it to the center of the plate. There are different combinations that can be used to achieve an attractive presentation.

Combining shapes breaks up the plate and helps to enhance presentation. To help this process, roughly sketching the plates on the menu will verify that all the desserts will not look the same. After sketching the desserts, analyze the shapes of the components and see if variety can be added. The available equipment can limit shapes of desserts; variety of shape can be added in the form of a round scoop of ice cream or a dot of sauce. Consider combining rounded smooth shapes with sharp rectangles or triangles.

Attractive plating using the same size and shape, called "**sameness**," can be very interesting. This style works best if all sizes are exactly the same, similar to what can be found in some modern art. The exactness of these items adds to the appeal.

When thinking about using shapes, several questions need to be answered.

What Shape Am I Trying to Achieve? As previously discussed, shape needs to be decided. This can be a simple rectangle or square cut out of a sheet, a round tart, or if a more intricate shape is desired, molds are available to the chef. Keep in mind that a complex shape being cut out of a larger sheet will incur product loss. When cutting out of sheets try to stick with squares, rectangles, parallelograms, or trapezoids. Also consider the size of the dessert—this will vary depending on the restaurant. A good starting point is 4 oz (120 g) for all components on the plate.

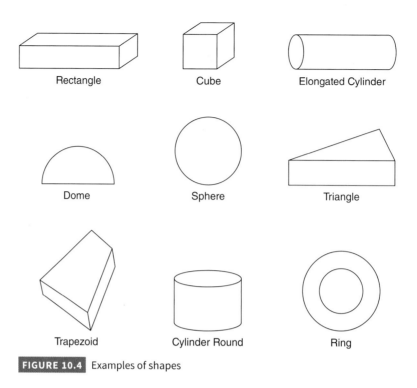

FIGURE 10.4 Examples of shapes

What Style of Food Does the Restaurant Serve? The style of food refers to the service level of the restaurant and the design of the food. This is inclusive of ingredients, technique, and service style.

Harmonizing the dessert with previous courses is important. Planning the dessert menu along with the main menu will provide continuity throughout the meal. It ensures that the courses continue to follow a progression and make sense. Knowing the style that the restaurant serves and, more importantly, serving shapes that are familiar to the diner are important. A traditional style restaurant may have a pie on the menu; this could be a slice or even an individual tart or pie. The diner would expect the shape to be a triangular wedge of pie or a round tart. Serving a square tart may be an option and provide a different look, but would be more fitting for a more contemporary restaurant.

Current trends present a more scattered plating style. This is visually attractive plating. Modern techniques can be easily utilized—ingredients can be changed based on availability, and the dessert is interactive for the guest. Pastry chefs can create different flavor combinations, as they experiment with the various components. While this style appears to have a haphazard approach, it requires knowledge of the ingredients and how to assemble in a timely manner. Desserts are plated **à la minute**, in a minute, meaning the order is placed and the dessert is plated. The complexity of the dessert means a longer time to plate up, which in turn means a longer wait for the guest. Consider the time plate-up will take when designing all desserts.

What Do the Other Desserts Look Like? The food a chef serves is art. Art is an expression of creativity, and as chefs we create with our minds and our hearts. We strive to present our creations to the guest to provide them an emotional experience, and please them. As with any form of art, it is subjective—trying to decide what is good art or bad art is entirely up to the guest. This brings about the next question.

What Is Your Personal Style as a Pastry Chef? All chefs have a style, and most evolve over the course of their career. Starting out, many young chefs imitate what they have encountered in their career, books, magazines, Internet, and television. As your career continues, you will begin to formulate your own style from the many experiences in your career.

Developing your own style helps to create your own brand. This is something that will develop over your career. Variety is important. Using the five components of dessert design will help you to diversify the menu. The best way to evaluate this is to lay out all the desserts on your menu together and look at what is on the table. The early step of sketching the plates helps to prevent too much repetition on the menu. Some items can still be overlooked, so once the menu is written and developed, assemble all the plates and evaluate what you have in front of you. If you notice repetition in these items, now is the time to make any necessary changes.

What Plate Am I Going to Use? A wide variety of plates is available. Plate selection is dependent on the size, shape, and layout of the dessert. It is much easier to create a dessert to fit on a plate, rather than having a plate and forcing a dessert to fit. The plate does not make the dessert, but it can impact the final design and at the same time, take away from the dessert. Many restaurants are limited by what plates they have. Investing in new plates can be expensive. Restaurants have been serving desserts in mason jars and martini glasses, creating new ways to use items found in restaurants and kitchens.

Finding a unique plate creates a challenge for the chef. A plate that does not fit the normal round, square, or rectangle is interesting and different. This can be a challenge met with mixed results. While the plate may be different, it may make the dessert too small or crowded on the plate. Keep in mind portion size and the ease of eating the dessert on the plate when selecting a plate.

Flat, rimless plates create a challenge to the diner: there is no place to push the food against to help scoop up the dessert. Additionally, items could fall off the plate on the way to the table or frozen components could melt and run off on the table. Alternately, deep bowls with large rims may make the portion size appear smaller, or make the dessert challenging to access. Glass bowls and plates provide an enticing view of the dessert from different angles. Ultimately, the plate should enhance the dessert presentation, not distract from or overwhelm it.

Getting Started

With so many choices to make, it can be overwhelming identifying what to do first. Here are some steps to getting started in developing a plated dessert:

1. Create an inventory of components.
2. Choose the main component for the dessert.
3. Select flavors.
4. Select garnish(es) and sauce.
5. Assemble dessert.
6. Evaluate final product.

Creating an Inventory

An inventory list will help to keep you organized as you move toward finalizing your creation. Using the techniques you have gained through the use of this text, categorize the items under main categories to create a visual reference. The inventory helps to reduce overusing items multiple times on the same menu. The items can be broken into main categories such as Sauces, Creams, Baked items, Fruit, and Frozen. These categories can be broken down into further sub categories. As an example, fruit can be broken down into color, preparation method, and shapes.

Component Inventory

Creams		
Chocolate Mousse—White, Milk, and Dark	Curd	Chiboust
Bavarian	Rice Pudding	Rice Pudding
Fruit Mousse	Flan	Cheesecake
Creaméux	Crème Brûlée	Blanc mange

Baked Items		
Cakes	Pain de Genes	Filo
Dacquoise	Doughs	Fried
Japonaise	Short Dough	Brioche
Jaconde	Struesel Based	Fritters
Pâte a Choux	Pie Dough	Churros
Macarons	Puff Pastry	

Frozen Items		
Parfait	Ice Cream	Granita
Semifreddo	Gelato	Ice Pops
Soufflé Glace	Sherbet	

Sauces		
Chocolate—Milk, White, Dark	Foams	Coulis
Sabayon	Infusion	Caramel
Anglaise	Reduction	Fluid Gel

Fruit				
Colors	**Preparation Method**	**Shapes**		
Red	Sauté	Sliced	Zest	
Yellow	Poach	Julienne	Supremes	
White	Dehydrate	Batonette		
Green	Stew	Tubes		
Purple/Blue	Roast	Ribbons		
Orange	Leather	Spheres		
	Compressed			

Choose Main Component

The main component is the focal point of the dessert. The number of desserts on a menu can range from as few as three up to seven. There is no set standard for the number of desserts offered; the basic goal should be to offer a little something for everyone. Once the number of dessert menu items has been determined, choose the main component. This could be a simple list at first; it will be developed as the process continues.

Determining this list can be as easy as evaluating what is currently on the menu or visiting other similar restaurants in the area and looking at the menu. If the menu has four items, choose basic ideas to start. Crème brûlée, cheesecake, tart or pie, and cake are a good start. These items are easily identifiable to most people and they provide a flexible foundation to build on.

Select Flavors

The flavor of the main component should be the dominant flavor on the plate. That does not mean that it has to be the strongest flavor. Orange could be a dominant flavor for the cheesecake. If a chocolate flavor is added to the plate, it should complement the orange, not overpower it. Once the main flavor is selected, choose two other flavors that will compliment it. In the example of the cheesecake, selecting milk chocolate and coriander would be good choices.

Select Garnishes

Garnishes on the plate need to have flavor and purpose. They can provide additional textures, temperatures, or visual appeal in the case of a **tuile**. Garnishes can include frozen components, tuiles, sauces, fried items, or fruit. This is the point when the dessert can develop into something more complex.

The main component has been selected as well as the three flavors, orange, coriander and milk chocolate. Next the flavors need to be incorporated into the remaining components of the dessert. The first thing to consider is the base of the cheesecake, traditionally this would be a graham cracker crust. The base of the dessert not only serves as crispy component on the plate, it also facilitates moving the cheesecake. Not having a base under the dessert makes it difficult to transfer from a sheet pan to the plate. The base can be the traditional graham cracker or another cookie crumble, thinly rolled and cut short dough, or even cake. Looking at the other components of the dish will help in deciding what the base should be. For this application chocolate short dough will be used. It will create an appealing color separation between the cheesecake and the plate; the dark color will help to convey the chocolate in the dessert.

The next step is to continue building on the flavors of orange and milk chocolate and incorporate the coriander. When using spices, use caution—these flavors can become very strong and overpowering. The goal is incorporating these flavors in a pleasant way and using them subtlety. As the ingredients are mixed and tasted, the flavors have not had a chance to mature. During the maturation, spices and herbs continue to infuse flavor. In the effort to provide a burst of coriander flavor, a good place to incorporate it would be a coriander crisp. Not only will it provide flavor, but also additional needed crunch.

In most restaurants, cheesecake is served with whipped cream. Using milk chocolate mousse is a playful way to incorporate an aerated component to the dish, mimicking the whipped cream. Since both cheesecake and mousse are creams, there may be a need to add lighter, less fatty components to the dessert. The high-fat percentage in the dessert creates a very rich and sometimes heavy dessert. In an effort to reduce this, a thin layer of cake can be placed on top of the cheesecake. Then it can be topped with the mousse and the coriander crisp on top. This style of component is often referred to as a **stack**, and precision in layering, cutting, and piping will all add to look of the final product.

The main component is now complete. The plate now has all the flavors and different textures but only one temperature—cold. In restaurant service, it can be difficult to include smaller warm components. Using a milk chocolate ice cream for this dessert will reinforce the milk chocolate flavor and add a different temperature item to the plate.

The ice cream can also build on the visual design of the plate. The chocolate color of the ice cream and smooth texture create additional eye appeal. While frozen components are often shaped using a scoop or **quenelle**, they can also be molded. Current plating trends utilize large curls of ice cream or sorbet. When innovating new shapes, be sure that the component will arrive to the guest in the manner it was intended. When applicable, flavor combinations of contrasting colors can be swirled together after freezing and scooped to add complexity to the plate.

Frozen components placed directly on a plate begin to melt and slide around like a hockey puck on ice. An easy solution would be to place the ice cream on top of the stack; this presentation works well with a round-shaped dessert. The stack on this dessert will be an elongated rectangle; it would be best to place the ice cream somewhere else on the plate. Bases for ice creams can be streusel, cake crumbs, granola, chocolate, fruit, or even a shaped tuile cookie. The ice cream does not need to be completely contained. There just needs to be something small placed under it to hold its position. To incorporate fresh fruit on this plate, a simple fruit salad of orange suprêmes (using the leftover orange from zesting), simple syrup, and tapioca pearls will provide a base for the ice cream.

The last component needed to pull the dessert together is a sauce. Sauces are used on the plate to add flavor, texture, color, design, and moisture to the plate. When selecting a sauce, choose one that will add to the flavors in the dessert. Saucing a plate can be done simply using a squeeze bottle, spoon, or paper cornet. Using other pastry tools such as brushes, round cutters, and piped chocolate can add a more complex design to the plate. Infusing a crème anglaise with coriander will provide another way to incorporate the coriander on the plate without overpowering the other components and will provide a thick sauce that will hold its shape.

At this point the dessert could be written on the menu as:

Orange cheesecake, milk chocolate mousse, coriander crisp, milk chocolate ice cream and orange tapioca "salad"

Garnishes can always be added or taken away—too much and the plate will become confusing; too little and the plate looks unfinished. Ultimately, the flavor of the dessert and the garnishes need to work together.

Now that flavor has been addressed, presentation must be considered. The color of the cheesecake is neutral. The chocolate and the orange go well together and the orange "salad" provides a brighter color as well as textural addition. The next step is to sketch the dessert and decide on shapes.

Assembly

Assembly is one of the final steps in the process of creating a dessert. As the dessert's components are prepared individually and then assembled together as a finished product tasting needs to be done. In addition to tasting, detailed notes must be taken for processing after the final dessert is presented for the menu. These notes will be used for developing a training manual for the restaurant.

Orange, Chocolate & Coriander

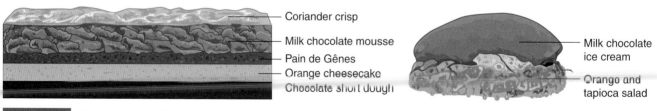

— Coriander crisp

— Milk chocolate mousse
— Pain de Gênes
— Orange cheesecake
Chocolate short dough

— Milk chocolate ice cream

— Orange and tapioca salad

FIGURE 10.5 Sketch for orange cheesecake

FIGURE 10.6 Picture of orange cheesecake, final

The final product should be a representation of the sketch produced earlier. Some changes may need to be made along the way. Creating a dessert is a process, and sometimes that process may be neverending. Documenting all the steps will help make sure all information is available for consistency with each order, as well as future plated desserts designs.

Evaluation

Even when the dessert is on the plate, the work continues. Everything needs to be evaluated: cost, time to produce components, plate-up time, flavor, time to train front of the house, and ultimately, a consideration of guest satisfaction. If any of these factors show a problem, changes must be made to the dessert. It may be noticed immediately or weeks later. Continue the process because, while the dessert may taste great to the pastry chef and executive chef, if guests are not ordering it, changes need to be made.

Creating a great dessert is not an easy task. Careful consideration and planning must be done first before entering the kitchen. Mastering four of the five elements of dessert design can make a good dessert, yet always remember that if flavor isn't there, the dessert will be unsuccessful.

Recipes

This chapter does not include yield and portion sizes for plated desserts. This was done intentionally as mold and portion sizes will vary.

Raspberry and Chocolate

Components

Reconstructed Hazelnut Base, page 228

Chocolate Pain de Genes, page 195

Chocolate Raspberry Creméux, page 283

Chocolate Raspberry Mousse, page 283

Chocolate Mirror Glaze, page 226

Raspberry Sauce, page 115

Sanded Almonds, page 298

Amaretto Ice Cream, page 283

Crispy Raspberry Foam, page 103

Procedure

1. Prepare reconstructed base recipe using pâte sablée, place a thin layer in a quarter sheet pan lined with parchment paper; allow to set.

2. Add 14 oz (400 g) of the chocolate raspberry creméux; refrigerate to set.

3. Place a piece of the chocolate pain de genes on the creméux and refrigerate.

4. Fill the remainder of the quarter sheet pan with 11.5 oz (325 g) of chocolate raspberry mousse and freeze.

5. Prepare the sanded hazelnut recipe (page 298) using slivered almonds in place of the hazelnuts.

6. Remove the chocolate raspberry mousse cake from the quarter sheet pan.

7. Apply the chocolate mirror glaze and refrigerate for 5 minutes to set the glaze.

8. Cut the cake into the desired shape.

9. Apply the raspberry sauce using a teaspoon.

10. Place a small pile of the sanded almonds and top with a quenelle of Amaretto ice cream.

11. Place a piece of the crispy raspberry foam onto the mousse cake.

FIGURE 10.7 Raspberry and Chocolate

Amaretto Ice Cream

Yield: 2 lb 3 oz (1008 g)

Portions: 36

Portion size: 1 oz (28 g)

Yield description: 36 scoops at 1 oz (28 g)

Ingredients	U.S.	Metric
Milk	1 lb 2.3 oz	520 g
Heavy Cream	6.7 oz	190 g
NFMS	1 oz	28 g
Casein	0.7 oz	20 g
Glucose Powder	1.8 oz	52 g
Granulated Sugar	5.3 oz	150 g
Ice Cream Stabilizer	0.28 oz	8 g
Amaretto (28% alcohol)	1.4 oz	40 g

Procedure

1. Ice cream base process (page 159).

Chocolate Raspberry Cremeux

Yield: 1 lb (465 g)

Portions: 1

Portion size: 1 lb (465 g)

Yield description: 1 portion at 1 lb (465 g)

Ingredients	U.S.	Metric
Heavy Cream	4.4 oz	125 g
Milk	3.5 oz	100 g
Sugar	0.9 oz	25 g
Egg Yolks	1.8 oz	50 g
Raspberry Purée	0.9 oz	25 g
Semisweet Chocolate 58%	4.9 oz	140 g

Procedure

1. Prepare a crème anglaise (page 124) with heavy cream, milk, sugar, and yolks.

2. Emulsify chocolate and anglaise.

3. Add purée and strain through a chinois.

Chocolate Raspberry Mousse

Yield: 1 lb 14 oz (875 g)

Portions: 1

Portion size: 1 lb 14 oz (875 g)

Yield description: 1 portion at 1 lb 14 oz (875 g)

Ingredients	U.S.	Metric
Half and Half	6 oz	170 g
Sugar	0.7 oz	20 g
Egg Yolks	1.2 oz	35 g
Semisweet Chocolate 58%	8.3 oz	235 g
Raspberry Purée	0.7 oz	20 g
Heavy Cream, whipped	13.9 oz	395 g

Procedure

1. Prepare using the chocolate mousse anglaise-based method (page 133).

Apple Consomme

Components

Clarified Apple Cider, page 88

Almond Financier, page 313

Compressed Granny Smith Apples, page 284

Brown Butter Ice Cream, page 169

Apple Chip, page 286

Pasta Dough, page 285

Ravioli Filling, page 285

Brown Butter Nuggets, page 113

Procedure

1. Prepare the apple cider using the gelatin clarification procedure on page 88.
2. Bake the almond financier in a 2.5-in. (65-mm) metal ring.
3. Place the compressed apples in the center of a bowl.
4. Stack the financier on the compressed apples.
5. Toss the three raviolis in the clarified apple cider and place in the bowl.
6. Add the clarified apple cider to the bowl.
7. Place a quenelle of brown butter ice cream on the financier.
8. Sprinkle with the brown butter nuggets and garnish with apple chip.

FIGURE 10.8 Apple Consomme

Compressed Apples

Yield: 12 oz (360 g)

Portions: 12

Portion size: 2.5 in. (65 mm)

Yield description: 12 portions at 2.5 in. (65 mm)

Ingredients	U.S.	Metric
Granny Smith Apples	11.6 oz	330 g
Brown Sugar	1.2 oz	33 g

Procedure

1. Peel the apples and slice on a vegetable lathe.
2. Layer the apple slices sprinkle a small amount of the brown sugar between each layer.
3. Repeat this to create five layers.
4. Place the apples in a vacuum bag and seal at 100% vacuum.
5. Refrigerate overnight.
6. Before serving remove the apple from the bag and dry off with a paper towel; cut into 2.5-in. (65-mm) rounds.

Pasta Dough

Yield: 7 oz (212 g)

Portions: 1

Portion size: 7 oz (212 g)

Yield description: 1 portion at 7 oz (212 g)

Ingredients	U.S.	Metric
Bread Flour	3.5 oz	100 g
Water	1.4 oz	40 g
Salt	0.04 oz	1 g
Egg Yolk	2.3 oz	65 g
Olive Oil	0.2 oz	5 g

Procedure

1. Combine bread flour and salt in a bowl.
2. Make a well in the center of the flour and add the wet ingredients.
3. Stir the wet ingredients with a fork; gradually begin working in the dry ingredients from the side of the bowl.
4. Once the dough begins to form, continue kneading by hand.
5. Wrap in plastic wrap and rest for 30 minutes.
6. Using a pasta roller, roll the dough to #2 and fold.
7. Turn the dough 90° and repeat two more times for a total of three folds.
8. Roll the dough to #6 on the pasta roller.
9. Cover in plastic wrap and refrigerate.

Ravioli Filling

Yield: 5 oz (155 g)

Portions: 62

Portion size: 0.08 oz (2.5 g)

Yield description: 62 portions at 0.08 oz (2.5 g)

Ingredients	U.S.	Metric
Ricotta Cheese	3.5 oz	100 g
Powdered Sugar	1.1 oz	30 g
Vanilla Paste	0.2 oz	5 g
Dried Cranberries, rehydrated and diced	0.7 oz	20 g
Salt	0.01 oz	0.5 g

Procedure

1. Combine ricotta cheese, powdered sugar, vanilla paste, and salt in a food processor.
2. Fold in cranberries.
3. Place 0.8 oz (2.5 g) of filling on the pasta dough.
4. Brush a thin layer of egg wash on the pasta dough around the filing.
5. Place a second piece of dough on top.
6. Remove any air bubbles and press to seal.
7. Cut with a 1.5-in. (40-mm) round fluted cutter.
8. Cook the ravioli in simmering salted water for 3 to 4 minutes or until al dente.
9. Cool in ice water, reserve for service.

Apple Chip

Yield: 7 oz (200 g)

Portions: 1

Portion size: 7 oz (200 g)

Yield description: 1 portion at 7 oz (200 g)

Ingredients	U.S.	Metric
Granny Smith Apples	2 each	2 each
Water	1 lb	480 g
Sugar	12 oz	360 g

Procedure

1. Using a French knife, cut the apple in half down the center.
2. Slice the apples $\frac{1}{16}$ in. (1.5 mm) thick on a meat slicer.
3. Combine water and sugar; bring to a boil.
4. Pour the boiling syrup over the apples.
5. Cover with plastic wrap and refrigerate overnight.
6. The following day remove the apples from the syrup.
7. Dry the apples on paper towels and place on a silpat.
8. Place the apples in a 150°F (65°C) oven for 3 to 4 hours or until dry.
9. To test for doneness, remove one of the apple slices from the silpat and allow to cool. The apple chip should snap cleanly. If it is flexible and bends, continue drying.
10. Store in an airtight container at room temperature.

Linzer Bombe

Components

Hazelnut Dough, page 225

Raspberry Sorbet, page 174

Cinnamon Parfait, page 287

Hazelnut Microsponge, page 288

Cinnamon Crème Anglaise, page 287

Raspberry Sauce, page 115

Fresh Raspberries

White Chocolate Spray, page 397

Procedure

1. Roll hazelnut dough to ⅛ in. (3 mm).

2. Cut with oval cutter and bake; reserve for assembly.

3. Prepare raspberry sorbet and freeze; portion into 0.6-oz (18-g) molds.

4. Assemble the cinnamon parfait.

5. Pipe mold half full with the parfait and insert the frozen raspberry sorbet.

6. Fill the remainder of the mold with the parfait and freeze for 4 hours.

7. Unmold the parfait and spray with white chocolate spray.

8. Prepare the hazelnut microsponge.

9. Place the parfait on the hazelnut dough.

10. Pipe various size dots of the raspberry sauce and cinnamon crème anglaise.

11. Cut raspberries in half to garnish the plate.

FIGURE 10.9 Linzer Bombe

Cinnamon Parfait

Yield: 1 lb 4 oz (580 g)

Portions: 24 portions

Portion size: 0.8 oz (24 g)

Yield description: 24 portions at 0.8 oz (24 g)

Ingredients	U.S.	Metric
Water	1.2 oz	35 g
Sugar	4.4 oz	125 g
Cinnamon Stick	1 each	1 each
Ground Cinnamon	0.01 oz	0.42 g
Vanilla Bean, split and scraped	1 each	1 each
Egg Yolks	3.4 oz	95 g
Heavy Cream, whipped	11.4 oz	325 g

Procedure

1. Combine water, sugar, cinnamon stick, cinnamon, and vanilla bean in a saucepan.

2. Make a pâte à bombe mixture with the egg yolks and sugar mixture (page 132). When sugar mixture reaches 220°F (105°C); carefully remove the cinnamon stick and vanilla bean.

3. When pâte a bombe is completely cooled, fold in cream.

Cinnamon Crème Anglaise

Yield: 12 oz (340 g)

Portions: 24

Portion size: 0.5 oz (14 g)

Yield description: 24 portions at 0.5 oz (14 g)

Ingredients	U.S.	Metric
Milk	4 oz	113 g
Heavy Cream	4 oz	113 g
Sugar	2 oz	57 g
Egg Yolks	2 oz	57 g
Cinnamon Stick	1 each	1 each
Vanilla Bean, split and scraped	0.5 each	0.5 each

Procedure

1. Crème anglaise procedure; add cinnamon stick and vanilla bean while cooking.

Hazelnut Microsponge

Yield: 13 oz (390 g)

Portions: 1

Portion size: 13 oz (390 g)

Yield description: 1 portion at 13 oz (390 g)

Ingredients	U.S.	Metric
Whole Eggs	5.6 oz	160 g
Cake Flour	2.4 oz	70 g
Sugar	2.8 oz	80 g
Hazelnut Paste	2.8 oz	80 g

Procedure

1. Combine eggs, sugar, and hazelnut paste with an immersion blender.

2. Using the immersion blender incorporate the flour.

3. Fill an ISI siphon halfway and fill with three nitrous oxide charges, shaking thoroughly between each cartridge.

4. Using a pairing knife, poke four holes in the bottom of the cup to release steam. The cake will not leak from the holes.

5. Fill the cup ¼ full with the cake batter.

6. Microwave for 40 seconds.

7. Turn the cup upside down on a cooling rack.

8. When completely cooled, remove the cake from the cup.

Banana and Chocolate

Components

Caramelized Bananas, page 290

Banana Mousse, page 173

Chocolate Pâte Sablée, page 246

Roasted Banana Sorbet, page 176

Caramel Sauce, page 290

Pliable Milk Chocolate Ganache, page 92

Banana Cake, page 289

Banana Chip, page 289

White Chocolate Spray
Colored Yellow, page 397

Procedure

1. Prepare pliable ganache using milk chocolate in place of the white chocolate and omit the orange blossom water.

2. Roll some of the pâte sablée to ⅛ in. (3 mm) and cut 1-in. (25-mm) discs and bake.

3. Grate additional pâte sablée on a box grater onto a silpat, freeze, for 30 minutes then bake.

4. Prepare banana mousse using the fruit mousse recipe mold in sphere molds and freeze.

5. After freezing spray the sphere in yellow white chocolate spray. Place onto the pâte sablée disc.

6. Place the sphere on the plate.

7. Cut the pliable milk chocolate ganache into a wedge shape and place it around the sphere.

8. Place the grated pâte sablée in the front curve of the pliable ganache to hold the ice cream.

9. Add the remaining items—caramel sauce, banana cake, caramelized bananas, banana chips, and quenelle of roasted banana sorbet.

FIGURE 10.10 Banana and Chocolate

Banana Cake

Yield: 1 lb 1 oz (488 g)

Portions: 1

Portion size: quarter sheet pan

Yield description: 1 quarter sheet pan

Ingredients	U.S.	Metric
Banana Purée	4 oz	113 g
Sugar	4 oz	113 g
All-Purpose Flour	4 oz	113 g
Whole Eggs	2 oz	57 g
Vegetable Oil	1.6 oz	45 g
Sour Cream	1.5 oz	43 g
Baking Soda	0.15 oz	4.3 g

Procedure

1. Sift dry ingredients.
2. Combine wet ingredients.
3. Add wet ingredients to dry and mix until combined.
4. Spread into paper lined quarter sheet pan and bake at 350°F (175°C) for 20 to 25 minutes.
5. Reserve for plating.

Banana Chip

Yield: 12 banana chips

Portions: 12

Portion size: 1 banana chip

Yield description: 12 banana chips

Ingredients	U.S.	Metric
Bananas	4 each	4 each
Lime Juice	As Needed	As Needed

Note: After slicing, reserve the extra banana for the banana cake.

Procedure

1. Peel banana and slice on a meat slicer ¹⁄₁₆ in. (1.5 mm) thick.
2. Place onto a silpat and brush with lime juice, to prevent oxidation.
3. Carefully lay another silpat on top of the bananas.
4. Place the bananas in a 150°F (65°C) oven for 3 to 4 hours or until dry.
5. Remove the top silpat after 2 hours.
6. To test for doneness, remove one of the banana slices from the silpat and allow to cool. The banana chip should snap cleanly. If it is flexible and bends, continue drying.
7. Store in an airtight container at room temperature.

Caramelized Banana

Ingredients	U.S.	Metric
Bananas	2 each	2 each
Sugar	As needed	As needed

Note: This must be done à la minute; the caramel will dissolve quickly due to the water in the banana.

Procedure

1. Slice the banana ¼ in. (6 mm) thick.
2. Coat one side of the banana in the sugar.
3. Caramelize the sugar with a blowtorch.

Caramel Sauce

Yield: 12 oz (343 g)

Portions: 24

Portion size: ½ oz (14 g)

Yield description: 24 portions at ½ oz (14 g)

Ingredients	U.S.	Metric
Sugar	4.8 oz	136 g
Water	1.3 oz	37 g
Heavy Cream	4 oz	113 g
Vanilla Bean, split and scraped	½ each	½ each
Butter, soft	2 oz	57 g

Procedure

1. Combine water and sugar in saucepan, bring to a boil.
2. Continue cooking the sugar until a dark caramel is reached; the darker the caramel, the more flavor the sauce will have.
3. Remove the pan from the heat; add the cream and vanilla bean.
4. Return the pan to a low heat to dissolve the caramel. Be careful to not boil the sauce.
5. Once the caramel is completely dissolved; add the butter, do not stir.
6. Let the sauce cool in the pan; once cooled, stir in the butter.
7. Strain through a chinois.

Warm Coffee Tart

Components

Chocolate Short Dough, page 247

Coffee Filling, page 291

Caramelized Pecans, page 366

Vanilla Ice Cream, page 167

Chocolate Pastry Cream, page 319

Chocolate Sauce, page 291

Crepe, page 292

Lemon Syrup, page 292

Procedure

1. Roll chocolate short to ⅛ in. (3 mm) thick and line 3.75-in. (9.5-cm) tart pans.

2. Blind bake shells halfway and cool.

3. Prepare Coffee Tart Filling; fill tart shells and refrigerate.

4. Caramelize the pecans using the caramelized hazelnut procedure (page 366), cool completely, and fold into the frozen vanilla ice cream.

5. Spread the chocolate pastry cream through a template onto a silpat.

6. Bake the pastry cream at 350°F (175°C) until the mixture looks dry.

7. Shape as desired while still warm; store in an airtight container.

8. For plating, bake the coffee tarts at 350°F (175°C) for 10 to 12 minutes.

9. While tarts are baking, warm the lemon syrup and toss the crepe strips in the syrup.

10. Place the tart just off center on the plate.

11. Add the chocolate sauce around the tart.

12. Next put the crepe strips to the right of the tart.

13. Put a quenelle of the candied pecan ice cream on the crepe and add the tuile.

FIGURE 10.11 Warm Coffee Tart

Coffee Tart Filling

Yield: 1 lb 15 oz (905 g)
Portions: 18
Portion size: 1.8 oz (50 g)
Yield description: 18 at 1.8 oz (50 g)

Ingredients	U.S.	Metric
Heavy Cream	2.3 oz	65 g
Ground Coffee	0.4 oz	10 g
Butter	2.6 oz	75 g
Semisweet Chocolate 58%	11.1 oz	315 g
Egg Yolks	5.3 oz	150 g
Egg Whites	7.9 oz	225 g
Sugar	2.3 oz	65 g

Procedure

1. Combine heavy cream and ground coffee; heat and cover.
2. Steep for 10 minutes, strain coffee.
3. Melt chocolate halfway over a double boiler.
4. Bring cream and butter to a boil; emulsify with chocolate.
5. Fold egg yolks into ganache.
6. Make a French meringue with the egg whites and sugar.
7. Fold meringue into ganache in three additions.

Chocolate Sauce

Yield: 11 oz (312 g)
Portions: 22
Portion size: 0.5 oz (14 g)
Yield description: 22 portions at 0.5 oz (14 g)

Ingredients	U.S.	Metric
Water	2 oz	57 g
Sugar	2.5 oz	71 g
Corn Syrup	1.5 oz	43 g
Cocoa Powder	1 oz	28 g
Semisweet Chocolate 58%	4 oz	113 g

Procedure

1. Combine water, sugar, and corn syrup in a saucepan.
2. Bring liquids to a boil; add chocolate and cocoa powder.
3. Strain through a chinois and cool.

Crepes

Yield: 1 lb 6.8 oz (647 g)

Portions: 1

Portion size: 1 lb 6.8 oz (647 g)

Yield description: 1 portion at 1 lb 6.8 oz (647 g)

Ingredients	U.S.	Metric
Cake Flour	2 oz	57 g
Bread Flour	2 oz	57 g
Sugar	0.75 oz	21 g
Salt	0.07 oz	2 g
Whole Eggs	4 oz	113 g
Egg Yolks	4 oz	113 g
Butter, Melted	2 oz	57 g
Milk, Warmed	8 oz	227 g

Procedure

1. Combine all ingredients in blender; mix until smooth. Strain through a chinois.
2. Refrigerate overnight.
3. Heat an 8-in. (20-cm) nonstick pan over medium heat; spray lightly with pan spray.
4. When pan is heated, add approximately 2 oz (60 g) of crepe batter.
5. Tilt the pan in all directions to evenly coat the pan.
6. When crepe can be easily shaken in the pan, flip to continue cooking the other side.
7. Place on parchment-lined sheet pan.
8. Once cooled, roll the crepe.
9. Using a French knife, cut the crepe into ¼-in. (6-mm) strips.
10. Wrap and store in the refrigerator.

Lemon Syrup

Yield: 14 oz (410 g)

Portions: 1

Portion size: 14 oz (410 g)

Yield description: 1 portion at 14 oz (410 g)

Ingredients	U.S.	Metric
Water	7 oz	198 g
Sugar	7 oz	198 g
Lemon Zest	0.5 oz	14 g

Procedure

1. Combine water, sugar, and zest in a saucepan.
2. Bring to a boil; cover and cool.
3. Store in refrigerator for service.

Tropical Stack

Components

Coconut Financier, page 293

Passion Fruit Curd, page 139

Chocolate Plaquette

Whipped White Chocolate Ganache, page 294

Mango Tuile, page 294

Mango Sauce, page 115

Coconut Sorbet, page 176

Procedure

1. Prepare the passion fruit curd using the lemon curd recipe.
2. Assemble the coconut financier and bake in a 3.25 in. (8.3 cm) savarin mold.
3. Cut chocolate plaquettes using a 3.25 in. (8.3 cm) round cutter.
4. Fill coconut financier with the passion fruit curd and place it in the center of the plate.
5. Place a round cutter slightly larger than the savarin on the plate.
6. Using a squeeze bottle, pipe dots of the sauce along the cutter.
7. Twist the cutter clockwise and lift straight up.
8. Pipe the whipped white chocolate ganache on the chocolate plaquette; place this on the coconut financier.
9. Place the mango tuile on the panna cotta and top with a scoop of coconut ice cream.

FIGURE 10.12 Tropical Stack

Coconut Financier

Yield: 2 lb 1 oz (955 g)

Portions: 18

Portion size: 1.8 oz (50 g)

Yield description: 18 portions at 1.8 oz (50 g)

Ingredients	U.S.	Metric
Desiccated Coconut	6.2 oz	175 g
Powdered Sugar	5.6 oz	160 g
Sugar	2.5 oz	70 g
Egg Whites	7.9 oz	225 g
Beurre Noisette, melted	3.2 oz	90 g
Butter, melted	3.9 oz	110 g
All-Purpose Flour	4.4 oz	125 g

Procedure

1. Combine desiccated coconut, powdered sugar, sugar, and all-purpose flour in a mixing bowl.
2. Add egg whites, beurre noisette, and butter to dry ingredients.
3. Mix until combined.
4. Fill savarin-shaped molds and bake at 350°F (175°C).
5. Cool and wrap; store at room temperature.

Whipped White Chocolate Ganache

Yield: 1 lb 4 oz (589 g)

Portions: 1

Portion size: 1 lb 4 oz (589 g)

Yield description: 1 portion at 1 lb 4 oz (589 g)

Ingredients	U.S.	Metric
Heavy Cream #1	6.2 oz	175 g
Inverted Sugar	0.6 oz	18 g
Glucose Syrup	0.6 oz	18 g
White Chocolate	4.2 oz	118 g
Heavy Cream #2	9.2 oz	260 g

Procedure

1. Combine heavy cream #1, inverted sugar, and glucose syrup. Bring to a boil.
2. Emulsify with white chocolate.
3. Add heavy cream #2 and emulsify.
4. Refrigerate for 2 to 3 hours.
5. Whip in a mixer before use.

Mango Tuile

Yield: 12 oz (385.5 g)

Portions: 1

Portion size: 12 oz (385.5 g)

Yield description: 1 portion at 12 oz (385.5 g)

Ingredients	U.S.	Metric
Powdered Sugar	6.5 oz	195 g
Cake Flour	1.7 oz	50 g
Mango Purée	2.3 oz	70 g
Butter, melted	2.3 oz	70 g
Yellow Pectin	0.02 oz	0.5 g

Procedure

1. Combine all ingredients in a food processor.
2. Spread the batter through a template onto a silpat through a template.
3. Bake the mango tuile at 350°F (175°C) until golden brown, shape as desired while still warm.
4. Store in an airtight container.

Strawberry Cheesecake

Components

Cheesecake, page 144

Graham Cracker Crust, page 295

Black Pepper Meringue, page 295

Fresh Strawberries

Clear Glaze, page 106

Vodka Foam, page 89

Strawberry Sauce, page 115

Procedure

1. Prepare the cheesecake base; add the zest of 1 orange to the base and bake in a half sheet pan.
2. Prepare the vanilla bean vodka foam.
3. Cut a 4-in. (10-cm) round from the cheesecake.
4. Cut strawberries into quarters and brush with clear glaze.
5. Place dots of the foam and sauce on top of the cheesecake.
6. Arrange the fruit and glaze.
7. Place the meringues.

FIGURE 10.13 Strawberry Cheesecake

Graham Cracker Crust

Yield: 14 oz (420 g)

Portions: 1

Portion size: 14 oz (420 g)

Yield description: 1 portion at 14 oz (420 g)

Ingredients	U.S.	Metric
Graham Cracker Crumbs	8.8 oz	250 g
Butter, melted	6 oz	170 g

Procedure

1. Combine graham cracker crumbs and butter.
2. Spread a thin layer of graham cracker crust in a half sheet pan.
3. Bake for 5 minutes at 350°F (175°C).
4. Once cooled, top with cheesecake batter and bake.

Black Pepper Meringue

Yield: 10 oz (300 g)

Portions: 1

Portion size: 10 oz (300 g)

Yield description: 1 portion at 10 oz (300 g)

Ingredients	U.S.	Metric
Egg White	3.5 oz	100 g
Sugar	7.1 oz	200 g
Black Pepper	As needed	As needed

Procedure

1. Prepare a Swiss meringue with the egg whites and sugar.
2. Once cooled, pipe into long tubes with a ¼-in. (6-mm) plain pastry tip onto parchment paper.
3. Grind black pepper onto meringue.
4. Dry in a 200°F (95°C) oven until completely dry.
5. Cut into pieces and store in an airtight container.

Pear and Hazelnut

Components

Gianduja Bavarian, page 296

Hazelnut Pain de Genes, page 297

Pear Williams Liquor Bonbon, page 378

Hazelnut Streusel, page 298

Sous Vide Pineapple, page 349

Hazelnut Croquant, page 298

Pineapple Sherbet, page 171

Candied Hazelnuts, page 366

Poached Pears, page 267

Orange Fluid Gel, page 298

Procedure

1. Place the frozen ring of gianduja Bavarian on the plate; allow 5 to 10 minutes to thaw.

2. Place the hazelnut pain de genes in the ring.

3. Using a spoon, add some of the hazelnut streusel and pine-apple confit.

4. Add the sliced poached pears and Pear Williams liquor bonbon.

5. Place four candied hazelnuts.

6. Pipe the orange fluid gel.

7. Quenelle the pineapple sherbet and add the hazelnut croquant.

FIGURE 10.14 Pear and Hazelnut

Gianduja Bavarian

Yield: 2 lb 4 oz (1026 g)

Portions: 12

Portion size: 3 oz (85 g)

Yield description: 12 portion at 3 oz (85 g)

Ingredients	U.S.	Metric
Milk	6.2 oz	175 g
Heavy Cream	6.2 oz	175 g
Egg Yolks	2.5 oz	70 g
Sugar	1.3 oz	36 g
Gianduja	6 oz	170 g
Gelatin Sheets, bloomed	4 each	4 each
Heavy Cream, whipped	14.1 oz	400 g

Procedure

1. Prepare using the Bavarian procedure (page 133).
2. Add the cooked Bavarian base to the gianduja and emulsify.
3. Using a pastry bag, pipe into 5.75-in. (14-cm) ring molds and freeze.

Hazelnut Marzipan

Yield: 14 oz (415 g)

Portions: 1

Portion size: 14 oz (415 g)

Yield description: 1 portion at 14 oz (415 g)

Ingredients	U.S.	Metric
Hazelnuts, lightly toasted	6.2 oz	175 g
Sugar	4.8 oz	136 g
Glucose	1.6 oz	45 g
Water	1.6 oz	45 g
Pear Williams Liqueur	0.5 oz	15 g

Procedure

1. Rough-chop hazelnuts in a food processor; place on a silpat-lined sheet pan.
2. Combine water, sugar, and glucose in saucepan and bring to a boil.
3. Cook sugar syrup to 239°F (115°C) and pour over hazelnuts.
4. Cool mixture completely.
5. Return mixture to food processor and add Pear Williams Liqueur (Poire William).
6. Grind to a fine paste.
7. Reserve for Hazelnut Pain de Genes.

Hazelnut Pain de Genes

Yield: 1 lb 11 oz (777.5 g)

Portions: 1

Portion size: half sheet pan

Yield description: 1 half sheet pan

Ingredients	U.S.	Metric
Hazelnut Marzipan, page 297	11.4 oz	325 g
Eggs	8.8 oz	250 g
Inverted Sugar	1.2 oz	35 g
Salt	0.08 oz	2.5 g
All-Purpose Flour	2.1 oz	60 g
Beurre Noisette	3.2 oz	90 g
Water	0.5 oz	15 g

Procedure

1. Place hazelnut marzipan in a mixer with paddle attachment.
2. Slowly add eggs one at a time, scraping between additions.
3. Add inverted sugar and scrape.
4. Add flour, salt, and beurre noisette.
5. Spread in half sheet pan lined with a silpat.
6. Bake at 325°F (165°C) for 8 minutes.
7. Cool and wrap, reserve for plating.

Hazelnut Croquant

Yield: 6 oz (175 g)

Portions: 1

Portion size: 6 oz (175 g)

Yield description: 1 portion 6 oz (175 g)

Ingredients	U.S.	Metric
Fondant	3.2 oz	90 g
Glucose	2.1 oz	60 g
Hazelnuts, toasted and chopped	0.9 oz	25 g

Procedure

1. Combine fondant and glucose in a saucepan and cook to a caramel.
2. Pour onto silpat and cool.
3. Grind to a fine powder in a food processor.
4. Sift powder onto a silpat and top with chopped hazelnuts.
5. Bake 350°F (175°C) until melted.

Hazelnut Streusel

Yield: 4 oz (121 g)

Portions: 1

Portion size: 4 oz (121 g)

Yield description: 1 portion at 4 oz (121 g)

Ingredients	U.S.	Metric
Butter	1.1 oz	30 g
Brown Sugar	1.1 oz	30 g
Orange Zest	½ each	½ each
Hazelnuts, ground	1.1 oz	30 g
Flour	1.1 oz	30 g
Salt	0.04 oz	1 g

Procedure

1. Cream butter, brown sugar, and zest with a paddle.
2. Add sifted dry ingredients.
3. Spread mixture onto a parchment lined half sheet pan.
4. Bake 350°F (175°C) until golden brown.

Orange Fluid Gel

Yield: 10 oz (301 g)

Portions: 20

Portion size: 0.5 oz (14 g)

Yield description: 20 portions at 0.5 oz (14 g)

Ingredients	U.S.	Metric
Orange Juice	5.3 oz	150 g
Pineapple Purée	1.8 oz	50 g
Agar	0.04 oz	1 g
Xanthan Gum	0.006 oz	0.18 g
Blood Orange Purée	3.5 oz	100 g

Procedure

1. Combine orange juice and pineapple purée.
2. Combine agar and xanthan gum; add to orange juice mixture with an immersion blender.
3. Bring this mixture to a boil.
4. Cool on an ice bath.
5. The sauce will gel to a solid. Use an immersion blender to break up the gel.
6. Adjust the consistency using the remaining blood orange purée.

Apricot Tart

Components

Pâte Sablée, page 246

Apricot Pectin Fruit Gelée, page 105

Pistachio Cream, page 300

Milk Chocolate Creméux, page 229

Caramelized White Chocolate Mousse, page 132 (pâte bombe mousse)

Caramelized White Chocolate Spray, page 300

Apricot Sorbet, page 176

Apricot Sauce, page 115

Caramel Popcorn, page 301

Procedure

1. Roll the pâte sablée to ⅛ in. (3 mm) thick.
2. Line a 3.5-in. (9-cm) tart shell and refrigerate.
3. Prepare the roasted white chocolate mousse mold into savarin molds and freeze.
4. Cut a disc of the apricot gel; place it in the bottom of the un-baked tart shell.
5. Pipe a thin layer of the pistachio cream on top of the apricot gelée and bake the shell.
6. After the shell has cooled, prepare the milk chocolate creméux and fill the shell to the top.
7. Unmold the caramelized white chocolate mousse and spray with the caramelized white chocolate spray; return to the freezer for 5 minutes.
8. Place the caramelized white chocolate mousse on the tart.
9. Pipe a layer of apricot sauce in the center of the savarin.
10. Place the tart on the plate and sauce.
11. Top the tart with a scoop of apricot sorbet.
12. Garnish with caramel popcorn.

FIGURE 10.15 Apricot Tart

Caramelized White Chocolate

Yield: 1 lb (480 g)

Portions: 1

Portion size: 1 lb (480 g)

Yield description: 1 portion at 1 lb (480 g)

Ingredients	U.S.	Metric
White Chocolate	1 lb	480 g

Procedure 1

1. Put white chocolate in a quarter sheet pan.

2. Place the pan in a 250°F (120°C) oven.

3. Stir every 10 minutes, cook for approximately 30 to 60 minutes or until the white chocolate becomes a deep caramel color.

4. After removing the chocolate from the oven, process with an immersion blender to remove any lumps.

Procedure 2

1. Place white chocolate in a vacuum bag and seal at 100%.

2. Fill a pressure cooker halfway full of water with the lid off; begin to heat the water.

3. Place the bag in the pressure cooker and seal; continue to heat according to the manufacturer's instructions.

4. Cook the white chocolate for 20 minutes.

5. Cool the pressure cooker and carefully remove the lid.

6. Dry the bag of chocolate and allow to cool.

7. Melt the caramelized white chocolate and process with an immersions blender to remove any lumps.

Pistachio Cream

Yield: 12 oz (360 g)

Portions: 1

Portion size: 12 oz (360 g)

Yield description: 1 portion at 12 oz (360 g)

Ingredients	U.S.	Metric
Butter	3.2 oz	90 g
Sugar	3.2 oz	90 g
Almond Flour	1.1 oz	30 g
Pistachio Flour	2.1 oz	60 g
Eggs	3.2 oz	90 g

Procedure

1. Combine butter, sugar, almond flour, and pistachio flour with a paddle on low speed.

2. Slowly add eggs one at a time, scraping between additions.

3. Refrigerate.

Caramel Popcorn

Yield: 12 oz (349 g)

Portions: 1

Portion size: 12 oz (349 g)

Yield description: 1 portion at 12 oz (349 g)

Ingredients	U.S.	Metric
Popcorn Kernels	1.9 oz	55 g
Vegetable Oil	As needed	As needed
Salt	0.2 oz	7 g
Butter	4.2 oz	120 g
Brown Sugar	2.5 oz	70 g
Honey	1.8 oz	50 g
Corn Syrup	1.6 oz	45 g
Baking Soda	0.08 oz	2.3 g

Procedure

1. Coat the bottom of a saucepan with vegetable oil and heat.
2. Add popcorn kernels and cover; continue shaking the pan until popping stops.
3. Toss the salt on the popcorn and cool on a sheetpan.
4. Melt butter and add brown sugar, honey, and corn syrup.
5. Cook to 300°F (150°C).
6. Add baking soda and quickly toss with popcorn.
7. Dry in a 200°F (93°C) for 10 to 15 minutes.
8. Press into metal cake ring, cool completely.
9. Slice on a meat slicer and store in an airtight container.

S'more Saint Honoré

Components

Puff Pastry, page 80

Pate au Choux, page 319

Graham Cracker Croustillant, page 302

Chocolate Ice Cream, page 167

Dark Chocolate Mousse

Dark Chocolate Creméux, page 302

Marshmallow, page 374

Graham Cracker Crème
Anglaise, page 302

Procedure

1. Prepare marshmallow and pipe with a 0.4-in. (10-mm) plain tip; cut and tie marshmallow into knots.

2. Prepare pâte au choux with graham cracker croustillant.

3. Roll puff pastry to ¹⁄₁₆ in. (2 mm) thick and dock. Bake between two silicone mats until golden brown.

4. Cut puff pastry into a strip 1.25 in. x 6 in. (3 cm x 15 cm)

5. Fill pâte au choux with chocolate creméux.

6. Attach the pâte au choux using caramel.

7. Using a star tip pipe the chocolate mousse between the pâte au choux; leave room at the end of the puff pastry for the chocolate ice cream.

8. Place the strip on the plate; use a small amount of mousse to secure the puff pastry to the plate.

9. Place the marshmallow knots on the top of the mousse.

10. Sauce the plate.

11. Place the quenelle of chocolate ice cream on the end of the strip.

FIGURE 10.16 S'more St Honore

Graham Cracker Croustillant

Yield: 12 oz (352 g)

Portions: 1

Portion size: 12 oz (352 g)

Yield description: 1 portion at 12 oz (352 g)

Ingredients	U.S.	Metric
Butter	3.5 oz	100 g
Brown Sugar	4.4 oz	125 g
Graham Cracker Crumbs	4.4 oz	125 g
Salt	0.07 oz	2 g

Procedure

1. Combine all ingredients with a paddle.
2. Roll to ¹⁄₁₆ in. (2 mm) thick between two sheets of parchment paper and freeze.
3. Cut with a round cutter to fit on piped pâte au choux.
4. Bake pâte au choux according to recipe.

Dark Chocolate Creméux

Yield: 2 lb (830 g)

Portions: 1

Portion size: 2 lb (830 g)

Yield description: 1 portion at 2 lb (830 g)

Ingredients	U.S.	Metric
Heavy Cream	8.8 oz	250 g
Milk	8.8 oz	250 g
Sugar	1.8 oz	50 g
Egg Yolks	3.5 oz	100 g
Semisweet Chocolate 58%	9.5 oz	270 g

Procedure

1. Prepare a crème anglaise (page 142) with the heavy cream, milk, sugar, and egg yolks.
2. Emulsify the crème anglaise with dark chocolate.
3. Strain through a chinois and store in the refrigerator for service.

Graham Cracker Anglaise

Yield: 13 oz (401 g)

Portions: 26

Portion size: 0.5 oz (14 g)

Yield description: 26 portions at 0.5 oz (14 g)

Ingredients	U.S.	Metric
Milk	4.2 oz	120 g
Heavy Cream	4.2 oz	120 g
Graham Crackers	1 oz	27.5 g
Brown Sugar	1.5 oz	43 g
Honey	0.5 oz	14 g
Egg Yolks	2 oz	57 g
Vanilla Bean, split and scraped	½ each	½ each

Procedure

1. Combine milk and heavy cream in a saucepan and scald.

2. Remove from heat and add vanilla bean and graham crackers (do not stir); cover with plastic wrap and steep for 5 minutes.

3. Strain the mixture through a chinois. Do not press the liquid out of the graham crackers; this will make the crème anglaise gritty.

4. Some of the milk and cream will be lost in the process of steeping in the cookies. Make up the difference with 50% cream and 50% milk to return the total weight of milk and cream to 8 oz (240 g).

5. Make a crème anglaise (page 142) with infused milk and cream mixture, brown sugar, honey, and egg yolks.

6. Strain through a chinois, chill on an ice bath.

Key Terms

Scattered
Flavor families
Umami
Monochromatic

Sameness
à la minute
Garnishes
Tuile

Stack
Quenelle

Questions for Review

1. Discuss the five key components of plated desserts. Which of these is the most important, and why?

2. What are the five basic tastes? How can they be used to help bring balance to a rich dessert?

3. Why is it important to use different textures and temperatures on the plate?

4. When creating a new plated dessert, there are six steps involved. Explain why the last step is important to the process.

5. Design a new dessert based on pumpkin pie, carrot cake, or banana split using the six steps of developing a new dessert.

CHAPTER 11

Petits-Fours

The wood-burning ovens of the 1800s didn't have the modern conveniences of today's ovens. It took a considerable amount of time to heat the oven. Once heated it was referred to as the *grand-four*, or large oven. After cooking all the larger items in the oven the heat source was extinguished but it took a long time for the oven to cool completely. Not wanting to waste resources, this gave the bakers the **petits-fours**, or small oven. The lower temperature was ideal for producing smaller cakes and pastries.

LEARNING OBJECTIVES

After reading this chapter, you should be able to:

1. **Define** the three categories of petits-fours.
2. **Design** a petits-fours buffet.
3. **Make** a selection of petits-fours sec, glacé, and contemporary.
4. **Produce** fondant and glaze petits-fours.

Introduction to Petits-fours

Petits-fours are smaller in size compared to other pastries and are intensely flavored. Literally named after the oven they are baked in and translating from the French to mean "small oven," these one- to two-bite pastries are broken down into three categories: sec, glacé, and contemporary. Oftentimes, chocolates and confections (Chapter 12) are served along with petits-fours. The three categories—sec, glacé, and contemporary—encompass pastries from a simple butter cookie dipped in chocolate to a fresh fruit tart. The combination of flavors, textures, and color of the petits-fours is only limited by the creativity of the chef.

Petits-fours are served as part of a dessert buffet, tea service, pre-dessert, room service amenity, or as a complimentary item along with the check. **Pre-dessert** is a plated presentation of one petit-four. This is a complimentary item served between the main course and dessert at fine dining restaurants. In a restaurant, a selection of petits-fours can also be served after the meal along with the check.

In some way, petits-fours can be compared to hors d'oeuvres. Originally hors d'oeuvres, translated to "outside the work," were prepared by the wait staff with leftover products given to them by the chef. The front of the house is no longer responsible for preparing food in this manner. However, part of the origin of the hors d'oeuvres tradition is still alive today.

Chefs create amuse bouche and hors d'oeuvres using the same approach of cross utilization of ingredients and recipes from menu items to assemble these small bites of food. The pastry chef employees the same approach, using base recipes such as lemon curd, pastry cream, cakes, tart dough, and fresh fruit.

Petits-fours are small complex pastries and some may take a considerable amount of time to assemble but this is what sets them apart from other pastries. Many times the flavors and components found in petits-fours may just be a smaller version of a plated dessert, cake, or tart. When building a production schedule for cakes or tarts, prepare additional fillings or doughs that can be reserved for petits-fours production. To save time, extra mousse from assembling cakes can be molded in flexipans and frozen for future use.

Sec

The category of **petits-fours sec** includes all dry products. It is the simplest form of petits-fours, including butter cookies, small cakes, and tuiles. The benefit of petits-fours sec is that they can be prepared in advance. Cookies can be made in advance, shaped and refrigerated or frozen and baked the day of the event. Cakes can also be mixed and pans filled to await baking at the last possible minute to ensure a fresh, moist product.

Sec items provide a petits-fours presentation with color, texture, and shapes that cannot be achieved with other petits-fours. Due to the simplicity of these items, the execution of the procedure must be perfect. Adding additional elements to these items can increase their complexity. Cookies can be filled; dried or macerated fruit can be added to cakes; a chocolate garnish can be added; or a piped rosette of ganache can be used to add flavor, texture, and design to the finished petits-fours.

Cookies and cakes included in this chapter can be used in many other items produced in the pastry shop. They can be utilized in plated desserts, tarts, cakes, and even as a garnish for other petits-fours. Macarons can be used unfilled to garnish the side of an entremets, or piped small and used as garnish for a contemporary petits-fours. Cookies such as speculaas can be baked and infused into a custard or cream, giving it the flavor of the cookie. It is important to consider cross utilization of flavors and products to be able to prepare the wide variety of items that come out of the pastry shop.

FIGURE 11.1 Presentation of petits-fours sec (clockwise from top): speculaas, sablé Breton, romias

Recipes

Romias

Yield: 1 lb 8 oz (694 g)
Portions: 50 cookies
Portion size: 0.43 oz (13 g)
Yield description: 50 cookies at 0.43 oz (13 g)

Ingredients	U.S.	Metric
Butter	8.8 oz	250 g
Powdered Sugar	3.5 oz	100 g
Vanilla Bean Powder	0.07 oz	2 g
Salt	0.07 oz	2 g
Egg Whites	1.4 oz	40 g
All-Purpose Flour	10.6 oz	300 g

Procedure

1. Cream butter and powdered sugar.
2. Add vanilla powder and salt.
3. Add egg whites in three additions; scrape between each addition.
4. Add flour and mix until ingredients are combined.
5. Pipe using a sultan tip onto a silpat-lined sheet pan.
6. Fill with nougatine mixture (see following recipe).
7. Refrigerate for 1 hour before baking.
8. Bake at 350°F (175°C) until light golden brown.

Romias Nougatine

Yield: 14 oz (400 g)
Portions: 50
Portion size: 0.28 oz (7.9 g)
Yield description: 50 portions at 0.28 oz (7.9 g)

Ingredients	U.S.	Metric
Glucose	3.5 oz	100 g
Brown Sugar	3.5 oz	100 g
Chopped Almonds	3.5 oz	100 g
Butter, cubed	3.5 oz	100 g

Procedure

1. Combine glucose and brown sugar.
2. Warm to dissolve sugar.
3. Add butter and chopped almonds.
4. Cool to room temperature and reserve for cookie assembly.

Speculaas

Yield: 1 lb (471 g)
Portions: 45 cookies
Portion size: 0.35 oz (10 g)
Yield description: 45 cookies at 0.35 oz (10 g)

Ingredients	U.S.	Metric
Butter	3.5 oz	100 g
Brown Sugar	3.5 oz	100 g
Sugar	1.1 oz	30 g
Speculaas Spice Blend, page 334	0.17 oz	5 g
Salt	0.04 oz	1 g
Eggs	0.9 oz	25 g
Milk	0.3 oz	7.5 g
All-Purpose Flour	7.1 oz	200 g
Baking Powder	0.1 oz	3 g

Procedure

1. Sift flour and baking powder.
2. Cream butter, brown sugar, and sugar.
3. Add spice mixture and salt.
4. Combine eggs and milk; add in three additions scraping between additions.
5. Add flour and mix until combined.
6. Refrigerate for a minimum 2 hours.
7. Roll to dough to a thickness of 1/8 in. (3 mm).
8. Cut with a star cutter and place onto silpat-lined sheet pan.
9. Lightly brush dough with water and sprinkle with granulated sugar.
10. Bake at 350°F (175°C) until light golden brown.

Speculaas Spice Blend

Yield: 4 oz (132 g)
Portions: 1
Portion size: 4 oz (132 g)
Yield description: 1 portion at 4 oz (132 g)

Ingredients	U.S.	Metric
Cinnamon	2.4 oz	67 g
Nutmeg	0.7 oz	19 g
Clove	0.7 oz	19 g
Ginger	0.5 oz	15 g
Cardamom	0.25 oz	7 g
White Pepper	0.18 oz	5 g

Procedure

1. Combine all ingredients.
2. Reserve for speculaas cookie recipe.

Sablé Breton

Yield: 3 lb 5.9 oz (1620 g)

Portions: 200 cookies

Portion size: 0.25 oz (8 g)

Yield description: 200 cookies at 0.25 oz (8 g)

Components

Sablé Breton, page 248

Powdered Sugar (as needed)

Procedure

1. Roll sablé Breton dough to 4 mm.

2. Cut with a plain 1.6-in. (4-cm) round cutter.

3. Place dough into a buttered 1.6-in. (4-cm) metal ring.

4. Bake at 350°F (175°C) 8–10 minutes.

5. Cool completely and dust with powdered sugar.

Lemon Viennese

Yield: 12 oz (346 g)

Portions: 57 cookies

Portion size: 0.2 oz (6 g)

Yield description: 57 cookies at 0.2 oz (6 g)

Ingredients	U.S.	Metric
Butter	4.4 oz	125 g
Powdered Sugar	1.8 oz	50 g
Salt	0.04 oz	1 g
Lemon, zested with microplane	2 each	1 each
Egg whites	0.7 oz	20 g
All-Purpose Flour	5.3 oz	150 g
Powdered Sugar, for dusting	As needed	As needed

Procedure

1. Cream butter and powdered sugar.

2. Add salt and lemon zest.

3. Add the egg whites in 3 additions; scrape between each addition.

4. Add flour mix until combined.

5. Pipe using a star tip in a "W" shape onto parchment-lined sheet pans.

6. After piping refrigerate for 1 hour.

7. Bake at 350°F (175°C) until light golden brown.

8. Cool completely and dust with powdered sugar.

FIGURE 11.2 Pistachio Diamond, Biscotti, Lemon Viennese, Orange Tuile

Pistachio Diamonds

Yield: 1 lb 14 oz (862 g)
Portions: 60 cookies
Portion size: 0.5 oz (14 g)
Yield description: 60 cookies at 0.5 oz (14 g)

Ingredients	U.S.	Metric
Butter	8.1 oz	230 g
Powdered Sugar	5.6 oz	160 g
All-Purpose Flour	14.1 oz	400 g
Pistachio Paste	1.1 oz	32 g
Pistachios, chopped	1.4 oz	40 g
Sugar	As needed	As needed

Procedure

1. Cream butter and sugar.
2. Add flour, pistachio paste and chopped pistachios; mix until combined.
3. Roll dough into logs 1.5 in. (40 mm) in diameter and freeze.
4. Remove dough from the freezer and moisten with water; roll in granulated sugar.
5. Allow dough to temper for a few minutes.
6. Cut into ¼ in. (7 mm) and place on a silpat-lined sheet pan.
7. Bake at 350°F (175°C) until light golden brown.

Orange Tuile

Yield: 9 oz (258 g)
Portions: 43 tuile
Portion size: 0.2 oz (6 g)
Yield description: 43 tuile at 0.2 oz (6 g)

Ingredients	U.S.	Metric
Powdered Sugar	3.5 oz	100 g
All-Purpose Flour	1 oz	28 g
Pectin Yellow	0.03 oz	0.8 g
Orange Juice	1.1 oz	30 g
Butter	1.4 oz	40 g
Almonds, chopped	1.8 oz	50 g
Candied Orange Peel, page 337	0.4 oz	10 g

Procedure

1. Combine flour, pectin, powdered sugar, chopped almond, and chopped orange peel.
2. Add melted butter and orange juice, mix until combined.
3. Refrigerate for 4 hours.
4. Scoop tuile batter into balls 0.5 in. (12 mm) in diameter and place a silpat-lined sheet pan.
5. Bake at 350°F (175°C) until the center of the tuile is a light golden brown.
6. Remove the sheet pan from the oven and allow to cool slightly.
7. Using an offset pallet knife, remove the warm tuile from the pan and place it over a rolling pin to shape.
8. After tuile has completely cooled store in an airtight container.

Candied Citrus Peel

Ingredients	U.S.	Metric
Oranges	12 each	12 each
Salt	0.6 oz	20 g
Water #1	2 lb 4.5 oz	1000 g
Sugar	3 lb 10 oz	1750 g
Water #2	1 lb 7 oz	750 g
Glucose	8.3 oz	250 g

Note: Any citrus fruit can be used in place of the orange. The candied orange peel will store for several months in a sealed container in the refrigerator.

Procedure

1. Wash the fruit thoroughly.
2. Using a French knife; remove the peel from the fruit.
3. Cut the peel into ¼-in. (7-mm) wide strips.
4. Bring water #1 and the salt to boil; blanch the peel for 5 minutes.
5. Strain and rinse the peels.
6. Combine the 2 lb 12 oz (1250 g) of sugar with water #2 and bring to a boil.
7. Pour over peel, place plastic wrap directly on top of syrup (the peel must be covered) and allow to cool overnight.
8. The next day, strain the syrup from the peel; reserve the syrup.
9. Add 4 oz (125 g) of sugar the strained syrup and heat just to a boil.
10. Pour over the peel, place plastic wrap directly on top of the syrup, and allow to cool overnight.
11. Repeat steps 8 to 10 for 3 more days.
12. On the fifth day strain the syrup from the peel and scale 2 lb 12 oz (1250 g).
13. Add the glucose to the syrup and bring to a boil.
14. Pour over the peel and cover directly with plastic wrap.
15. The peel can be dried overnight on glazing racks and stored in the syrup under refrigeration or in the freezer.

Biscotti

Yield: 3 lb 3 oz (1476 g)
Portions: 147 cookies
Portion size: 0.3 oz (10 g)
Yield description: 147 cookies at 0.3 oz (10 g)

Ingredients	U.S.	Metric
Butter	5.7 oz	163 g
Sugar	12 oz	340 g
Salt	0.09 oz	2.5 g
Vanilla Extract	0.9 oz	25 g
Eggs	5.8 oz	165 g
All-Purpose Flour	1 lb 1.9 oz	508 g
Baking Soda	0.2 oz	5 g
Baking Powder	0.2 oz	5 g
Sliced Almonds	8.8 oz	250 g
Orange Zest	0.4 oz	10 g

Procedure

1. Cream butter and sugar.
2. Add salt and vanilla extract.
3. Add eggs in three additions scraping between each addition.
4. Sift flour, baking soda, and baking powder.
5. Add sifted flour mixture, sliced almonds, and orange zest.
6. Mix until combined.
7. Scale dough into 9-oz (250-g) pieces.
8. Roll into logs 12 in. (30 cm) long.
9. Bake at 350°F (175°C) on parchment paper lined sheet pans until golden brown.
10. Remove from oven and let bars cool.
11. While still warm, slice with a serrated knife to desired thickness.
12. Lay sliced biscotti on a parchment-lined sheet pan and continue baking until dried.

Chocolate Pistachio Biscotti

Ingredients	U.S.	Metric
Chocolate Chips	4.4 oz	125 g
Pistachios	5.3 oz	150 g

Variation

Replace almonds and orange zest with chocolate chips and pistachios.

Hazelnut Financier

Yield: 1 lb 2 oz (510 g)
Portions: 25 cakes
Portion size: 0.7 oz (20 g)
Yield description: 25 cakes at 0.7 oz (20 g)

Ingredients	U.S.	Metric
Hazelnut Flour	1.8 oz	50 g
Powdered Sugar	4.4 oz	125 g
All-Purpose Flour	1.8 oz	50 g
Egg Whites	4.2 oz	120 g
Butter	4.4 oz	125 g
Honey	1.4 oz	40 g
Griottine Cherries	25 each	25 each

Note: Hazelnut flour can be replaced with almond or pistachio flour.

Procedure

1. Brown butter in a heavy-bottom saucepan to make beurre noisette.

2. Combine dry ingredients.

3. Add egg whites to dry ingredients followed by beurre noisette.

4. Refrigerate overnight.

5. Pipe into 1.5-in. (3.8-cm) molds; place one griottine cherry in the center of each.

6. Bake at 350°F (175°C).

FIGURE 11.3 Macaron, financier, madeleine (clockwise from top)

French Macaron

Yield: 2 lb 10 oz (1122 g)
Portions: 186 cookies (93 sandwiched cookies)
Portion size: 0.2 oz (6 g)
Yield description: 186 cookies (93 sandwiched cookies)

Ingredients	U.S.	Metric
Almond Flour	10.6 oz	300 g
Powdered Sugar	10.6 oz	300 g
Egg Whites #1	3.9 oz	110 g
Sugar	8.8 oz	250 g
Corn Syrup	1.8 oz	50 g
Water	2.6 oz	75 g
Egg Whites #2	3.9 oz	110 g
Egg White Powder	0.07 oz	2 g

Note: Liquid or powder color can be added to the meringue during mixing.

Procedure

1. Combine almond flour and powdered sugar in a food processor; grind for 1 minute.
2. Add water, corn syrup, and sugar to heavy-bottom saucepan.
3. Combine egg whites #2 and egg white powder in a stand mixer.
4. Cook sugar mixture to 240°F (114°C).
5. Turn egg whites on high speed, continue cooking sugar mixture to 245°F (118°C).
6. Add cooked sugar mixture to egg whites; cool to 110°F (44°C).
7. Fold egg whites #1 into almond flour and powdered sugar mixture; this paste will become stiff if left too long.
8. Fold meringue into mixture in three additions.
9. The finished batter should run slightly. If it is stiff, use a rubber spatula to remove some of the air from the batter.
10. Place into pastry bag fitted with a ⅜-in. (10-mm) plain tip.
11. Pipe onto a silpat-lined sheet pan 1 in. (25 mm) in diameter.
12. Allow the macaron to dry at room temperature for 30 minutes.
13. Bake at 330°F (165°C) for 13 to 15 minutes; the cookie should not have any browning
14. Fill with flavored ganache or buttercream.

Chocolate Macaron

Ingredients	U.S.	Metric
Cocoa Paste	2.8 oz	00 g

Variation

1. Heat cocoa paste to 100°F (38°C).
2. Incorporate cocoa paste during step 7 above.

Madeleine

Yield: 1 lb 10 oz (762 g)
Portions: 115 portions
Portion size: 0.2 oz (6.5 g)
Yield description: 115 portions at 0.2 oz (6.5 g)

Ingredients	U.S.	Metric
Butter	6.3 oz	180 g
Sugar	5.1 oz	145 g
Brown Sugar	0.7 oz	20 g
Salt	0.07 oz	2 g
Honey	1.1 oz	30 g
Eggs	7.1 oz	200 g
All-Purpose Flour	6.3 oz	180 g
Baking Powder	0.2 oz	5 g

Procedure

1. Cream butter, sugar, brown sugar, and salt.
2. Sift flour and baking powder.
3. Add honey to creamed mixture.
4. Add eggs in three additions, scraping between each addition.
5. Add flour and mix until combined.
6. Brush madeleine molds with soft butter and dust with flour.
7. Pipe batter into mold, fill ¾ of the way.
8. Refrigerate for 1 hour.
9. Bake at 400°F (205°C) for 5 to 7 minutes.
10. Immediately remove madeleines from pans.

Glacé

The next category, **petits-fours glacé**, includes items that are glazed. The glaze can come in the form of poured fondant, chocolate glaze, fruit glaze, or caramel. The glaze on these pastries gives them a bright shine, adds flavor, and protects the product underneath from drying out while on the buffet. To further prevent glazed items from looking dry, coat cakes in a thin layer of marmalade or thinly rolled sheet of marzipan. The marzipan will provide a smooth surface for the glaze as well as prevent the cake to absorb water from the glaze.

Oftentimes, when customers refer to petits-fours, they do not understand the wide variety of pastries that this includes. They immediately think of the small square or round cakes that are enrobed in pouring fondant. Pouring fondant is very sweet, so it's important to consider this when using it as part of a petits-fours. Pairing fondant with a pastry that has an acidic filling or one that is not overly sweet works best.

Pouring fondant is a product that can be made in the pastry kitchen or purchased from a supplier. It is a mixture of water, sugar, glucose, and acid that is cooked and cooled on a marble table. As the fondant begins to cool it is agitated, similar to fudge. During this stage, the sugar begins to crystalize. The temperature the fondant syrup is cooked to and the ingredients, glucose and acid, control the crystallization. Agitation creates small crystals in the syrup, making the mixture opaque.

When working with pouring fondant, the ideal working temperature is 110°F (43°C). If the fondant is too thick when heated, water or sugar syrup can be added to adjust the consistency. Exceeding this temperature will begin to melt the crystals out of the fondant. As the fondant cools and dries, it will not shine, due to the reduced amount of crystals. Dull fondant can occur if the fondant is overheated or placed in the refrigerator. The shine of the fondant indicates a freshly made product; dull fondant is associated with an older product.

FIGURE 11.4 Improperly glazed petits-fours (left), properly glazed petits-fours (right)

Recipes

Traditional Petits-Fours Glacé

Yield: 54 cakes at 1.25 × 1.25 in. (3.1 × 3.1 cm)

Portions: 54 cakes

Portion size: 1.25 × 1.25 in. (3.1 × 3.1 cm)

Yield description: 54 cakes at 1.25 × 1.25 in. (3.1 × 3.1 cm)

Components

Petits-Fours Cake, page 345

Marzipan, page 344

Pouring Fondant, page 344

Raspberry Marmalade

Procedure

1. Spread a thin layer of raspberry marmalade on the top of cake.
2. Cut the cake in half and stack the layers.
3. Roll a piece of marzipan to thinly cover the top of the cake.
4. Freeze the cake.
5. Turn the cake upside down and cut into 1.25-in. (3.1-cm) squares or using round cutter.
6. Glaze with pouring fondant.

FIGURE 11.5 Top to bottom: White chocolate pineapple, opera, citron, traditional petits-fours glacé

Marzipan

Yield: 4 lb 12 oz (2180 g)

Portions: 1

Portion size: 4 lb 12 oz (2180 g)

Yield description: 1 portion at 4 lb 12 oz (2180 g)

Ingredients	U.S.	Metric
Almond Paste	2 lb 3 oz	1000 g
Glucose	6 oz	180 g
Powdered Sugar, sifted	2 lb 3 oz	1000 g

Procedure

1. Using a paddle attachment mix almond paste with glucose on low speed.
2. Begin adding powdered sugar, not all of the powdered sugar will be needed; add enough to form a soft dough.
3. Wrap tightly in plastic wrap and store in the refrigerator.

Pouring Fondant

Yield: 3 lb 1 oz (1421 g)

Portions: 1

Portion size: 3 lb 1 oz (1421 g)

Yield description: 1 portion at 3 lb 1 oz (1421 g)

Ingredients	U.S.	Metric
Water #1	1 lb 9 oz	720 g
Sugar	2 lb 10 oz	1200 g
Glucose	7.8 oz	220 g
Cream of Tartar	0.04 oz	1 g
Water #2	1 lb 5 oz	600 g

Procedure

1. Lightly oil a marble table and metal bars, prepare a frame to hold the cooked syrup.
2. Combine water #1 and sugar; bring to a boil.
3. Cook the mixture to 225°F (107°C).
4. Warm the glucose and add to the cooking sugar; continue cooking to 240°F (116°C).
5. Pour onto oiled marble and sprinkle with water #2.
6. Cool the mixture to 110°F (43°C) and table as with tempering chocolate (page 347).
7. Once the syrup has crystallized, store it in a plastic container; cover the top of the fondant with a thin layer of water. Allow fondant to rest for 24 hours before use.

Reheating Fondant

1. Pour off the syrup from the top of the fondant.
2. Warm the fondant over a double boiler to 110°F (43°C). If the fondant is too thick once warmed, add a small amount of the syrup that was on top of the fondant.

Petits-Fours Cake

Yield: 2 lb 6 oz (1080 g)
Portions: 1
Portion size: half sheet pan
Yield description: 1 half sheet pan

Ingredients	U.S.	Metric
Almond Paste	1 lb 1 oz	480 g
Butter	8.5 oz	240 g
Sugar	2.1 oz	60 g
Eggs	8.5 oz	240 g
Cake Flour	2.1 oz	60 g

Procedure

1. Cream almond paste, butter and sugar with a paddle on medium speed.
2. Slowly add eggs, scraping between additions.
3. Add flour on low speed; mix until combined.
4. Spread onto a greased half sheet pan lined with parchment paper.
5. Bake at 350°F (175 °C) 15 to 20 minutes.

Chocolate Filled Pâte au Choux

Portions: 50
Portion size: 1.5 inch (3.8 cm)
Yield description: 50 portions at 1.5 inch (3.8 cm)

Components

Pâte au Choux, page 346
Chocolate Pastry Cream, page 346
Fondant, page 344

Procedure

1. Prepare pâte au choux; pipe into 0.75-in. (1.9-cm) rounds and bake.
2. Fill pâte au choux with chocolate pastry cream.
3. Prepare fondant; add unsweetened chocolate as desired to make chocolate fondant.
4. Glaze the top of the pâte au choux.

Pâte au Choux

Yield: 1 lb 10 oz (761.5 g)

Portions: 50

Portion size: 0.5 oz (14 g)

Yield description: 50 portions at 0.5 oz (14 g)

Ingredients	U.S.	Metric
Milk	7.9 oz	225 g
Heavy Cream	0.9 oz	25 g
Butter, cubed	4.4 oz	125 g
Sugar	0.2 oz	5 g
Salt	0.05 oz	1.5 g
All-Purpose Flour	2.3 oz	65 g
Bread Flour	2.3 oz	65 g
Eggs	8.8 oz	250 g

Procedure

1. Combine milk, heavy cream, butter, sugar, and salt in saucepan.
2. Heat to a boil.
3. Add all-purpose flour and bread flour; stir and cook for 2 minutes.
4. Transfer the mixture to a mixer with the paddle attachment, mix until temperature is 140°F (60°C).
5. Add eggs and mix until combined.
6. Pipe into desired shape on a siplat.
7. Bake at 300°F (150°C) until golden brown.

Chocolate Pastry Cream

Yield: 1 lb 11 oz (790 g)

Portions: 1

Portion size: 1 lb 11 oz (790 g)

Yield description: 1 portion at 1 lb 11 oz (790 g)

Ingredients	U.S.	Metric
Pastry Cream, page 140	1 lb 8 oz	700 g
Chocolate 60%	3.2 oz	90 g

Procedure

1. Prepare pastry cream (page 140).
2. Place warm pastry cream and chocolate in a mixing bowl fitted with a paddle attachment.
3. Mix on low to combine and cool the pastry cream.
4. Cover with plastic wrap and store in the refrigerator.

Citron

Yield: Forty-five 1.5 inch tarts

Portions: 45

Portion size: One 1.5-in. tart

Yield description: Forty-five 1.5-in. tarts

Components

Sablé Breton, page 248

Italian Meringue, page 253

Lemon Mousseline, below

Fondant, page 344

Candied Lemon Zest, page 337

Procedure

1. Roll sablé Breton dough to 0.2 in. (5 mm) thick.
2. Cut the sablé Breton using a 1.5-in. (40-mm) round cutter and bake.
3. Using a sultan tip, pipe Italian meringue and brown with a torch.
4. Prepare fondant and color yellow.
5. Place a toothpick into the frozen lemon mousseline and dip in the warmed fondant.
6. Place on the meringue.
7. Remove the toothpick and cover the hole with a thin slice of candied lemon zest.

Lemon Mousseline

Yield: 15 oz (450 g)

Portions: 45

Portion size: 0.35 oz (10 g)

Yield description: Forty-five 1-in. (2.5-cm) spheres

Ingredients	U.S.	Metric
Lemon Curd, page 139	8.1 oz	230 g
Butter	7.8 oz	220 g

Procedure

1. Cream butter on medium speed using a paddle attachment.
2. Slowly incorporate lemon curd.
3. Continue mixing until light and fluffy.
4. Pipe into 1-in. (2.5-cm) sphere mold and freeze.

Opera

Portions: 100 cakes

Portion size: 1.25 × 1.5 in. (2.5 × 3.8 cm)

Yield description: 100 cakes at 1.25 × 1.5 in. (2.5 × 3.8 cm)

Components

Dark Chocolate, melted

Jaconde, page 196

Coffee Syrup, page 348

Coffee Buttercream, page 348

Dark Chocolate Ganache, page 351

Chocolate Mirror Glaze, page 226

Procedure

1. Cut jaconde into half sheet pan pieces.
2. Spread the melted chocolate on one of the layers of jaconde. Allow this to crystallize; then place chocolate side down.
3. Generously soak cake with coffee syrup.
4. Spread a layer of the coffee buttercream on the jaconde.
5. Place a sheet of jaconde on top of the buttercream and soak with coffee syrup.
6. Spread a layer of ganache on the jaconde.
7. Place a sheet of jaconde on top of the buttercream and soak with coffee syrup.
8. Spread a layer of coffee butter cream on the jaconde.
9. Refrigerate the assembled cake for 2 hours to set the buttercream and ganache.
10. Glaze the top of the cake with the chocolate mirror glaze and refrigerate for 5 minutes to set the glaze.
11. Cut into 1.25 × 1.5 in. (2.5 × 3.8 cm) rectangles.

Coffee Syrup

Yield: 1 lb 5 oz (600 g)

Portions: 1

Portion size: 1 lb 5 oz (600 g)

Yield description: 1 portion at 1 lb 5 oz (600 g)

Ingredients	U.S.	Metric
Water	5.3 oz	150 g
Sugar	5.3 oz	150 g
Coffee Extract	10.6 oz	300 g

Procedure

1. Combine water and sugar.
2. Heat to dissolve, then cool.
3. Add coffee extract.
4. Reserve for assembly.

Coffee Buttercream

Yield: 1 lb 6 oz (630 g)

Portions: 1

Portion size: 1 lb 6 oz (630 g)

Yield description: 1 portion at 1 lb 6 oz (630 g)

Ingredients	U.S.	Metric
Swiss Buttercream	1 lb 5 oz	600 g
Coffee Extract	1.1 oz	30 g

Procedure

1. Combine buttercream and extract with a paddle on low speed.
2. Reserve for assembly.

White Chocolate Pineapple

Yield: Fifty portions at 1.75 in. (4.4 cm) dome

Portions: 50

Portion size: 1.75-in. (4.4-cm) dome

Yield description: Fifty 1.75-in. (4.4-cm) domes

Components

Hazelnut Dough, page 225

Sous Vide Pineapple, page 349

White Chocolate Mousse, page 135

Colored White Chocolate Glaze, page 349

Jaconde, page 196

Procedure

1. Roll hazelnut dough ⅛ in. (3 mm) thick, cut with a fluted cutter 1.75 in. (4.4 cm) and bake.
2. Drain sous vide pineapple.
3. Cut jaconde with a 1-in. (25-mm) round cutter.
4. Fill a 1.75-in. (4.4-cm) silicone dome mold ¾ full with white chocolate mousse, place a small amount of pineapple inside followed by a piece of the jaconde and freeze.
5. Unmold and glaze with colored white chocolate glaze, tinted yellow.

Sous Vide Pineapple

Yield: 13 oz (375 g)

Portions: 1

Portion size: 13 oz (375 g)

Yield description: 1 portion at 13 oz (375 g)

Ingredients	U.S.	Metric
Pineapple, brunoise	7.1 oz	200 g
Water	4.4 oz	125 g
Sugar	1.8 oz	50 g
Vanilla Bean, split and scraped	1 each	1 each

Procedure

1. Combine water, sugar, and vanilla bean.
2. Cool completely; pour over pineapple in vacuum bag.
3. Seal bag at full vacuum and cook at 190°F (88°C) for 1 hour.
4. Cool and reserve in bag for assembly.

Colored White Chocolate Glaze

Yield: 2 lb 14 oz (1335 g)

Portions: 1

Portion size: 2 lb 14 oz (1335 g)

Yield description: 1 portion at 2 lb 14 oz (1335 g)

Ingredients	U.S.	Metric
Water	6.9 oz	195 g
Sugar	10.5 oz	300 g
Glucose	10.5 oz	300 g
Sweetened Condensed Milk	7.6 oz	215 g
Gelatin Sheets, bloomed	7.5 each	7.5 each
White Chocolate	11.4 oz	325 g
Food Coloring	As needed	As needed

Procedure

1. Combine water, sugar, and glucose; bring to a boil.
2. Add the sweetened condensed milk and gelatin.
3. Pour over white chocolate and emulsify.
4. Add coloring as needed.
5. Glaze at 86°F (30°C).

Contemporary

Contemporary petits-fours contain more components than sec or glacé. They are assembled with a minimum of three components: base, cream, and garnish. Cakes, cookie dough, macaron, or chocolate are suitable bases for a contemporary petits-fours. The base of the petits-fours is in place to facilitate transferring during production, providing both a textural element and the design of the petits-fours. The most important role of the base is to provide a way for the guest to pick up the pastry. In addition to a cookie base, baked items such as cake or meringue may also be used.

The flavor of the petits four is introduced through the creams. Custards and creams can be used much in the same way they are incorporated in an entremets in Chapter 8. Combing stirred custard with a mousse will give the petits-fours different textures and flavors. To maintain the quality and moisture of the cream, a glaze or chocolate spray can be applied.

The last component is the garnish. The garnish needs to represent the flavors contained inside the petits-fours. Products that contain nuts can be garnished with the nut contained in the pastry. This conveys the flavor and also alerts the guest that have nut sensitivities that there are nuts in the pastry. A light sugar twist or delicate chocolate garnishes provide a nice finish to contemporary petits-fours.

Pastry chefs continue to develop new and innovative ways to present their petits-fours. **Verrines**, petits-fours assembled in glasses, continue to be a popular item. The petits-fours is assembled in a glass using creams, mousses, streusels, cakes, coulis, and even edible flowers. The use of verrines allows for different textures, creams can have a reduced amount of gelatin making the texture very soft and loose. The use of a clear container allows for creative layering of the dessert, showing all the colors, textures and flavors of the desserts. While glass containers provide excellent carriers for verrines, there are many plastic glasses and plates available in different sizes, shapes, and colors to create new designs.

Recipes

Lime and White Chocolate Verrine

Yield: Thirty 2-oz (57-g) glasses

Portions: 30

Portion size: 2-oz (57-g) glasses

Yield description: Thirty 2-oz (57-g) glasses

Components

Lime Gelée, page 352

White Chocolate Creamy, page 352

Raspberry Cloud, page 89

Candied Sunflower Seeds, page 353

Procedure

1. Fill the glass with 10 g of lime gelée and refrigerate until set.

2. Top the gelée with 10 g of white chocolate creamy and refrigerate until set.

3. Repeat steps 1 and 2 to create 4 layers in the glass.

4. Using a spoon apply the raspberry cloud.

5. Sprinkle with candied sunflower seeds.

FIGURE 11.6 Lime and White Chocolate Verrine

Lime Gelée

Yield: 1 lb 7 oz (656 g)

Portions: 1

Portion size: 1 lb 7 oz (656 g)

Yield description: 1 portion 1 lb 7 oz (656 g)

Ingredients	U.S.	Metric
Lime Juice	5.8 oz	165 g
Sugar	4.6 oz	130 g
Water	12.7 oz	360 g
Vanilla Bean Powder	0.04 oz	1 g
Gelatin Sheets, bloomed	5 each	5 each

Procedure

1. Combine water, sugar, and vanilla bean powder in saucepan.
2. Heat to dissolve sugar.
3. Remove from heat; add gelatin and lime juice, and strain through a chinois.
4. Reserve for assembly.

White Chocolate Creamy

Yield: 1 lb 8 oz (690 g)

Portions: 1

Portion size: 1 lb 8 oz (690 g)

Yield description: 1 portion at 1 lb 8 oz (690 g)

Ingredients	U.S.	Metric
Milk	6.5 oz	185 g
Heavy Cream	6.5 oz	185 g
Egg Yolks	2.6 oz	75 g
White Chocolate, chopped fine	8.6 oz	245 g
Gelatin Sheets, bloomed	2.25 each	2.25 each

Procedure

1. Prepare a crème anglaise (page 143) with the milk, heavy cream, and egg yolks.
2. Add the crème anglaise to the white chocolate; emulsify.
3. Next add the bloomed gelatin and strain through a chinois.
4. Reserve for assembly.

Candied Sunflower Seeds

Yield: 9 oz (238.5 g)

Portions: 1

Portion size: 9 oz (238.5 g)

Yield description: 1 portion at 9 oz (238.5 g)

Ingredients	U.S.	Metric
Sugar	2.5 oz	70 g
Water	1.2 oz	35 g
Sunflower Seeds	5.8 oz	165 g
Cocoa Butter	0.1 oz	3.5 g

Procedure

1. Combine water and sugar in a saucepan and cook to 240°F (115°C).

2. Remove from the heat; add the sunflower seeds and stir with a heat-resistant rubber spatula.

3. The sugar will crystallize, creating a thin coating of sugar on the seeds.

4. Return the pan to a medium-high heat; continue stirring the seeds until the sugar caramelizes.

5. Stir in the cocoa butter.

6. Pour the sunflower seeds onto a silpat-lined sheet pan.

7. Allow seeds to cool completely; store in airtight container.

Cherry Chocolate Verrine

Yield: Forty 2.5-oz (70-g) glasses

Portions: 40

Portion size: 2.5-oz (70-g) glasses

Yield description: Forty 2.5-oz (70-g) glasses

Components

Pectin Cherry Gelée, page 105

Buttermilk Panna Cotta, page 139

Chocolate Flourless Cake, page 356

Chocolate Streusel Base, page 232

Chantilly (Stabilized), page 251

Chocolate Meringue, page 356

Procedure

1. Prepare the pectin cherry gelée; place half of the mixture into ¼-in. (6-mm) sphere molds.

2. Cut the chocolate flourless cake with a 1.6-in. (4.2-cm) round cutter.

3. Angle the glass; place five spheres of the pectin cherry gelée and then fill with 0.9 oz (25 g) panna cotta; refrigerate.

4. Place the glass flat and fill the open area with the chocolate streusel.

5. Top with the Chantilly and add some chocolate meringue.

FIGURE 11.7 Cherry Chocolate Verrine

Chocolate Flourless Cake

Yield: 1 lb 9 oz (735 g)

Portions: 1

Portion size: half sheet pan

Yield description: 1 half sheet pan

Ingredients	U.S.	Metric
Heavy Cream	2.1 oz	60 g
Butter	8.5 oz	240 g
Sugar	4.2 oz	120 g
Chocolate 50%	4.2 oz	120 g
Cocoa Powder	1.6 oz	45 g
Eggs	5.3 oz	150 g

Procedure

1. Whip eggs and half the sugar on high speed for 10 minutes.
2. Combine heavy cream, butter, chocolate, remaining sugar, and cocoa powder.
3. Melt over a double boiler.
4. Fold the whipped eggs into the melted chocolate mixture.
5. Spread onto a silpat-lined half sheet pan.
6. Bake at 350°F (177 °C) for 10 to 15 minutes.

Chocolate Meringue

Yield: 10 oz (310 g)

Portions: 1

Portion size: 10 oz (310 g)

Yield description: 1 portion at 10 oz (310 g)

Ingredients	U.S.	Metric
Egg Whites	3.5 oz	100 g
Sugar #1	3.5 oz	100 g
Cocoa Powder	0.7 oz	20 g
Sugar #2	3.2 oz	90 g

Procedure

1. Sift second sugar and cocoa powder.
2. Make a common meringue with the egg whites and first sugar.
3. Fold the cocoa powder mixture into the meringue.
4. Pipe onto a parchment-lined sheet pan.
5. Bake at 212°F (100°C) until dry.

Macaron Surprise

Yield: Forty 1.5-in. (3.8-cm) macaron surprise

Portions: 40

Portion size: 1.5-in. (3.8-cm) macaron surprise

Yield description: Forty 1.5-in. (3.8-cm) macaron surprise

Components

Chocolate Macaron, page 314

Speculaas Cream, page 358

Poached Apples Spheres, page 358

Clear Glaze, page 106

Milk Chocolate Spray, page 397

Chocolate Décor

Procedure

1. Prepare chocolate macaron and pipe to 1.75-in. (4.4-cm) diameter.

2. Unmold the speculaas cream and spray with milk chocolate spray to achieve a velvet texture.

3. Return the speculaas cream to the freezer for 10 minutes.

4. Place the speculaas cream on the chocolate macaron.

5. Using a toothpick, dip the apple in the clear glaze.

6. Place the apple on the speculaas cream.

7. Top with the chocolate décor.

FIGURE 11.8 Clockwise starting at top: White Chocolate and Raspberry Purse, Apricot Creme Fraiche, Fruit Tart, Macaron Surprise, Pistachio Crunch

Speculaas Cream

Yield: 1 lb (475 g)

Portions: 40

Portion size: 0.4 oz (11 g)

Yield description: Forty 1.75-in. (4.4-cm) savarin molds

Ingredients	U.S.	Metric
Heavy Cream	5.8 oz	165 g
Milk	5.8 oz	165 g
Baked Speculaas Cookies	2.6 oz	75 g
Brown Sugar	1.2 oz	35 g
Egg Yolks	1.3 oz	38 g
Gelatin Sheets, bloomed	1.5 each	1.5 each

Procedure

1. Combine milk and heavy cream in a saucepan and scald.

2. Remove from heat; add baked speculaas cookies (do not stir), cover with plastic wrap, and steep for 15 minutes.

3. Strain the mixture through a chinois. Do not press the liquid out of the cookies; this will make the cream gritty.

4. Some of the milk and cream will be lost in the process of steeping in the cookies. Make up the difference with 50% cream and 50% milk to return the total weight of milk and cream to 10.8 oz (330 g).

5. Make a crème anglaise (page 124) with infused milk and cream mixture, brown sugar, and egg yolks.

6. Add the bloomed gelatin and strain through a chinois.

7. Deposit the cream into 1.75-in. (4.4-cm) savarin molds and freeze.

Sous Vide Poached Apples

Yield: 40 apple spheres

Portions: 40

Portion size: 0.8-in. (2.2-cm) spheres

Yield description: Forty 0.8-in. (2.2-cm) spheres

Ingredients	U.S.	Metric
Granny Smith Apples, peeled	4 each	4 each
Water	15 oz	450 g
Rum	1.7 oz	50 g
Sugar	4.2 oz	125 g
Vanilla Bean, split and scraped	1 each	1 each
Cinnamon Stick	1 each	1 each

Procedure

1. Combine water, rum, sugar, vanilla bean, and cinnamon stick in a saucepan, bring to a boil.

2. Cover and cool completely on an ice bath.

3. Use a 0.8-in. (2.2-cm) parisienne scoop to portion the Granny Smith apples.

4. Combine the apples and syrup in a vacuum bag and seal at a full vacuum.

5. Cook in a thermal circulator at 185°F (85°C) for 90 minutes. Test the doneness of the apples by gently squeezing them through the bag.

6. Place the vacuum bag on an ice bath to cool.

7. Reserve for assembly.

Fruit Tart

Yield: Forty 1.9-in. (4.8-cm) tarts

Portions: 40

Portion size: 1.9-in. (4.8-cm) tart

Yield description: Forty 1.9-in. (4.8-cm) tarts

Components

Pâte Sablée, page 246

Almond Cream, page 78

Pastry Cream, page 140

Clear Glaze, page 106

Fresh Seasonal Fruit

Procedure

1. Roll pâte sablée to ⅛ in. (3 mm) thick.

2. Line 1.9-in. (4.8-cm) tart shells and refrigerate.

3. Pipe a thin layer of almond cream in the shell.

4. Bake at 350°F (177°C) until golden brown.

5. After shells have cooled spread a thin layer of pastry cream on top of the almond cream.

6. Arrange the fresh fruit.

7. Apply a thin layer of clear glaze to the fruit.

Pistachio Crunch

Yield: Thirty 1.5 in. (3.8 cm) pistachio crunch

Portions: 30

Portion size: 1.5 in. (3.8 cm) pistachio crunch

Yield description: Thirty 1.5 in. (3.8 cm) pistachio crunch

Components

Pistachio Crunch Base, page 360

Pistachio Buttercream, page 360

Pistachio Crunch Florentine, page 361

Procedure

1. Using a star tip, pipe pistachio buttercream on the pistachio crunch base.

2. Place the pistachio crunch Florentine on top of the buttercream.

Pistachio Crunch Base

Yield: 14 oz (427 g)

Portions: 30

Portion size: 1.25-in. (3.1-cm) cakes

Yield description: Thirty 1.25-in. (3.1-cm) cakes

Ingredients	U.S.	Metric
Butter	3.5 oz	100 g
Sugar	3.5 oz	120 g
Almond Flour	1.1 oz	30 g
Eggs	2.5 oz	70 g
All-Purpose Flour	3.5 oz	100 g
Baking Powder	0.07 oz	2 g
Rum	0.2 oz	5 g

Procedure

1. With the paddle attachment, cream butter, sugar, and almond flour.
2. Add eggs in two additions, scraping between each addition.
3. Sift baking powder and all-purpose flour.
4. Add rum to mixer.
5. Add sifted ingredients, mix to combine.
6. Pipe into 1.25-in. (3.1-cm) round silicone molds.
7. Bake at 350°F (177 °C) for 8 to 10 minutes.

Pistachio Crunch Buttercream

Yield: 15 oz (450 g)

Portions: 1

Portion size: 15 oz (450 g)

Yield description: 1 portion at 15 oz (450 g)

Ingredients	U.S.	Metric
Italian Buttercream	14.1 oz	400 g
Pistachio Paste	1.8 oz	50 g

Procedure

1. Soften buttercream in a mixer with a paddle.
2. Incorporate pistachio paste into buttercream.
3. Reserve for assembly.

Pistachio Crunch Florentine

Yield: 8 oz (240 g)

Portions: 30

Portion size: 1.25-in. (30-mm) rounds

Yield description: Thirty 1.25-in. (30-mm) rounds

Ingredients	U.S.	Metric
Glucose	2.1 oz	60 g
Brown Sugar	2.1 oz	60 g
Pistachios, chopped	2.1 oz	60 g
Butter	2.1 oz	60 g

Procedure

1. Warm glucose in a saucepan over a medium heat, do not cook.
2. Add brown sugar, pistachios, and butter; heat until sugar dissolves.
3. Pour Florentine onto a sheet of parchment paper.
4. Roll between two pieces of parchment paper.
5. Refrigerate on a sheet pan, this will facilitate removing the top parchment.
6. Bake on double sheet pans at 350°F (177°C) until Florentine is golden brown.
7. Cut 1.25-in. (30-mm) circles from the Florentine.
8. Reserve for assembly.

White Chocolate and Raspberry Mousse Purse

Yield: Fifty 1.4-in. (35-mm) cakes

Portions: 50

Portion size: 1.4-in. (35-mm) cake

Yield description: Fifty 1.4-in. (35-mm) cakes

Components

Sacher Biscuit, page 195

White Chocolate Mousse
(Pâte à Bombe), page 135

Fresh Raspberries

Raspberry Marmalade

Dark Chocolate Wrap, page 362

Cocoa Powder

Procedure

1. Cut the sheet of sacher biscuit in half; place one piece into a half sheet pan.
2. Spread a thin layer of raspberry marmalade on the cake.
3. Place the raspberries on the cake.
4. Prepare the white chocolate mousse; spread to fill the pan.
5. Place the remaining piece of sacher biscuit on top of the mousse and freeze.
6. Cut the frozen cake into 1.4-in. (35-mm) rounds.
7. Wrap in Dark Chocolate Wrap.
8. Lightly dust with cocoa powder.

Dark Chocolate Wrap

Yield: 9.1 oz (275 g)

Portions: 2

Portion size: sheet pan

Yield description: 2 sheet pans

Ingredients	U.S.	Metric
Dark Chocolate 58%	1 lb 1 oz	500 g
Vegetable Oil	1.8 oz	50 g

Procedure

1. Combine chocolate and vegetable oil.
2. Melt over a double boiler to 110°F (43°C).
3. Warm a sheet pan to 110°F (43°C).
4. Spread the chocolate mixture onto the back of the sheet pan, refrigerate until set.
5. Remove the sheet pan from the refrigerator and allow to warm.
6. Once the sheet pan warms to room temperature, use a scraper to test that the chocolate will roll up off the pan.
7. After the test strip is successful, scrape a strip of chocolate and wrap the cake.
8. Using your finger, pinch the top of the chocolate.
9. Once the cakes are wrapped, return to the refrigerator.

Apricot Crème Fraiche

Yield: Forty 1.3-in. (35-mm) apricot crème fraiche

Portions: 40

Portion size: 1.3 in. (35 mm)

Yield description: 40 portions at 1.3 in. (35 mm)

Components

Apricot Caramel, page 363

Pâte Sablée, page 246

Italian Meringue, page 253

Pain de Genes, page 194

Apricot Halves

Green Cocoa Butter Color

White Chocolate

Italian Meringue, page 253

Procedure

1. Prepare apricot caramel and freeze.
2. Roll pâte sablée to ⅛ in. (3 mm), cut into 1.3-in. (35-mm) rounds, and bake.
3. Place apricot caramel on layer of pain de genes.
4. Cut apricot with a 1.1-in. (3-cm) round cutter.
5. Brush a piece of acetate with green cocoa butter.
6. After the cocoa butter has set, spread a thin layer of tempered white chocolate on the acetate.
7. Wrap the bottom of the assembled apricot stack.
8. Allow chocolate to crystallize; remove the acetate band.
9. Place the wrapped apricot stack on the pâte sablée.
10. Pipe Italian meringue and torch.
11. Top the creméux with a slice of the apricot.

Apricot Caramel

Yield: 1 lb 13 oz (1235 g)

Portions: 1

Portion size: Half hotel pan

Yield description: 1 half hotel pan

Ingredients	U.S.	Metric
Apricots, IQF	1 lb 8 oz	700 g
Pectin NH	0.8 oz	23 g
Water	1.2 oz	35 g
Sugar	3.7 oz	105 g

Note: Apples, pear, pineapple, or peaches can be used in place of the apricots.

Procedure

1. Mix the pectin and sugar.
2. Place the apricots in a half hotel pan.
3. Sprinkle the pectin mixture over the fruit and toss lightly.
4. Pour the water over the fruit.
5. Cover the top with a silpat.
6. Bake at 350°F (43°C) until golden brown.
7. Once cooled, freeze.

Petits-Fours Presentations

Petits-fours presentations can be very attractive, whether they are a small amenity or a large buffet table. The presentation can vary from a pre-dessert, room service amenity, passed, or buffet presentation. There are seven guidelines to help develop a petits-fours buffet.

In most cases the guests specify that they would like a buffet table without specifying the items. Be sure to incorporate a wide variety of flavors—the buffet should have something for everyone. Chocolate items are always popular, but not everyone likes chocolate—and the same holds true for fruit. Consider all options when developing a selection for petits-fours presentations.

Petits-Fours Guidelines

1. **Size:** The proper size of the petits-fours should be 1 to 2 bites. The assortment presented on the buffet should all be in the same range.

2. **Shape:** Using contrasting and complimentary shapes will help to create a visually appealing buffet. Molds limit the shapes that can be made, based on what is available in the pastry shop. Full sheet pan assembled cakes can be cut into squares, rectangles, triangles, parallelograms, or trapezoids. Avoid cutting these sheets with round cutters to minimize waste.

3. **Flavor:** Due to the small size of the petits-fours, intense flavor is needed. Incorporating too many flavors will muddle the flavors, making them difficult to distinguish. Try to avoid duplicating flavors on the buffet.

4. **Color:** Naturally occurring colors can make the buffet very attractive. Purées, marmalades, glazes, and chocolate can produce attractive colors. If possible, avoid adding large quantities of food coloring.

5. **Garnish:** The garnish helps to set petits-fours apart from simple pastries. Garnishes made from chocolate, fresh fruit, chopped nuts, or candied fruit can add interest to the pastries.

6. **Precision:** When presented to the guest, the petits-fours are lined up. When assembling the individual pastries, focus on precision to ensure they are the same. Accuracy during every step of the process—assembling, garnish placement, and positioning on the platters—is extremely important to the final presentation.

7. **Quantity:** Calculating how many pieces to make can be challenging. Overproduce and money is lost, underproduce and a customer will be unhappy. For a standard pastry buffet served after a full meal, three to four pieces per person is adequate. A reception setting that serves hors d'oeurves will require more pieces per person. The lighter meal eaten at a reception requires five to six pieces per person. This may not seem like enough food, but this is based on the average number of pieces eaten.

Pre-Dessert

Pre-desserts continue to gain popularity in fine dining restaurants and beyond. Just as the chef sends out a complimentary amuse bouche, the pastry chef sends out a complimentary pastry before dessert arrives. This sampling begins the transition from savory to sweet courses and allows the pastry chef to show their creativity. The pre-dessert can be a way to experiment with new flavors and techniques. It gives the pastry chef the opportunity to research what appeals to the customer and insight into what may be successful on future menus. Pre-desserts can be more complex and include frozen components due to being served à la minute.

Room Service Amenity

Room service amenities are provided to very important guests, repeat guests, or groups attending a conference at a resort or hotel. In some cases, the petits-fours amenity will be served with

FIGURE 11.9 Room service amenity platter with sugar showpiece

a chocolate or sugar showpiece themed to the event. The amenity is placed in the room prior to the guest arriving. When selecting petits-fours for room service, amenities choose those that will not require refrigeration and will not decrease in quality rapidly. Petits-fours sec, chocolates, and confections are excellent options.

Passed Presentation

Smaller receptions may request that the food is passed, or presented butler style. In this format, servers carry trays with petits-fours and present them to the guest. Passing food offers a personal touch to the service, as the server stops with the petits-fours they provide a brief description of the item. It is best to arrange items for **passed presentation** with one or two different petits-fours per tray. This simplifies the refilling process and allows the server to move throughout the room. More than two items results in slowing down the server's ability to move through the room.

Buffet Presentation

The most common presentation method of petits-fours is a buffet. Buffet presentations can be elaborate, including different elevations, props, fresh flowers, or large showpieces. Regardless of all the decorations on the table the petits-fours are the true star of the show. The petits-fours can be presented on trays, plates, tiles, mirrors, or large silver platters. Large platters and mirrors give the petits-fours a dramatic presentation. The pastries are carefully lined up in straight rows or curves. Although this is a very attractive layout for the petits-fours, it is difficult to refill. Large serving platters can hold as many as 100 pieces, and it looks great at the beginning of the reception. Toward the end of the event, the platter will start to look picked over and somewhat messy. It is not possible to refill the platter, and is difficult to remove it during the event because of the large size.

Smaller plates give the buffet the look of a pastry shop. Items are presented with one type of pastry on a plate. The plates are worked on and around the elevations and props. The small plates make it easy to refill the buffet and keep it clean, avoiding the picked-over look of the larger platters.

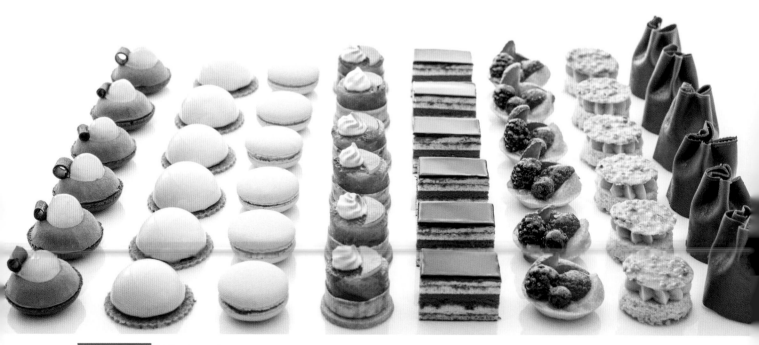

FIGURE 11.10 Petits-fours platter

Key Terms

Petits-fours

Pre-dessert

Petits-fours sec

Petits-fours glacé

Pouring fondant

Contemporary petits-fours

Verrines

Passed presentation

Questions for Review

1. Identify the three categories of petits-fours and give an example of each.

2. Design a menu for a buffet reception for 250 people. Create two petits-fours from each category and determine the correct number of pieces to produce.

3. What are the three components of a contemporary petits-fours?

4. What will happen if pouring fondant is heated too high?

5. What is the benefit of creating a verrine?

CHAPTER 12

Chocolate and Confections

The history of chocolate being used in beverages can be traced back more than 4,000 years. It played an important part in religious ceremonies, and was even used as currency. As cocoa beans traveled around the world, new production methods and techniques were created to produce chocolate. World War II saw chocolate used by the United States as a way to boost the energy of soldiers. Today, chocolate is an affordable luxury enjoyed by many. From mass-produced chocolates to small artisan chocolatiers, there is a chocolate for everyone.

LEARNING OBJECTIVES

After reading this chapter, you should be able to:

1. **Prepare** a variety of chocolates and confections.
2. **Demonstrate** how to temper milk, white, and dark chocolate using the tabling and seeding methods.
3. **Describe** the process of manufacturing chocolate.
4. **Explain** what cocoa percentage represents.
5. **Describe** the differences between crystalline, noncrystalline, aerated, and jelly confections.

Introduction to Chocolates and Confections

Chocolates and confections have increased in popularity in recent years. Oftentimes they are served along with a petits fours buffet, offered as dessert after a meal, or sold in chocolate shops.

Equipment

Chocolate Warmer

A chocolate warmer uses heat to melt chocolate slowly and evenly. A melter cannot temper chocolate, but it can hold chocolate that has been melted to keep it fluid.

FIGURE 12.1 Chocolate melter (Credit: Photo courtesy of Tomric Systems, Inc.)

Chocolate Tempering Machine

A chocolate tempering machine melts the chocolate and tempers the chocolate. There are two types of tempering machines—one version batch tempers the chocolate and the other continually tempers. A batch-tempering machine tempers all the chocolate at once. Running this machine for a long period of time will cause the chocolate to overcrystallize and become thick. A continuous tempering machine remelts the chocolate as it enters the storage tank and then tempers as needed. This reduces the possibility of overcrystallization and provides a fluid chocolate.

FIGURE 12.2 Chocolate tempering machine (Credit: Photo courtesy of Tomric Systems, Inc.)

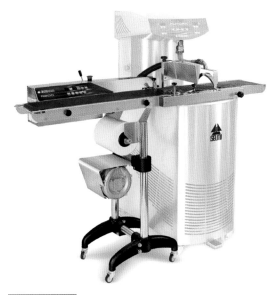

FIGURE 12.3 Chocolate enrober (Credit: Photo courtesy of Tomric Systems, Inc.)

Chocolate Enrober

A chocolate enrober is used to coat bonbons in chocolate. The enrober is used along with a tempering machine. Many tempering machine companies also distribute enrober systems that connect to the tempering machine. A series of belts are used to coat the bottom and top of the chocolate in a thin coating of chocolate.

Manufacturing Chocolate

Chocolate is an upscale product that travels a long distance before it is delivered to pastry shop. The journey begins in the tropical regions, encompassing the areas 20 degrees to the north and south of the equator. The warm climate, high humidity, and frequent rainfall produce the ideal growing environment for the cocoa tree. Because the cocoa trees are sensitive to excessive sunlight and high winds, they are planted among larger trees to protect them. The majority of cocoa beans originate in West Africa, South America, and Southeast Asia.

Several factors contribute to the flavor of the cocoa beans produced. The first factor is the type of bean: Criollo, Forastero, and Trinitario. Just as we see with wine, the terroir, geography, geology, and climate all affect the flavor. Just as important as where the cocoa beans are grown and which type is grown, the manufacturing process will be used to develop the flavor of the beans. Chocolate is made from a blend of cocoa beans, which helps to create a balanced flavor. Beans are blended based on variety and the location of their place of origin.

Cocoa Bean Varieties

Bean	Flavor	Origin	Percentage of World Crop	Characteristics
Criollo	Caramel, nuts, vanilla, and tobacco	South America	1%	Rarest of cocoa beans; very flavorful
Forastero	Strong cocoa, bitter	Africa, Ecuador, and Brazil	80%	Good base bean
Trinitario	Spicy, earthy, fruity	Mexico and South America	15%	Hybrid of Criollo and Forastero; it is more resistant to disease.

It can take as long as two to three years for the cocoa tree to produce blossoms. Once the blossoms are pollinated, they will grow into cocoa pods—it can take as long as six months for the pods to mature. The tropical climate allows the cocoa tree to produce pods year round. Cocoa trees have the ability to produce cocoa pods for up to 30 years. Each pod contains 35–40 cocoa beans. This may seem like a lot, but it takes 200 cocoa beans to yield 1 pound of chocolate. The process of transforming cocoa beans into chocolate takes seven steps.

Harvesting

When the cocoa pods are fully ripened they are harvested. The workers cut the pod from the tree using a machete. They are then split, revealing the contents of cocoa beans and white pulp. The beans and pulp are collected and transferred to the fermentation house.

Fermentation

The collected beans and pulp are placed in covered wood boxes for fermentation. Fermentation can last from 5 to 7 days depending on the bean. During this time, the beans are transferred between the boxes every 24 to 36 hours. This prevents mold from forming on the beans and ensures that the beans are fermented equally. Yeast and bacteria break down the white pulp to the point it is almost completely dissolved. The dark brown color and flavor of the bean is developed during the fermentation process. Too long of fermentation and the beans are destroyed; too short and the flavor is not developed.

The fermentation process also prevents the beans from being able to germinate, essentially killing the bean. Once fermentation is completed, the beans are dried, ceasing fermentation and preparing the beans for transportation to the manufacturer. About 75 percent of the world's cocoa production is processed in Europe and the United States, requiring the chocolate to be shipped long distances. Drying the cocoa beans makes certain they will arrive to the manufacturing facility in good condition.

Roasting

When the beans arrive at the factory, they are cleaned to remove any rocks or other debris. Roasting the cocoa beans continues to develop the flavor—as many as 400 flavors can be released at this time. The beans are roasted for 20 to 30 minutes at temperatures ranging from 212 to 284°F (100 to 140°C), depending on the type of bean.

Shelling and Winnowing

In the next step, the beans are shelled, removing the outer husk of the bean. The beans are extremely fragile after roasting and are easily broken during the shelling process. To separate the bean from the husk, air is blown into the mixture forcing the lighter husk material to separate from the bean. This is known as **winnowing**. The broken bean pieces are now called cocoa nibs. The nibs are further processed through a series of perforated screens to remove any additional husk.

Grinding, Blending, and Mixing

The nibs are then blended, combining different varieties of beans from different locations to achieve the desired flavor profile of the final chocolate. The beans are then ground, and the friction of grinding melts the cocoa butter. This unsweetened mass is known as chocolate liquor.

The liquor can now be processed in two different ways. In the production of dark chocolate, sugar is added, or to produce milk chocolate, sugar, and milk solids are added. The chocolate is then further refined to reduce the particle size.

In the second part of the process, the chocolate liquor is pressed under high pressure. This removes the cocoa butter from the cocoa solids. The pressed solids can then be ground into cocoa powder. In some manufacturing processes, all chocolate liquor is pressed to remove the cocoa butter. The cocoa butter and cocoa solids are recombined during the manufacturing process.

Conching

The chocolate is now ready for further refining in a conche. While in the conche, the chocolate is ground into smaller particles by large stone rollers or mixing blades that stir the chocolate. **Conching** changes the flavor and viscosity of the chocolate. At the beginning of the process the chocolate has a doughlike consistency but by the end, the chocolate resembles a thick fluid. The size of the solid particles is reduced with every pass through the conche, which helps to coat the solid particle in cocoa butter, while at the same time improving the mouthfeel of the final product by reducing the size. The conche continually agitates the chocolate as a result of the friction from mixing temperatures can range from 120°F (49°C) for milk chocolate to 180°F (82°C) for dark chocolate.

During this process the chocolate undergoes three phases. In the first phase, the mix is dry and the agitation of the conche coats the dry particles in fat. Through the mixing process, air is incorporated, removing unwanted acids developed during the fermentation process and any remaining water that may have been present in the cocoa beans after roasting. The second phase increases the speed of the conche, and coating of the solid particles in fat continues. In the third phase, additional cocoa butter and lecithin are added to adjust the viscosity of the chocolate. The speed of the machine is reduced and the chocolate begins to cool.

Tempering

Once conching is complete, the chocolate is tempered. Tempering is the process of heating and cooling chocolate to develop the proper cocoa butter crystallization. Tempering gives the chocolate its characteristic snap and sheen. Pages 345–349 will provide more detailed information about tempering. After the chocolate is tempered and cooled completely, it is packaged and ready for shipping.

Chocolate Percentages

In the United States, the FDA regulates the classifications of chocolate. The following table provides the minimum percentages of chocolate liquor and milk solids required to label a product as chocolate. If a manufacturer uses the minimum percentages, the remaining quantity would be sugar. Using the dark chocolate with 35% chocolate liquor as an example, the remaining 65% would be sugar. This would result in a very sweet product.

While chocolates can range from inexpensive to costly for a good quality, there is a higher quality product called couverture. **Couverture** comes from the French word *couvrir* meaning "to cover." Couvertures are made with the highest-quality beans and are conched for longer periods of time, decreasing the particle size even further. They also contain more cocoa butter, 36% to 39%, creating a more fluid product that is ideal for producing a thin coating on chocolates.

FDA Minimum Requirements for Chocolate

Type	Minimum Chocolate Liquor	Minimum Milk Solids
Dark, Semisweet	35%	N/A
Milk	10%	12%
White	20% (cocoa butter only)	14%

Manufacturers identify their products with a name and a percentage on the label. There is much confusion as to what this percentage actually represents. For this example we will look at a 58% semisweet couverture. This percentage represents the amount of cocoa in the couverture. Additional information on the label may include the amount of cocoa butter, which in this case is 38% cocoa butter.

Chocolate liquor is made of cocoa butter and cocoa solids, so to determine the amount of cocoa solids, perform the following:

Cocoa% – Cocoa butter% = Cocoa solids%

58% – 38% = 20%

The amount of sugar in the recipe is calculated by subtracting the 58% from 100%:

100% – Cocoa% = Sugar%

100% – 58% = 42%

We can determine that there is 42% sugar, and a minimal percentage of lecithin and vanilla flavoring. Once all the numbers are calculated, it will give a better idea of the sweetness of the chocolate. As the percentage of chocolate liquor increases, the percentage of sugar decreases.

The chocolate liquor percentage contains both cocoa solids and cocoa butter. These ingredients are blended and adjusted based on the different chocolates. A chocolate that is formulated for coating will have more cocoa butter to produce a chocolate with a lower viscosity. Increasing the amount of cocoa solids will intensify the flavor of the chocolate, as well as increase the viscosity.

The example in Figure 12.4 demonstrates cocoa percentages. All the cylinders contain 42% sugar. The first cylinder has chocolate that is made from only ground cocoa beans with sugar added. A cocoa bean is 55% cocoa butter and 45% cocoa solids. The second cylinder is made from adding cocoa butter to the chocolate liquor, resulting in a couverture that is ideal

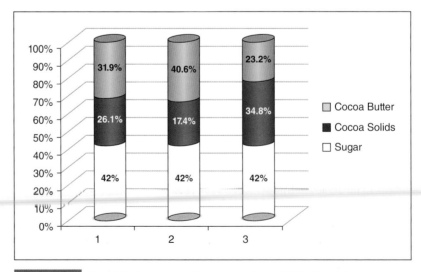

FIGURE 12.4 Chocolate liquor percentage comparison of 58% chocolate

for coating. Moving on to the third cylinder, there are more cocoa solids; consequently, this chocolate will have a strong flavor and be thicker than the first two. As you can see, these are completely different products that can all be labeled as a 58% chocolate.

There is another variable at work as well. The percentage and manufacturer's label provide insight into what the chocolate is suited for. The other variable that needs to be examined is the origin of the bean and type of bean. A 58% chocolate with the same percentage of cocoa butter and cocoa solids made by different manufacturers will taste completely different. One may have a fruity flavor while the other may have a strong chocolate flavor. The blend of beans and manufacturing process will change the flavor of the final chocolate. It is important to remember which chocolate is used when developing recipes and note this on the recipe. This will ensure the consistency of the final products. There are all-purpose chocolates that can be used to flavor mousses or enrobe candies. It is not necessary to have 15 different chocolates in the pastry shop.

Tempering Chocolate

Cocoa butter is what gives chocolate its shine and characteristic snap when eaten. It is a **polymorphic** fat, meaning that the fat can form many different crystals. There are six different crystals the cocoa butter can form: four are unstable and two are stable. Unstable crystals produce chocolate that blooms, has a crumbly texture, and melts easily when handled. **Fat bloom** occurs when improperly tempered cocoa butter begins to crystallize, producing white streaks in the chocolate. Stable crystals produce a chocolate with sheen, snap, and strong contraction when molding.

Cocoa Butter Crystal Characteristics

	Crystal	Melting Point	Characteristic
Unstable	I	63°F (17°C)	Soft, crumbly, melts too easily
	II	70°F (21°C)	Soft, crumbly, melts too easily
	III	79°F (26°C)	Firm, poor snap, melts too easily
	IV	82°F (28°C)	Firm, good snap, melts too easily
Stable	V	93°F (34°C)	Glossy, firm, best snap, melts near body temperature 98.6°F (37°C)
	VI	97°F (36°C)	Hard, takes weeks to form

Through the process of tempering, the pastry chef cools and stirs the chocolate, encouraging the growth of stable cocoa butter crystals. Tempering consists of the three components: time, temperature, and agitation. When properly tempered, cocoa butter crystallization occurs quickly. In its stable forms the tempered cocoa butter attracts the remaining crystals to quickly form solid tempered chocolate. Chocolate that is not tempered properly takes too long to crystallize. This causes the chocolate to become streaky and develop a white haze as the cocoa butter forms the unstable crystals.

Temperature is critical. Stable crystals form when the chocolate is cooled to below 82°F (27.7°C). This can be achieved through tabling or seeding—both will be discussed in detail in the following section. If the chocolate were left alone on a table and allowed to cool, stable crystals would have formed. But still there would not be enough: This is when agitation comes into play. The stirring of the chocolate causes the highly attractive stable crystals to attract more crystals. This creates a reaction of more stable crystals forming quickly, which causes the chocolate to set faster. Too much agitation can cause the chocolate to over crystallize.

FIGURE 12.5 Properly tempered dark chocolate (left); improperly tempered bloomed chocolate (right)

When working with chocolate for a long period of time, it may thicken even when held at the proper temperature. Adding additional melted chocolate to the tempered chocolate, or melting and tempering again can correct this.

Improperly stored chocolate can also develop **sugar bloom**, which occurs when moisture is absorbed by the chocolate. High humidity forms condensation on the exterior of the chocolate and pulls the sugar to the surface. As the water evaporates, the sugar crystallizes leaving a white haze on the surface. Storing chocolate in the refrigerator or freezer will cause sugar bloom. It is best to store chocolate tightly wrapped at 70°F (21°C) to reduce the chances of sugar bloom.

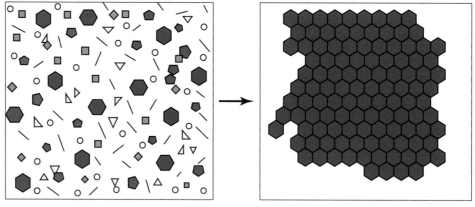

Soft, dull, untempered chocolate

Hard, shiny, tempered chocolate

FIGURE 12.6 Improper cocoa butter crystallization (left); properly aligned cocoa butter crystals (right)

Tempering Methods

There are two methods of tempering: tabling and seeding. The chocolate in the **tabling method** is spread on a marble surface and cooled to the desired temperature. The **seeding method** adds chopped chocolate into the melted chocolate to decrease the temperature. Both achieve the same results so the decision of which method to use is based on personal preference.

Melting

Regardless of which method is used, the work area and all equipment must be clean and dry. The smallest amount of water can cause the chocolate to seize. **Seizing** occurs when water is absorbed by sugar in the chocolate. This creates a syrup that then traps the cocoa solids. Once there is water in the chocolate, it cannot be removed.

There are three ways to melt chocolate: in a chocolate melter, over a double boiler, or in a microwave. It is best to melt the chocolate slowly, overnight in a chocolate melter. To fully melt all the cocoa butter crystals, a temperature of 115°F (45°C) for 12 hours is necessary and will ensure a better temper. When using a double boiler, the heat source should be on a low setting to prevent burning and steam from getting into the chocolate. A double boiler is an excellent conductor of heat and can easily burn the chocolate. The steam produced from excessive heat will travel up and over the sides of the bowl and then get trapped in the chocolate. A microwave is an excellent way to melt smaller quantities of chocolate. Reduce the power to 50% and melt for no longer than 15 to 20 seconds. The microwave heats from the inside out, so the chocolate must be removed and stirred. Not stirring the chocolate may cause the center to overheat and burn.

Once the chocolate is fully melted, the tempering process can be started. In order for the chocolate to properly crystalize, it must be cooled using the tabling or seeding methods. A portion of the chocolate is then cooled to 80 to 82°F (27 to 28°C), and rewarmed to the proper working temperature depending on the chocolate being used. The following table shows temperature ranges for dark, milk, and white chocolate.

Tabling Method

Equipment needed: Offset pallet knife, 5-in. metal scraper, thermometer, heat gun, marble, and rubber spatula:

1. Pour two-thirds of the melted chocolate on the marble.

2. Using the offset pallet knife spread the chocolate.

3. Push the chocolate back toward the center, make sure to work the chocolate back into one mound and clean off tools by scraping against each other when working. Chocolate left on the marble or tools can harden and create lumps in the tempered chocolate.

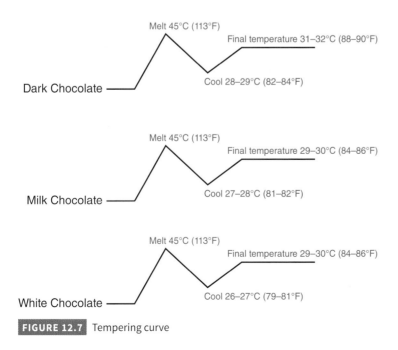

FIGURE 12.7 Tempering curve

4. Repeat steps 2 and 3 until the chocolate appears thickened.

5. Scrape the chocolate from the marble back into the bowl.

6. Quickly stir the chocolate and check the temperature.

7. If the temperature is too high, return some of the chocolate to the marble and repeat steps 2 through 6, until the correct temperature is reached.

8. If the temperature is below the chocolate's working temperature, use a heat gun on low and warm the chocolate.

9. Use a small piece of parchment paper to test the temper of the chocolate. The test strip should set within two minutes. The chocolate should set without showing any signs of streaking.

10. If this does not produce a clean test, check the temperature again. If the temperature is correct, vigorously stir the chocolate for 30 seconds and test again.

FIGURE 12.8a–d

1. Pouring chocolate on marble

2. Spreading chocolate with pallet knife

3. Using scraper to work chocolate into center

4. Checking temperature

Seeding Method

Equipment needed: Rubber spatula, thermometer, and immersion blender:

1. Prepare seeding chocolate by chopping in a food processor. It will take about 25% of the weight of the chocolate to be tempered in seed. If you are tempering 4 lb, you will need 1 lb of seed. *Note:* Seeding chocolate must be tempered.

2. Add seed to the melted chocolate until the temperature reaches 95°F (35°C). There should still be seed that has not melted. This indicates that stable cocoa butter crystals are present that will seed the melted chocolate.

3. Use an immersion blender to remove any small pieces of unmelted seed. Be sure to keep the immersion blender completely submerged in the chocolate to avoid incorporating any air. If the chocolate is too cool when using the immersion blender the chocolate will over crystallize quickly and become very thick. This will make it difficult to work with.

4. Using a small piece of parchment paper or metal scraper, test the temper of the chocolate. The test strip should set within two minutes. The chocolate should set without showing any signs of streaking.

5. If this does not produce a clean test, check the temperature again. If the temperature is correct, vigorously stir the chocolate for 30 seconds and test again.

Chocolates

The term *chocolates* is often used to refer to various chocolate products such as **bonbons** and **truffles**. *Bonbon,* translated from French to English, means "good good" and can refer to any candy that is coated in chocolate. Bonbons can be filled with a wide assortment of fillings, including ganache, marshmallow, buttercream, fruit creams, caramels, and nougat. They can be flavored with fruits, nuts, or liqueurs. Truffles are often hand-rolled and are filled with **cream ganache** or **butter ganache**.

When making chocolates, the formula can have as few as three ingredients: whipping cream, chocolate, and flavoring. The ingredients are the "stars" of these items. High-quality ingredients combined with proper technique will ensure the smoothness and flavor of the chocolates come through.

Ingredients

Chocolate

Chocolate is the main ingredient in ganache. It is not only used to flavor—it provides the texture and the firmness of the ganache. The use of couverture for ganache is recommended, due to the flavor and higher content of cocoa butter. Chocolates used in the production of ganache are selected based on the flavor profile and cocoa percentage. The flavor of the couverture should complement the other flavors used in assembling the ganache. Formulas are balanced based on these two factors. If a change in chocolate is necessary, adjustments may need to made to the liquids in the recipe.

Cream

The cream used for ganache should be 35% Whipping Cream. Cream is the primary source of water in the ganache. The water functions as a buffer in the ganache, dispersing the fat. This prevents the ganache from breaking. Fat found in the cream helps to soften the texture of the ganache. Higher-fat creams will not only produce a softer ganache—the increased fat can make the ganache unstable and more susceptible to breaking.

Sweeteners

Sweeteners give the ganache more than sweetness. They can prevent crystallization, soften ganache, and caramelize. The smooth texture of the ganache is also improved with the use of sweeteners.

Sweeteners

Type of Sweetener	Origin	Function
Granulated Sugar	Sugar beets or sugar cane	Most common sweetener used Flavor and color when caramelized
Glucose	Corn, potato, or wheat	Retains moisture Prevents crystallization
Invert Sugar	Sugar heated with an acid	Prevents crystallization Smoother ganache
Sorbitol (Sugar Alcohol)	Apples, pears, and berries	Emulsifier Sugar replacer

Butter

Butter is used in ganache to stabilize the emulsion. Incorporating butter into the ganache will soften the fat of the cocoa butter and reduce the melting temperature. Recipes that include purée, liquor, or other water-based flavorings employ butter to replace the fat for these ingredients. When adding a water-based flavoring to a ganache, incorporate half the weight of the flavoring in butter.

Butter as a product is an emulsion. Butter becomes soft at room temperature and when heated it separates. When using butter in a ganache, it is critical that the butter does not become overheated. To avoid overheating, the butter is added after the other ingredients have been combined and cooled.

Ganache

Ganache was discussed briefly in Chapter 6 to be used for a base in chocolate mousse. The production of ganache for chocolates is more involved, with different ratios and numbers of ingredients. There are two types of ganache used as fillings: cream and butter. Either of these can be used in molded, enrobed, slabbed, and piped productions.

Cream Ganache

Cream ganache is a fat-in-water emulsion that contains whipping cream, chocolate, and flavorings, with a shelf life of 3 weeks. This is the ganache most often used to fill bonbons in the United States.

Cream Ganache Method

1. Place chocolate in a food processor and grind to small pieces. Be careful to not process too long to avoid melting the chocolate.

2. Place whipping cream in a heavy-bottom saucepan and heat to just below a boil. Boiling the cream will reduce the water in the cream.

3. Pour the hot cream over the chopped chocolate and allow it to sit for 1 to 2 minutes. This melts the chocolate while the cream cools. The ideal temperature for mixing is 90 to 110°F (32 to 44°C).

4. Begin stirring the mixture in the center to create the emulsion. Once the center has come together, start to widen the stirring motion to the edges of the bowl. Stirring the mixture too quickly will incorporate air into the ganache; stir slowly to avoid this. Air bubbles facilitate the growth of bacteria.

5. Allow the ganache to cool to 92°F (33°C); add the softened butter and mix slowly to incorporate.

6. Use an immersion blender to finish the ganache. Place the blade of the immersion blender at the bottom of the container to avoid incorporating any air. Move the blender in the ganache to mix easily. This can also be done in a measuring pitcher to reduce incorporating air.

FIGURE 12.9a–b

1. The beginning of the emulsion

2. The properly emulsified ganache

Butter Ganache

Butter ganache is a water-in-fat emulsion that contains butter and chocolate and is typically flavored with liquor. Compared to cream ganache, the butter ganache will crystallize and firm faster, allowing dipping within 30 minutes of being prepared. The final texture will be firmer and have a longer shelf life of 6 to 8 weeks.

Butter Ganache Method

1. Temper chocolate and rewarm to make sure it is at the maximum working temperature. Dark chocolate 90°F (32°C), white, and milk 88°F (31°C).
2. In another bowl, use a rubber spatula to mix the softened butter at 86°F (30°C).
3. Fold in the tempered chocolate; the temperature of the ingredients makes it easy to fold them together before the chocolate sets.
4. Add the liquor and stir to combine.
5. Mix ganache with an immersion blender.

Molded Ganache

Molds allow the pastry chef to create bonbons with unique shapes, colors, and fillings. Color can be added in the form of sprayed colored cocoa butters, edible luster dusts or a brush of white chocolate on a dark-shelled bonbon. The process for applying color is described in Chapter 13, page 385. Molded bonbons are easily produced in large quantities as long as molds are available. The shell provides a way to retain softer fillings such as Pistachio Crunch Buttercream (page 332) or softer-setting ganache.

Polycarbonate chocolate molds are available from a wide variety of suppliers. While molded chocolates are easy to mass produce, there is a high cost associated with the molds. Taking care of these molds is important to their longevity. Washing should not be needed if the molds are used properly. If washing is necessary, use hot soapy water and a clean soft cloth. Never use abrasive scrubbing pads or paper towel—this will cause scratches in the mold, reducing the shine of the final chocolates. Molds that have been used retain a small amount of cocoa butter in them and they are seasoned much like a cast iron skillet is with fat; washing removes this coating. After washing and between uses, the molds should be buffed with cotton or cheesecloth.

FIGURE 12.10 Assorted molded bonbons

Molding Method

Equipment needed: Offset pallet knife, 8-in. metal scraper, parchment paper, ladle, plastic acetate sheet, rolling pin:

1. Fill the mold with tempered chocolate. Use an offset pallet knife to spread the chocolate, be sure to fill all the molds.

2. Use the metal scraper to remove excess chocolate.

3. Tap the side of the mold with the plastic handle of the scraper; this will remove any bubbles from the mold.

4. Turn the mold; pour out the extra chocolate. Tap the mold with the plastic handle of the scraper.

5. With the scraper, remove any excess chocolate.

FIGURE 12.11a–e Bonbon filling procedure:

Filling bonbon mold with chocolate (step 1)

Emptying the chocolate from the mold (step 4)

Scraping the bottom of the mold (step 6)

Filling the mold (step 8)

Sealing the mold and rolling with rolling pin (step 11)

6. Place a piece of parchment paper on a flat work surface and place the mold upside down, allowing the excess chocolate in the mold to drain out. Before the chocolate sets, remove the mold from the paper. Scrape again if necessary.

7. While the chocolate is crystallizing in the mold, prepare the filling.

8. When the ganache has cooled to 86°F (30°C), fill the molds using a disposable pastry bag. Do not fill the mold to the top; leave a gap of ⅛ in. (3 mm) for capping.

9. Allow the ganache to crystallize at room temperature. This may take up to 24 hours.

10. Spread a thin layer of tempered chocolate over the molds, making sure all remaining space is filled. Scrape off excess chocolate.

11. Place a sheet of parchment paper or acetate sheet on the mold and smooth with rolling pin or bench scraper.

12. Allow the chocolate to crystallize completely. If necessary, place the molds in the refrigerator for 15 minutes to release the chocolate from the mold.

Enrobed Ganache

Coating a bonbon filling in couverture is known as **enrobing**. The fillings for enrobed bonbons need to be firmer to stand up to the dipping process. In this process, the ganache (or other filling) is made prior to dipping—in some cases, as much as 24 hours earlier. This gives the ganache sufficient time to crystallize. Crystallization of the ganache is necessary before dipping. Ganache may be shaped by using the slabbed, piped, or hand-rolled techniques.

Slab Ganache

Slab ganache is poured out into a metal frame and spread to ensure an even thickness. The ganache is then allowed to crystallize. The length of time it takes the ganache to crystallize is dependent on the temperature of the room. In a warmer room it will take longer; a cooler room will speed up crystallization. Placing the ganache in the cooler or freezer is not recommended. While this may make the ganache firm faster, it will quickly soften when returned to room temperature.

On the second day, spread a thin base coat of tempered chocolate on the ganache. The purpose of the base coat is to allow the ganache to easily be moved and dipped. When hand dipping, the thin layer of chocolate prevents the dipping fork from becoming stuck in the soft ganache. After the base layer has crystallized, the ganache is ready to be portioned. Smaller production facilities will use a ruler and knife to cut the ganache to the correct size. The final dipped weight of a bonbon should be 0.5 oz (14 g). Larger production facilities will use a guitar. A **guitar** is a machine that quickly portions slabs of ganache into equal sizes using metal wire. After cutting, space the ganache apart letting the cut edges dry slightly to ease handling.

Piped Ganache

Piping ganache enables the pastry chef to create different shapes without the need of costly molds. When making the slabbed ganache, a base was added to prevent the dipping fork from becoming stuck in the ganache. Piped ganache has the same requirement. Tempered chocolate is spread in a thin layer on acetate and cut with a round cutter or knife into the shape the ganache will be piped. Once the chocolate base has crystallized fully, the prepared ganache is piped into the desired shape and allowed to dry slightly before dipping.

FIGURE 12.12 Piping butter ganache on the disk center

Dipping Method for Enrobing Slabbed and Piped Fillings

The cut or piped ganache is ready to dip after it has had some time to crystallize. Crystallizing allows the ganache to maintain its shape while being handled. Couverture should always be used for enrobing. This will ensure a thin shell:

1. Set up a dipping station. Working left to right, place the undipped center to the left. Place the bowl of tempered couverture in the center, and on the right, place a silpat-lined sheet pan for the finished bonbon. If left-handed, place the undipped centers on the right and the finished product on the left.

FIGURE 12.13a–e Hand-dipping procedure:

Placing ganache in tempered chocolate (step 2)

Coating the ganache in chocolate (step 3)

Tapping to remove excess chocolate (step 4)

Cleaning the bottom of the chocolate on the bowl (step 5)

Placing onto a silpat (step 6)

2. Place ganache in the tempered couverture.

3. Place the dipping fork under the ganache. Leave ¼ of the ganache off the fork; coat the ganache completely in couverture. This will make it easier to slide the dipped piece off the fork and prevent it from falling off.

4. Using an up-and-down motion, lift the ganache out of the couverture. This up-and-down tapping motion helps to remove excess chocolate. With each tap, the dipped center should be removed slightly higher. This should be done 3 to 4 times per piece.

5. Slide the fork along the rim of the bowl to remove excess couverture. This excess couverture will begin to coat the edge of the bowl, and it makes it difficult to keep lumps out of the couverture. To prevent this, attach a thin wire at the top of the bowl to clean the bottom of the chocolates. The small surface area of the wire will prevent excess chocolate from building up.

6. Transfer the dipped bonbon to the silpat-lined tray. Touch the front of the bonbon on the tray and carefully slide the fork out.

7. Continue this process until all the pieces are dipped, being careful to monitor the temperature of the couverture while dipping.

Hand-Rolled Ganache

Hand-rolled ganache can be done in one of two ways. In the first method, the ganache is placed in a hotel pan overnight. When the ganache has crystallized, use a scoop to portion the ganache and roll it by hand into spheres. In the second method, the ganache is piped and then rolled. Both of these methods require the ganache to be crystallized before portioning. Hand-rolled ganache does not require a base before enrobing.

Enrobing Hand-Rolled Filling Method

Hand-rolling is a fast and easy way to enrobe ganache. Often, hand-rolled ganache is referred to as a truffle. The look of the chocolate truffle is similar to that of the black truffles used in savory applications:

1. *Set up a dipping station.* Working left to right, place the undipped center to the left. Place the bowl of tempered couverture in the center, and on the right, place a silpat-lined sheet pan for the finished bonbon. If left handed, place the undipped centers on the right and the finished product on the left.

2. *Wear gloves.* Using two fingers on your right hand spread a small amount of chocolate in the center of your left hand.

3. *Take one of the rolled centers and place it in your left hand.* Carefully roll the ganache in the chocolate. Maintain the shape and be sure to coat the entire piece. This will serve as a base coat.

4. *After the base coat has crystallized, apply another layer of chocolate.* This layer can be slightly thicker than the first.

5. *Once the pieces are coated, the truffle can be rolled in cocoa powder, powdered sugar, toasted chopped nuts or chocolate shavings.* This must be done immediately after rolling in chocolate to make sure the coating sticks.

Chocolate Recipes

Pistachio Cinnamon Ganache

Yield: 2 lb 12 oz (1270 g)
Portions: 90 pieces
Portion size: 0.5 oz (14 g)
Yield description: 90 pieces at 0.3 oz (8.5 g)

Ingredients	U.S.	Metric
Heavy Cream	11.3 oz	320 g
Trimoline	1.3 oz	36 g
Pistachio Paste	3.2 oz	90 g
Ground Cinnamon	0.14 oz	4 g
White Chocolate	1 lb 7.6 oz	670 g
Butter, room temperature	5.3 oz	150 g

Procedure

1. Combine ground cinnamon and pistachio paste.
2. Place white chocolate in a bowl over a double boiler and melt halfway.
3. Bring heavy cream and Trimoline to a boil.
4. Pour cream mixture over white chocolate; emulsify.
5. Add pistachio mixture to ganache.
6. Cool to 86°F (30°C).
7. Add butter and emulsify with immersion blender.
8. Fill bonbon mold premolded in tempered white chocolate.
9. Allow ganache to crystallize for 12 hours.
10. Seal the molds with tempered white chocolate.

Passion Fruit Bonbon

Yield: 1 lb 9 oz (710 g)
Portions: 50 pieces
Portion size: 0.5 oz (14 g)
Yield description: 50 pieces at 0.5 oz (14 g)

Ingredients	U.S.	Metric
Passion Fruit Purée	6 oz	170 g
Glucose	0.9 oz	25 g
Butter	2.5 oz	70 g
White Chocolate	14.6 oz	415 g
Cointreau	1.1 oz	30 g

Procedure

1. Line bonbon mold with tempered white chocolate.
2. Combine purée, glucose and butter, bring to a boil.
3. Pour over white chocolate to form a ganache.
4. Cool mixture to 95°F (35 C).
5. Add Cointreau and emulsify with immersion blender.
6. When mixture has cooled to 82°F (28 C), pipe into molds.
7. Allow passion fruit ganache to crystallize for 12 hours.
8. Seal the molds with tempered white chocolate.

Orange Coriander Bonbon

Yield: 2 lb 3 oz (1016 g)

Portions: 65 pieces

Portion size: 0.5 oz (14 g)

Yield description: 65 pieces at 0.5 oz (14 g)

Ingredients	U.S.	Metric
Coriander Praline	8.8 oz	250 g
Coriander Praline Crunch	12 oz	350 g
Orange Caramel Ganache	1 lb 7 oz	666 g

Procedure

1. Line bonbon mold with tempered milk chocolate.
2. Prepare coriander praline.
3. Prepare coriander praline crunch.
4. Prepare orange caramel ganache, fill mold two-thirds full with ganache.
5. Top with coriander praline crunch.
6. Allow coriander praline crunch to crystallize for 12 hours.
7. Seal the molds with tempered milk chocolate.

Orange Caramel Ganache

Yield: 1 lb 7 oz (666 g)

Portions: 65 portions

Portion size: 0.3 oz (10 g)

Yield description: 65 portions 0.3 oz (10 g)

Ingredients	U.S.	Metric
Sugar	3.5 oz	100 g
Glucose	0.9 oz	25 g
Orange Juice	6.3 oz	180 g
Orange Zest	0.04 oz	1 g
Milk Chocolate, finely chopped	6.3 oz	180 g
Cocoa Butter, finely chopped	1.8 oz	50 g
Butter	1.8 oz	50 g
Grand Marnier	1.8 oz	50 g
Sorbitol Liquid	1.1 oz	30 g

Procedure

1. Combine sugar and glucose, cook to a light caramel.
2. Deglaze with orange juice; add purée and sorbitol.
3. Pour over milk chocolate and cocoa butter, emulsify with immersion blender.
4. Add butter and Grand Marnier.
5. Reserve for assembly at 77°F (25°C).

Coriander Praline

Yield: 1 lb 5 oz (620 g)
Portions: 2.4 portions
Portion size: 8.8 oz (250 g)
Yield description: 2.4 portions at 8.8 oz (250 g)

Ingredients	U.S.	Metric
Water	1.2 oz	35 g
Sugar	6 oz	170 g
Glucose	2.3 oz	70 g
Salt	0.04 oz	1 g
Whole Coriander	0.3 oz	9 g
Hazelnuts, toasted	11.8 oz	335 g

Procedure

1. Combine water, sugar, and glucose in a pan and caramelize.
2. Remove from heat and add coriander.
3. Place hazelnuts on a silpat-lined pan and pour caramel over nuts.
4. After cooling completely, mix in food processor to a smooth paste.
5. Reserve for coriander praline crunch; store any additional product in the refrigerator.

Coriander Praline Crunch

Yield: 12 oz (350 g)
Portions: 85 portions
Portion size: 0.14 oz (4 g)
Yield description: 85 portions at 0.14 oz (4 g)

Ingredients	U.S.	Metric
Coriander Praline, page 360	8.8 oz	250 g
Milk Chocolate	1.1 oz	30 g
Cocoa Butter	1.6 oz	45 g
Feuilletine	0.9 oz	25 g

Procedure

1. Melt milk chocolate and cocoa butter; combine with coriander praline base.
2. Fold in feuilletine.
3. Reserve for assembly at 77°F (25°C).

Peanut Butter Banana Bonbon

Yield: 2 lb 12 oz (1280 g)
Portions: 90 pieces
Portion size: 0.5 oz (14 g)
Yield description: 90 pieces at 0.5 oz (14 g)

Ingredients	U.S.	Metric
Peanut Butter Ganache	1 lb 6 oz	640 g
Banana Ganache	1 lb 6 oz	640 g

Procedure

1. Line bonbon mold with tempered dark chocolate.
2. Fill halfway with peanut butter ganache.
3. Fill the shell with banana ganache.
4. Allow banana ganache to crystallize for 12 hours.
5. Seal the molds with tempered dark chocolate.

Peanut Butter Ganache

Yield: 1 lb 7 oz (670 g)
Portions: 95 portions
Portion size: 0.25 oz (7 g)
Yield description: 95 portions at 0.25 oz (7 g)

Ingredients	U.S.	Metric
Sugar	8.8 oz	250 g
Glucose	1.8 oz	50 g
Water	1.4 oz	40 g
Butter, softened	3.5 oz	100 g
Heavy Cream	5.3 oz	150 g
Peanut Butter	2.8 oz	80 g

Procedure

1. Combine water, sugar, and glucose in a pan and bring to a light caramel.
2. Pour caramel onto a silpat. Cool completely and grind in a food processor.
3. Add finely ground caramel mixture to cream and warm to dissolve.
4. Cool caramel to 95°F (35°C).
5. Add peanut butter and softened butter; emulsify with immersion blender.
6. Reserve for assembly at 80°F (27°C).

Banana Ganache

Yield: 1 lb 6 oz (640 g)

Portions: 90 portions

Portion size: 0.25 oz (7 g)

Yield description: 90 portions at 0.25 oz (7 g)

Ingredients	U.S.	Metric
Heavy Cream	5.3 oz	150 g
Trimoline	1.1 oz	30 g
White Chocolate	11.8 oz	335 g
Butter, softened	1.4 oz	40 g
Dark Rum	0.4 oz	10 g
Banana Purée	2.6 oz	75 g

Procedure

1. Place white chocolate on a double boiler and melt 25%.
2. Bring cream to a boil.
3. Pour over chocolate and form a ganache.
4. Cool ganache to 95°F (35°C).
5. Add butter, Trimoline, banana purée, and rum.
6. Reserve for assembly at 80°F (27°C).

Yogurt Berry Bonbon

Yield: 2 lb 3 oz (1030 g)

Portions: 70 pieces

Portion size: 0.5 oz (14 g)

Yield description: 70 pieces at 0.5 oz (14 g)

Ingredients	U.S.	Metric
Berry Compote	10.4 oz	295 g
Yogurt Ganache	1 lb 9 oz	735 g

Procedure

1. Line bonbon mold with tempered milk chocolate.
2. Pipe berry compote.
3. Fill mold with yogurt ganache.
4. Allow yogurt ganache to crystallize for 12 hours.
5. Seal the molds with tempered milk chocolate.

Berry Compote

Yield: 1 lb 3 oz (561 g)
Portions: 140 portions
Portion size: 0.14 oz (4 g)
Yield description: 140 portions at 0.14 oz (4 g)

Ingredients	U.S.	Metric
Raspberry Purée	6.9 oz	195 g
Black Currant Purée	3.5 oz	100 g
Dried Blueberries	1.8 oz	50 g
Sugar	4.6 oz	130 g
Pectin NH	0.2 oz	6 g
Water	2.8 oz	80 g

Procedure

1. Combine pectin NH with 30 grams of sugar.
2. Combine remaining sugar, water, purées, and dried blueberries, and warm.
3. When purée mixture reaches 125°F (50°C), add pectin/sugar mixture.
4. Boil this mixture for 2 minutes, stir constantly.
5. Pour onto a silpat on a marble table to cool completely.
6. Purée mixture using an immersion blender.
7. Reserve for assembly.

Yogurt Ganache

Yield: 1 lb 9 oz (735 g)
Portions: 73 portions
Portion size: 0.35 oz (10 g)
Yield description: 73 portions at 0.35 oz (10 g)

Ingredients	U.S.	Metric
Heavy Cream	5.6 oz	160 g
Butter	1.4 oz	40 g
Sorbitol	1.4 oz	40 g
Lecithin	0.03 oz	0.75 g
White Chocolate (41%)	12.3 oz	350 g
Cocoa Butter	1.1 oz	30 g
Greek Yogurt 2% fat	3.5 oz	100 g
Yogurt Powder	0.5 oz	15 g
Citric Acid Solution	10 drops	10 drops

Note: Citric Acid Solution can be made using the formula for Tartaric Acid Solution on page 373, replace tartaric acid with citric acid.

Procedure

1. Combine cream, sorbitol, butter, and lecithin, and warm.
2. Combine white chocolate and cocoa butter, melt over a double boiler.
3. Emulsify white chocolate and cream mixture.
4. Add Greek yogurt, yogurt powder, and citric acid solution; emulsify.
5. Pipe into shells at 84°F (29°C).

Palet d'Or (piped)

Yield: 1 lb 10 oz (750 g)

Portions: 50 pieces

Portion size: 0.5 oz (14 g)

Yield description: 50 pieces at 0.5 oz (14 g)

Ingredients	U.S.	Metric
Heavy Cream	9.2 oz	260 g
Dark Chocolate 68%	12.7 oz	360 g
Trimoline	1.8 oz	50 g
Butter, softened	2.8 oz	80 g

Procedure

1. Combine cream and Trimoline in a saucepan, bring to a boil.
2. Pour over chocolate; combine to form a ganache.
3. Cool ganache to 95°F (35°C), add butter.
4. Mix with an immersion blender to emulsify.
5. Place plastic wrap directly on top of ganache and crystallize for 12 hours.
6. Pipe ganache onto a sheet of acetate with a 0.5-in. (1.3-cm) plain tip the size of a quarter.
7. Place another sheet of acetate on top of piped ganache and flatten to 0.3 in. (8 mm) thick.
8. Allow ganache to crystallize for 12 hours.
9. Remove acetate sheet and spray ganache with a cocoa butter spray (recipe page 397).
10. Dip in tempered dark couverture.

FIGURE 12.14 Hand-dipped bonbons (left to right): Rocher, coffee and lemon, Cognac kiss, Palet d'or.

Cognac Kiss (piped)

Yield: 1 lb 10 oz (740 g)

Portions: 50 portions

Portion size: 0.5 oz (14 g)

Yield description: 52 portions at 0.5 oz (14 g)

Ingredients	U.S.	Metric
Feuilletine Base, page 364	50 each	50 each
Cognac Butter Ganache, page 365	1 lb 10 oz	740 g

Procedure

1. Attach feuilletine base to a piece of parchment paper with a dot of chocolate.
2. Prepare cognac butter ganache
3. Pipe cognac butter ganache using a 0.5-in. (1.3-cm) plain tip.
4. Allow ganache to crystallize for 12 hours.
5. Dip in tempered milk chocolate.

Feuilletine Base

Yield: 1 lb 1 oz (490 g)

Portions: 50

Portion size: ¾-in. (20-mm) round

Yield description: 50 pieces at ¾-in. (20-mm) round

Ingredients	U.S.	Metric
Cocoa Butter	1.4 oz	40 g
Milk Chocolate	2.6 oz	75 g
Praline Paste, page 365	4.4 oz	125 g
Feuilletine	8.8 oz	250 g

Procedure

1. Combine cocoa butter and milk chocolate; melt over a bain marie.
2. Add melted chocolate mixture to praline paste.
3. Fold in feuilletine.
4. Spread mixture onto parchment paper and roll to ⅛ in. (3 mm) thick.
5. Allow the feuilletine mixture to set; cut with a ¾-in. (20-mm) round cutter.
6. Reserve for assembly.

Cognac Butter Ganache

Yield: 1 lb 10 oz (740 g)
Portions: 50 portions
Portion size: 0.5 oz (14 g)
Yield description: 52 portions at 0.5 oz (14 g)

Ingredients	U.S.	Metric
Butter	5.6 oz	160 g
Cognac	3.3 oz	80 g
Milk Chocolate	1 lb 1.6 oz	500 g

Procedure

1. Soften butter in a mixer with a paddle attachment.
2. Melt and temper milk chocolate, add to butter.
3. Fold in cognac.
4. Reserve for assembly.

Rocher (hand rolled)

Yield: 2 lb 6 oz (1104 g)
Portions: 140 pieces
Portion size: 1 Rocher
Yield description: 140 Rochers

Ingredients	U.S.	Metric
Praline Paste	1 lb 4 oz	575 g
Caramelized Hazelnut	4.5 oz	129 g
Craquelin	14 oz	400 g

Procedure

1. Pipe praline paste onto acetate sheets approximately 0.7 in. (18 mm).
2. Place caramelized hazelnut in the praline paste.
3. Allow praline paste to set.
4. Roll the praline paste in your hand to cover the hazelnut.
5. Hand roll once in melted milk chocolate and immediately roll in craquelin.
6. Allow the milk chocolate to fully crystallize overnight.
7. Dip the Rocher in tempered milk chocolate.

Praline Paste

Yield: 1 lb 4 oz (575 g)
Portions: 1 portion
Portion size: 1 lb 4 oz (575 g)
Yield description: 1 portion at 1 lb 4 oz (575 g)

Ingredients	U.S.	Metric
Hazelnuts	8.8 oz	250 g
Sugar	8.8 oz	250 g
Water	2.2 oz	63 g
Cocoa Butter	2.6 oz	75 g

Note: Purchased praline paste can be used in place of this recipe.

Procedure

1. Combine water and sugar; caramelize to a dark brown.
2. Pour over hazelnuts; cool completely.
3. Grind hazelnuts and caramel to a paste in a food processor.
4. Add melted cocoa butter.
5. Reserve for assembly.

Caramelized Hazelnut

Yield: 4.5 oz (129 g)
Portions: 140 (approximate)
Portion size: 1 hazelnut
Yield description: 140 hazelnuts (approximate)

Ingredients	U.S.	Metric
Hazelnuts, peeled, whole, toasted	3.5 oz	100 g
Sugar	0.9 oz	25 g
Water	0.7 oz	20 g
Cocoa Butter	0.14 oz	4 g

Procedure

1. Warm nuts to 200°F (93°C).
2. Combine sugar and water; cook to thread stage, 230°F (110°C).
3. Take pan off the stove and stir in nuts; continue stirring to crystallize the sugar.
4. Pour the crystallized nuts onto a silpat-lined sheet pan and allow to cool.
5. Sift off excess sugar and return to a clean pan.
6. Constantly stir nuts over a medium high heat. The sugar will begin to dissolve and caramelize.
7. Once a light amber color has been reached, remove the pan from the stove and stir in the cocoa butter.
8. Pour nuts onto a silpat-lined sheet pan and cool completely.
9. Reserve in an airtight container for assembly.

Craquelin

Yield: 14 oz (400 g)
Portions: 1
Portion size: 14 oz (400 g)
Yield description: 1 portion at 14 oz (400 g)

Ingredients	U.S.	Metric
Almonds, chopped, lightly toasted	7.1 oz	200 g
Sugar	7.1 oz	200 g
Water	1.8 oz	50 g

Procedure

1. Warm nuts to 200°F (93°C).
2. Combine sugar and water; cook to thread stage, 230°F (110°C).
3. Take pan off the stove and stir in nuts. Continue stirring to crystallizes the sugar.
4. Pour the crystallized nuts onto a silpat-lined sheet pan and allow to cool.
5. Sift off excess sugar.
6. Reserve in an airtight container for assembly.

Coffee and Lemon (slab)

Yield: 2 lb 4 oz (1019 g)
Portions: 69 pieces
Portion size: 1-in. (25-mm) square
Yield description: 69 portions at 1-in. (25-mm) square

Ingredients	U.S.	Metric
Lemon Ganache, page 367	1 lb 12 oz	794 g
Coffee Nougatine, page 367	8 oz	225 g

Procedure

1. Attach the coffee nougatine to the bottom of the lemon ganache squares using melted chocolate.
2. Hand dip in dark chocolate.

Lemon Ganache

Yield: 1 lb 12 oz (794 g)
Portions: 69 portions
Portion size: 0.4 oz (11.5 g)
Yield description: 69 portions at 0.4 oz (11.5 g)

Ingredients	U.S.	Metric
Heavy Cream	7.1 oz	200 g
Glucose	0.7 oz	20 g
Sorbitol	0.7 oz	20 g
Chocolate 64%	2.1 oz	60 g
Milk Chocolate	14.5 oz	410 g
Lemon Juice	2.5 oz	70 g
Lemon Zest	0.1 oz	4 g
Butter	0.4 oz	10 g

Procedure

1. Melt milk and dark chocolate half way over a double boiler.
2. Bring heavy cream, glucose and sorbitol to a simmer.
3. Emulsify chocolate and cream mixture.
4. Add lemon zest, juice, and soft butter; emulsify.
5. Pour ganache into 8 × 9.5 in. (20 × 24 cm) frame with 0.5-in. (13-mm) thick metal bars.
6. Allow ganache to crystallize for 12 hours.
7. Cut into 1-in. (25-mm) squares.

Coffee Nougatine

Yield: 1 lb 2 oz (538 g)
Portions: 69
Portion size: 1-in. (25-mm) square
Yield description: 69 portions at 1-in. (25-mm) square

Ingredients	U.S.	Metric
Water	0.4 oz	10 g
Glucose	4.9 oz	140 g
Honey	1.4 oz	40 g
Sugar	5.6 oz	160 g
Salt	0.04 oz	1 g
Yellow Pectin	0.1 oz	3 g
Butter	1.4 oz	40 g
Hazelnuts, roasted, finely chopped	4.9 oz	140 g
Arabica Coffee, finely ground	0.1 oz	4 g

Procedure

1. Combine pectin, sugar, and salt in a bowl.
2. Place water, sugar, honey, and glucose in a saucepan; add dry ingredients.
3. Caramelize the mixture.
4. Add hazelnuts, coffee, and butter to caramel.
5. Place nougatine between two sheets of parchment paper and roll thin. If mixture becomes too cool to roll, place in a 350°F (175°C) oven for 2 to 3 minutes to warm.
6. Cut into 1-in. (25-mm) squares and allow to cool.
7. Reserve in an airtight container for assembly.

Troubleshooting for Chocolates

Issue	Cause/Solution
Chocolate blooms when temperature is correct.	1. Not enough tempered chocolate was added during the seeding of the chocolate. Add additional seed to chocolate.
	2. The chocolate was not stirred enough during the tempering process. Stir chocolate more.
	3. The chocolate was not tested. Test before use.
Molded chocolate will not release.	1. The chocolate was not tempered correctly. Temper chocolate properly.
	2. Shell is too thin; recast with a slightly thicker shell.
	3. The chocolate was properly tempered but not allowed enough time in the mold. Allow chocolate to fully crystallize.
Ganache has a grainy texture.	1. Ganache was stirred when it was cool. Stir ganache less.
	2. The recipe was not scaled accurately or too much water was removed during the cooking process. Add more liquid to emulsify.
Butter ganache loses shape when piped.	The ganache is not crystallized. Allow mixture to crystallize longer before piping.

Confections

Confections are defined by the presence of sweeteners—most often in the form of sugar. They can be broken down into four main categories: crystalline, noncrystalline, aerated, and jellies. Hard candies, caramels, fudge, pâte de fruit, and marshmallows are all forms of confections. What sets these categories apart is the role the sweetener plays in the recipe. Sweeteners will always contribute to flavor; applications in confections may create a smooth, creamy caramel or a fudge.

Crystalline

Crystalline confections are identified by the presence of crystallized sugar in the final product. The ingredients used in the formula create a system that controls the size of the crystals. Fudge, fondant, and liquor bonbons are all examples of crystalline confections. Fondant is made through a process of cooking sugar, water, and glucose to a specific temperature, then cooling. Once the fondant has cooled, it is worked on a marble table, and the agitation creates many small crystals that make the fondant opaque.

Sugar is the main ingredient in crystalline confections. Applying heat to a sugar solution allows more sugar to dissolve in the solution. As the sugar solution cools, it now contains more sugar than could have previously been dissolved. This is now a **supersaturated** solution. In this solution, there is not much buffering for the sugar molecules. If the mixture is agitated or stirred, the sugar will begin to recrystallize back out of the solution. This is a desired effect for some crystalline confections. However, not controlling this crystallization is a problem. Ingredients like glucose and inverted sugar help to create smaller crystals that will maintain the creamy texture of the confections. Another factor in controlling crystallization is cooking the ingredients to the proper temperature.

Noncrystalline

Noncrystalline confections have sugar present in an amorphous form. This means the sugar is lacking form—it is dissolved in the confection and is free of crystals. The sugar provides noncrystalline confections with sweetness and hardness of the final product. A formula for brittle may contain sugar, glucose, water, butter, and nuts, and have a hard candy type consistency. Caramels will have the same ingredients with the addition of dairy. The dairy products contribute color and flavor to the candies while giving them a softer consistency.

Aerated

Aerated confections require the incorporation of air into a cooked sugar syrup. There are three ways the air can be incorporated: mechanical, chemical, or pressure. Mechanical is achieved through the use of a mixer and chemical is done through the use of baking soda. Mechanically aerated confections require a whipping agent and stabilizer. The whipping agent comes in the form of egg whites stabilized by gelatin. These two methods are used for smaller batch production; pressure aeration is reserved for large manufacturers. Marshmallows and nougat are included in aerated confections.

Jellies

Jellies are confections that contain a high percentage of sugar and are set with agar, pectin (yellow or apple pectin), or gelatin. More information about the hydrocolloids used to set jellies can be found in Chapter 4. The high percentage of sugar in products like gummy bears, jelly beans, pâte de fruit, and gumdrops contributes to their long shelf life.

As the name implies, many of these products have a sticky exterior until a final coating of oil or granulated sugar is applied. An inexpensive way to create different shapes from the jellies is to use a cornstarch mold. The following method will explain how to use cornstarch as a mold for gummies, pâte de fruit, and liquor bonbons (crystalline confection).

Cornstarch Mold Method

1. Dry cornstarch in a low temperature oven 100°F (38°C).
2. Sift starch into a wooden framed starch box; level of the top of the starch using a metal bar pulled along top of the frame.
3. Press the molds into the cornstarch and carefully lift straight up.

   Note: Plaster of Paris works best for casting molds. A positive mold will need to be made by casting plaster of Paris into a well-oiled chocolate or silicone mold. Make several castings of the mold and glue the cured plaster onto a wooden stick, leaving space between the molds.

4. Return the cornstarch to the oven to keep it warm and dry before filling.
5. Larger molds can be filled with a fondant funnel, while smaller molds can be filled with a pipette. Deposit the liquid into the mold.
6. Sift additional cornstarch over the liquid. Allow the confections to remain in the starch box overnight.
7. Carefully remove confections from starch and clean off excess cornstarch using either a brush or compessed air.

FIGURE 12.15a–e

1. Sifting the starch

2. Leveling the starch

3. Pressing the mold into the starch

4. Depositing the syrup

5. Sifting to cover the syrup

Confection Recipes

Apricot Passion Pâte de Fruit

Yield: 7 lb 7 oz (3392 g)

Portions: 160 pieces

Portion size: 0.7 oz (20 g)

Yield description: 160 pieces at 0.7 oz (20 g)

Ingredients	U.S.	Metric
Apricot Purée	1 lb 8.7 oz	700 g
Passion Fruit Purée	1 lb 8.7 oz	700 g
Yellow Pectin	1.1 oz	30 g
Sugar #1	5.3 oz	150 g
Glucose	10.6 oz	300 g
Sugar #2	3 lb 4.9 oz	1500 g
Tartaric Acid Solution, page 373	0.4 oz	12 g
Superfine Sugar	As needed	As needed

Procedure

1. Combine first sugar 5.3 oz (150 g) amount with pectin.
2. Combine second sugar 3 lb 4.9 oz (1500 g) and glucose.
3. Place purées in a heavy-bottom saucepan and heat to 104°F (40°C).
4. Add pectin/sugar mixture and bring to a boil.
5. From this point on the mixture must remain boiling.
6. Slowly add sugar/glucose mixture while whisking.
7. Once all this mixture is incorporated cook to 225°F (107°C), or 75°Brix.
8. Add the tartaric acid solution, immediately pour into molds or paper lined half sheet pan.
9. Allow pâte de fruit to cool to room temperature overnight.
10. Unmold or cut into desired shapes and dredge in superfine sugar.

FIGURE 12.16 Banana, Raspberry, and Apricot Passion Pâte de Fruit

Banana Pâte de Fruit

Yield: 8 lb 8 oz (3780 g)
Portions: 180 pieces
Portion size: 0.7 oz (20 g)
Yield description: 180 pieces at 0.7 oz (20 g)

Ingredients	U.S.	Metric
Pear Purée	2 lb 3.3 oz	1000 g
Yellow Pectin	1.2 oz	35 g
Sugar #1	5.3 oz	150 g
Glucose	10.6 oz	300 g
Sugar #2	3 lb 4.9 oz	1500 g
Banana Purée	1 lb 13.7 oz	750 g
Lemon Juice	0.5 oz	15 g
Tartaric Acid Solution	1.1 oz	30 g
Superfine Sugar	As needed	As needed

Procedure

1. Combine first sugar 5.3 oz (150 g) amount with pectin.
2. Combine second sugar 3 lb 4.9 oz (1500 g) and glucose.
3. Place pear purée in a heavy-bottom saucepan and heat to 104°F (40°C).
4. Add pectin/sugar mixture and bring to a boil.
5. From this point on the mixture must remain boiling.
6. Slowly add sugar/glucose mixture while whisking.
7. Once all this mixture is incorporated cook to 233°F (112°C).
8. Add the banana purée.
9. Continue cooking to 225°F (107°C) or 75°Brix, add lemon juice and tartaric acid solution. Immediately pour onto paper lined half sheet pan or molds.
10. Allow pâte de fruit to cool to room temperature overnight.
11. Unmold or cut into desired shapes and dredge in superfine sugar.

Raspberry Pâte de Fruit

Yield: 7 lb 8 oz (3405 g)
Portions: 160 pieces
Portion size: 0.7 oz (20 g)
Yield description: 160 pieces at 0.7 oz (20 g)

Ingredients	U.S.	Metric
Raspberry Purée	2 lb 3.3 oz	1000 g
Fresh Raspberries	14.1 oz	400 g
Pectin	1.1 oz	30 g
Sugar #1	5.3 oz	150 g
Glucose	10.6 oz	300 g
Sugar #2	3 lb 4.9 oz	1500 g
Tartaric Acid Solution	0.9 oz	25 g
Superfine Sugar	As needed	As needed

Procedure

1. Combine first sugar 5.3 oz (150 g) amount with pectin.
2. Combine second sugar 3 lb 4.9 oz (1500 g) and glucose.
3. Place raspberry purée and fresh raspberries in a heavy-bottom saucepan and heat to 104°F (40°C).
4. Add pectin/sugar mixture and bring to a boil.
5. From this point on the mixture must remain boiling.
6. Slowly add sugar/glucose mixture while whisking.
7. Once all this mixture is incorporated, cook to 225°F (107°C) or 75°Brix.
8. Add the tartaric acid solution; immediately pour into molds or paper lined half sheet pan.
9. Allow pâte de fruit to cool to room temperature overnight.
10. Unmold or cut into desired shapes and dredge in superfine sugar.

Tartaric Acid Solution

Yield: 4.2 oz (120 g)

Portions: 1

Portion size: 4.2 oz (120 g)

Yield description: 1 portion at 4.2 oz (120 g)

Ingredients	U.S.	Metric
Tartaric Acid	2.1 oz	60 g
Water, boiling	2.1 oz	60 g

Note: Tartaric acid solution easily crystallizes. Make sure all equipment and storage containers are cleaned before use.

Procedure

1. Bring 8 oz (240 g) of water to a rolling boil.
2. Place tartaric acid in a bowl.
3. Scale boiling water directly into tartaric acid; stir gently to dissolve.
4. Cover container and allow to cool. Store at room temperature.

Marshmallow

Yield: 15 oz (425 g)

Portions: 75

Portion size: 0.2 oz (5.6 g)

Yield description: 120 knots at 0.2 oz (5.6 g)

Ingredients	U.S.	Metric
Water or purée #1	1.5 oz	42.5 g
Sugar #1	1.5 oz	42.5 g
Vanilla Bean, split and scraped	1 each	1 each
Water or purée #2	7.5 oz	212.5 g
Sugar #2	4.5 oz	127.5 g
Sheet Gelatin, bloomed for 15 minutes	9 each	9 each
Powdered Sugar	As needed	As needed

Procedure

1. Combine water or purée #1 and sugar #1 in a mixer with a whip.

2. Heat water or purée #2 and sugar #2 to a boil.

3. Pour boiling mixture into stand mixer.

4. Add melted gelatin to mixture.

5. Whip until completely cool.

6. Pipe lines with a 0.4-in. (1-cm) plain tip onto powdered sugar dusted sheet pans.

7. Dust the top of the marshmallow with additional powdered sugar.

8. Let marshmallow rest for 3 to 4 hours.

9. Cut into 2-in. (5-cm) pieces.

10. Tie into a knot and store in an airtight container at room temperature.

FIGURE 12.17 Clockwise from top: Coconut macadamia brittle, chocolate nougat, marshmellow, toffee, nougat

Nougat

Yield: 1 lb 13 oz (840 g)
Portions: 60 pieces
Portion size: 0.5 oz (14 g)
Yield description: 60 pieces at 0.5 oz (14 g)

Ingredients	U.S.	Metric
Egg White Powder	0.2 oz	5 g
Sugar	0.5 oz	15 g
Egg Whites	0.9 oz	25 g
Sugar	6.7 oz	190 g
Glucose	2.1 oz	60 g
Water	1.8 oz	50 g
Vanilla Bean, split and scraped	1 each	1 each
Honey	4.1 oz	115 g
Cocoa Butter	1.8 oz	50 g
Whole Almonds	3.5 oz	100 g
Hazelnuts	1.2 oz	35 g
Pistachios	2.8 oz	80 g
Sliced Almonds	1.2 oz	35 g
Dried Apricot, diced	1.9 oz	55 g
Dried Cranberries	2.6 oz	75 g

Procedure

1. Toast nuts.
2. Combine first sugar with egg white powder; add to egg whites in a mixer with whip attachment.
3. Combine second sugar, glucose, water, and vanilla bean in a saucepan.
4. Cook honey to 222°F (106°C); turn mixer on high. Continue cooking to 248°F (120°C).
5. Begin cooking sugar mixture; add cooked honey to whipped egg whites.
6. Cook sugar mixture to 323°F (162°C) and add to egg white mixture.
7. Allow to mix for 3 to 5 minutes; add melted cocoa butter.
8. Warm fruit and nut mixture to 248°F (120°C).
9. Fold nut mixture into meringue.
10. Roll the nougat between two pieces of parchment paper into a 7 × 9 in. (18 × 23 cm) frame with 0.5-in. (13-mm) thick metal bars.
11. Allow nougat to cool to room temperature, cut into 1-in. (2.5-cm) squares.

Chocolate Nougat

Yield: 2 lb 3 oz (1020 g)
Portions: 70 pieces
Portion size: 0.5 oz (14 g)
Yield description: 70 pieces at 0.5 oz (14 g)

Ingredients	U.S.	Metric
Sugar 1	13.4 oz	380 g
Water	3.4 oz	95 g
Honey	8.1 oz	230 g
Sugar 2	0.7 oz	20 g
Egg Whites	1.8 oz	50 g
Vanilla Bean, split and scraped	1 each	1 each
Unsweetened Chocolate 100%	4.4 oz	125 g
Whole Almonds	2.6 oz	75 g
Pistachios	2.3 oz	65 g
Hazelnuts	2.6 oz	75g

Procedure

1. Combine first sugar, water and vanilla bean, bring to a boil.
2. Begin whipping egg whites with second sugar.
3. Bring honey to a boil cook to 248°F (120°C) and add to whipped egg whites.
4. When sugar reaches 323°F (162°C), add to egg white mixture.
5. After incorporating sugar, paddle the mixture to cool.
6. Add the melted chocolate.
7. Warm fruit and nut mixture to 248°F (120°C).
8. Fold in nuts.
9. Roll the nougat between two pieces of parchment paper into an 8 × 9.5 in. (20 × 24 cm) frame with 0.5-in. (13-mm) thick metal bars.
10. Allow nougat to cool to room temperature, cut into 1-in. (2.5-cm) squares.

Toffee

Yield: 1 lb 3 oz (540 g)
Portions: 45 pieces
Portion size: 0.4 oz (11 g)
Yield description: 45 pieces at 0.4 oz (11 g)

Ingredients	U.S.	Metric
Butter	8.8 oz	250 g
Sugar	8.8 oz	250 g
Glucose	1.1 oz	30 g
Salt	0.07 oz	2 g
Vanilla Extract	0.3 oz	8 g
Chocolate 64%, tempered	As needed	As needed
Sea Salt	As needed	As needed

Procedure

1. Combine butter, glucose, salt, and sugar in a heavy-bottom saucepan and heat.

2. Stir with a rubber spatula or wooden spoon, while bringing to a boil.

3. Cook to a temperature of 295°F (146°C).

4. Remove from heat and add vanilla extract. If mixture is broken, stir to emulsify.

5. Deposit toffee into 1.4-in. (3.5-cm) molds and cool completely.

6. Dip toffee in tempered chocolate and sprinkle with sea salt.

Coconut Macadamia Brittle

Yield: 1 lb 8 oz (578 g)
Portions: 50 pieces
Portion size: 0.4 oz (11 g)
Yield description: 50 pieces at 0.4 oz (11 g)

Ingredients	U.S.	Metric
Water	4.1 oz	115 g
Glucose	6 oz	170 g
Sugar	8.5 oz	240 g
Butter	0.4 oz	10 g
Dessicated Coconut, lightly toasted	2.6 oz	75 g
Macadamia Nuts, toasted and chopped	2.6 oz	75 g
Vanilla Paste	0.2 oz	5 g
Baking Soda	0.1 oz	3 g

Procedure

1. Combine the water, glucose, sugar, butter, and salt in heavy-bottom saucepan. Bring to a boil.

2. Cook this mixture without stirring to 240°F (115°C).

3. Add coconut and macadamia nuts; stir constantly.

4. Continue cooking to 290°F (143°C).

5. Remove from heat and add baking soda and vanilla paste.

6. Pour the brittle onto a silpat-lined sheet pan. Use an offset pallet knife to spread the mixture.

7. Once the brittle starts to set, use your hands to pull it thinner.

8. Cool completely and break into pieces. Store in an airtight container at room temperature.

Liquor Bonbon

Yield: 12 oz (350 g)

Portions: 40 pieces

Portion size: 0.3 oz (8.5 g)

Yield description: 40 pieces at 0.3 oz (8.5 g)

Ingredients	U.S.	Metric
Sugar	8.8 oz	250 g
Water	3 oz	85 g
Liquor (min 40% alcohol)	3.5 oz	100 g

Procedure

1. Warm cornstarch to 110°F (43°C) in an oven.
2. Prepare a cornstarch mold (page 370).
3. Cook water and sugar to 243°F (117°C).
4. Remove from heat; add liquor and cover for 5 minutes.
5. Gently transfer syrup between two bowls to mix the syrup, a minimum of three times.
6. Deposit syrup into warm cornstarch mold.
7. Sift additional cornstarch on top of the mold to cover the syrup.
8. Return the cornstarch mold to warm oven to maintain a temperature of 110°F (43°C).
9. After 6 hours, carefully turn the liquor bonbons over to create an even crystallization.
10. Place the tray back in the oven overnight.
11. Remove the liquor bonbon from the cornstarch and brush off any excess cornstarch.
12. Dip in tempered chocolate.

Key Terms

Winnowing
Conching
Couverture
Polymorphic
Fat bloom
Sugar bloom
Tabling method

Seeding method
Seizing
Bonbons
Truffles
Cream ganache
Butter ganache
Enrobing

Slab ganache
Guitar
Crystalline confections
Supersaturated
Noncrystalline confections
Aerated confections
Jellies

Questions for Review

1. What are the qualities of properly tempered chocolate?

2. Describe the differences between milk, white, and dark chocolate.

3. What does cocoa percentage represent?

4. What happens when chocolate is overcrystallized?

5. What is the difference between crystalline and noncrystalline confections?

CHAPTER 13

Chocolate Work

Art is defined as the expression of human creative skill and imagination, typically in visual form. Pastry chefs create art every day that transcends vision, creating something that appeals to the sense of smell, taste, and feel. Chocolate work allows the pastry chef to demonstrate their ability to create works of art from a premium product usually reserved for consumption.

LEARNING OBJECTIVES

After reading this chapter, you should be able to:

1. **Assemble** a chocolate showpiece.
2. **Demonstrate** how to build a variety of chocolate flowers.
3. **Prepare** a variety of chocolate garnishes.
4. **Explain** how to design a showpiece.

Introduction to Chocolate Work

Chocolate provides an excellent medium for creating garnishes and showpieces. Chocolate garnishes are delicately used on cakes, tarts, desserts and petits fours to add an attractive visual element to the dessert. The **garnish** can add color, movement, and height to pastries. Many of these garnish elements can be incorporated into a chocolate showpiece for a room service amenity or a larger buffet decoration.

Chocolate as a Medium for Sculptures and Garnishes

Chocolate can be easily molded, sculpted, and shaped to create a wide variety of components from solid support structures to delicate flower petals. A sculpture can be created using basic kitchen equipment, hand tools, and some equipment from the local hardware store. The one challenge associated with chocolate is that it is dark and solid, which leads to a heavy showpiece. Because chocolate is a strong medium, structural pieces tend to be overbuilt. This not only increases the cost of the piece, but adds to the weight of the piece. Reducing the weight of the structure will add to the visual appeal of the piece while reducing the overall weight, making transportation easier, and reduce cost.

Chocolate Selection

The pastry chef uses garnishes and showpieces to demonstrate skill and mastery of chocolate. Chocolate garnishes are strictly used as decoration: they provide color, texture through the snap of the chocolate, and the flavor of the chocolate. There is no set rule as to which chocolate should be used for a garnish. The flavor of chocolate goes with almost every other flavor, it is acceptable to use chocolate as a garnish even if there is not chocolate it the dessert. However, if there is chocolate in the dessert the garnish can be used as a way to reflect this. A pastry that has white chocolate mousse should use a white chocolate garnish, additional color can be added with the use of edible luster dusts and cocoa butter colors.

A showpiece requires additional thought in selecting the correct chocolate. Milk and white chocolate contain milk products and a higher percentage of sugar compared to dark chocolate. These additional ingredients reduce the amount of cocoa butter in the chocolate. Cocoa butter provides the strength and structure to hold the showpiece up. Milk chocolate is rarely used in the production of chocolate sculptures. Dark chocolate is the primary chocolate used for chocolate sculptures, while white chocolate is used as an accent due to its decreased strength.

If dark chocolate is the best chocolate to build a showpiece with and cocoa butter makes the piece stronger, then a high cocoa percentage chocolate is the best chocolate, right? Wrong. Just as different cocoa percentage chocolates have different flavor profiles, they also have different characteristics when building a showpiece.

A 55% to 58% couverture can be used to assemble a strong showpiece. The amount of sugar in the chocolate makes it easy to temper, and, at the same time, the amount of cocoa butter makes it strong. This chocolate will be slightly thicker than the next example. The ease of tempering is a benefit for using a semisweet chocolate. The other benefit is the length of working time when tempered. Chocolate with a high percentage of cocoa butter can easily become overcrystallized. This will cause the chocolate to become very thick, reduce the ability to flow, and make it difficult to work with.

Using a bittersweet couverture, 60% to 64% cocoa solids, will give a better flow for molding. This chocolate will require more attention while tempering. The additional cocoa butter present will create a stronger structure. There is a drawback associated with higher cocoa percentage chocolates. It can easily become overcrystallized when working with the chocolate. This occurs after several hours of working with the tempered chocolate. Melting the chocolate and repeating the tempering process can reverse the overcrystallized cocoa butter and return it to a fluid state.

Garnishes

Garnishes can be used for sculptures or as a decorative element for pastries. These pieces are edible and added for decorative purposes and can be made using white, milk, or dark chocolate.

Chocolate Cigarette

Equipment needed: Offset pallet knife, straight blade slicing knife, and metal scraper:

1. Spread a thin layer of tempered chocolate onto a piece of marble. It is important that the chocolate be spread as evenly as possible. Thinner areas will set too quickly and will also be too soft to come off the knife.
2. Using the metal scraper, clean the edges of the spread chocolate. The width of the chocolate should be 4 to 6 in. (10 to 15 cm).
3. Allow the chocolate to set; rub your hand over the chocolate to rewarm slightly.

4. Place the knife on the chocolate, starting ½ in. (1.5 cm) in from the end of the chocolate on the right side.

5. Push down and away toward the right. The chocolate will roll off in the shape of a cigarette.

Variation: To make two-colored cigarettes, spread dark chocolate first then scrape with a metal comb. After the chocolate has set to the point it will not smear, spread a layer of tempered white chocolate over the top.

Chocolate Plaquettes

Equipment needed: Offset pallet knife, airbrush, skewer, paring knife, round cutters, two flat cutting boards, parchment paper, plastic acetate sheet:

1. Wipe the cutting board with a wet towel. Place the acetate on the cutting board, using your hand to remove any large bubbles that may have formed under the acetate. Then, using a clean dry towel, wipe the acetate to remove any water that might have gotten on top. The water left underneath the acetate will be enough to hold it in place.

2. Spray the acetate with a darker cocoa butter color (green).

3. Use a clean rubber eraser or artist's blending tool to draw circles in the cocoa butter.

4. Spray a lighter cocoa butter color (yellow) next and allow the cocoa butter to crystallize.

5. Spread a thin, even layer of tempered chocolate over the cocoa butter.

6. When the chocolate sets, cut out desired shapes using the back of a paring knife or round cutters. This prevents cutting through the acetate.

7. Place a sheet of parchment paper on top of the chocolate, followed by the other cutting board. Chocolate will contract as it crystallizes; the weight placed on top will keep the decorations flat.

8. Let the chocolate crystallize overnight before removing the acetate.

Variations: 1. In place of the cocoa butter, use white, milk, and dark chocolate. 2. Use a paintbrush to splatter cocoa butter on the acetate. 3. A sponge can be used to apply colors. 4. Textured plastic sheets can also be used to create a different effect.

FIGURE 13.1 Chocolate spread on marble with a portion already made into cigarettes on the left and the remainder of the strip in the process

Colored Chocolate Spheres

Equipment needed: Polycarbonate sphere mold, offset pallet knife, metal scraper, half sheet of parchment paper, colored cocoa butters:

1. Wearing gloves, smear a thin layer of colored cocoa butter in the mold with your finger.

2. Fill the molds with tempered chocolate.

3. Scrape off any excess chocolate and tap the mold with the plastic handle of the scraper to remove any bubbles.

4. Let the filled mold sit for 1 to 2 minutes.

FIGURE 13.2a–d

1. Applying swirls on first color of acetate (step 3)

2. Spreading chocolate (step 5)

3. Cutting chocolate (step 6)

4. Finished assorted colored decors (step 8)

5. Turn the mold over and tap with the plastic handle of the scraper, removing the extra chocolate.

6. Place the mold on a sheet of parchment paper and allow the chocolate to drip down to form a lip. This will make it easier to seal the two halves together.

7. Before removing from the paper, be sure that the chocolate has crystallized enough that the lip remains with the mold.

8. Scrape the mold again, removing any excess chocolate. This will ensure the chocolate will be able to contract properly during crystallization.

9. Leave the chocolate in the mold overnight and release the following day; this will ensure a good shine. If needed sooner, the mold can be placed in the refrigerator for 10 to 15 minutes to release the chocolate.

10. Remove the sphere halves from the mold.

11. Using a warm, flat surface, approximately 100°F (38°C), melt the edge of both pieces of the chocolate.

12. Press the halves together and place the sphere back in the mold, allow the seam to set fully before moving.

Variations: 1. Use an airbrush to spray the cocoa butter colors in the mold. 2. Use a brush to add the cocoa butter color by brushing or splashing in color.

FIGURE 13.3a–d

1. Applying the color into the mold (step 1)

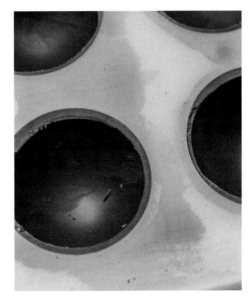

2. Showing the lip inside the mold after scraping (step 7)

3. Melting the halves and placing them in the mold to set (step 11)

4. Finished piece with spheres

Colored Chocolate Triangles

Equipment needed: Acetate plastic sheet, half sheet of parchment paper, paring knife, offset pallet knife, paintbrush, piece of tape:

1. Drizzle colored cocoa butter onto the sheet of acetate. Immediately brush the cocoa butter across the acetate. The cocoa butter needs to be 88°F (31°C). It does not need to be tempered; the process of brushing will temper the cocoa butter.

2. After the cocoa butter has crystallized, spread a thin layer of tempered chocolate.

3. As the chocolate crystallizes, it will become firm enough to cut cleanly and still remaining pliable. This can be checked by touching the chocolate with your finger—it should not stick to your finger.

4. Using the back side of the paring knife (this avoids cutting the acetate), cut the chocolate into triangles, approximately 1 × 4 in. (2.5 × 10 cm).

FIGURE 13.4a–d

Brushing on the cocoa butter (step 1)

Cutting the chocolate (step 4)

Wrapping the curls (step 5)

An example of chocolate curls with modeling chocolate roses.

5. Place the piece of parchment paper on top of the chocolate and roll diagonally. Place a small piece of tape to secure the roll.

6. Allow the chocolate to crystallize overnight. This will ensure the triangles will have an excellent shine. Unroll tubes as needed to protect them.

Variations: 1. After drizzling the cocoa butter color spread with an offset pallet knife. 2. In place of the colored cocoa butter, use white or milk chocolate.

Chocolate Curls

Equipment needed: 2.5 × 12 in. (6.5 × 30 cm) acetate strip, offset pallet knife, plastic comb, half plastic tube, paper cornet:

1. Place the acetate strip on the table. To adhere the strip to the table, use a wet towel and place the acetate on top. Wipe with a clean dry towel to remove any water. This will prevent the acetate from moving.

2. Spread a thin layer of chocolate onto the acetate strip.

3. Pull the plastic comb down the length of the strip.

4. Pipe small dots of chocolate between the lines to hold the twist together.

5. Twist the acetate and place in the half plastic tube and let the chocolate crystallize.

6. Carefully remove the acetate from the curl.

Variations: 1. Brush acetate with colored cocoa butter. 2. Do not pipe the dots between the lines. The curls can be used individually.

FIGURE 13.5 Garnish from entremets

FIGURE 13.6a–b

1. Piping chocolate on the vermicelli (step 2)   **2.** The finished decorations

Piped Decors

Equipment needed: Piping bag, half sheet pan, chocolate vermicelli:

1. Spread the chocolate vermicelli on the half sheet pan.
2. Pipe the chocolate directly onto the vermicelli. Piping can be in circles or lines.
3. Allow the chocolate to crystallize before removing the decoration.

Sculpture Design

Chocolate sculptures offer the pastry chef a way to demonstrate their creativity and knowledge of chocolate. The size of these pieces can vary from a small room service amenity to a large piece meant for display on a buffet. Regardless of size there are three parts to constructing a sculpture: structure, color, and theme.

When setting out to start creating showpieces, planning is the most important step. Everyone creates art differently; you may be inspired by a drawing or searching for images online. Once your ideas are collected, draw the piece to scale. This does not have to be a perfect drawing. It is a starting point from which templates will be made to start assembling the sculpture. The next step in the process is to assemble the sculpture from cardboard templates. Any design changes are easy to make. At this point, your idea goes from paper to three dimensions. A great deal about the piece can be learned from these additional steps that should make building the piece from chocolate faster.

Structure Design

Base

As with any other form of construction the base is the foundation of the piece. The base can easily be overlooked when creating the sculpture. It not only provides a sturdy foundation to build on, but also stabilizes the piece. Small and large pieces constructed with a weak base will be more likely to fail. In the case of larger pieces, the weight of the base makes transporting the piece easier. The base is not just a block of chocolate, it can be molded and sculpted to reinforce the theme of the piece.

Include the base in the sketch of the piece so that there is a point of reference for the height of the base. The base should be no more than 30 percent of the total structure. As part of the construction of the base include a small chocolate pedestal or feet. This piece should be just slightly smaller then the size of the base; if it is too small the piece may not be stable enough. From a design standpoint, this pedestal lifts the piece off the display table and gives the sculpture a lighter feel. It also provides a way to easily lift the piece when transporting.

Structure

The **structure** of the piece provides the height and strength of the piece. When designing a sculpture this is the first step. It is important to design a structure that is strong to hold the theme elements. The most common shaped structures are J, C, E, and S. These shapes provide a flow to the design of the sculpture—straight lines are also used to create structures.

It is important to consider the shape of the structure and how it impacts the overall design of the piece. The structure should catch the eye of the viewer and help their eye to move through the piece. The movement should come from the top and bottom of the piece towards the middle, ultimately directing them back to the focal point.

Focal Point

In addition to supporting the sculpture the structure is also used to guide the viewer's eye to the focal point. The **focal point** is the point of interest on the piece that makes the sculpture unique. Most often, the focal point is a flower or pastries presented on the piece. The focal point should be located 50% to 60% of the height from the base of the sculpture. This is a guideline for sculptures placed on a buffet table with a height of 30 in. (76 cm). This is a guideline for large sculptures; smaller amenity pieces do not have to follow this guideline and an attractive design can be created.

It is important to consider the height of the table and placement of the table (against a wall or in the middle of the room, etc.) when designing a piece. The table height and position will impact how the decorative elements are positioned. Decorative elements and focal point should be placed in a way that they are easily viewed.

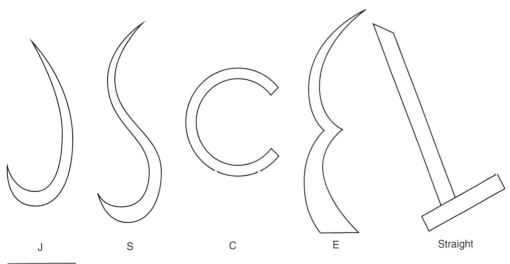

| J | S | C | E | Straight |

FIGURE 13.7 Drawing of J, S, C, E and straight lines

Optimal Viewing Position

For example, a flower placed on a sculpture should be positioned in a way that the center of the flower is facing the viewer. This is known as the **optimal viewing position (OVP)**. Some refer to this simply as the front of the piece. When considering the OVP, most of the elements on the piece should be visible from this position. Not all elements need to be in clear view from the front of the piece. At the same time the piece should not have a "back" that is void of any decoration. Elements from the front of the piece should catch the eye and draw the observer to inspect what is on the other side the piece. A perfectly designed piece should be just as interesting on the back as it is from the OVP.

Incorporating Design in the Structure

While the primary purpose of the structure is to hold the piece up, it can also help to carry the theme through the piece. A curved piece at the top of an S-curved structure could be made to look like a bow with arrows flowing around it. A straight vertical line can add to the piece by taking on the appearance of a steel beam. The possibilities are endless. Keep an open mind when practicing assembling the piece as it will evolve and change with every assembly.

Theme

When thinking about how to design a sculpture for a buffet, consider the theme of the buffet. Holidays such as Christmas, Valentine's Day, Thanksgiving, Easter, and New Year's Eve all have easily recognizable themes. What makes the showpiece unique is how the themes are incorporated.

Consider New Year's Eve as a theme, what ideas come to mind? A clock, champagne flutes, horns, hats, and noisemakers immediately come to mind. A visit to the library or museum, as well as searching online, may provide additional ideas. Using any three of these elements should be enough to convey the theme of the holiday buffet.

To build the New Year's Eve themed sculpture we will use the decorative elements of the clock, champagne bottle, and confetti. It is now time to decide on the structure of the piece. It is best to decide on decorative elements and the purpose of the piece before selecting the structure. This piece will be a strictly decorative piece on the buffet. Selecting the S curve, E, or straight-line designs will work for this piece. If the piece requires a cake or pastry to be displayed on the piece, the J or C shape will work well. For this application, the S curve will be selected. The piece can now be sketched using the decorative elements and structure (see Figure 13.8).

Color

Creating color on a chocolate sculpture can be easily achieved with the use of colored cocoa butter. The biggest challenge when working with chocolate is creating a piece that is not bulky and heavy. Design, along with color, can be used to create a chocolate sculpture that is light and flows. Color can be used to draw attention to areas like the focal point while taking attention from larger structural pieces.

An attractive showpiece can be built using the natural colors of white, milk, and dark chocolate. This holds true with a piece using black and white colors. Cocoa butter colors are available in a wide variety of colors, and they can also be blended to create many additional colors. Primary colors, such as red, blue, and yellow, can be used to create almost any other color. Mixing the primary colors together creates secondary colors of orange, green, and purple. The color wheel in Figure 13.9 shows primary, secondary, and tertiary colors and their corresponding complementary colors. The complementary colors are located directly across from each other.

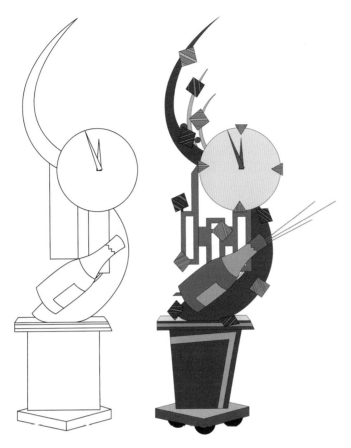

FIGURE 13.8 Sketch of piece with decorative elements

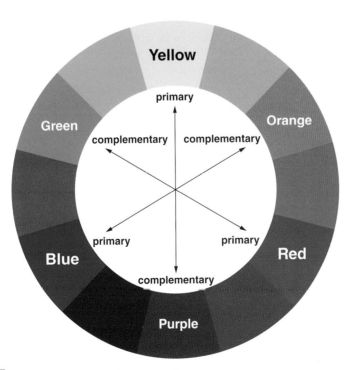

FIGURE 13.9 Color wheel with complementary colors

FIGURE 13.10 Finished piece made from chocolate

While colors are easily applied to the chocolate, it is good to leave some of the chocolate of the piece showing. In some cases, this may be the only indication to the observer that it is in fact chocolate.

Incorporating color into a showpiece can be done in several ways: through the use of colored garnishes, by adding color to white chocolate, using a paintbrush or airbursh, or adding edible luster dusts. When applying color to chocolate the color of the chocolate will change the applied color. If red cocoa butter color is sprayed on dark chocolate, it will have a deeper red color from the brown color behind it. The same is true when adding color to white chocolate, the natural yellow from the cocoa butter will combine with the color. For example, adding blue to white chocolate will produce a green-blue color. Depending on the desired final color, another spray or primer, may need to be applied. For the red spray to be a true red on the dark chocolate, white must first be applied. Experimenting with different color combinations will help to make the sculpture more unique.

The design of the piece continues by adding color to the sketch. A set of colored pencils or markers can get the colors close to what the cocoa butter colors will achieve. When adding color to the piece, refer back to the complimentary colors as a starting point. For example, the face of the clock will be a tan color, the numbers and arms black, the champagne bottle will have a green color, and the confetti will be colored red and blue. More color can be added by the accent pieces that will represent fireworks.

Assembly

After all the ideas have been put down on paper, it is time to get the templates together. Chocolate is an excellent medium to work with because it does not require much equipment to build an elaborate piece. The templates can be cut from poster board or cake boxes; in fact, any piece of flat, sturdy cardboard will work. Transfer the designs to the cardboard. At this point, the cardboard templates can be taped together, giving a preview of what the final piece will look like.

Once the templates are assembled, any necessary changes can be made. The following procedure explains the chocolate **cutout method**, how to cut out the chocolate using templates.

Chocolate Cutout Method

Equipment needed: Paring knife, 2 each 0.25-in. (6-mm) metal bars, offset pallet knife, cardboard template, parchment paper, newsprint:

1. Place the newsprint on a flat board, with the metal bars on the side. The metal bars will ensure that the chocolate is even thickness, which is very important for structural pieces. The chocolate will also crystallize at the same rate, making it easier to cut.

2. Ladle tempered chocolate on the newsprint and spread it with an offset pallet knife. Quickly drag a metal bar across the top of the 0.25-in. (6-mm) bars. This will level out the chocolate.

3. Wait for the chocolate to crystallize. When the chocolate looks like it is setting, test with your gloved finger. The chocolate should not stick. At this point, it is ready to cut.

4. Place the template on top of the chocolate and cut with the paring knife. Do not press down; the newsprint under the chocolate should not be cut. Make additional relief cuts once the template is cut.

5. Place the parchment paper on top of the chocolate and flip the board over.

6. Remove the newsprint from the chocolate. The chocolate should remove cleanly from the paper. You will notice the newsprint is greasy. This is caused by the cocoa butter from the chocolate. If parchment paper were used in place of newsprint, the parchment would have become wrinkled from the absorption of the cocoa butter and this would have transferred to the chocolate.

7. Remove excess chocolate from around the cutout piece. Allow the structural piece to crystallize fully before moving.

The cut pieces require several hours to crystallize fully. Moving the pieces prematurely may cause the chocolate to bend slightly, forming small cracks that may not be visible. Over time, these cracks will weaken the structure to the point that it could break.

FIGURE 13.11a–c

1. Spreading the chocolate between the bars (step 2)

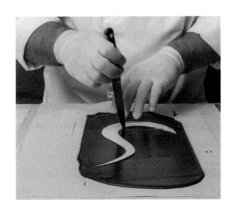

2. Cutting the chocolate (step 4)

3. Removing the paper from the flipped cut out (step 6)

Connecting Pieces

Although it is said that the chocolate is used to "glue" the pieces together, this is not entirely true: The chocolate acts as more of a weld. When connecting pieces, the goal is to get them to become one, not just two pieces with some chocolate between them holding them together. To achieve this, the chocolate pieces are warmed slightly at the connection point, a thin line of tempered chocolate is piped at the connection point, and the pieces are placed together. Be careful how much chocolate is piped to avoid overfilling. The extra chocolate will be pressed out of the seam and leave an unsightly mess, or worse, drip onto another part of the piece. Any extra chocolate can be cleaned using a gloved finger or a small pallet knife. The seam needs to be as clean as possible, even if it is not in clear view on the piece. Practicing making a clean seam is good for when the seam will be visible.

To help set the seam quickly, cold spray can be used. Cold spray is compressed air in a can that sprays cold air. This product can be helpful in assembling a piece quickly. However, it is often abused and overused by the inexperienced. A quick blast of cold spray can set the chocolate enough for the remainder of crystallization to occur without the piece moving or falling. Over-spraying can cool the chocolate too rapidly and create a false set, as the piece warms back up the chocolate returns to a liquid state and the piece falls off. Since the chocolate crystallizes better without the use of cold spray, it is recommended to only use it when absolutely necessary.

Connecting Pieces Method

Equipment needed: heat gun, paper cornet, paring knife:

1. Place the pieces being glued together and use the paring knife to mark a line where the pieces line up.
2. Warm the connection areas with the heat gun. A slight warming will not take the chocolate out of temper; instead, it will warm the chocolate to fuse the two pieces together.
3. Pipe a small line of chocolate where the two pieces will meet.
4. Connect the pieces pressing firmly; hold until set.
5. Clean any excess chocolate that may have ran out.
6. Go back over the seams with the paper cornet and pipe a line of chocolate along each side of the piece. Immediately clean the excess with a gloved finger.

FIGURE 13.12a–c Attaching technique:

1. Warming the pieces (step 2)   **2.** Piping the chocolate (step 3)   **3.** Cleaning the seam (step 5)

Component Inventory

When designing a showpiece, it is important to get the ideas down on paper. After the sketch is completed, the design moves into the next phase. Utilizing different techniques and components in the piece will help to create a more interesting piece. If a chocolate sculpture is made from flat cutout pieces and sprayed, it would still look good. However, incorporating different techniques like molded spheres, flowers, and piped chocolate can give the piece more life. Creating a component inventory of techniques will help make sure that nothing is overlooked during the planning process.

Component Inventory for Chocolate Showpieces

Molded	Cutouts	Piped
Shiny	Dull	Sprayed flat
Sprayed velvet	Carved	Food processor rollouts
Brushed	Hand painted	Rocks
Chocolate pastillage	Flower	

When designing a sculpture, it is important to take into consideration what is truly needed and what is not. The hardest skill to learn in designing a showpiece is editing. Not every item on the component needs to be included in the design.

Techniques

Spraying with Cocoa Butter

When working with chocolate, whether it is molded pieces or cutouts, the piece will need to be finished with a cocoa butter spray. It is inevitable that smudges or fingerprints will get on the piece. While spraying will cover small marks, any large dents or chips will become more pronounced after spraying. Cocoa spray provides a way to cover up these small blemishes and at the same time give the structural elements the same color.

Spraying a showpiece is not the same as the delicate work of airbrushing. The sprayer is larger and more powerful. There are several models of spray guns available from most hardware stores. The spray is propelled in one of two ways: an electric sprayer uses a small piston to push the paint through a nozzle, while a compressor forces air through a small opening to propel the chocolate. Compressor-powered sprayers spray a more even coat than the electric version, but they are considerably more expensive.

Always test the spray gun before spraying the piece to confirm the gun is operating properly. Start with the gun off to the side of the piece and begin spraying. Slowly move the gun over the piece and continue past. Continue spraying the piece in passes, being careful to go past the piece when switching directions. If direction is changed while the spray is directed at the piece it will become oversprayed in this area. This will lead to drips and an uneven coating of color.

The spray guns operate at a high pressure. It is recommended to create a spraying station with a large cardboard box or other material to reduce clean up time. After spraying the piece, move the piece carefully—any contact will result in fingerprints on the piece.

Velvet Spraying

Spraying can be used to achieve different textures in the piece. By placing the chocolate in the freezer for 15 minutes and then spraying the piece, it will have a velvet finish. As the cocoa butter spray comes in contact with the frozen chocolate piece, it immediately sets. Then, as more spray is added, it continues to build up. Be careful when handling velvet-sprayed chocolate. It is very delicate and easily damaged.

FIGURE 13.13 A properly sprayed piece (left), oversprayed (center), and velvet texture (right)

Modeling Chocolates

Modeling Chocolate

Molds help to speed up the production of chocolate sculptures. There are some items that cannot be made with molds. A delicate chocolate rose is impossible to make from chocolate and the shape cannot be replicated with a mold. The only way to assemble a rose out of chocolate is to use **modeling chocolate**, a combination of chocolate and sugar syrup that allows the chocolate to remain flexible. Modeling chocolate can also be used to create leaves and figurines. After sculpting, the modeling chocolate will dry and hold its shape. Larger pieces tend to weep over time, but modeling chocolate will set as hard as chocolate. Modeling chocolate is used mostly for decorative showpieces, and is not allowed in competitions.

White or Milk Modeling Chocolate For white modeling chocolate, use white or milk chocolate in place of the dark chocolate and add 100 g of cocoa butter to the chocolate. During the tabling process, the cocoa butter will separate out from the chocolate. This is normal. Table the cocoa butter separately; once crystallization has begun, add it back to the chocolate and continue tabling as with dark modeling chocolate.

Modeling Chocolate Rose Method Equipment needed: Metal spoon, paring knife:

1. Knead the modeling chocolate back to a workable consistency and roll to ⅛ in. (3 mm) thick.

2. Using a round cutter, cut 10 disks 1.5 in. (40 mm) and one solid sphere ¾ in. (20 mm) in diameter.

3. Shape the sphere into a teardrop shape, slightly flatten the larger end so it will stand without falling over.

4. Use the spoon to thin out the edge of the disks. Thinning the edges will give the flower a more lifelike appearance. The petals can easily be removed from the marble with a paring knife.

5. Wrap the first petal completely around the teardrop. Be sure to cover the entire teardrop.

6. Place the middle of the second petal directly across from the seam of the first petal, and slightly lower. The center of the flower should always be the highest point.

7. The next layer will have three petals. These petals will be slightly lower than the second petal. Place the left side of the petal against the rose bud and roll back the right side with your finger. The next petal goes under the right side of the previous petal. All three petals will interlock. When spaced evenly, the bud will remain round. Flowers are always assembled with odd numbers of petals to prevent the flower from becoming boxy and to provide a natural appearance.

8. The remaining five petals are shaped by pinching the bottom to create a small-cupped petal. The top of the outer petals is pinched slightly in the center and rolled back.

9. Attach the petals, making sure they are evenly spaced and slightly lower than the previous layer.

10. Freeze the finished flower and spray with red cocoa butter color.

FIGURE 13.14a–d

1. Flattening the petals with a spoon (step 4)

2. Cupping the outer petals (step 8)

3. Bud; bud with 2 wrapped petals; bud with 3 petals; bud with 5 petals

4. Finished rose piece with sprayed rose

Food Processor Modeling Chocolate **Food processor modeling chocolate** gives the chef a faster alternative to traditional modeling chocolate. Using the food processor eliminates the need for making the modeling chocolate and waiting for it to crystallize and then having to dry it. Food processor modeling chocolate uses the friction of the food processor to melt the cocoa butter to the point that it is malleable but still tempered. The chocolate has the consistency of clay and is easily rolled into smooth shapes. It cannot be used for creating the delicate petals of a rose because the chocolate crystallizes too quickly. Instead, it is used for larger showpiece decorations like rollouts and loops.

There are two methods to making food processor chocolate. Solid tempered chocolate can be placed directly in the food processor. Chocolate pistoles from the manufacturer work best, as they arrive tempered and are uniform in size. The second method uses the formula below with cocoa powder and cocoa butter. Using these methods has two advantages: There is minimal preparation time and the chocolate crystallizes within 15 minutes of rolling.

White Food Processor Rollouts To make white chocolate rollouts, replace the cocoa powder with potato starch. Cocoa butter colors can be added to the white chocolate mixture in the food processor.

Note: Due to the inclusion of potato starch, the white chocolate rollout recipe cannot be used in competitions.

Food Processor Rollout Method

1. Place ingredients or chocolate in food processor.
2. Mix until the chocolate forms a paste.
3. Knead on a wood table to make sure the all the paste is slightly melted. It should not stick to the table, if it sticks to the work surface the cocoa butter has melted too much.
4. Roll the chocolate into a long rope. These can be even or tapered at one end. A piece of cardboard can be used to smooth out and indentations left from fingers.
5. Quickly form the chocolate, as it will begin setting within minutes.

FIGURE 13.15a–c Food processor rollout method:

1. The consistency of chocolate in food processor (step 2)

2. Rolling out the chocolate (step 4)

3. Finished piece with rollouts

Chocolate Pastillage

Chocolate pastillage is a relatively new medium used on chocolate showpieces. It is similar to pastillage used on sugar sculptures, with the addition of cocoa powder. The use of chocolate pastillage is restricted to display pieces, and not allowed in competitions. There are many advantages to using chocolate pastillage on chocolate sculpture. It can be rolled thinner than modeling chocolate and will dry completely. It holds the shape it is formed in and is extremely light.

Chocolate pastillage can be shaped in the same way pastillage is shaped in Chapter 14. Once the pieces have dried, they are attached to the showpiece using tempered chocolate. Spraying the chocolate pastillage will give it a darker color, and it will blend with the rest of the piece.

Chocolate Flowers

Flowers made from chocolate provide a way to add color and lighten up a showpiece. Flowers, like a modeling chocolate rose, mimic a real flower, while modern chocolate flowers can add volume to a showpiece with minimal weight. Volume refers to the space the flower fills on the piece. Flowers are open with thin petals; therefore, they minimize the amount of weight. Petals can be positioned to create a swirling motion or placed straight and look more like an explosion.

There are four techniques used to create flower petals: chablon, dipped-knife, cutout, or scraped. A **chablon** is a thin mat that chocolate is spread on. This method creates petals of even thickness that are thinned on the edges. The knife-dipped flowers use a paring knife, or any long object, dipped into chocolate then placed on an acetate sheet. These petals can be left flat or curved. Cutout petals are spread onto paper the same way pieces are cut out for structures, only the chocolate is spread thinner, cut, and shaped. The scraped method uses round cutters or scrapers to shape the chocolate directly off the marble table. All of these methods offer interesting ways to create flowers, which can be small to as large as 12 in. (30 cm) across.

Chablon Method A chablon is a thin mat of rubber or flexible material with shapes cut out. The thickness of the chablon will depend on the size of the final flower—the bigger the flower, the thicker the mat will need to be. For most flowers, a mat that is ⅛ in. (3 mm) thick is good.

Equipment needed: Newsprint, chablon, piping bag, metal scraper, mold for shaping:

1. Place the chablon on a piece of newsprint.
2. Pipe a line of tempered chocolate on top of the chablon.
3. Drag the metal scraper across the top of the chablon. Do this only once.
4. Remove the chablon immediately after spreading.
5. Pick up diagonally opposite corner and tap the newsprint. This will smooth out the chocolate.
6. Shape the chocolate petals and let them set in the mold.
7. Remove the petals from the newsprint and reserve for assembly.

Dipped-Knife Method The dipped-knife method uses a paring knife, offset pallet knife, or painter's knife (available at craft stores) to make the petals. The knife is dragged through the tempered chocolate and then placed on an acetate sheet and shaped. Flowers can be with twisting petals or several rows of multiple petals.

Equipment needed: Acetate strips, paring knife, mold for shaping:

1. Wipe a wet towel along the edge the table. Place the acetate strip on the wet table and smooth. Use a clean, dry towel to remove excess water.
2. Dip the knife into tempered chocolate the full length of the blade and drag through the chocolate.

FIGURE 13.16a–c

Dipping the knife in the chocolate (step 2)   Placing the knife on the acetate (step 3)   Unmolded petals (step 6)

3. Place the chocolate-covered knife blade on the acetate sheet; do not press all the way down to the plastic.

4. Lift the knife straight up and pull straight back. This will create a ridge on what will be the inside of the petal, providing structural support.

5. Place the petals in the shaping mold and let the chocolate crystallize.

6. Remove the petals from the acetate and reserve for assembly.

Assembly of Chablon and Dipped-Knife Flowers   Chablon and dipped-knife flowers are assembled in the same way. They are attached to a series of spheres that will hold the flower up, allowing for easy placement on the showpiece. This assembly will require two 1-in. (2.5-cm) spheres and two 2-in. (5-cm) half spheres solid cast. One of the half spheres will be used for assembling the flower, the other is attached to the showpiece as a mounting point for the finished flower.

Equipment needed: Cold spray, 8 in. (20 cm) cake board, paper cornet:

1. Build the center of the flower, start with one of the half sphere on the bottom followed by the two 1-in. (2.5-cm) spheres. Place the seams of the spheres vertically.

2. Once the spheres have crystallized fully, turn the assembly upside down and dip in tempered chocolate, return to the cake board. This dipping solidifies the spheres, reducing the possibility of breakage. It also creates a rough surface to attach the petals.

3. Begin placing the petals on the center. Dip the end of the petal in tempered chocolate and place on the bottom of the top sphere. Use a quick shot of cold spray to attach the petal. Continue placing a total of five petals in the first row. The first row of petals is strictly for positioning purposes. It is a common mistake to begin placing the first row of petals too close together to fill in the space between the petals. The remaining rows will be positioned between the openings of the previous row.

4. The second row of five petals is placed in between the petals from the first row and positioned so the tips of the petals are slightly lower. This will create an open flower. A flower that is too open is associated with a flower that is past its prime and beginning to die.

5. Continue using the same method for attaching the third row of petals.

6. Freeze and spray the flower with colored cocoa butter.

FIGURE 13.17a–c

1. The stack of spheres, one dipped the other not (steps 1 and 2)

2. Placing the first petals (step 3)

3. Series of the flower showing the progress of each row

7. The remaining half sphere is used to attach the flower to the showpiece. Place the half sphere with the flat side facing out.

8. Warm the flat portion of the sphere with a heat gun and pipe a small amount of tempered chocolate.

9. Pick the flower up from under to petals and press into place, quickly with a shot of cold spray to set the chocolate.

Scraped Flower Method The scraped flower method creates a flower that closely resembles a peony. The ruffled curls of the petal set this flower apart from the rest. When making chocolate cigarettes, the chocolate demonstrates a certain flexibility before setting. The same procedure is used to create flower petals using the scraped method.

Equipment needed: Round cutter, offset pallet knife, paper cornet, 8-in. (20-cm) cake board, parchment paper square 6 in. (15 cm):

1. Spread tempered chocolate on a marble table. Be sure the chocolate is spread to an even thickness.

2. Once the chocolate is beginning to set, test with the round cutter. The chocolate should peel off the marble and still be flexible.

3. To scrape the petals, hold the side of the cutter closest to you with both hands. Pull the cutter toward you while pressing down firmly. Lifting the cutter up will create a tight curl; holding the back end down will create a more open curl. A tight curl is needed for the center; the remaining curls will need to be open. Continue scraping the chocolate.

4. Let the curls crystallize before assembling the flower.

5. Place the parchment square on the cake board and pipe a dot of chocolate to attach the flower center.

6. Begin building the flower around the center with small tighter curls, eventually opening to the larger curls. Pipe chocolate on the paper to attach the petals.

7. Once the chocolate has crystallized, remove the flower from the paper before spraying with colored cocoa butter.

FIGURE 13.18a–d

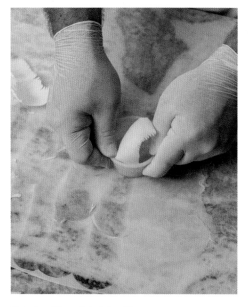

Scraping the petals (step 2)

Showing the scraped petals

Beginning to assemble the flower (step 6)

The airbrushed finished flower

Additional Chocolate Techniques

Chocolate Rocks Creating texture on a showpiece that is primarily smooth adds visual appeal to the piece. Chocolate Rocks, also referred to as chocolate concrete, adds color and texture to the piece. The inclusion of sugar is acceptable for competition use, since sugar is an ingredient in chocolate. To produce chocolate cement, the mixture is cast into a mold and then scuffed to reveal the texture of the granulated sugar. For rocks, the mixture is rolled to an even thickness. Once the mixture has crystallized, it is broken into pieces and scuffed, bringing out the texture.

Chocolate Branches Creating **organic forms** in chocolate pieces can be challenging. Organic forms are those with a natural look or flowing or curving appearance. There are no commercial molds available to shape chocolate into twists and curves. These chocolate branches are easily made using equipment in every kitchen.

Gelatin Molds

A showpiece can be built without the use of molds. However, there is a place and time for molds. Custom molds take time to order and there is a price associated with them. A quick, temporary mold can be created using gelatin. These molds are usually good for two moldings—then they will begin to lose shape. Gelatin molds can used to cast three-dimensional molds of figurines or bottles. Castings can also be made from shapes and placed inside molds to create a negative impression. Gelatin molds provide the pastry chef a way to practice molding before moving on to working with more expensive silicones.

Issue	Cause/Solution
When molding chocolate spheres with colored cocoa butter, the color does not release from the mold.	1. The cocoa butter was not tempered when applied to the mold. Temper the cocoa butter before spraying 2. The chocolate was too cool to release the cocoa butter. Use tempered chocolate that is at the higher end of the tempered range.
When making chocolate cigarettes the chocolate sticks to scraper instead of rolling up.	The chocolate has not set enough. Wait 30 seconds and try again.
Cocoa butter spray on a showpiece begins to bloom after several weeks.	The chocolate spray was not tempered and has bloomed. Temper spray before applying.
When kneading modeling chocolate there is a gritty texture.	The cocoa butter was not fully emulsified in the modeling chocolate. 1. Cool the chocolate before adding the syrup. 2. Table the mixture longer to ensure emulsification.
Modeling chocolate is soft.	There is not enough cocoa butter in the chocolate. Use a higher cocoa percentage chocolate, or add some additional cocoa butter.
When spraying velvet spray the spray comes off of the chocolate.	1. The chocolate was too cold when spraying. Take out of the freezer sooner. 2. The spray was applied too heavily, and it flakes off. Spray less chocolate the next time.
Chocolate pastillage is dry and not coming together in the mixer.	Add a small amount of water to pull the dough together.
Chocolate pastillage is too sticky.	1. The liquid may have been too hot when added, just warm to dissolve the gelatin. 2. The recipe was not scaled accurately. Add additional potato starch to get proper consistency.
Chocolate pastillage has small lumps.	Gelatin was not bloomed and dissolved properly.

Recipes

Cocoa Butter Spray

Yield: 10 oz (300 g)

Portions: 1

Portion size: 10 oz (300 g)

Yield description: 1 portion at 10 oz (300 g)

Ingredients	U.S.	Metric
Milk, White, or Dark Chocolate	7.1 oz	200 g
Cocoa Butter	3.5 oz	100 g

Procedure

1. Combine chocolate and cocoa butter, and melt.
2. Strain through a warmed chinois; this will prevent the sprayer from becoming clogged.
3. Cool to 88°F (31°C), spray is ready to use.

Modeling Chocolate

Yield: 3 lb 4 oz (1500 g)

Portions: 1

Portion size: 3 lb 4 oz (1500 g)

Yield description: 1 portion at 3 lb 4 oz (1500 g)

Ingredients	U.S.	Metric
Dark Chocolate 63%	2 lb 3 oz	1000 g
Sugar	4.4 oz	125 g
Water	2.6 oz	75 g
Glucose Syrup	10.6 oz	300 g

Procedure

1. Combine sugar and water in a saucepan.
2. Melt chocolate and cool to 84°F (29°C). The cooler the chocolate is, the better the emulsification between the syrup and chocolate.
3. Heat the sugar and water to simmer; be sure all sugar is dissolved. Add the glucose syrup.
4. Combine the syrup with the melted chocolate and stir.
5. Pour the modeling chocolate onto a marble surface and table in the same method as tempering. This cools the modeling paste quickly and promotes crystallization.
6. After the modeling chocolate has been tabled and cooled sufficiently, wrap tightly in plastic wrap.
7. Rest modeling chocolate for 2 hours at room temperature to fully crystallize.

Dark Food Processor Roll Outs

Yield: 15 oz (450 g)

Portions: 1

Portion size: 15 oz (450 g)

Yield description: 1 portion at 15 oz (450 g)

Ingredients	U.S.	Metric
Cocoa Powder	10.6 oz	300 g
Cocoa Butter	5.3 oz	150 g

Note: This formula produces a rollout that is stronger than the straight chocolate rollout method.

Procedure

1. Combine cocoa powder and cocoa butter in a food processor.
2. Mix until the friction of the food processor melts the cocoa butter. At this point, it will still be tempered.
3. Roll out to desired thickness and shape.

Chocolate Pastillage

Yield: 2 lb 8 oz (1155 g)

Portions: 1

Portion size: 2 lb 8 oz (1155 g)

Yield description: 1 portion at 2 lb 8 oz (1155 g)

Ingredients	U.S.	Metric
Powdered Sugar	1 lb 10 oz	735 g
Potato Starch	4.4 oz	125 g
Cocoa Powder	4.8 oz	135 g
Gelatin Sheets	7 each	7 each
Cold Water	4.2 oz	120 g
Glucose Syrup	0.9 oz	25 g
White Vinegar	0.5 oz	15 g
Additional Potato Starch for Dusting		

Note: Chocolate pastillage is suitable for display pieces. It is not approved for use in most competitions. Refer to the rules before using.

Procedure

1. Bloom gelatin in the cold water specified in the recipe.
2. Combine powdered sugar, potato starch, and cocoa powder and sift.
3. Combine the gelatin and water mixture with glucose syrup and vinegar in a saucepan.
4. Warm gelatin mixture to dissolve gelatin, do not overheat.
5. Place dry ingredients in a mixer with paddle attachment.
6. While mixing on low, add wet ingredients to dry ingredients; mix until combined.
7. Remove the mixture from the bowl and knead on a table dusted with potato starch.
8. Wrap pastillage tightly in plastic wrap, then in a damp towel and again in plastic wrap to prevent drying.
9. Allow pastillage to rest overnight before using.

Chocolate Rocks

Yield: 1 lb 12 oz (800 g)

Portions: 1

Portion size: 1 lb 12 oz (800 g)

Yield description: 1 portion at 1 lb 12 oz (800 g)

Ingredients	U.S.	Metric
Dark Chocolate	14.1 oz	400 g
Granulated Sugar	14.1 oz	400 g

Procedure

1. Combine melted dark chocolate and granulated sugar.
2. Cast into a mold or roll out between parchment paper to a uniform thickness; allow to crystallize.
3. Unmold and use a small wood rasp to scuff the chocolate.

FIGURE 13.19a–b

1. Spreading the chocolate mixture

2. Scuffing the chocolate to reveal the texture

Chocolate Branches

Yield: 15 oz (450 g)

Portions: 1

Portion size: 15 oz (450 g)

Yield description: 1 portion at 15 oz (450 g)

Ingredients	U.S.	Metric
Cocoa Powder	10.6 oz	300 g
Cocoa Butter, melted	5.3 oz	150 g

Procedure

1. Create a mold for the branch using a cylinder; size will vary, depending on the final size needed.
2. Place plastic wrap on the cylinder and secure with tape.
3. Combine cocoa powder and melted cocoa butter, and place in a pastry bag.
4. Pipe mixture over the plastic wrap in multiple passes.
5. Let the mixture crystallize for 2 hours at room temperature before moving.

FIGURE 13.20a–b

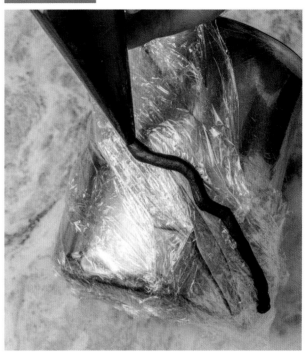

Piping the mixture (step 4)

Finished branch

Gelatin Mold

Yield: 2 lb 5.3 oz (1110 g)

Portions: 1

Portion size: 7 oz (210 g)

Yield description: 1 portion at 7 oz (210 g)

Ingredients	U.S.	Metric
Gelatin Powder	5.9 oz	170 g
Sugar	7.4 oz	210 g
Glucose	1.8 oz	50 g
Water	1 lb 7 oz	680 g

Note: If a firmer mold is needed, gelatin can be increased; to make the mold softer, decrease the amount of gelatin. The gelatin mold can be melted down and reused.

Procedure

1. Combine sugar and gelatin.
2. Add glucose to water and whisk in gelatin.
3. Bloom for 10 to 15 minutes; cover with plastic wrap.
4. Heat gelatin in a double boiler until liquid.
5. Pour gelatin mixture into mold and refrigerate for 5 to 15 minutes. This will depend on the size of the mold.
6. Unmold and allow gelatin to warm to room temperature before filling with chocolate.Troubleshooting for Chocolate Work

FIGURE 13.21a–d

1. Casting the gelatin

2. Removing the molded piece

3. Filling the gelatin mold with chocolate

4. Finished pieces made from gelatin mold

Key Terms

Garnish

Structure

Focal point

Optimal viewing position (OVP)

Cutout method

Modeling chocolate

Food processor modeling chocolate

Chablon

Organic forms

Questions for Review

1. What is the difference between optimal viewing position and focal point?

2. What is the function of a chocolate garnish?

3. When designing a showpiece, why is it important to assemble a scale model from cardboard?

4. What is the role of the base of a showpiece?

5. What are the advantages and disadvantages of using chocolate to create a showpiece?

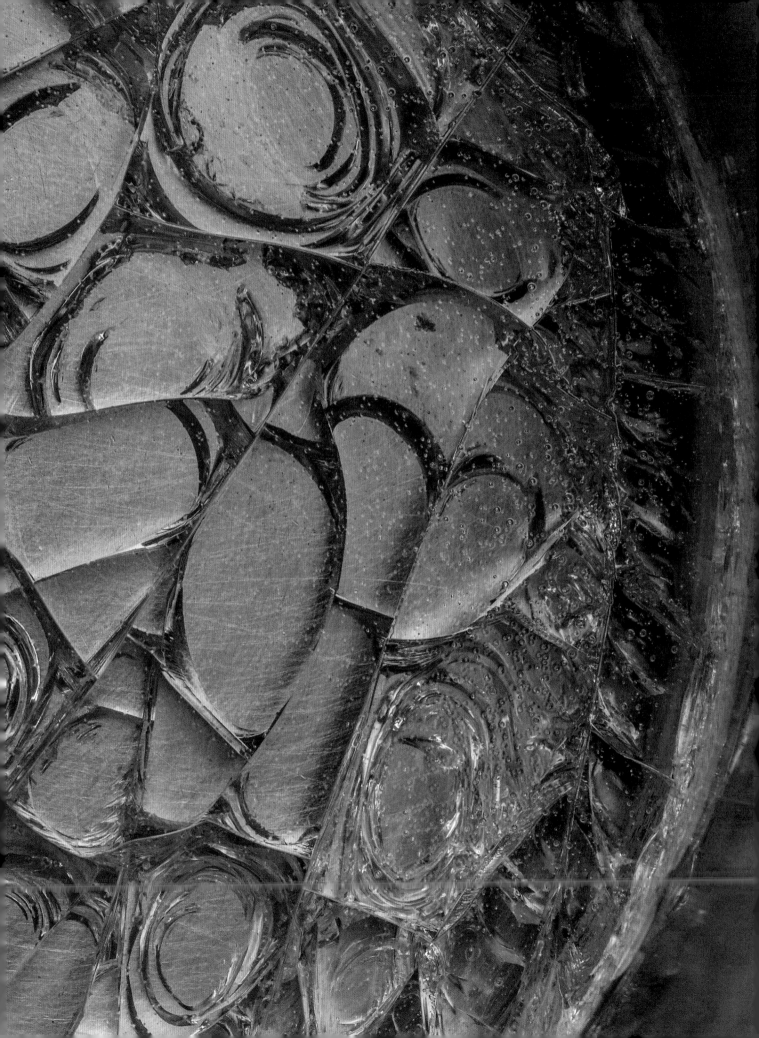

CHAPTER 14

Sugar Work

Dale Chihuly, the most celebrated glassmaker in the United States, was quoted saying, "I'm an artist, a designer, a craftsman, interior designer, half architect. There's no one name that fits me very well." Sugar work closely resembles glass work, and Chihuly's work can be referenced for innovative ideas in glass that have been replicated in sugar. Pastry chefs are more than just chefs—they must be chef, artist, designer, architect, innovator, student, and teacher all at the same time.

LEARNING OBJECTIVES

After reading this chapter, you should be able to:

1. **Cook** sugar for casting, pulling, and blowing.
2. **Make** crystallized sugar and bubble sugar.
3. **Assemble** a showpiece from pastillage.
4. **Demonstrate** how to make a sugar rose.
5. **Assemble** a sugar showpiece.
6. **Demonstrate** how to cast, pull, and blow sugar.

Introduction to Sugar Work

Artistic showpieces constructed from sugar bear a strong resemblance to a sculpture made from glass. Warmed sugar can be cast into forms, blown with air, or pulled and shaped by hand. Sugar work can be found on elaborate competition showpieces, hotel lobby displays, or used as a garnish on pastries. A small garnish on a plated dessert or a large showpiece, this fragile medium will capture the attention of the guest and demonstrate the skill and artistry of the pastry chef.

Sugar as a Medium for Sculptures and Garnishes

Sugar work is used primarily for decorative showpieces, but it also can serve the function of a garnish on pastries. Thin, wispy hoops, ribbons, or even sugar roses can be used to decorate wedding cakes and plated desserts. There are many forms of sugar that can be used for sugar work. Granulated sugar is used to create the cast, blown, crystallized, and pulled components, while powdered sugar is used to make pastillage.

Introducing textures into the sugar work can be achieved through the use of crystalline sugar, pressed sugar, propagated sugar crystals, or even pressed brown sugar. The most important area to consider when working with sugar is moisture. Many of the mediums used for sugar work are **hygroscopic**, meaning they can readily absorb moisture from the air and direct contact with water. High humidity will cause the sugar to become sticky and cause the sugar to become dull and hazy, which could ultimately lead to the structural failure of the piece.

Cooking Sugar

In order to work with sugar, it must first be cooked. When it comes to showpieces, cooking sugar holds as much importance as chocolate tempering. An inability to do both makes it difficult to create the piece. Cooking sugar is not as easy as dropping a thermometer into the pan and following directions. Mise en place of ingredients and equipment will facilitate the cooking of sugar and assembling of a showpiece.

Guidelines

1. Cooked sugar is extremely hot and can cause serious burns, so it is critical to use extreme caution when working with sugar. It is recommended to wear gloves when working with sugar. The gloves can easily be removed if hot sugar gets on your hands.

2. Thoroughly clean all equipment and surfaces that will be used for cooking and working with the sugar.

3. Calibrate the thermometer to ensure the sugar is cooked to the proper temperature.

Ingredients

Sugar

Sugar purity and cleanliness are two factors that must be considered when preparing to cook sugar. Granulated sugar is available from two sources: cane and beet. While both are sucrose, the higher quality and more pure sugar is cane and should be selected for cooking. The storage of the sugar in the shop contributes to the cleanliness. A dry-ingredient storage bin containing granulated sugar will also contain trace amounts of flours and other products in the pastry shop. These contaminants could cause the sugar to crystallize or discolor during cooking. A separate storage area for sugar used for cooking is recommended.

Granulated sugar is the low-cost alternative to using isomalt. When working with sugar, avoid overheating the sugar under the heat lamp or working it too long. The sugar is less forgiving than isomalt, and is prone to crystallize under these conditions. Crystallized sugar has a cloudy appearance and will begin to form large sugar crystals. As the sugar crystallizes the once pliable warm sugar will become solid even when warmed, this sugar should be discarded.

Isomalt

Isomalt is a sugar alcohol that is resistant to humidity and crystallization. It was first used as a bulking agent in sugar-free candies. Isomalt has half the sweetness of granulated sugar, but performs the same physical function as sugar in a recipe.

Resistance to crystallization and humidity make it ideal for sugar work. Isomalt can be cooked to higher temperatures and maintain a clear or pure white due to its resistance to browning. All of these benefits come at a cost, as isomalt is considerably more expensive than granulated sugar. However, its benefits outweigh the cost.

Cooking time and amount of water may need to be adjusted to ensure all crystals are fully dissolved during cooking. Be careful when increasing the quantity of water because boiling the isomalt for an extended period of time will make the isomalt brittle.

Water is the only additional ingredient added to the isomalt. It does not require any glucose syrup or tartaric acid solution. When using isomalt, the same formula is used for pulling, blowing, and casting. Another advantage of using isomalt is that it can be cooked repeatedly. If a batch cooked for pulling contains crystals, more water can be added to this sugar and it can be cooked again with no loss of quality.

Isomalt is cooked slightly higher than sugar, and will be more liquid when hot. Additional cooling time is necessary for isomalt, but the same honey-like consistency should be used to determine when to cast. All working techniques that are done with sugar can be done the same way with isomalt.

Water

Water that is high in mineral content will discolor the cooked sugar or isomalt. As the water evaporates during cooking, the minerals concentrate and may give the sugar a yellow tint. Using distilled water will help to prevent this from occurring. Distilled water has many of the impurities and nutrients removed from the water.

The formulas in this chapter contain specific amounts of water and sugar or isomalt. The amount of water may need to be increased or decreased, depending on the strength of the burner. Cooking sugar is not about speed. It is important that all the crystals dissolve. By increasing the amount of water, the cooking time will be extended. When working with granulated sugar, cooking time should not exceed 20 minutes. The longer the sugar boils, the more likely it is to have a yellow tint.

Glucose Syrup

Glucose syrup is an inverted sugar produced through the hydrolysis (breaking down) of starch from wheat, corn, or potato. The resulting syrup is used to prevent crystallization in the cooked sugar. Too much glucose syrup can have a detrimental effect on the sugar, making it soft. When cooking sugar formulas with glucose syrup, it must be added after the sugar is dissolved in the water. If added too early, the sugar will not dissolve. It is not necessary to add glucose to isomalt.

Tartaric Acid

Acid is used when cooking granulated sugar to prevent crystallization and soften the sugar to ease pulling. Including too much acid will make the sugar soft and sticky; too little will make the sugar brittle. **Tartaric acid** is used when cooking sugar. The reaction of the acid is immediate, and the acid can be added at the end of cooking. Tartaric acid is available in a white powder form and must be dissolved in water prior to use.

Tartaric acid is not the same as cream of tartar. Cream of tartar is slower acting and must be added at the beginning of cooking. It is not necessary to add tartaric acid to isomalt.

Color

Food coloring is added to the sugar during cooking. Liquid food colorings contain acid as a preservative. The additional acid from the food coloring can weaken the cooked sugar. Water-soluble powder colors are available in a wide variety of colors. The powder cannot be directly added to the sugar, it must be dissolved in water or alcohol first.

Mise en Place for Cooking Sugar

Cooking sugar takes a great deal of preparation and attention to the process. Mise en place of the workstation and ingredients will help to ensure a successfully cooked batch of sugar. This includes thoroughly cleaning all equipment and work stations. Any contaminants, such as flour or grease can cause the sugar to crystallize or become dull.

Induction versus Gas Stoves

Many kitchens contain both induction and gas stoves, and there is a great deal of discussion about which is better for cooking sugar. Induction technology requires special pans in order to work, and these burners are more powerful than gas stoves. Induction burners provide a constant heat source, and a great deal of temperature control can be achieved.

The heat of an induction burner is focused only on the bottom of the pan and does not heat the sides, which is good and bad. Heating the sides of the pan can result in caramelizing the sugar because the thin wall of the saucepan quickly transfers the heat. Although too much heat up the side of the pan is not good, some heat is needed. A gas stove that heats the sides of the pan will help dissolve sugar crystals along the sides of the pan.

The type of heat source used to cook the sugar is not as important as focusing on the technique of cooking. While the heat source and type of pan used may have an impact on how the sugar cooks, the pastry chef ultimately controls the outcome. When working with new equipment, conduct test batches to see what works best, check and record heat settings and times. Once the cooking of the sugar has been mastered, the focus can be placed on the techniques of pulling and blowing.

Casting Sugar

Cast sugar is made using granulated sugar, water, and glucose syrup. There is no additional acid added to cast pieces to ensure these pieces are solid. Cast pieces provide the structural support to the showpiece and do not require the flexibility needed for pulled and blown pieces.

Procedures for Casting Sugar

Cast sugar is used to create base and structural elements for showpieces. Sugar can be cast into many shapes, using silicone noodles, metal bars, flexipans, silicone molds, and metal cake rings. To create a bottom of the mold, these forms are placed on silicone mats or vinyl sheets.

It is important that the casting surface is flat and level, so the casting is the same thickness the entire length of the piece. Pieces that are cast flat can be rewarmed and bent to give more dimension. To create more dramatic effects, using multiple colors when casting can enhance cast components, creating a marbleized design. Inlays of airbrushed pastillage can be placed inside clear cast sugar, creating a design that looks as if it is trapped in glass. This technique also gives the pastillage a shiny finish.

Casting Method

Equipment needed: Rubber gloves, vinyl sheet, parchment paper, blowtorch, frame:

1. Place a sheet of parchment paper under the silicone mold, vinyl sheet, or silpat. If a silicone mold is not available, use metal bars of metal cake rings to create the desired shape.

2. Cook the sugar and cool to a honey-like consistency, which will ensure that it is bubble free. If the sugar is too cold, it will not flow into the mold evenly and will trap air and create bubbles in the sugar. Pour the sugar into the mold, starting at one end. Slowly pour the sugar until the mold is filled.

3. Quickly pass a blowtorch over the top of the piece, which will remove any surface bubbles.

4. Allow the piece to cool completely; a slightly warm piece will bend a little before cracking. Once the sugar has set, a fan can be used to shorten cooling time.

5. Carefully remove the silicone mold from the sugar. If using a silpat or vinyl sheet, slide the vinyl to the edge of the table and pull down. The vinyl will peel off of the sugar while leaving the sugar flat. Turn the vinyl sheet and remove the other half of the cast piece from the vinyl. Trying to lift the sugar off of the vinyl will break the sugar.

FIGURE 14.1a–c

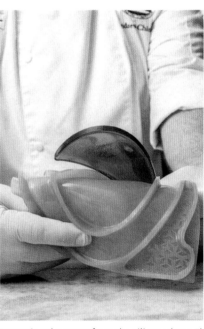

| Pouring the sugar into the mold (step 2) | Blow torching to remove the bubbles (step 3) | Removing the sugar from the silicone (step 5) |

Casting into Vinyl Tubing Method

Casting sugar into vinyl tubing creates a perfect cylindrical tube of clear sugar. This method can be used to create hoops and cylinders used for decoration or support. When cutting and shaping temperature is critical. If the sugar is too hot, the tube will lose shape. Too cold and it will snap, this can be remedied by placing the tube under the warming lamp.

Equipment needed: ⅝ in. inside diameter vinyl tubing, masking tape, pitcher, utility knife, rubber gloves, 8-in. cake ring, parchment paper, silpat:

1. Warm the vinyl tube under a heat lamp until it becomes pliable. Warming the tube will help the sugar to flow better.
2. Tape both ends of the tube to the side of the worktable, make sure it is secured well.
3. Transfer the cooked sugar to a pitcher. For this technique, the sugar needs to be thinner than other casting methods.
4. Pour the sugar into the tube from one end, continuing until the tube is full.
5. Let the sugar cool until the tube is still flexible but not hard, at this point the sugar will not run out of the ends of the tube.
6. Remove the tube from the table, use the box cutter and cut along the length of the tube.
7. Remove the sugar from the tube and shape around the cake ring.
8. Allow the ring to cool completely before moving.
9. Cut the tube to the desired length with a hot knife.

FIGURE 14.2a–d

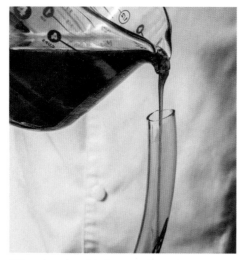

Filling the tube with the sugar (step 4)

Cutting the vinyl tube (step 6)

Shaping the sugar (step 7)

The finished cooled tube

Casting into Sugar Method

Creating larger pieces and new shapes can sometimes be challenging when just starting out working with sugar. Granulated sugar can be used to create a variety of organic shapes, with the texture of the granulated sugar.

Equipment needed: stainless steel bowl or hotel pan, granulated sugar, rubber gloves:

1. Fill the stainless steel bowl ¾ full with granulated sugar.
2. Create a form in the sugar using your hand.
3. Cast the liquid sugar.
4. Cover the cast sugar with the granulated sugar; be careful as the cast sugar is extremely hot.
5. Allow the sugar to cool until it is almost solid.
6. Carefully move the cast piece while it is still in the granulated sugar.
7. Let the piece fully cool and remove from granulated sugar.

FIGURE 14.3a–c Casting into sugar:

Creating the shape in the granulated sugar (step 2)

Casting the sugar (step 3)

The finished piece

Bending Cast Sugar Method

Equipment needed: Silpat, warming lamp, form to shape sugar:

1. After the sugar has completely cooled, unmold and transfer to a silpat.
2. Place the silpat and sugar on the warmer or in a 160°F (70°C) oven.
3. As the sugar warms, it will become flexible, while maintaining the shape. The goal is to warm the sugar and keep the clean edges.
4. Place the warmed sugar on the mold, in this case a rolling pin, and cool completely.

FIGURE 14.4a–b Bending cast sugar:

Sugar placed over rolling pin (step 4)

Finished cooled piece

Procedures for Bubble Sugar

Bubble sugar can be produced through casting or by melting isomalt in the oven. Both methods give slightly different looks. Bubble sugar provides a filler to showpieces to create volume, the look of water to an underwater themed piece, or as abstract leaves.

Bubble Sugar Casting Method

Equipment needed: 2 half sheets of parchment paper, rubber gloves:

1. Crumple up one of the sheets of parchment and flatten out. The creases in the paper will trap the air that will form the bubbles.
2. Pour sugar along one side of the crumpled paper.
3. Lift the paper so the sugar runs down; hold this over the other piece of parchment in case some of the sugar drips off.
4. Let the sugar cool, then remove from the paper.

FIGURE 14.5a–c Bubble sugar casting:

Pouring the sugar on the crumpled paper (step 2)

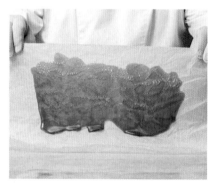

Lifting the paper (step 3)

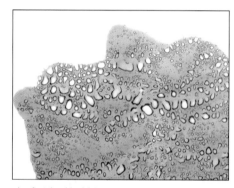

The finished bubble sugar

Bubble Sugar Oven Method

Equipment needed: 2 half silpats, half sheet pan:

1. Place one silpat on the sheet pan and sprinkle with isomalt. At this point color can be added by very lightly dusting the isomalt with powder food coloring.

FIGURE 14.6a–b Bubble sugar oven method:

Sprinkle isomalt onto silpat-lined sheet pan (step 1)

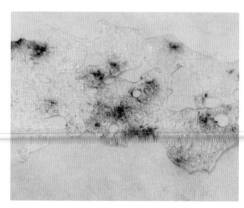

Finished bubble sugar

2. Place the other silpat on top.

3. Bake in the oven at 350°F (175°C) for 10 minutes. Check to see that the isomalt has all melted. If not, you will be able to see crystals through the silpat. If there are still crystals, place back in the oven for 2 more minutes.

4. Allow the isomalt to cool before removing silpat.

Pulling and Blowing Sugar

Pulled and blown sugar is manipulated by hand to create delicate ribbons and flowers. Properly cooked sugar will maintain a brilliant shine and be free from crystals. This formula is the same with the addition of the tartaric acid solution, which helps to increase the flexibility of the sugar when it is warm and prevent crystallization.

When cooking sugar for pulling and blowing, it is important that the sugar cook for approximately 20 minutes. The quantity of water and intensity of the heat can be adjusted to reach the correct time. The quality of the sugar will also have an impact on the boiling time. If cooked too quickly, the sugar crystals may not be fully dissolved before reaching the final temperature. Due to the thin nature of pulled sugar elements, crystals can easily be seen. When casting, the cooking time is not as important because these pieces tend to be thicker and opaque.

Satinizing Sugar

Satinizing is the process of folding air into the sugar. This makes the sugar opaque and creates the shine of **pulled sugar**. After cooking, the sugar is poured onto a silpat-covered marble slab to decrease the cooling time. The cooling starts from the outside edge of the sugar while the middle remains hot. When the edges of the sugar harden slightly, fold them into the center of the hot sugar. Leaving this outer edge to cool completely before folding in can result in sugar crystals in the pulled sugar. It is difficult to melt these crystals once they form; cooling the mass of sugar in a uniform way will prevent this.

Sugar that is not satinized will have a glassy appearance. In the same way, overworking the sugar or folding in too much air will cause the sugar to have a dull finish. The cooler the sugar is, the better for satinizing. As the sugar cools it retains the air better, creating a more reflective sugar. All colors can be satinized with the exception of black—incorporating air into black sugar creates gray.

Satinizing Method

Equipment needed: Rubber gloves, scissors:

1. Fold the sugar over onto itself on the silpat to cool. Continue folding until the sugar no longer moves but is still soft.

2. Roll the sugar into a cylinder.

3. Pick up the ends of the sugar, place one hand at each end.

4. Pull the sugar out from the center, fold in half and twist.

5. Pull again out from the center, fold, and twist again. Continue doing this until the sugar is opaque and shiny.

6. Lay the sugar out flat and cut with scissors; completely cool the sugar.

7. Store the sugar in zippered plastic bags and reserve for pulling or blowing.

FIGURE 14.7a–d

Folding the sugar (step 1)

Pulling the sugar (step 4)

Twisting to incorporate air (step 4)

Finished satinized sugar

Pulled Sugar

Pulling sugar is an art form that relies on touch to determine when the sugar is the correct temperature for creating ribbons, flowers, and other decorations. Practicing and perfecting the skills are truly the only way to master them.

Sugar Ribbon Method

A sugar ribbon requires multiple colors of sugar to be heated to the same consistency. It is critical that the different colors be consistent in feel so they will stretch at the same rate. It is a delicate balance of temperature, warm enough to be pliable and connect when folded over, but not too hot that the sugar loses the sheen. Work with single colored ribbons to get the feel for temperature and learning the process. Once a good single-colored ribbon can be made, add more colors.

Equipment needed: Heat lamp, knife, blowtorch, wet towel, rubber gloves:

1. Roll five pieces of colored satinized sugar into cylinders approximately 1 in. (3 cm) in diameter and 5 in. (12.5 cm) long, and one piece of black sugar the same length and ⅓ in. (1 cm) in diameter.
2. Lay the pieces side by side and connect them.
3. Pick up the ends of the ribbon, place one hand at each end.
4. Stretch the ribbon out from the center.
5. Fold the ribbon in half and connect in the middle.
6. Repeat the stretching and folding two more times.
7. Pull the ribbon out to the desired thickness and lay it flat on a marble table.

8. Using the blowtorch heat the knife to cut the ribbon. The knife must be hot enough to cut through the sugar without discoloring the sugar or sticking. Wipe the knife on the wet towel between cuts to clean the blade.

9. Rewarm the ribbon under the heat lamp, shape as needed.

FIGURE 14.8a–d

Lining up the sugar (step 2)

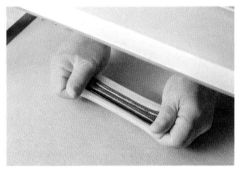

Pulling out the strands (step 4)

Cutting with hot knife (step 8)

Assorted ribbons

Sugar Rose Method

When making a sugar rose refer to a picture of a real rose. The goal is to capture the thin edges, the shape, positioning and beauty of how the petals come together to form the flower. When pulling a sugar rose be sure that each layer has odd numbers, to keep the rose round. When moving from one row of petals to the next the petals should increase in size and become more rounded.

Equipment needed: Sugar warmer, silpat, scissors, alcohol burner:

1. Shape a piece of sugar into a teardrop shape to form the center of the rose.
2. To pull the petals, stretch a thin edge on the sugar using two hands; this will give the flower a delicate look.
3. Pinch the sugar between the thumb and index finger and pull out.
4. Cut the sugar off and position around the flower center.
5. The next row is composed of three petals, pulled slightly wider than the previous row. The right edge of each of these petals will be curled back slightly.
6. Connect the petals by slightly melting the bottom over the burner.
7. The outer set of petals will need five petals. These petals have a more pronounced, cupped shape formed by pressing the petal into the left palm with the right thumb. The top of the petal is pinched in the center and the edges are curled out.
8. Connect the petals by slightly melting the bottom over the burner.

FIGURE 14.9a–d

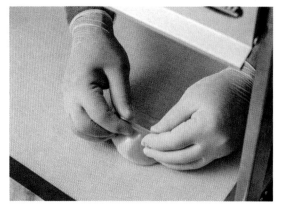

Thinning the edge of the sugar (step 2)

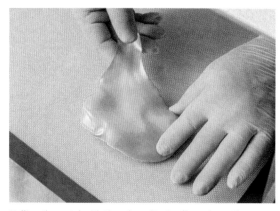

Pulling the petal with thumb and index finger (step 3)

Attaching the petal to the bud (step 4)

One picture showing all the petals and layers of the rose from bud to finished

FIGURE 14.10a–b

Placing the sugar in the press (step 3)

Removing the sugar from the press (step 4)

Pressed Leaves Method

Silicone and metal molds can be used to give pulled sugar texture. These molds can replicate a leaf or create a diamond pattern in the sugar. The extra lines pressed into the pulled sugar create different angled surfaces to refract light. Pulled sugar that will be pressed can be pulled slightly thicker, keeping it warm and flexible while in the press.

Equipment needed: Scissors, mold, warming lamp:

1. To pull the petals, stretch a thin edge on the sugar using two hands.
2. Pull the petal out and cut with scissors to the desired shape.
3. Quickly place the sugar on the press and close the mold; press firmly.
4. Remove the leaf and shape as desired.

Blown Sugar

Blown sugar, the most challenging of the three sugar working techniques, requires the use of a pump to inflate the sugar to create hollow spheres, flowers, figurines, and fruits. When working with blown sugar, it is important to understand the vital role of temperature. It is difficult to state the temperature at which the sugar is ready to be placed on the pump. The complexity of the piece and skill of the pastry chef must also be considered. A piece that is more complex needs to be warmer, to allow for additional working time to shape the sugar. The same holds true with a novice sugar worker—it will take longer to form the sugar and therefore it will need to be warmer. Over time, you will build the skills to work with the sugar at a cooler temperature and retain more of the shine.

Sugar blowing is not just about pumping air into sugar. As the air is blown into the sugar, the pastry chef must shape the sugar. For example placing sugar on a pump and blowing in air will not create a sphere. The air is pumped in slowly into the sugar; carefully watch the sugar to see how it is expanding. Hold the piece at eye level and turn so you can observe all sides. Keeping one hand on the pump and the other on the sugar will help to steady the sugar while still being able to add more air if needed.

The sugar may start to slowly bulge on one side. This is due to the sugar being slightly thinner and/or warmer. The thinner the sugar, the less resistance there is for the air to push it outward. To control this, place a hand over the bulge. The temperature of your hand is lower than that of the sugar and it begins to cool the sugar making it expand less. If the sugar is too cool, it can be warmed slightly under the heat lamp to make it more flexible. After the piece has been shaped, cool it completely using a fan or hair dryer that has a cool setting.

Placing Sugar on the Pump Method

Before placing the sugar on the pump, it is critical that the sugar temperature be equalized. This can be done by folding the sugar to make sure the internal temperature matches the external temperature. A consistent temperature will cause the sugar to expand at a more even rate.

Equipment needed: Warming lamp, sugar pump, fan, scissors, rubber gloves, alcohol burner:

1. Fold the sugar onto itself to equalize the temperature and smooth the outside of the sugar.
2. Cut a ball off the edge of the sugar with room-temperature scissors (hot scissors will stick to the sugar).
3. Press a finger into the bottom of the ball (cut end). Pushing too far will cause a thin spot to form at the top of the sugar.

4. Warm the opening of the sugar over the alcohol burner and attach the sugar. Do not push the end of the tube all the way into the sugar, as the tube will become clogged and the sugar will not expand. Quickly press the sugar onto the tube.

5. Pump a little air into the sugar to be sure it is sealed.

FIGURE 14.11a–c Placing sugar on the pump:

Cutting the ball of sugar (step 2)

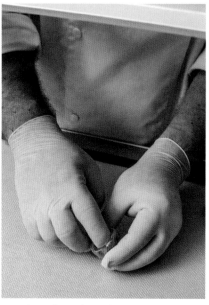

Inserting a finger (step 3)

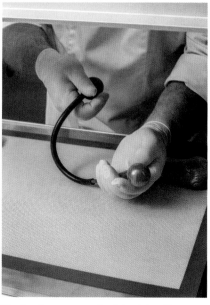

Placing the sugar on the tube (step 4)

Blowing a Sphere Method

A sphere may look like a simple shape, but learning to blow a sphere is a foundational element of blowing sugar. The simplicity of the shape makes it challenging, as any inconsistencies in the sphere can be easily noted. The goal is to create a perfectly round sphere with walls of even thickness. More advanced blown forms like fruit also start out as spheres.

Equipment needed: Warming lamp, sugar pump, fan, scissors, rubber gloves, alcohol burner:

1. After checking that the sugar is completely sealed on the tube, slowly pump a little air into the sugar.

2. Check the sugar to see if it is expanding equally in all directions. If the sugar is expanding too much in one area, cool it by placing your hand on the warm spot. Sugar that is too thin will eventually cool and pop when more air is added. If the sugar is too thin, remove it from the pump and start again.

3. When the sphere is expanding equally, pump in some more air.

4. Using your hand, begin pushing the sphere away from the tube; be careful to not pinch the sugar close by the tube.

5. Use your hand to round the sphere.

6. Continue pumping air into the sugar until the desired size has been reached.

7. Completely cool the sphere.

8. To remove the sphere, warm the sugar near to the tube and cut with scissors.

FIGURE 14.12a–d Blowing a sphere:

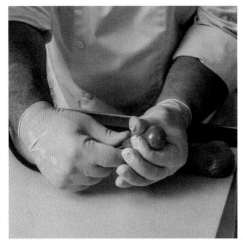

Sliding the sugar up from the pump (step 4)

Using a hand to round the sphere (step 5)

Continue filling the sphere with air (step 6)

Finished sphere

Blown Sugar Flower Center

Blown sugar can be used to add volume to a showpiece. These larger pieces carry a visual weight from the size of the piece. As a result of being hollow, they do not carry any physical weight—therefore, the impact on the physical structure of the showpiece is low.

Equipment needed: Warming lamp, sugar pump, fan, scissors, rubber gloves, alcohol burner, blowtorch, knife, wet towel:

1. After checking that the sugar is completely sealed on the tube, slowly pump a little air into the sugar.

2. Shape the sugar into a cylinder on the tube; add a small amount of air.

3. Pinch the top of the sphere about a quarter of the way down the cylinder. The sugar should now look like a bowling pin.

4. Add some more air. While doing this, continue to work the sugar away from the pump. Pulling the piece away from the pump will develop an elegant long piece. Adding air and not pulling will result in a more rounded shape.

5. Hold the tube in one hand, and with the other pull the pinched piece out to elongate the thinner portion.

6. Quickly cut the tip of the sugar off. The remaining heat will seal the sugar.

7. Continue pumping in air until the desired size is reached.

8. Remove the sugar from the tube and cut the thinner section with a hot knife.

FIGURE 14.13a–d

Elongating the sugar (step 3)

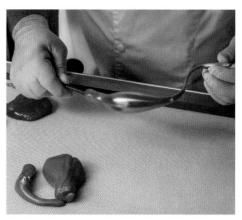

Stretching out the pinched piece (step 5)

The blown piece attached to the blowing tube

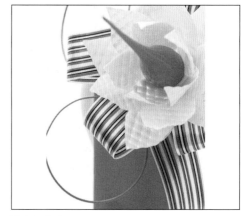

Finished piece

Crystalline Sugar

Sugar showpieces are characterized by their clarity, shine, and bright colors. Granulated sugar and **propagated crystals** are ways to add texture and color to a showpiece. Granulated sugar can be added to a showpiece by folding into pulled sugar, coating pulled or cast sugar, or by pressing.

Pressed Sugar

Pressed sugar closely resembles the texture of a sugar cube. Granulated sugar is combined with a small amount of water and pressed into a mold and allowed to dry.

Propagated Crystals

Propagated crystals are formed by submerging an item into a sugar syrup for several days or weeks. A blown piece of sugar or a sculpted piece of shortening is coated in sugar and placed in the sugar syrup. The submerged item forms a seed and attracts more sugar crystals to it. Over a period of time the water in the container evaporates, increasing the sugar concentration and causing the crystals to form at a faster rate. When the finished product is removed from the syrup and allowed to dry it resembles rock sugar and can be used to decorate a showpiece.

Pastillage

Pastillage is used to create showpieces as well as accent pieces for a sugar showpiece. What makes a sugar showpiece beautiful and attractive is the transparency of the cast pieces and the sheen of pulled elements. Pastillage is used to add different textures and opacity to a sugar showpiece through the use of very thin decorative elements with a flat finish. It is pure white and can be easily painted or airbrushed. Pastillage can be rolled with a rolling pin and cut, texturized, shaped on curved forms, hand rolled, or pressed into molds. Before use, the pastillage must be fully dried. Thin pieces can dry within an hour, while larger pieces may take days.

Pastillage Cutout Method

Equipment needed: X-acto knife, vodka, potato starch sachet, templates, rolling pin:

1. Knead the pastillage to soften. This will make it easier to roll.
2. Roll the pastillage to the desired thickness. Pastillage is very strong when dry. Decorative elements can be rolled thin and will dry quickly.
3. Dip the X-acto knife in the vodka and shake off excess. The alcohol will help the blade to cut cleanly; any excess left on the pastillage will evaporate quickly.
4. Cut the pastillage using the templates.
5. Place the pastillage on foam to dry, or over molds to create bends.
6. Pastillage can be sanded if needed.

FIGURE 14.15a–c Pastillage cutout method:

 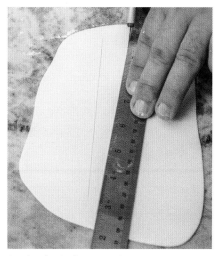 

Rolling (step 2)   Cutting (step 4)   Finished pastillage

FIGURE 14.16a–b Pastillage rollout method:

Rolling (step 2)   Finished assorted rollout shapes

Pastillage Rollout Method

Equipment needed: Paring knife, cake board:

1. Knead the pastillage to soften. This will make it easier to roll.
2. Roll out a small piece of pastillage so it is tapered at one end.
3. Use the cake board toward the end of rolling to remove any marks left from fingers.
4. Trim the end of the pastillage and shape immediately.

Pastillage Rock Method

Pastillage can be used to create shapes other than by rolling and cutting. Sculpting can also be used to shape pastillage. A simple form to sculpt is rocks. More complex figurines and animals can be made as well, but work must be done quickly before the pastillage dries out and begins to crack.

FIGURE 14.17a–d Pastillage rock method:

Pastillage rocks being
airbrushed (step 2)

Water being applied (step 3)

Dipping the rocks (step 5)

Finished piece with rocks

Equipment needed: Airbrush, brush, dipping fork, silpat:

1. Shape pastillage with your hands into smooth river-rock shapes.
2. After the pastillage has dried, airbrush with two to three colors.
3. Apply water to rocks using a paintbrush; allow to dry.
4. Warm up clear sugar, the sugar needs to be hot and free of bubbles.
5. Dip the pastillage into the sugar, using the fork transfer the rock to the silpat.

Assembling Pastillage

Before assembling a pastillage piece, be sure that the pastillage is completely dry and free of any dust from rolling or sanding. There are three methods that can be used to attach pastillage: royal icing, cooked sugar, or pastillage glue. **Royal icing** is a mixture of egg whites and powered sugar that dries hard. In addition to gluing, it can be used for decorative string work or piping on a sugar piece. Microwaving pastillage to a liquid state makes pastillage glue. Both pastillage glue and cooked sugar will set very quickly.

Sculpture Design

Designing a sculpture from sugar is similar to designing a piece from chocolate. Both mediums have several similarities: structural shape, importance of color, focal point, OVP, and incorporating theme. What really sets a sugar piece apart from chocolate is the use of transparent or clear sugar. A strong sugar piece can be created, and using clear sugar will make parts of the piece appear to float while being firmly connected.

Structure Design

Base

The bases of a sugar piece can be made from cast sugar or pressed sugar. The overall height of the piece needs to be considered when creating the base. A tall, slender showpiece with a small base will need enough weight to anchor the piece and prevent it from falling over. For larger pieces, it is important to remember that the base should include elements of the theme and not just be a supporting piece. Hot sugar can be used to attach the showpiece to the display base, providing additional support.

Structure

Sugar pieces follow the same structural shapes as were discussed in Chapter 13 on page 389, J, C, E, S and straight line. There are some differences in how the structure can be assembled, taking advantage of the clarity of the sugar. Rather than casting one large thick piece, multiple panes of sugar can be cast and spaced apart. Using this approach gives the piece the stability and strength needed. It also enhances the design of the piece; the empty space between the cast sugar adds to the lightness of the piece.

Incorporating Design in the Structure

The clarity of the sugar provides another way to incorporate the theme of the showpiece into the structure. Pastillage can be cut, painted, and airbrushed to incorporate theme elements into the structural pieces. Placing silicone molds or vinyl cutouts down before casting the sugar will create a negative impression in the backside of the sugar. Using vinyl will make the design clear; silicone will create small bubbles in the sugar.

Color

When working with color on sugar work, refer to "Color" in Chapter 13 on pages 390–392. The rules of selecting color apply the same way. When working with sugar, many shades of the same color can be used on the same piece. An attractive piece can be created using only white and various shades of pink, this would be difficult to achieve with chocolate colors. Structural pieces can be cast in lighter shades of pink, then moving to darker shades of pink and white within the flowers. When working with color, experiment with the colors each time the piece is practiced to see what works and what does not.

A batch of casting sugar can be colored with a few drops of blue, just giving it a light tint, so it will resemble a pane of glass. Adding additional blue will continue to deepen the color. The sugar can be made opaque by adding titanium dioxide along with the blue. When adding color to pulling sugar, the color must be strong. As the sugar is satinized, the color will lighten. It is better to have dark pulled sugars that can be lightened by mixing with other pulled sugar. White pulled sugar does not have any color added; the air that is worked into the sugar makes it opaque.

FIGURE 14.18 Cast sugar with a lot of blue (top), a piece with a few drops of blue (center), a piece of the blue with titanium dioxide added (bottom)

Assembly

Assembling sugar pieces requires a great deal of care to make sure that the pieces are affixed properly. Sugar pieces are very strong when bonded properly. Both pieces need to be warmed to create a solid fusion.

It is important to consider temperature when attaching sugar pieces. A piece that was made a day prior to assembly or one that is in a cold room will be more fragile than one that was just cast. The heat of a torch is extremely hot compared to a room-temperature piece of sugar. This amount of heat can cause areas of the sugar to expand while others do not—this is called **thermal shock**. The cracks may not be visible but may be heard during assembly. This will weaken the structure of the piece. To prevent this from happening, the pieces can be warmed slightly under a heat lamp.

Assembling Sugar Method

Equipment needed: Silpat, small torch:

1. Place the pieces being assembled on a silpat. When assembling pieces, there may be enough heat to melt a piece and have it stick to the worktable.
2. Test-fit the pieces to see where the sugar will need to be heated.
3. Pull a thread of sugar the length of the pieces being attached.
4. Warm the edge of the sugar and place the pulled sugar thread. This small thread will help to fill any low spots in the seam and make the connection stronger.
5. Heat both pieces of sugar where they will connect. A small butane torch makes it easier to direct the heat directly where it is needed. Overheating the sugar will cause it to drip.
6. Quickly place the warmed areas together; press firmly to make sure the connection is solid. Pressing too hard may crack the sugar.
7. Use a fan to blow cool air on the seam.

Sugar is difficult to work with in humid environments and will not only stick to your gloves but also to itself. Sticky sugar can create the feeling that the pieces are properly attached but then they will fall apart shortly after. When melting sugar to attach a piece, the sugar should begin to bubble but not drip. Doing this with both surfaces will ensure a solid connection.

FIGURE 14.19a–c

Placing the thread on the sugar (step 4)

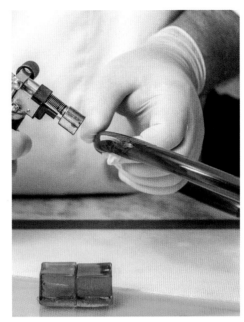

Melting the thread (step 5)

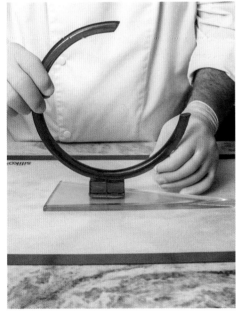

Placing the pieces together (step 6)

Component Inventory

When designing a showpiece, it is important to get the ideas down on paper. After the sketch is completed, the design moves into the next phase. Utilizing different techniques and components in the piece will help to create a more interesting piece.

Component Inventory for Sugar Showpieces

Cast	Pulled	Blown
Pressed Sugar	Vinyl Tubes	Bent
Pastillage	Ribbon	Molded

When designing a sculpture, it is important to take into consideration what is truly needed and what is not. The hardest skill to learn in designing a showpiece is editing. Not every item on the component needs to be included in the design.

Troubleshooting for Sugar Work

Issue	Cause/Solution
Sugar has a yellow tint.	1. The flame was too high and sugar on the edge of the pan caramelized. Use a smaller pan or reduce heat. 2. The sugar cooked for too long. Turn the heat up slightly to reduce cooking time. 3. There were minerals in the water. Use filtered water for cooking sugar.
Sugar is sticky.	1. Too much acid. Decrease amount for next batch. 2. Sugar was not cooked to the correct temperature. Calibrate thermometer and cook another batch.
Sugar is dull.	1. There were impurities in the sugar. Be sure to skim the sugar when cooking. 2. Sugar was too hot when pulled. Allow the sugar to cool more before satinizing.
Crystals can be seen in the sugar.	The sugar did not fully dissolve. Let the syrup sit for 24 hours before cooking.
Sugar piece collapses.	1. Too much acid was added to the sugar. Decrease the amount of acid. 2. Sugar was not cooked to the proper temperature. Calibrate thermometer and cook another batch of sugar.
Sugar is brittle.	1. Not enough acid. Increase the amount of acid. 2. Sugar was cooked too high. Calibrate thermometer and cook another batch of sugar.
Crystals can be seen in isomalt.	1. Isomalt was not cooked long enough. Increase the amount of water and cook the isomalt again. 2. Heat was too high. Reduce heat and cook slower to dissolve crystals.
Isomalt is brittle and hot when pulling.	When cooking, the isomalt boiled too long. Increase the heat and cook the isomalt again.

Recipes

Isomalt

Yield: 2 lb 8 oz (1150 g)

Portions: 1

Portion size: 3 lb 6 oz (1550 g)

Yield Description: 1 portion at 3 lb 6 oz (1550 g)

Ingredients	U.S.	Metric
Isomalt Type M	2 lb 3.3 oz	1000 g
Water	5.3 oz	150 g

Note: Total water can be increased to 9 oz (250 g). When pulling or blowing isomalt, some undissolved crystals may be present during the satinizing of the isomalt. This can result from the isomalt being cooked to quickly. Since all stoves do not have the same intensity, adjustments may need to be made to the level of heat, amount of water, or cooking time. This will ensure that all isomalt crystals have fully dissolved.

Procedure

1. Place water in a heavy-bottom saucepan.
2. Add a small amount of the isomalt and stir until dissolved.
3. Gradually add more isomalt; using this method will cook the isomalt faster than adding it all in the pan at the beginning.
4. Use cold water to clean any isomalt crystals off the sides of the pan.
5. Add food coloring once all isomalt is dissolved.
6. Cook to 330°F (165°C).
7. Immediately shock the pan in ice water to prevent carry overcooking.
8. When the isomalt is free of bubbles and it has a honey-like consistency, it is ready for casting.

Tartaric Acid Solution

Yield: 4 oz (120 g)

Portions: 1

Portion size: 4 oz (120 g)

Yield Description: 1 portion at 4 oz (120 g)

Ingredients	U.S.	Metric
Tartaric Acid Powder	2.1 oz	60 g
Water	2.1 oz	60 g

Note: Tartaric acid solution can easily crystallize. All containers should be thoroughly cleaned before using. After storage, the solution may begin to crystallize. If this occurs, discard the solution.

Procedure

1. Scale the tartaric acid and place in a container.
2. Boil more water than needed, after the water has boiled scale the required quantity directly into the tartaric acid.
3. Store the Tartaric Acid Solution in a glass dropper bottle.

Sugar for Casting

Yield: 3 lb 6 oz (1550 g)

Portions: 1

Portion size: 3 lb 6 oz (1550 g)

Yield Description: 1 portion at 3 lb 6 oz (1550 g)

Ingredients	U.S.	Metric
Granulated Sugar	2 lb 3.3 oz	1000 g
Water	12.3 oz	350 g
Glucose Syrup	7.1 oz	200 g

Procedure

1. Combine sugar and water in a heavy-bottom saucepan. Warm slowly to dissolve sugar.
2. Once the sugar is dissolved add the glucose syrup and continue cooking.
3. Skim the surface with a tea strainer to remove any impurities.
4. Using a clean brush and cold water, clean the sides of the pan to remove any crystals that may have formed.
5. Continue cooking and add color at 285°F (140°C). To create opaque cast sugar, combine titanium dioxide with water and add to the sugar.
6. Cook the syrup to 320°F (160°C).
7. Immediately shock the pan in ice water to prevent carryover cooking.
8. When the sugar is free of bubbles and the sugar has a honey-like consistency, it is ready for casting.

Sugar for Pulling and Blowing

Yield: 3 lb 8 oz (1600 g)

Portions: 1

Portion size: 3 lb 8 oz (1600 g)

Yield description: 1 portion at 3 lb 8 oz (1600 g)

Ingredients	U.S.	Metric
Granulated Sugar	2 lb 3.3 oz	1000 g
Water	14.1 oz	400 g
Glucose Syrup	7.1 oz	200 g
Tartaric Acid Solution	10 drops	10 drops

Procedure

1. Combine sugar in water in a heavy-bottom saucepan. Warm slowly to dissolve sugar.
2. Once the sugar has dissolved, add the glucose syrup and boil.
3. Skim the surface with a tea strainer to remove any impurities.
4. While the sugar syrup is still hot, cover the pan with plastic wrap and allow the syrup to rest for 24 hours at room temperature. Resting the syrup overnight will help dissolve any remaining sugar crystals.
5. Bring the syrup to a boil and clean the sides of the pan, using a clean brush and cold water.
6. Add the Tartaric Acid Solution. Continue cleaning the pan as needed with the brush.
7. Add colors at 285°F (140°C); adding the color too early in the cooking process may change the color.
8. Cook the syrup to 320°F (160°C).
9. Immediately shock the pan in ice water to prevent carryover cooking.
10. Pour the syrup onto a silpat.

Pressed Sugar

Yield: 1 lb 3 oz (550 g)

Portions: 1

Portion size: 1 lb 3 oz (550 g)

Yield description: 1 portion at 1 lb 3 oz (550 g)

Ingredients	U.S.	Metric
Granulated Sugar	1 lb 1.6 oz	500 g
Water	1.8 oz	50 g

Note: Powder color can be added as needed to the water.

Procedure

1. Combine sugar and water; mix to a wet sand consistency.
2. Fill mold and pack the sugar into the mold.
3. Scrape the bottom of the mold to remove excess sugar.
4. Carefully unmold immediately.
5. Allow pressed sugar to dry completely 2 to 3 days.

FIGURE 14.14 Assorted pressed sugar

Pastillage

Yield: 2 lb 8 oz (1160 g)

Portions: 1

Portion size: 2 lb 8 oz (1160 g)

Yield description: 1 portion at 2 lb 8 oz (1160 g)

Ingredients	U.S.	Metric
Powdered Sugar	1 lb 12 oz	800 g
Potato Starch	7.1 oz	200 g
Gelatin Sheets	7 each	7 each
Cold Water	4.2 oz	120 g
Glucose Syrup	0.9 oz	25 g
White Vinegar	0.5 oz	15 g
Additional Potato Starch, for dusting		

Procedure

1. Bloom gelatin in the cold water.
2. Sift powdered sugar and potato starch.
3. Combine the gelatin and water mixture with glucose syrup and vinegar in a saucepan.
4. Warm gelatin mixture to dissolve gelatin, do not overheat.
5. Place dry ingredients in a mixer with paddle attachment.
6. While mixing on low, add wet ingredients to dry ingredients; mix until combined.
7. Remove the mixture from the bowl and knead on a table dusted with potato starch.
8. Wrap pastillage tightly in plastic wrap, then in a damp towel, and again in plastic wrap to prevent drying.
9. Allow pastillage to rest overnight before using.

Royal Icing

Yield: 1 lb 5 oz (600 g)

Portions: 1

Portion size: 1 lb 5 oz (600 g)

Yield Description: 1 portion at 1 lb 5 oz (600 g)

Ingredients	U.S.	Metric
Powdered Sugar	1 lb 1.6 oz	500 g
Egg Whites	3.5 oz	100 g
Cream of Tartar	0.02 oz	0.5 g

Note: Increasing egg whites will create a looser icing; decreasing will produce a stiffer icing.

Procedure

1. Sift dry ingredients into a mixing bowl.
2. Using the paddle attachment, start mixing on low while adding egg whites.
3. Continue mixing until the desired consistency is reached and icing is smooth.
4. To store royal icing, cover the surface with a moist towel, then wrap tightly with plastic wrap.

Key Terms

Hygroscopic
Isomalt
Glucose syrup
Tartaric acid
Cast sugar

Bubble sugar
Satinizing
Pulled sugar
Blown sugar
Propagated crystals

Pastillage
Royal icing
Thermal shock

Questions for Review

1. Why is glucose added after the sugar has dissolved?

2. Describe the process of satinizing sugar.

3. What is the purpose of tartaric acid in pulled sugar?

4. What are the benefits of using isomalt for sugar work?

5. What are the structural shapes that are used for sugar pieces?

Index